KU-300-960

WITHDRAWN

Consumer Behavior

Consumer Behavior

An Information Processing Perspective

Brian Sternthal
Northwestern University

C. Samuel Craig
New York University

Prentice-Hall, Inc., Englewood Cliffs, New Jersey   07632

Library of Congress Cataloging in Publication Data

STERNTHAL, BRIAN.
   Consumer behavior, an information processing perspective.

   Bibliography: p.
   Includes index.
   1. Consumers. I. Craig, C. Samuel. II. Title.
HB820.S73   658.8′342   81-13809
ISBN 0-13-169284-4   AACR2

Editorial/production supervision and interior design by Steven Young
Manufacturing buyer: Ed O'Dougherty

Cover design by 20/20 Services, Inc.

© 1982 by Prentice-Hall, Inc., Englewood Cliffs, N.J.   07632

All rights reserved. No part of this book may be reproduced in any form or by any means without permission in writing from the publisher.

Printed in the United States of America

10 9 8 7 6 5 4 3 2 1

ISBN 0-13-169284-4

Prentice-Hall International, Inc., *London*
Prentice-Hall of Australia Pty. Limited, *Sydney*
Prentice-Hall of Canada, Ltd., *Toronto*
Prentice-Hall of India Private Limited, *New Delhi*
Prentice-Hall of Japan, Inc., *Tokyo*
Prentice-Hall of Southeast Asia Pte. Ltd., *Singapore*
Whitehall Books Limited, *Wellington, New Zealand*

NAPIER COLLEGE OF COMMERCE AND TECHNOLOGY

AC 84 0093869 /01   RC 192

SIGHTHILL

658.8342 STE   CAT X

CON 0131692844   PR 7D 22-90

To

Sara and Ben Sternthal

and

Charles and Catherine Craig

Contents

Preface   xvii

Part I

Introduction   1

Chapter 1

The Nature and Scope of Consumer Behavior   3

    Consumer Behavior Theory   6

        Consumer Behavior Defined   6
        Consumer Decision Making   7

    Summary   13
    Questions   14

Chapter 2

Consumer Research: Describing, Explaining, and Evaluating Consumer Response   16

Descriptive Research   17

Archives   17
Survey   20
Observation   23
Summary   24

Explanatory Research   24
Evaluative Research   28

True Experiments   28
Quasi-Experiments   30

Theoretical Research and Policy Decisions   32
Summary   34
Questions   35

Part II

Theory Development and Modeling Consumers' Behavior   37

Chapter 3

Theories of Consumer Behavior   39

Monadic Models   40

Microeconomic Model   40
Psychoanalytic Model   41
Perceived Risk Model   42

Multiple Variable Models   44

Engel-Kollat-Blackwell Model   44
Webster-Wind Model   46
Howard-Ostlund Model   49

The Relationship among Multiple Variable Models   51
Summary   54
Questions   54

⁜ **Chapter 4**

A Framework for Analyzing Consumer Behavior   **56**

Purchasing an Iron   57
The Framework   59

Information Acquisition from Others   *59*
Exposure to Information   *60*
Information Reception   *61*
Cognitive Analysis   *62*
Acquisition of Attitudes from Behavior and Behavioral
    Circumstances   *65*
Information Organization   *66*
Information Utilization   *68*
Individual Differences   *69*

Implications of the Framework   70
Measuring Consumer Response   72

Information Acquisition   *72*
Information Utilization   *76*

Summary   77
Questions   77

Part III

Consumer Decision Making   **79**

Chapter 5

Information Acquisition   **81**

Information Exposure   82

The Case for Underexposure   *82*
Patterns of Exposure to Information   *83*
Factors Related to Information Seeking   *85*

Information Reception   88

Arousal   *88*
Attention   *91*

Cognitive Analysis   94

    Comprehension   94

    Cognitive Response   97

    Evidence for Cognitive Response   102

    Implications of Cognitive Response   107

Summary   113

Questions   114

Chapter 6

Information Acquisition from One's Own Experiences   **116**

The Self-Perception Process   117

    The Effect of One's Own Behavior on Decision Making   117

    Own versus Others' Behavior as Determinants of Decision
      Making   121

    The Effect of Circumstances on Self-Perception   122

Self-Perception and Information Processing   124

    The Single Process View   124

    The Multiple Processes View   127

Information Acquisition from One's Own Behavior and Marketing
    Strategy   129

    Guidelines for Using the Foot-in-the-Door Technique   129

    When Foot-in-the-Door Fails   130

Summary   130

Questions   131

Chapter 7

Organization of Information for Decision Making   **132**

The Abstraction Process   134

    Masculinity-Femininity   135

Social Class   *138*
Performance   *138*
Multiple Abstractions   *141*

The Aggregation Process   141

Linear Model   *142*
Lexicographic Model   *146*
Conjunctive Model   *148*
Disjunctive Model   *148*
Situational Effects on Information Aggregation   *149*

Summary and Strategic Implications   151
Questions   153

Chapter 8

Explaining and Predicting Consumers' Behavior   **155**

The Prediction of Behavior from Attitudes   156
Improving the Prediction of Behavior from Attitudes   159

Selecting the Attitude Measure   *159*
The Behavior Measure   *161*
Other Variables to Improve the Prediction of Behavior   *163*
Normative Beliefs   *163*
Judged Influence of Extraneous Events   *165*

Evaluation of the Behavioral Prediction Model   166
The Effect of Subliminal Stimuli on Behavior   168
Predicting Long-Term Behavior   170

Environmental Forecasting   *172*
Technological Forecast   *176*
*An Integrated Approach to Predicting Long-Term
Behavior*   *179*

Summary   180
Questions   181

Part IV

Consumers as Individuals and Groups   **183**

Chapter 9

Consumer Individual Differences   **185**

Freud's Psychoanalytic Theory   186

Personality Structure   186
Personality Development   187

Consumption-Tailored Personality Measures   189
The Impact of Individual Differences on Consumer Information
        Processing   192

Personality Characteristics   193
Demographic Characteristics   195

Summary   198
Questions   199

Chapter 10

Demographic Trends and Consumption   **200**

Fertility Rates   201
Households   205
Women in the Work Force   208
Mobility and Migration   209
Education, Income, and Occupation   211
Summary and Conclusions   213
Questions   214

Chapter 11

The Impact of Groups on Consumer Behavior   215

Social Stratification   216

Demographic Classification of Social Class   216
Social Class and Consumption   221
Summary and Conclusions   225

Family Decision Making   226

Family Consumption Roles   226
Division of Buying Roles   228
The Family Life Cycle   229

Summary   231
Questions   232

Part V

Influencing Consumer Decision Making   235

Chapter 12

Product Strategy   237

Product Characteristics Influencing Choice   238

Price as a Product Cue   238
Product Presentation   242

New Product Strategy   245

New Product Characteristics and Adoption   246
Targets for New Product Adoption   248
Competitive Analysis   251

Summary   256
Questions   256

Chapter 13

Message Strategies   **259**

Message Content Strategies   261

    *Consumer Oriented vs. Product Oriented Attribute
       Selection   261*

    Message Discrepancy   263

    Attributes Sensitive to Social Norms   265

    Opposing Attributes   265

Message Execution   266

    Threatening Appeals   266

    Humorous Messages   271

    Labeling   275

Message Structure   277

    Message Repetition   277

    Order of Presentation   282

Silent Messages   284

    Proxemics   286

    Kinesic Behavior   287

    Paralanguage   289

Summary   291

Questions   292

Chapter 14

Communication Source and Modality Strategies   **293**

The Communication Source   294

    Source Attractiveness   294

    *Expertise and Trust as Persuasive Facilitators and
       Nonliabilities   295*

    Credibility as a Persuasive Liability   303

Communication Modality   304

    Consumer Response   305
    Competitive Environment   308
    Other Factors in Modality Selection   309

Summary   309
Questions   309

Part VI

Summary and Conclusion   311

Chapter 15

Information Processing Theory: Marketing Strategy   313

Consumer Information Processing   313

    Exposure and Reception   314
    Retrieval and Rehearsal   314
    Individual and Group Differences   318

Problem Solving from an Information Processing Perspective   319

    Controlling the Effects of Rumors   319
    Stimulating Energy Conservation   320

Summary   325
Questions   325

Bibliography   327

Index   343

Preface

Consumer behavior as a field of inquiry has expanded dramatically in the past decade. The different theories used to develop an understanding of consumers' behavior, the varied contexts in which consumers' behavior is examined, and the burgeoning empirical research have all conspired to make it difficult to provide an adequate discussion of all facets of the field in one book. To deal with this diversity, we have taken a particular perspective called *information processing,* which interprets consumption behavior in terms of how people acquire, organize, and utilize information to make judgments. This approach provides a parsimonious means of organizing and integrating knowledge of consumers' behavior.

The adoption of an information processing perspective might seem to indicate that some important topics in consumer behavior are not discussed. However, this is not necessarily the case. Throughout the book we have sought to develop a common language that enables an information processing interpretation of issues not previously examined from this perspective. For example attribution theory, which describes how people perceive the causes of behavior and act upon these perceptions, is addressed by examining how behavior affects the thoughts on which consumers' judgments are predicated. The effect of demography, personality, and social class on consumption is examined in terms of how these individual differences influence *what* and *how* information is used to make decisions.

The book is intended primarily as a graduate-level text for a course in consumer behavior. It may also be useful to advanced undergraduates in consumer behavior and in social psychology courses with an applied social cognition perspective. No knowledge of behavioral science is assumed, and only a rudimentary understanding of marketing concepts is required. We develop in a step-by-step manner those behavioral science constructs that are required to explain and predict consumers' behavior. Moreover, the strategies implied by information processing theory are described and illustrated using familiar examples.

In describing consumers' behavior, we have stressed the link between theory and strategy. This approach is predicated on our belief that theory provides an efficient means of distinguishing variables likely to impact consumers' judgment from the myriad of nondeterminant variables present in everyday decision contexts. Moreover, it is our belief that the effects of variables on consumers' behavior can be deduced more accurately on the basis of theory than they can by relying on intuitive or empirical induction. Finally, we believe that illustrating the strategic applications of theory facilitates understanding and appreciation of theory.

The book is divided into six major sections. Part I explains what consumer behavior is about, why it is of interest to managers, and how it may be studied. An overview of the particular approach to the study of consumer behavior is developed, as well as the critical role of research in developing an understanding of consumers' behavior. In Part II consumer behavior as a field of inquiry is placed in historical perspective. Its development from the earliest single construct models to the more recent multiple variable models is traced. The key aspect of Part II is development of an information processing model of consumer behavior. This model serves two purposes. It organizes what is known about consumers' behavior, and it provides the structure for the remainder of the book. Part III begins the elaboration of the model by describing how consumers make decisions. Consumers' acquisition of information is examined in terms of external sources and their own experience. The ways in which consumers organize and utilize their information in making decisions is discussed.

Part IV examines consumers as individuals and as they exist in groups. The ways consumers make choices differ depending on the individual. To examine this, individual difference in decision-making and changing demographic trends are considered. The ways consumers are influenced by the groups to which they belong is described.

Part V applies the knowledge of consumer behavior developed earlier in the book to the design of strategies aimed at influencing individuals' consumption choices. This involves the development of product strategies to stimulate demand for new and existing products. Message strategies are considered in terms of communication content, execution, and structure. The source of the message and the particular modality used to deliver the message are also considered. Finally, Part VI summarizes the main features of the information processing perspective and highlights the applicability of information processing principles in addressing marketing problems.

This book has had a long gestation and its final form is a far cry from its initial design. Its present form reflects the evolution of the field of consumer behavior and the evolution of our own thinking about the field. In addition it bears the imprint of all those who influenced us in our graduate studies and colleagues who have continued to stimulate our intellectual development. At the risk of omitting some, we do want to acknowledge our deep sense of gratitude to those who made this book a reality.

Professor James F. Engel, Wheaton College, Professors Anthony Greenwald and Roger D. Blackwell, Ohio State University, and David T. Kollat, The Limited, all provided direction and inspiration in our study of consumer behavior. Professor Clark Leavitt, Ohio State University, provided considerable intellectual stimulation in the early development of this book. Professors Bobby J. Calder, Sidney J. Levy, and Alice M. Tybout, Northwestern University, helped refine our thinking about numerous issues in consumer behavior. The senior author would also like to gratefully acknowledge the support of his current and former colleagues at Northwestern University—Richard M. Clewett, John Hauser, Philip Kotler, Trudy Murray, Louis W. Stern, Gerald Zaltman, and Adris A. Zoltners.

We are very grateful for the many helpful comments made by those who reviewed the manuscript. Professors Joel Cohen, University of Florida, Michael L. Ray, Stanford University, and Ivan Ross, University of Minnesota, made detailed and very helpful comments on an earlier draft. These comments enabled us to make substantial revisions and improve the overall quality. Professors Michael K. Mills, University of Southern California, Jerry Olsen, Pennsylvania State University, and Carol Scott, UCLA, made insightful comments on the current version. Their suggestions helped us to refine the manuscript further.

We are grateful for the capable people at Prentice-Hall who assisted us through the many steps. We would like to acknowledge Judy Rothman, who started the project with us, and John Connolly and Steve Young, who saw it to completion.

A number of our graduate students have made valuable contributions to the book. Professors Lynn Phillips, Stanford University, and Richard Yalch, University of Washington, have made many useful suggestions. We are also grateful for the contribution of Teri Phillips, Lori Simon, and Carin Gendell, who read and critiqued the manuscript from a pedagogical perspective. Richard Crowe provided valuable assistance in the preparation of the instructor's manual. Greg Brill helped in tracking down and verifying exhibits and citations.

Finally, we would like to acknowledge the able typing assistance provided through many drafts by Mrs. Marion Davis and the secretarial staffs at Ohio State University, Cornell University, New York University, and Northwestern University.

Brian Sternthal

C. Samuel Craig

Consumer Behavior

Part I

Part I indicates what consumer behavior is about, why it is of interest to managers, and how it may be studied. Chapter One identifies the domain of consumer behavior inquiry. Consumer behavior is viewed as a process by which people acquire, organize, and use information to make purchase decisions. This process is of interest to managers because it suggests strategies that can be used to influence consumers' choices. Chapter Two examines the role of research in learning about consumers and in designing influence strategies. Research helps the manager describe and explain consumption behavior. The strategies that emerge from this analysis are subjected to research approaches that can evaluate the effectiveness of various strategic alternatives.

Introduction

Chapter 1

The Nature and Scope of Consumer Behavior

Jay Black, the brand manager for Flex ready-to-eat cereal, addressed the members of the corporate planning committee.

> . . . As you know, there has been a proliferation in the brands of ready-to-eat cereals during the last decade. At last count, there were more than 100 brands on the market. And, Flex has not been able to hold its share-of-market in this environment. In fact, Flex's share has dropped from its high of 6 percent in 1965 to its present low of 2.2 percent. While many of you are in favor of cutting off all market support for this brand, market and consumer research have given us some insights about how we may revitalize the brand. I'd like to review these data now . . .

Black then presented the information collected by corporate research. Relying on consumer research, he described the way consumers purchase ready-to-eat cereals. This description indicated that the majority of cereal purchases are made by housewives. They tend to decide which brand of cereal to buy when they pass the cereal section in the store. On the average, cereal purchases were made about twice a month; over the course of a year, the typical consumer purchased about ten different brands. Consumers' choice of brands was based on flavor, nutrition, and texture or crispness. Black then described the information obtained for the Flex brand. He noted that ninety percent of consumers were aware of the Flex brand. Nine out of ten consumers responded to the question "What kind of product is Flex?" with the answer "a cereal." Further, forty percent of consumers had purchased Flex during the past year. But despite this high awareness and one-time purchase, top-of-mind awareness (that is, mentioning Flex when asked to name brands of cereal) was poor. Only eight percent of the people questioned spontaneously mentioned Flex when asked to name all the ready-to-eat cereals they could think of. Consumers who taste tested either wheat, rice, or corn Flex all indicated that the major reason for buying these brands was that they stayed crisp in milk.

Before outlining his strategy to revitalize Flex, Mr. Black reviewed the marketing strategy of Flex and its competitors in the ready-to-eat cereal market. These data are shown in Table 1.1. Both Flex and its competitors spent ten percent of their sales dollar on advertising, or about $1.5 million for each share-of-market point. Furthermore, most of the marketing effort was focused on advertising. Promotions, such as discounts to the trade and consumer deals (for example, cents-off marked price, media-distributed coupons), constituted only a small portion of the total marketing allocation for both Flex and its competitors. Finally, advertising for Flex emphasized different attributes for each of the brands in the line—wheat, corn and rice. For this purpose, three different sixty-second television commercials were used. In contrast, competitors typically stressed flavor and the vitality delivered by their brands.

Black concluded his presentation by outlining the strategy he favored for halting the decline in Flex's share-of-market.

> . . . On the basis of the information we have about how consumers buy ready-to-eat cereals, the factors related to the purchase of Flex, and the competitive situation, I feel we have a good chance of turning the Flex brand around. Therefore, I suggest that we:
>
> 1. *Maintain our current marketing budget.* Investment spending is not warranted because the brand is late in its life cycle, but neither is total retraction of support. Remember that each share point generates $15 million in revenue.
>
> 2. *Adjust the advertising to promotion ratio from its current 80:20 level to a 50:50 level.* This would involve stepping up both trade incentives and the deals we give consumers when they purchase Flex. This is a radical departure from industry tradition and our own practice, but a justifiable departure. It allows us to stimulate demand where it occurs—in the store. More than half the brand decisions for ready-to-eat cereals are made at the shelf.
>
> 3. *Alter our advertising approach so that it has impact despite the significant reduction in the advertising allocation.* Here I suggest using a single theme to sell wheat, rice, and corn rather than the individual brand sell used previously. This would involve emphasizing the fact that Flex stays crisp in milk—the common attribute for the three brands in our line. In addition, we can maintain our advertising

TABLE 1.1. Marketing Strategy: Flex and Competitors

Marketing Strategy	Flex	Competitors
Advertising as a percent of sales	10%	10%
Advertising to promotion ratio	80:20	90:10
Brand attributes stressed	Wheat — Vitality Corn — Taste Rice — Texture	Flavor and vitality

presence in relation to competition by using thirty-second commercials instead of the sixty-second commercials previously used. There should be no problem in communicating the crispness attribute in thirty-second commercials.

. . . In sum, research indicates that while most consumers know about our brand and many consumers purchase it at least once a year, it is not one of the brands in their purchase set for ready-to-eat cereals; when naming cereals only 8 percent indicate top-of-mind awareness of Flex. By stepping up our promotions in relation to those offered by competitors, and at the same time maintaining a strong advertising presence, we shall increase the number of consumers who consider Flex when purchasing cereals. The bottom line will be increased sales and market share for roughly the same level of marketing effort.

After some discussion of where the Flex advertising would appear, how often advertising would be aired, the specific promotions that would be used, and the budget that would be needed, corporate planning accepted Black's program. After one year, sales of the Flex brand had increased by about fifty percent.

The Flex case provides an indication of how the field of consumer behavior is approached in this book. The view is that consumer behavior is the basis for developing strategies to influence individuals' purchase and consumption choices. An integral part of this view is the pivotal role of research in the design and evaluation of such strategies. Guidance and direction for this research is based on a theory of consumer decision making, that is, a set of interrelated concepts about the determinants of consumption behavior.

Applying this view to the Flex case, it is apparent that Mr. Black's interest in consumer behavior was motivated by the desire to develop a strategy that would revitalize the Flex brand. Research was conducted to achieve this goal. Research on the ready-to-eat cereal category told him that people purchased the category frequently, switched brands often, and did little planning about what to buy before going to the store. This information implied that to be effective, a strategy would have to combat consumers' tendency to switch brands. Furthermore, the strategy would have to be consistent with consumers' propensity to make in-store brand choices, or it would have to stimulate planning of cereal choices prior to the shopping trip.

Research pertaining to consumers' knowledge and reactions to the Flex brand was also useful in strategy selection. It indicated that many consumers knew about the brand and had purchased it during the past year. But repeat purchase of Flex was low. Thus, a strategy that stimulates repeat purchase was required. Consumer promotions meet this criterion. Moreover, choice of an appropriate promotion, such as a coupon in the package good for the next purchase of Flex, would stimulate consumers to make their brand choice prior to visiting the store and reduce brand switching.

Finally, research might be used to assess the effectiveness of Black's strategy. Here, the focus centers on determining the sales response to one promotion strategy in relation to some other strategy. Black found that sales increased fifty percent in response to his strategy, although factors other than the new strategy may have caused this outcome.

The research conducted by Black was based on a simple theory of consumer behavior. According to this theory, consumers' choice of Flex was based on their top-of-mind awareness of the brand. In turn, top-of-mind awareness depended on consumers' knowledge of Flex's existence. This theory led Black to include questions about brand awareness and top-of-mind awareness. Finally, Black developed a strategy for Flex by interpreting consumers' response to these questions in accord with his theory.

The Flex case underscores the importance of research and theory in the study of consumer behavior. The role of research is considered in Chapter Two. In the remainder of this chapter, we provide an overview of the theory that will guide our study of consumer behavior. This involves identifying the major determinants of consumers' behavior and indicating how these determinants are interrelated. To facilitate understanding of the theory, each determinant of consumers' behavior is illustrated by an example drawn from actual practice.

CONSUMER BEHAVIOR THEORY

A wide variety of theories have been offered to explain consumers' behavior. Some theories account for consumers' behavior in terms of risk reduction, others in terms of utility maximization, and still others in terms of achieving consistency. This diversity of theories poses a problem. One must decide which theory or theories best explain consumers' behavior.

A number of approaches are available to resolve this problem. The most popular approach among authors of consumer behavior texts is to provide a brief description of most, if not all, of the theories that have been advanced to explain consumers' behavior. Although this has the advantage of documenting the breadth of inquiry undertaken to interpret consumers' behavior, it also has a severe limitation: the reader is not given a clear indication of how various theories interface. Rather, it is left to the reader's discretion to determine whether theories are competitive or complementary and to ascertain when it is appropriate to invoke each theory.

To remedy this limitation, we shall rely primarily on a single theory of consumer behavior called *information processing theory*.[1] This theory was chosen because it provides a testable explanation for a wide variety of consumer behavior phenomena and because it provides a basis for designing strategies to influence consumer response. Its choice, however, does not imply the exclusion of other theoretical views. Quite the contrary, a wide variety of consumer behavior theories will be represented by interpreting them in information processing terms. The presumption is that by using the language of information processing theory as a means of linking seemingly disparate theories, a coherent and comprehensive theory of consumer behavior can be developed.

Consumer Behavior Defined

In describing consumer behavior theory, we begin with a formal definition that reflects the information processing view. *Consumer behavior is the study of the process by which consumers make decisions. More specifically, it is concerned with how con-*

---

[1]For a detailed description of information processing, see Bettman (1979) and Olson (1978).

sumers acquire, organize, and use information to make consumption choices. This definition requires amplification to clarify who is being referred to by the term consumer, what are the behaviors of interest, and what is the nature of the process involved in decision-making.

Consumers Defined. Two terms have been used in the literature to describe those individuals who purchase or consume products and services: buyers and consumers. The more general term, *buyers,* refers to people who are acting as either ultimate, industrial, or institutional purchasers. The term *consumer* is more restrictive. It denotes people who purchase for ultimate use.

This text focuses on the behavior of ultimate consumers. This emphasis does not imply that industrial and organizational buyer behavior is of little interest. Quite the contrary, the ability to predict and explain these behaviors is of great importance. However, industrial and organizational buyer behavior occurs in settings where purchase decisions are often made by several people acting in their formal roles. The analyses of this behavior requires the discussion of concepts beyond those needed to understand consumer behavior. Rather than provide a superficial analysis of all types of buyer behavior, we shall concentrate on presenting a detailed description of consumer decision making. The discussion of industrial and institutional buyer behavior is limited to those situations where consumer behavior concepts are equally applicable to other types of buyers.[2]

Behavior Defined. Behaviors performed by consumers refer to those overt activities employed to facilitate and consummate the exchange of objects that have meaning for consumers. Behaviors of interest include such diverse actions as the use of a particular service, purchase of a particular brand, voting for a candidate, and signing a petition in support of an issue. But, because most students of consumer behavior are particularly interested in overt actions pertaining to economic goods and services, these social objects receive greater emphasis in this text.

Consumer Decision Making

The approach to understanding the processes involved in decision making is based on human information processing theory. This theory interprets consumers' choices as a function of three processes that occur in memory: information acquisition, information organization, and information utilization. Because our purpose here is to highlight the nature of these processes and their interrelationships, they are represented in a highly simplified form. As Figure 1.1 shows, information about some product or service is acquired from other people (including mass media) in the form of incoming information, as well as on the basis of one's own experience. These bits of information are then organized. Organization systemizes what a person knows so that it can be used to evaluate some object. Once information is organized, it is utilized to make a purchase choice.

[2]For a detailed discussion of industrial buyer behavior, see Webster and Wind (1972).

Figure 1.1. The Consumer Decision Making Process

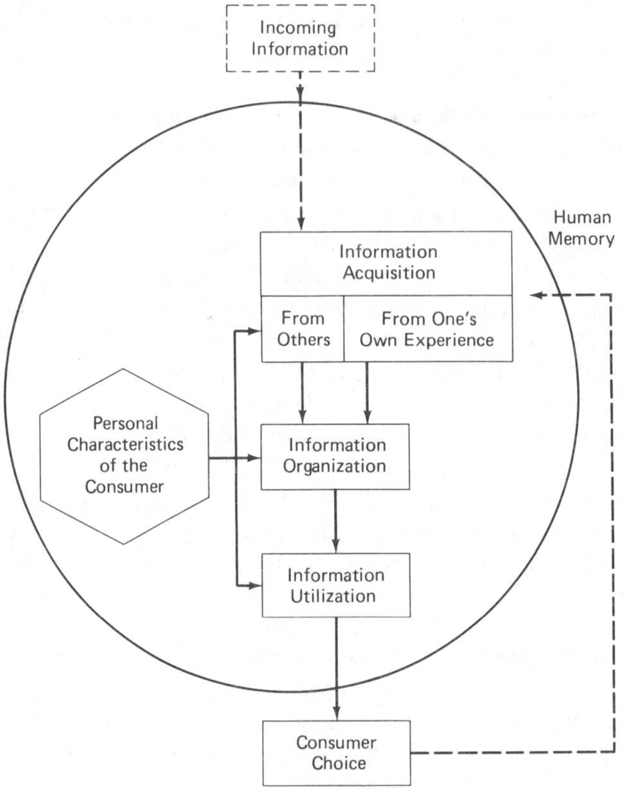

Although all people process information in this way, they differ in the specific information they acquire, how they organize it, and how they use it. These differences are depicted by the Personal Characteristics of the Consumer box in Figure 1.1

Information Acquisition. Consumers' behavior is determined, in part, by the information they acquire from external sources. These sources may include family members, friends, salespeople, and mass media. Whatever the external source of information, it must be represented in memory if it is to affect decision making. This representation is in the form of thoughts or propositions that link an object to an attribute. For example, Flex stays crisp in milk is a thought linking the object "Flex" to the attribute "stays crisp in milk." The following case identifies some of the factors involved in acquiring information from others.

During the mid 1960s the soft-drink industry experienced rapid growth. The post World War II baby boom had significantly increased the number of heavy soft-drink consumers in the fourteen- to twenty-four-year-old age segment. This population trend, however, had very little effect on the sales of 7UP, a lemon-lime soft drink.[3] The growth of 7UP's sales languished far behind that of its major competitors, Coca-Cola and Pepsi-Cola. To remedy this situation, research was conducted to identify the reasons behind 7UP's slow growth. The following problems were identified. Consumers did not regard 7UP as a soft drink. When asked to list all of the soft drinks they could name, 7UP frequently was not mentioned. Unlike Coke and Pepsi, 7UP typically was not viewed as appropriate to serve with meals, snacks, or to company. Rather 7UP was seen as a mixer and a good remedy for indigestion and other after-effects of too much drinking. 7UP also was perceived to have a taste that quenched thirst better than its cola competitors.

Consumer perceptions of 7UP led management to conclude that a communication was needed that informed the consumer of two things. First, 7UP is a soft drink like the colas. Second, it is superior to other soft drinks because of its thirst-quenching taste. Execution of these ideas was done in the form of television commercials, one of which is shown in Figure 1.2. As this figure illustrates, focus centered on representing 7UP as a soft drink like the colas but superior to the colas in taste. This "uncola" approach was quite successful. 7UP's sales growth exceeded that of the industry for several years following the introduction of the uncola campaign.

The 7UP case illustrates the importance of transmitting information to consumers that is useful for decision-making. Consumers apparently acquired the thought that 7UP had a thirst-quenching taste and used this information in making their soft-drink choices. In Chapter Five, we shall consider how consumers acquire information. Of particular concern is understanding how consumers acquire attitudes about products and services on the basis of information presented by others—family members, friends, salespeople, media, and the like. Among the questions addressed are:

1. What determines whether or not people will be exposed to information?
2. What determines whether people will process the information to which they are exposed?
3. What determines their acceptance of the information conveyed as a basis for decision making?

A second source of information may also influence consumer decision making. This information is acquired on the basis of consumers' experiences and the circumstances in which those experiences occur. The introduction of a newspaper illustrates this mode of information acquisition.

To examine different ways of selling subscriptions to a weekly newspaper in a new community, a publisher had his telephone-calling staff contact community residents.[4] Some residents were offered a two-week trial subscription of the paper at the full price. Others were offered the trial for half price and a third group was offered a free trial. After the trial period, all of these people were recontacted and asked to subscribe to the newspaper at full price. In addition, a group of residents were contacted and asked to

[3]The 7UP case was adapted from Mandell (1974).
[4]The study reported in this case was conducted by Scott (1976).

Figure 1.2. Uncola Commercial

J. WALTER THOMPSON COMPANY

DATE: July, 1969
PRODUCER: Weissman-Franz, New York

CLIENT: The Seven-Up Company
PRODUCT: Seven-Up
FILM #/TITLE: 5118/"Uncola Nuts" :60
JOB #:   5118

1. (Jingle sfx under) GENTLEMEN: These are cola nuts. They grow here.

2. They're used to make cola-flavored soft drinks.

3. These, on the other hand, are Uncola nuts. They grow here, too,...

4. ...but, as you can see, they're a bit different from cola nuts.

5. Rather larger, for one thing. Rather juicier too, I'd say.

6. Marvelous little things, Uncola nuts. We use them, of course, to make The Uncola...Seven-Up.

7. It's the Uncola nut...

8. ...that helps give The Uncola its...

9. ...je ne sais quoi. You know... fresh,...clean taste.

10. No aftertaste.

11. Wet. Wild. All that.

12. (Silent)

13. Marvelous. Absolutely marvelous. Just try making something like that out of a cola nut.

14. Why...it's even prettier than a cola.

15. Nuttier than a cola, actually. (Laughs)

Courtesy of the Seven-Up Company.

subscribe to the newspaper without prior trial. It was found that the free offer resulted in more people trying the newspaper for two weeks than the other two approaches. However, the half price trial was most effective in stimulating actual subscriptions. In fact, eighteen percent of those who had been offered a half price trial eventually subscribed to the newspaper, whereas only nine percent of those who were merely asked to subscribe complied with this request.

This illustration underscores the importance of people's experience and the circumstances in which that experience occurs on their subsequent actions. When consumers reflect on their previous behavior and the reasons for that behavior they generate new thoughts about the object of the behavior. In turn, thoughts acquired in this way guide future actions. In Chapter Six we shall examine how consumers use their experience as a basis for inferring thoughts and directing subsequent purchase decisions.

Information Organization. A second subprocess of consumer decision making involves the *organization* of the information acquired from various sources. Organization entails combining the bits of information that the consumer has acquired. In this process, information about the physical characteristics of a product are converted into subjective impressions that are useful for evaluating a product. The Pringle's case illustrates this process.

Procter and Gamble decided to introduce a new kind of potato chip, Pringle's. This decision was predicated on several factors. Taste tests had revealed that Pringle's was perceived to be as good-tasting as competitors' brands. The chips were nongreasy, unbroken, and uniform in shape and texture. They came in a resealable pack, which allowed the consumer to store the product and maintain its freshness.

Consumers' initial reaction to the product was quite favorable. Pringle's attained a substantial share of the potato chip market after several months. Thereafter, however, sales began to slump. People who tried the product claimed that it tasted artificial. This complaint was somewhat surprising in that, when the brand was tasted without visual inspection, Pringle's taste was rated to be as good as other brands.

The difficulties faced by Pringle's appear to be related to the way people organize information. Specifically, the physical characteristics of the product, such as the uniform shape and texture, may have led consumers to infer that they were artificial and therefore not as good-tasting as other chips. In Chapter Seven we discuss how individuals interpret physical product cues and how they combine the various bits of information they have acquired in order to choose among purchase alternatives.

Information Utilization. Once consumers have acquired and organized information, they are in a position to make a decision. This entails a consideration of factors beyond their thoughts about choice alternatives. This point is illustrated in the Frost 8/80 case.

Ever since World War II, there has been a growing awareness among manufacturers of hard liquor that young adults and women of all ages dislike the taste of whiskey. Nevertheless, young adults and women constituted a significant segment of potential consumers of hard liquor. To take advantage of this opportunity, Brown-Foreman produced a dry white whiskey called Frost 8/80. It was believed that the bland taste of this product would be ideal when combined with an appropriate mixer. Some $500,000 was spent to determine consumers' preferences regarding the color, taste, and package design for Frost 8/80.

On the basis of these extensive preintroductory tests, sales of 300,000 cases were forecasted for the first two years. An advertising agency was hired which developed the theme "the color is white, the taste is dry, the possibilities endless." Unfortunately, consumers found the possibilities quite limited; they did not know what to do with a product that looked like vodka but tasted like whiskey. When sales lagged, another advertising agency was hired to rectify the problem. A new approach was taken to educate potential users about how to use Frost 8/80. Ads suggested that Frost 8/80 should be mixed with a sugary pineapple and grapefruit concoction to form a Sigmund Frost. Playing on the Freudian theme, this drink was described as "the crazy, mixed-up drink" and "the drink that defies analysis." This strategy was also unsuccessful. After two years sales had reached only about one-third of the forecasted level. When Brown-Foreman retracted the product, approximately $6.5 million had been spent on the product, $2.5 million of which was estimated to be lost.

The failure of Frost 8/80 was due, in part, to the fact that individuals' thoughts about a product's taste, color, and package design may not be adequate to predict their behavior accurately. During the past few years progress has been made in identifying factors that are important in predicting and explaining behavior, other than consumers' thoughts about a product *per se*. These are covered in detail in Chapter Eight.

Personal Characteristics. In order to make decisions all consumers must acquire, organize, and use information. But these commonalities in the decision making process do not mean that all consumers make the same consumption choices. Characteristics unique to individuals or groups—such as personality and demographics—affect consumers' behavior. These characteristics influence behavior by affecting what information is acquired, how it is organized, and the way it is used. The blue-collar family case illustrates the role of personal characteristics in consumption behavior.

The heads of blue-collar households tend to hold jobs requiring manual activity. Like other social classes, the blue-collar family purchases their home in an area where neighbors are for the most part of the same ethnic, religious, and educational background and hold similar occupations. However, blue-collar families tend to utilize the rooms of their homes in a distinct manner.

Because much of their home-life centers around the consumption of food, the kitchen is perhaps the most important room in the blue-collar home. Not only are meals prepared and served in the kitchen, but the room also serves as the entertainment center for visitors. The blue-collar wife perceives her existence to be focused on providing for her children and husband. As a consequence, blue-collar kitchens are often equipped with the latest avocado-colored or harvest gold-colored appliances. They are as modern as any in town. The importance of food is also reflected in the blue-collar wife's reliance on national brands when purchasing food items.

The living room often serves as the television viewing center in the blue-collar home. It is furnished with simple, bulky, but comfortable furniture, translucent curtains, and floral carpets. The walls are often painted in bright colors. The few paintings that are hung deal with religious topics. A large color television set often dominates the room. In fact, blue-collar families purchased a disproportionately large number of color television sets when they were initially introduced to the American public in the late fifties. If there is a piano in the living room, it is generally an upright. A chair rather than a piano bench is most often used when one is seated at the piano. Bowling trophies are often prominently displayed in the living room.

Finally, the bedrooms in the blue-collar home are utilized almost solely for sleeping. (This is contrary to college students' use of bedrooms as entertainment centers.) The bedroom is furnished with inexpensive and simple furniture. Frequently the pieces in the room were purchased one at a time and consequently are not well-coordinated. The emphasis is on obtaining the nicest or prettiest item at the best price.

The manner in which blue-collar families utilize the rooms in their homes has a significant bearing on their purchase behavior. They are prime segments for the purchase of electrical appliances and televisions, but poor targets for expensive and coordinated furniture, rugs, and objects d'art. Apparently, personal characteristics of the consumer affect the thoughts they have about various products and, thus, their propensity to purchase them. In Chapters Nine to Eleven, we shall consider the impact of personal characteristics on consumption behavior. Among the questions of particular concern are the following:

How do consumers' personality characteristics influence their purchase behavior?

What major demographic trends will emerge in the American population over the next decade and how will these trends affect consumption?

What strategies are appropriate to influence the behavior of specific segments of the population?

SUMMARY

The study of consumer behavior encompasses a broad range of topics and activities. In this chapter, we have identified the scope of consumer behavior inquiry. It is concerned with an understanding of individuals' purchase and consumption activities. This requires a knowledge of how people acquire information through their own, and others', experience. It involves study of how they organize the acquired information and how it is used to make purchase decisions. It also requires a knowledge of how personal characteristics of the buyer affect the acquisition, organization, and utilization processes. Using this information, strategies may be developed to affect consumers from both a marketing manager's and a consumer advocate's perspective.

In this book, information processing theory serves as a basis for describing how consumers make consumption choices. It also is employed to guide development of strategies that can influence consumers' behavior. Taking this approach does not imply that perspectives other than information processing are inappropriate for understanding and influencing consumers' actions. However, focus on a single perspective provides an integrated view of how people make decisions. Moreover, other perspectives are not ignored. Rather, they are reinterpreted within the information processing framework.

To highlight various issues that are considered part of the domain of consumer behavior and to describe the information processing approach used to address consumer behavior phenomena, a number of illustrative cases were presented. The 7UP case and the newspaper solicitation example provide examples of how an understanding of the information acquisition process may be used to develop effective marketing strategies. In contrast, the following two examples point out how a lack of understanding of consumer decision making may result in poor consumer response. The Pringle's case emphasizes the importance of how individuals organize information to make decisions, whereas the Frost 8/80 case illustrates the importance of factors apart from consumers' thoughts about specific product attributes in predicting their behavior. The final illustration, which describes blue-collar consumption, emphasizes the important role of personal characteristics in consumption behavior.

QUESTIONS

1. What are some of the differences between buyers and consumers?

2. Describe each of the subprocesses involved in consumer decision making (for example, information acquisition, information organization). For each, indicate how an understanding of the subprocess may be used in developing marketing strategies.

3. Read the following description of Bill Boggs' buying behavior and answer the questions posed:

Bill Boggs retired from his job as an auto mechanic last year at the age of sixty-five. Bill's life had changed substantially in the last ten years. Shortly after his retirement his wife died, so he lived alone in his small suburban home. His only daughter, Mary, had married when he was fifty and lived about ten miles away with her husband and children. The neighborhood, too, was changing, with many young families moving into it. Bill was cordial to these people, but did not socialize with them.

When Bill's wife died, he assumed many of the household chores that she had done. One of these was washing. While doing the wash one day, the machine began to make an ominous sound. Bill reached into the washer with his hand to see if any of the clothing might be stuck under the rotary blade.

> . . . When I stuck my hand in the machine I darn near got electrocuted. I pulled the plug and called my daughter. She suggested I call a repairman, and she gave me the number of the one she used. It turned out that it was going to cost me one hundred dollars to fix. It was then I knew I had two choices—buy a new one or use the laundromat on the corner. I decided not to spend the money, so I tried the one at the laundromat for a few weeks. It turned out to be too much trouble—you know, lugging the laundry down there, sitting in the hot store, with that loud music playing. That's when I decided I'd get me a new machine. I do most things myself, especially fixing things. You know I had forty years' experience

as a mechanic. But what do I know about washing machines? So I called my daughter Mary. She told me that Sears had good machines and good service. I went to Sears and looked at the machines. They all looked about the same to me except for the price. A salesman pointed out the advantages of the top-of-the-line washer but I figured who needs three water temperatures and two wash cycles? Still I liked him. He had been a mechanic like me before he hurt his back. I thought when I bought a machine I'd give him the first shot.

I didn't buy a machine then. I looked in some other stores and saw some ads on TV. But the ads didn't help any, until I read about a sale Sears was having on washing machines. I called my daughter and she met me at the Sears store. After talking to the same salesman as before and getting my daughter's opinion, I decided to purchase one. Had it three weeks and it works fine. It sure beats going down to the laundromat or getting electrocuted!

a. Use this description to construct a model of consumer decision making.

b. To test the adequacy of the model developed show that the way consumers behave in the Flex illustration can be accommodated by your model.

c. Develop strategies you would employ to attract Bill Boggs to a brand other than Sears.

d. Develop strategies you could employ in your role as a consumer advocate to increase the likelihood that Bill Boggs made a judicious purchase decision.

Chapter 2

Consumer Research: Describing, Explaining, and Evaluating Consumer Response

Effective marketing strategy requires a thorough understanding of the market. Consider, for example, the information needs of automobile manufacturers. Planning an efficient production schedule requires a knowledge of automobile demand. Product development, price, and promotion decisions require a description of potential buyers and their motivations for purchasing. An efficient dealer location strategy requires information about the geographic locales where demand is likely to be greatest.

These information needs may be obtained by conducting three types of research (Table 2.1). *Descriptive* research provides factual information about consumers and their purchase behavior. It is useful in identifying who potential purchasers are, and in establishing facts about their behavior. *Explanatory* research provides insight into why people purchase. On the basis of descriptive and explanatory research, product, price, distribution, and promotional policies can be developed. To determine the effectiveness of these strategies, *evaluative* research is required. It provides a basis for determining the efficacy of strategic alternatives.

The strategist is often faced with a dilemma in pursuing these research procedures. Descriptive and explanatory research may suggest a myriad of strategies. But firms have the resources to conduct evaluative research on only a small subset of these strategies. To deal with this problem, it is often possible to use findings from theoretical consumer research. Such findings provide a way of identifying strategic alternatives that are most likely to be effective (Table 2.1).

In this chapter, we shall examine how consumer research is used to guide corporate

TABLE 2.1. Consumer Research: Describing, Explaining and Evaluating

RESEARCH APPROACH	STRATEGIC USE
DESCRIPTIVE RESEARCH • Describes consumers' purchase behavior	Estimation of demand Identification of target
EXPLANATORY RESEARCH • Identifies causes of consumers' behavior	Selection of potential product, price, promotion, and distribution strategies
THEORETICAL RESEARCH • Specifies the relationship among theoretical constructs	Identification of most viable strategies
EVALUATIVE RESEARCH • Identifies consumer response to marketing strategy	Estimation of strategy effectiveness

policy-making. Descriptive, explanatory, and evaluative research procedures are outlined, and their role in the corporate policy-making process is discussed. Then the role of *theoretical* consumer research in policy formulation is examined. To illustrate these approaches, we shall rely on an account of a manager's deliberations in marketing full-size automobiles.

DESCRIPTIVE RESEARCH

The development of an effective marketing program begins with the acquisition of facts about potential consumers: who they are, where they buy, when they buy, and the like. To learn these facts, three types of procedures are typically used: archives, observation, and surveys.

Archives

Archival data is usually collected as part of on-going business activity. Although it is not accumulated to address any specific issue, it may be useful in answering a variety of managerial questions. Perhaps the most common type of archival data is corporate sales. Firms commonly accumulate sales data and categorize it by the various regions in which their brand is sold. This information indicates the total demand for a brand. It is also useful in assessing the relative demand for various regions of the country. For this purpose a Brand Development Index (BDI) is developed. The BDI is computed by dividing the brand sales per thousand people in a particular region by the average brand sales per thousand people in the country as a whole. This quotient is multiplied by 100. BDI may be represented as follows:

$$\text{BDI} = \frac{\text{Sales of a brand in a region per 1,000 people}}{\text{Average sales of a brand in the country per 1,000 people}} \times 100$$

Thus, if the brand sales for the Chevrolet automobile are 5 per 1000 people in Buffalo and they average 4 per 1000 in the country as a whole, the BDI for Buffalo would be 125 (5/4 × 100). In general, BDIs over 100 indicate that the sales of a brand in a region are better than brand sales for the country as a whole, whereas BDIs under 100 indicate that a region is weaker than the country as a whole. By computing the BDI for all regions in which a brand is sold, the strategist is able to identify strong and weak markets.

Sales archives are also useful for detecting trends in demand. An examination of monthly sales records gathered over a period of several years can be used to identify seasonal sales patterns. In addition, business cycles lasting from several months to several years can be detected.

In sum, a firm's sales archives are useful in determining the aggregate demand for a brand, the relative contribution of various regions to demand, and the times at which demand for a brand is likely to be strong and weak. To interpret these facts, it is useful to compare them to industry sales performance. Although corporations do not usually collect this information, it is often readily available to them through industry trade associations and syndicated services, such as Neilsen and SAMI. The industry sales data collected provide a basis for estimating total product demand, product seasonality and cycles, and a firm's market share. Moreover, by examining industry sales one can compute a Category Development Index (CDI). Conceptually, the CDI is identical to the BDI. However, it reflects the sales of the category rather than the brand. Thus, the CDI of a particular region is represented as:

$$CDI = \frac{\text{Sales of the product category in a region per 1,000 people}}{\text{Average sales of the product category in the country per 1,000 people}} \times 100$$

Examination of CDI and BDI concurrently provides the manager with some preliminary strategic insights. As Figure 2.1 shows, when both the CDI and BDI in a region are high, the manager must be concerned about saturation. Thus, there is a need to resist the temptation to invest heavily in a high BDI-high CDI region because it may result in diminishing marginal returns. When CDI is low but BDI is high, the appropriate action is likely to be a maintenance strategy, where the brand attempts to hold its preferred position. In some instances it may be appropriate for a firm to attempt stimulation of

Figure 2.1.   CDI and BDI Analysis

Category Development Index

		High	Low
Brand Development Index	High	Saturation	Maintenance or Category Stimulation
	Low	Competition	Opportunity?

category demand in low CDI, high BDI areas. When CDI is high but BDI is low, a firm must determine the factors underlying its poor performance. Finally, when both CDI and BDI are low, it must be ascertained whether the area constitutes a poor opportunity or an opportunity that has not been exploited.

To illustrate the use of sales archives, consider the sales trend data shown in Figure 2.2 for the Chevrolet Impala and other full-size cars (for example, Ford LTD) in relation to mid-size cars, (for example, Oldsmobile Cutlass). These data were generated from archival records. They indicate that the Impala has maintained about a thirty-one percent share of the full-size car market between 1976 and 1980. Moreover, the unit sales for full-size cars have dropped during this period. Mid-size car sales have increased. It seems apparent from these data that consumers are switching from full-size to mid-size cars. This conjecture seems quite reasonable in light of the rapidly escalating price of gasoline; people are switching from full-size gas guzzlers to more fuel efficient mid-size cars. But it should be noted that sales archives do not rule out another interpretation of consumers' behavior. Specifically, it may be that rather than switching from full-size to mid-size cars, consumers who have traditionally bought full-size cars have taken themselves out of the market. Perhaps they are holding onto their current cars longer than they have in the past. The increase in mid-size sales may be due to the entry of first-time purchasers into the market.

The automobile example underscores several important features of archival sales

Figure 2.2.   Full-size and Mid-size Unit Sales, 1971–1980

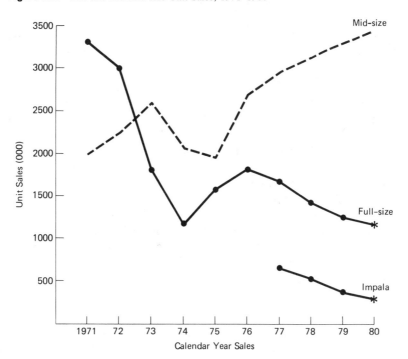

data. It provides factual information about a brand's performance over time and in relation to other brands. The pattern of sales may also suggest an explanation for consumers' response. But in many cases, it cannot rule out plausible rival explanations. This is because the aggregate nature of sales archives (and most other archives) does not allow detection of individual consumer's behavior. A survey approach, which we shall discuss in the next section, is needed for this purpose.

Sales archives categorized by regions of the country provide further insight about the problem faced by Impala. In high BDI and CDI areas such as the East, Great Lakes, and Southwest, sales losses for full-size cars between 1976 and 1980 have been most substantial. If Impala seeks to halt the decline, these regions are prime candidates for a new strategy.

Survey

A second approach to conducting descriptive research involves the use of surveys. A survey provides factual information about individual consumers. This information may pertain to their demographic profile (for example, age, income); their consumption behavior with respect to products, services, and media; their knowledge of various issues, and their attitudes toward them. By examining the relationships among the responses consumers provide in a survey, a description of purchase behavior can be developed.

Marketing managers frequently use surveys conducted by syndicated services. These services make the results of their surveys available to their clients for a fee. The data provided by such services is often helpful in describing more fully patterns of consumer response observed in archival records. The Roper service, for example, annually collects and analyzes survey information about consumers' purchase intentions for a variety of products. Among the questions asked in the Roper survey are ones pertaining to consumers' automobile purchase intention. The results of this survey are shown in Figure 2.3. They indicate that the decline in full-size car sales is related to the fact that owners of full-size cars intend to buy fewer full-size cars and more mid-size cars in the future.

Syndicated service data is often useful in describing the market. The Simmons service collects survey information about consumers' demographic characteristics, product consumption practices, and media consumption behaviors. By cross-classifying this information, one is able to build a demographic profile of the good and poor prospects. For example, Simmons data indicates that owners of full-size cars are people between the ages of thirty and forty-four, whose incomes are $20,000 and who live in the more rural areas of the country as well as suburban metropolitan areas. These inferences emerge by categorizing people according to the size of car they indicated owning in the Simmons survey and examining the demographic characteristics of full-size car owners. Good prospects for full-sized cars are determined by inspection of index numbers.[1] An index number provides a numerical representation of the incidence of some group in a con-

---

[1]See Scissors and Petray (1976) for a more detailed discussion of index numbers.

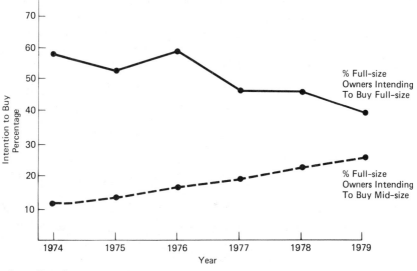

Figure 2.3. Full-size Car Owners Intent To Buy 1974–1979

% Full-size
Owners Intending
To Buy Full-size

% Full-size
Owners Intending
To Buy Mid-size

Source: Roper Survey

sumption category in relation to the incidence of that group in the population. For computational purposes, an index number can be expressed as follows:

$$\text{Index number} = \frac{\text{Percent of some group engaging in some behavior}}{\text{Percent of the population made up of some group}} \times 100$$

To clarify the meaning of index numbers, consider the age group thirty to forty-four. Suppose this age group composes forty percent of all full-size car owners but only twenty percent of the population. The index number in this instance is 200 (40/20 × 100). It indicates that the age group thirty to forty-four composes twice the number of full-size car owners as one would expect on the basis of the incidence of thirty to forty-four year olds in the population. Thus, index numbers over 100 indicate a disproportionately high representation of some group (say thirty to forty-four year olds) on some consumption behavior (say full-size car purchase). In contrast, index numbers under 100 indicate disproportionately low representation of some group with respect to some consumption practice. We characterized the full-size car owner as a thirty to forty-four year old with an income of $20,000 because the index numbers for full-size car ownership were above one hundred for people with these characteristics.

The rationale for using index numbers as a basis for targeting is that it is efficient to focus on those people who have a disproportionately large chance of being consumers of the product being marketed. Although this rationale has appeal, several precautions must be taken when index numbers are used to identify prospects. First, it is important to verify that a target is large enough to warrant a separate strategy. Suppose a group comprises one percent of full-size car buyers, and .5 percent of the population. The index number is 200, which would make the group appear attractive, but because it is comprised of so few people, it is not.

A second and related precaution that is necessary in using index numbers is to insure that the target as a whole is substantial. Suppose people with each of the following characteristics exhibit high index numbers with respect to subcompact car ownership.

Age: 18–24

Income: $30,000 and up

Family Size: Three or more children

Although the index number for each characteristic is high, this target is unlikely to be an attractive one. The problem is that there are very few people who possess all three characteristics. One way to overcome this problem is to alter the specification on one or more attributes. Thus, if we broaden the age characteristic to say eighteen to thirty-four years of age, the index number may fall somewhat, but the number of people possessing all three demographic characteristics is likely to be greater than the number in the eighteen to twenty-four-year-old group.

Syndicated survey data provide an efficient way to learn some basic facts about the consumers. It can be used to identify who uses the product category and what brands they use. Nevertheless, there are instances when syndicated survey research is not adequate. One such instance occurs when a new product introduction is being planned. Here, syndicated data are useful only to the extent one is willing to make inferences based on people's consumption of existing products. And these inferences may be wrong. Syndicated data are also unlikely to be adequate when interest centers on knowing the information consumers are using in making consumption decisions.

To address these issues, firms often conduct their own surveys. A new product survey may entail describing the product being considered for introduction or showing consumers a prototype of the new product and asking for their reactions. (This topic is covered in greater detail in Chapter Twelve.) This information yields some preliminary indication of the reception the product is likely to get when it is introduced, the demographic characteristics of the people who are likely to be good prospects, and the reaction to specific product features. For existing products, surveys may be used to discern how aware consumers are of a product or brand, their understanding of its function, and their evaluation of its performance. In effect, this information amplifies the description of consumer behavior that one obtains from syndicated and archival data. Specifically, it describes consumers' response on factors that might underlie an observed sales response. For example, a corporate survey may indicate that the weak sales of the Impala among people under thirty observed from syndicated data is associated with the fact that they do not value interior roominess, or that they do value the sportiness of smaller cars.

Observation

Observation provides an inexpensive approach to enhancing our understanding of consumers' behavior.[2] Observational research can be conducted as part of the everyday activities that are performed in running a business. It may involve the direct observation of consumers' behavior; who purchases, what roles other people play in the purchase decision, when consumers purchase, and the issues or concerns they have in purchasing can be determined by a direct observation approach.

Another form of observation entails the inspection of physical traces left by consumers. In consuming, people often use up resources (that is, erosion) as well as leave behind residual evidence of their presence (that is, accretion). By observing the physical traces due to erosion and accretion, clues regarding consumers' behavior may be observed.

To illustrate the observation approach, consider the decision to purchase an automobile. Direct observation on the showroom floor yields valuable insights about the characteristics of the target audience. The amount of showroom traffic during various days of the week and times of day is useful in planning the sales staffing requirements. The customers' approximate age, sex, and make of the customers' current automobile is useful in identifying good prospects. These data are also useful in choosing advertising content and media. Direct observation helps identify the person responsible for various aspects of the car purchase decision. It may be observed, for example, that the husband is the primary decision maker with respect to car make, engine size, and price. The wife may be responsible for the particular model, accessories, and color. This knowledge is useful in deciding the content of the salesperson's presentations and advertising appeals made to the various participants in the purchase decision. Finally, consumers' problems and concerns in making the purchase decision can be observed. Recurrent questions about financing, service, warranty, and the like may suggest that some action must be taken by the manager to facilitate sales.

Physical traces are also a valuable means of observing consumers' behavior. The daily erosion of sales brochures from the showroom provides some indication of the models people are interested in. The rate of erosion of tiles or carpeting in different areas of the showroom indicate patrons' traffic patterns. Strategic placement of cars to conform to these traffic patterns increases the likelihood they will be seen by customers. Accretion, too, may be useful. For example, a Chicago Chevrolet dealer, Z. Frank, routinely has his mechanics check the station to which car radios are tuned when customers bring their cars in for servicing. By repeating this procedure for all service customers, the radio stations on which advertising is most likely to be heard can be determined. Moreover, by checking the customers' odometers and model year, the salesperson can identify and contact likely new car prospects.

Observational research provides an efficient means of obtaining information about consumers. Direct observation and physical traces can be used to supplement previously

[2]See Webb et al. (1965) for a detailed discussion of observational methods.

conducted survey research by filling in details about such issues as when people are likely to purchase, and the purchase roles assumed by various family members. Observational methods may also be useful when conducted prior to survey research. Observational methods provide some initial indication about the kind of people who should be surveyed, and the types of issues that should be addressed in survey research. But observational research can seldom be used in lieu of surveys. Observation is not a sufficient basis for describing consumers because it gives little indication of the generality of the behaviors that have been observed or the incidence and nature of behaviors that have not been observed.

Summary

Three approaches to describing consumers' behavior have been identified. Archives are particularly useful in describing consumer responses, and particularly their sales response. Surveys supplement archival information by providing demographic and geographic profiles of category and brand users. Surveys may also be used to identify people's cognitive reactions to product offerings; that is, the awareness of a product, their understanding of its use, and their assessment of its features. Observational research is useful if conducted prior to surveys in that it suggests the types of people and issues that might be addressed in survey work. Observational research is also valuable in supplementing the description of consumer behavior inferred from surveys.

EXPLANATORY RESEARCH

Descriptive research provides factual information pertaining to consumers' behavior. It describes which consumers purchase, when they purchase, how much they purchase, and what they know or believe about a product. On the basis of such description, one might infer why people do what they do. But such inferences often involve great leaps of faith. Or, if the inferences are more conservative, they provide only a superficial explanation of consumers' behavior. For example, consider the descriptive fact that consumers are switching from full-size Impalas to mid-size cars because of the latters' superior fuel economy. Survey data can be gathered to support this view by showing that consumers value fuel economy and that mid-size cars are rated higher on this dimension than full-size cars. But this explanation provides little insight about what Chevrolet might do to halt the switch to smaller cars. What is needed is an explanation for consumers' belief that large car fuel economy is poor and their belief that good fuel economy is an important consideration in making the car purchase decision. A guess can be made about the cause of these beliefs, but it will be based on assumptions not apparent from descriptive research.

To generate defensible insights about the motivations for consumers' behavior, explanatory research is useful. This entails implementing a qualitative research approach.[3]

---

[3]See Calder (1977) for a detailed discussion of this topic.

One type of qualitative research is *depth interviewing*. Potential consumers are interviewed individually regarding their thoughts and actions pertaining to the product of interest. Depth interviewing is often longitudinal in character in that research participants are asked to trace their thoughts and actions before, during, and after purchase. Thus, it allows the researcher to construct an event sequence that explains individuals' behavior.

A second type of qualitative research involves *focus groups*. Between six and ten potential purchasers are typically recruited for a focus group session. As in depth interviewing, they are asked to discuss their thoughts and actions pertaining to some consumption issue. But focus groups are not simply depth interviews done six or ten at a time. Rather, focus groups provide the opportunity for consumers to learn about the experience of others and to use this information as a stimulus in developing and expressing their own thoughts. The views individuals express in focus groups are reactions to the thoughts expressed by others.

Whether one uses depth interviewing or focus groups, two types of explanation for consumers' behavior may be sought. One is *everyday explanation*. Here consumers indicate what they believe has caused their behavior. The reasons they give may not be the actual causes of behavior. Nevertheless, everyday explanations are useful because they put the manager in touch with consumers. From such explanation managers learn about consumers' experience from a consumer's perspective. They learn the vocabulary consumers use to describe and account for their experience. This knowledge is useful in developing marketing programs that are adaptive to consumers' perspectives.

To obtain useful everyday explanations, several guidelines should be followed. The person conducting the depth interviews or focus groups should have empathy for the views of research participants. This orientation will make it easier for the interviewer to stimulate a full discussion of the research issue. People who participate in focus group research at one time should hold similar perspectives so as to maximize the extent to which a particular point of view is articulated. The generality of this view can be examined by repeating the qualitative research with diverse groups, each of which is homogeneous.

A second use of qualitative research is as a basis for *scientific explanation*. As such, it provides evidence about the relationship between constructs postulated by some theory. To the extent qualitative research provides theory-supporting evidence, we may invoke the theory to design marketing strategy. In essence, qualitative research yields insight about the appropriate scientific explanation. Having identified this explanation, we may then proceed to develop strategies suggested by it.

In using qualitative research to develop scientific explanation, it is important that the interviewer be an expert in consumer behavior theory. This knowledge is needed if research participants are to be asked questions that will indicate the appropriate scientific explanation. How similar or different the people recruited are depends on the scientific explanations being considered. If the scientific explanation specifies that outcomes depend on characteristics distinguishing people from one another, research participants should reflect different degrees of the characteristic on which outcomes are thought to depend. Otherwise, a homogeneous group of research participants is adequate.

The value of qualitative research as a basis for explaining consumer motivation is illustrated by the following results of depth interviews and focus groups.[4] These techniques were used to explain the motivations underlying consumers' switching from full-size to mid-size cars noted earlier in archival research. In the depth interviews, people in the market for a new car were asked to talk about their deliberations in making car purchase decisions. The purpose is to provide an everyday explanation for switching from full- to mid-size cars. A focus group with ten prospective new car buyers also was conducted to provide a scientific explanation for the same behavior.

From the depth interviews, it was learned that room and comfort were attractive features of a full-size car. When describing their current full-size cars, consumers said:

> . . . The thing I like best is that it is a big car and I'm able to do a lot of shopping at once because I have room to carry lots of packages. I need a big car—or a small car and a small truck.
>
> . . . What I like best is that it can carry six adults with no problem. We can go out with other couples and we don't need two cars.
>
> . . . The car is very comfortable. It accommodates long-legged people. I have a 6'2" son and a 5'10" daughter. It's helpful to have a big car for family trips.

Apparently, switching to mid-size cars was occurring despite consumers' appreciation for the room and comfort of full-size cars. Some insight about the reasons for this trend emerged when consumers who had switched from a full- to mid-size car described their new car purchase deliberations in depth interviews. As one consumer put it:

> The gasoline situation was getting worse. The old car was getting under ten miles per gallon. I had planned a trade-in anyway, and so I decided that this time I should get a mid-size car.

Consumers were equating automobile size with fuel economy; the smaller the car, the more economical it was perceived to be. The depth interviews also suggested that mass media advertising was promoting this concept. As a consumer who was considering her new car purchase decision said, "I've really been watching the ads on TV. And a car that would have good (gas) mileage is primarily on my mind."

Depth interviewing provides a description of consumers' experience in making a car purchase decision. Consumers who were considering the purchase of a full-size car face a dilemma. While it has the room and comfort they like, it is also viewed as providing poor fuel economy. This view appears to be one that was adopted on the basis of exposure to television ads. Despite this description of consumers' experience, we are uncertain about the specific causes of their behavior. We know that television advertising plays a role in car choice. But the details of television advertising effects are sketchy.

To address this issue, a focus group was conducted. The group was composed of ten people who were in the market for a new car and were considering a full-size car.

---

[4]This research was conducted at Northwestern University as part of a competition sponsored by General Motors. Researchers included Sherri Bergman, Robert Clark, Clay Cookerly, James Eiche, Robert Ewing, Rikki Horne, Tyler Johnston, Kim Leventhal, Georgia Lyman, Robert Nunez, and Paul Romer.

Among the issues addressed were the reasons people buy a small car. Part of the conversation went as follows:

Member 1:   You hear the propaganda all the time, you know . . . 'You've got to drive a small car, the American public must learn to drive small cars.' It's pounded into us day and night. Pretty soon, we start to think that way.

Member 2:   You become trained, or you become brainwashed, or whatever, by advertising that a small car or a medium-sized car is the thing to do. And now that GM is downsizing the larger, more luxurious-sized cars, you start believing the story.

Member 3:   That's right. I think Detroit has abandoned the full-size car. I have yet to see one commercial for an Impala that I can remember.

Member 4:   We've got to use less gasoline is what it comes down to. And to use less gas, that's why you go to a small car.

These focus group comments indicate that consumers feel they are being forced to buy small cars. They feel that they are being brainwashed into believing that fuel economy means a small car. The media are perceived to be so one-sided in delivering this message that it is accepted, even though consumers appear to be skeptical about the veracity of the small car message.

The focus group findings are consistent with the scientific explanation provided by information processing theory. According to this view, consumer behavior is a function of the behavior-relevant thoughts people have in memory. And because the media are dominated by a "think small car" mentality, such thoughts are most readily available to consumers. As a result, consumers are switching to smaller-sized cars. To offset this trend, our explanation implies the use of a strategy that will make the virtues of large cars dominant in consumers' minds. One way to achieve this objective is to combat the smaller car advocacy by using heavy media weights (that is, high levels of repetition) in advertising full-sized cars. In effect, this would make information supportive of full-size car purchase more available to consumers. Another strategy emerging from our scientific explanation entails providing consumers with arguments to counter small-car propaganda. For example, full-size car advertising might note that the difference in fuel economy between a full-size and mid-size car is about the same as the cost of a cup of coffee a day. From an information processing perspective, this strategy is expected to be effective because it will provide consumers with thoughts to counter small car advocacies.

In sum, qualitative research serves as a basis for two types of explanation. It provides an everyday explanation that consumers use to explain their experiences. This explanation enables the manager to share consumers' experience. Qualitative research also enables a determination of a scientific explanation for consumers' behaviors. Scientific explanation then serves as a guide to developing marketing strategy. One question that emerges from this is, where do scientific explanations come from? Before we can address this issue, we need to examine evaluative research methods, which are an integral part of scientific explanation development.

EVALUATIVE RESEARCH

Once a strategy has been selected, its effectiveness requires evaluation. At issue in evaluation research is whether some strategy caused a desired outcome. To demonstrate causation, three conditions must be met. First, the causal agent or strategy must precede the outcome it is supposed to have induced. Second, the outcome must co-vary with the presence of the causal agent; that is, some outcome is present when a strategy is present, but not when that strategy is absent. Third, plausible rival explanations for the observed outcome must be ruled out.

In attempting to conform to these criteria researchers often face a dilemma. They can conduct a true experiment that satisfies these criteria, but is often very costly. Or they can use quasi-experiments, which are less costly, but may compromise strong causal inferences. To understand how one may deal with this dilemma judiciously, the nature of true experiments and quasi-experiments is examined.

True Experiments

The distinguishing characteristic of true experiments is that consumers are randomly assigned to different strategies and the impact of each strategy on some outcome is measured.[5] Random assignment permits a strong causal inference that strategy X caused outcome Y. This is so because random assignment insures that people assigned to receive different strategies are equivalent, except with respect to the strategy they receive. This is not to say that individuals do not differ from each other. They do. But by randomly assigning enough of them to strategies, these differences are equally represented in each strategy condition examined.

True experiments conform to the criteria we have set for making strong causal inferences. Random assignment minimizes the chances that there will be plausible rival explanations for the observation that a strategy caused the observed result. Moreover, true experiments are conducted so that the strategy is presented before outcomes are measured. And, by statistical analysis, we can measure the extent of co-variation between strategy and outcome.

True experiments are used to evaluate a variety of marketing strategies. In controlled laboratory settings, true experiments are used to assess alternative product formulations. Consumers are randomly assigned to evaluate products varying in color, odor, flavor, and other characteristics. A laboratory setting is also used to assess experimentally the relative effectiveness of different advertising appeals. The laboratory setting is chosen as the site for true experiments, because it provides an inexpensive means of assessing strategy. It also reduces the likelihood that competitors will become aware of a firm's strategy prior to its introduction.

True experiments are also conducted in natural settings. This research, which is

[5]See Sternthal and Craig (1975) for a detailed discussion of experimentation.

generally referred to as test marketing, involves choosing several cities that are representative of the target population and that afford containment of marketing strategy. Containment refers to the fact that mass media advertising and distribution cover the area where the strategy is being tested with minimum spillover into other areas. Without containment of distribution, for example, it would be very difficult to estimate the impact of advertising strategy on sales. Some people would have access to the product but be outside of the area reached by advertising. Thus, their sales response would not reflect the advertising effort. Some cities that conform to the representativeness and containment criteria are Spokane, Milwaukee, Columbus, and Erie. In doing test marketing, some cities would be randomly assigned to receive the strategy to be tested, while others would serve as controls and receive no incremental marketing effort. Strategies might include variations in product, price levels, distribution, and promotion.

To illustrate the issues involved in conducting true experiments, consider a car manufacturer's evaluation of a strategy to promote a line of full-size automobiles. Two cities are randomly chosen to receive the strategy, which involves spending $100,000 to promote the fact that the difference in fuel cost per day between a full-size and mid-size car is the same as a cup of coffee. In addition, a rebate program of one hundred dollars is offered for each full-size car purchased. In the two control cities, no advertising or rebate program is instituted.

Suppose it is found that sales of full-size cars are on the average twenty percent higher in the cities receiving the strategy than in the control cities during the month following the strategy introduction. We can conclude that the advertising and rebate program caused this outcome. In contrast, suppose there were no difference in sales between strategy and control cities. It may be appropriate to conclude that the strategy was ineffective. Alternatively, it may be that the strategy may be effective under normal conditions, but in this instance was swamped by some other factor, such as a shortage of cars, or a recession.

It may be concluded that true experiments are highly informative when differences are observed between strategy and nonstrategy conditions. When no differences are observed, the conclusion is more equivocal. The strategy may be no more or less effective than others to which it is being compared. Or, it may be that some factor unknown to the researcher is producing the null effect, and in the absence of this factor the strategy would be effective.

Another experimental issue illustrated by the advertising and rebate strategy relates to the construct represented by a strategy. If a true experiment reveals that the advertising and rebate strategy yield a greater sales response than some other strategy alternatives, we may conclude that the strategy caused sales. But there is a problem in labeling the causal agent. Specifically, it is not known whether it was the advertising, the rebate, or the combination of the two that caused sales. Thus, the experimental finding compels the strategist to use the entire strategy. If just the rebate portion of the strategy were being considered, research would be required in which this strategy was varied independently of advertising. Eight cities would be needed for this research rather than the four needed to identify the joint effect of advertising and rebate (Figure 2.4).

Figure 2.4. Testing Strategy Effectiveness Using a True Experiment

Advertising Strategy

		Yes	No
Rebate Strategy	Yes	2 Cities	2 Cities
	No	2 Cities	2 Cities

Quasi-Experiments

True experiments, particularly ones conducted in natural settings, are expensive and require a significant amount of time to complete. To circumvent these problems, quasi-experimental procedures may be employed.[6] Quasi-experiments are similar to true experiments except for the fact that experimental units (people, cities) are not randomly assigned to the conditions being tested. As a result, plausible rival explanations for an observed effect often emerge. To the extent that these rival explanations can be ruled out, one can make causal inferences about a strategy's effect with confidence. While they do suffer from some limitations, quasi-experiments offer certain advantages, a major one being that their cost is often substantially lower than true experiments.

Before-After. Perhaps the simplest quasi-experimental procedure is the before-after design. It entails measuring some outcome (for example, sales) before a strategy is introduced and again some time after it is introduced. For example, one may assess full-size car sales in the month prior to and the month following the introduction of a rebate program for full-size cars. An increase in sales coincidental with the rebate program may imply that the program caused the sales increase. But rival explanations, such as variation in weather conditions, competitors' practices, seasonal fluctuations in sales, must be ruled out before one can assume with confidence that the rebate caused the sales increase.

To rule out at least some of the rival explanations, it is useful to include a control group in the before-after design. The control group is one that does not receive the strategy. Even though the control group is not randomly selected, the observation that the strategy yielded greater outcomes than the control is likely to be due to the strategy, if the control and strategy conditions are comparable. Variations in such factors as seasonality, weather, and competitive activity should affect both strategy and control groups equally. Thus, an increase in differences between the strategy and control conditions from the before to the after measure is likely to be attributable to the strategy.

The addition of a control group reduces the plausibility of most rival explanations.

[6]See Cook and Campbell (1979) and Phillips and Calder (1979, 1980) for a detailed discussion of quasi-experimental methods.

But because experimental units were not randomly assigned, all plausible rival explanations are not ruled out. Suppose it is observed that the difference in outcomes for strategy and control conditions increases between the before and after measures. It may be due to different local histories. The control group was exposed to some nonstrategy factor that the strategy condition did not receive. Or the strategy and control conditions involve different outcome trends. It may be that the units in the control condition were at their highest outcome level at the time of the before measure, whereas the units in the strategy condition were at their lowest outcome level at the time of the before measure. Even without the strategy introduction, it might be expected that the outcome would increase in the strategy condition, but not in the control condition. Or, it may be that the rate of change in outcomes differs between control and strategy conditions, such that the rate is greater in the strategy condition.

One way to minimize the plausibility of local history and trend explanations is to use multiple control groups. The idea is that by having several control groups the probability that control and strategy conditions will have unique histories or trends is minimized. The problem with this approach is that it is not subject to empirical verification. One must assume that multiple control groups minimize unique nonstrategy factors. A more compelling approach is to increase substantially the number of outcome observations beyond the two used in the before-after procedure. This involves the use of a time series approach.

Time Series. Time series analysis with control group extends the before-after design by including multiple observations of outcomes both before and after strategy introduction. This feature can be used to rule out trend differences between strategy and control conditions as a plausible explanation for observed outcomes. Moreover, by switching the groups that are designated as strategy and control, local history can be ruled out as a plausible explanation. But to implement the time series approach, a minimum of fifty outcome observations is required. Either one must have good archives, or be willing to pay the cost to collect the required outcome data to implement the time series approach.

To illustrate the time series approach, consider the effect of a full-size car rebate program. After an initial monitoring period (Figure 2.5, t_0–t_{10}) the rebate strategy is introduced in the strategy condition, but not in the control condition. The result is an increase in sales of full-size cars in the strategy condition relative to the control. This outcome cannot be due to trend (Figure 2.5). But it can be due to such local history factors as more advertising in the strategy condition. To minimize the plausibility of this explanation, the strategy is retracted from the strategy condition, in effect making it the control. Moreover, the strategy is introduced to what was formerly the control (Figure 2.5, t_{10}–t_{30}). The idea of this switching maneuver is to determine whether the strategy effect still holds. If it does, it is likely to be due to the strategy and not local history. For this latter explanation to be plausible, it would be necessary for the local history that was first associated with one condition to become disassociated with it and associated with the other. Such an occurrence is unlikely.

Time series analysis allows relatively strong causal inferences, despite the absence of random assignment. Moreover, if multiple observations of the outcome data are already

Figure 2.5. Time Series Data for Automobile Promotion Strategy

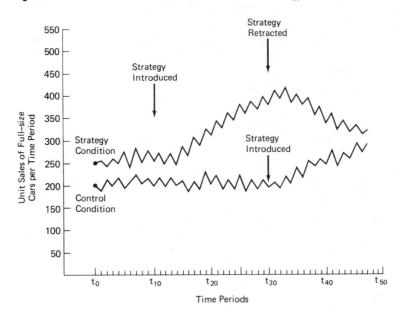

being collected as part of routine business operation (for example, car sales), the time series approach is inexpensive in relation to true experimental procedures. When it is not routinely collected, it may be more feasible to resort to a before-after approach with multiple control groups.

THEORETICAL RESEARCH AND POLICY DECISIONS

Until now, we have examined research approaches useful in making policy decisions. As we noted, research that describes and explains consumers' behavior serves as a basis for strategy development and evaluative research is useful in assessing the relative efficacy of the strategies developed. But there is a problem inherent in this approach. Descriptive and explanatory research often suggest many more strategies than can be evaluated. Guidance in deciding which strategies to evaluate comes from theory testing research.

The goal of theory testing research is to provide the conditions that allow falsification of the relationships between constructs postulated by a theory. Theories that have repeatedly escaped rigorous falsification attempts are the best candidates for guiding strategy selection. In effect, such theories inform managers about the relationship they can expect between some strategy and some outcome. It is left to the manager's creativity to devise the strongest possible application of the theory for his or her particular situation.

Theory testing research bears some similarity to the evaluative research procedures discussed earlier. It usually involves the performance of true experiments in laboratory settings. What is being evaluated in this instance, however, is not the effectiveness of some strategy, but rather whether the relationships postulated by a theory escape falsification.

To illustrate the nature and role of theory testing research, let us reconsider the situation described earlier where the goal was to stimulate the demand for full-size cars. The problem was to choose strategies that would offset the belief that full-size cars yield poor fuel economy. One solution to this problem may be to use a heavy advertising schedule that presents the facts about the fuel economy of the full-size car.

The manager can determine the effectiveness of this strategy empirically by conducting evaluative research described in the previous section. But given the cost of evaluation, it is important to evaluate only those strategies that have a good chance of being effective. Results of theory testing research not only suggest whether a strategy is likely to be effective, but also the conditions under which outcomes are likely to be optimal.

To anticipate the effect of increasing advertising for full-size cars, we shall rely on information processing theory. According to this theory, the content of a message is processed and stored as thoughts in memory. When an individual is faced with a car purchase decision, these thoughts are activated and used in evaluating choice alternatives. Up to a point (that is, low message redundancy), the greater the amount of message repetition, the greater the likelihood that these thoughts will be stored and the greater the likelihood of their use in evaluation. And because the message advocates purchasing a full-size car, the likelihood of positive evaluation and purchase of a full-size car increases as the message is repeated. Beyond a certain number of repetitions (that is, high message redundancy), the message may lose its information value. Subsequent repetitions cause people to think about their own thoughts rather than the ones contained in the message. Because the message is likely to provide a stronger advocacy for full-size cars than one's own thoughts, evaluation becomes less favorable (Figure 2.6).

Information processing theory thus postulates a nonmonotonic relationship (inverted U) between a construct we shall call information redundancy and a construct termed evaluation. Initial message repetitions (low redundancy) increase the favorableness of evaluation, whereas subsequent repetitions reduce it. In the typical test of this theory, college students are assigned to low, moderate, or high levels of message repetition. After reading or viewing the persuasive appeal, they are asked to rate their feelings about the position being advocated. As we shall see in Chapter Thirteen, the results of these theory tests have reliably shown the pattern presented in Figure 2.6.

Several features of the theory testing procedure described are worthy of note. The use of students as research participants is appropriate. The information processing theory described above does not specify differences between people. In testing this theory, it is therefore appropriate to select as homogeneous a group as possible, so as to minimize the effect of nontheoretical variables on outcomes. Students conform to this criterion. While nonstudents' responses may differ from those given by students, the nature of the relationship is not expected to be affected by the type of research respondents used. It should also be noted that theory testing research assesses whether relationships postulated by the theory are observed, but does not yield parameter estimates; that is, how much repetition will yield how much demand. Thus, we can determine whether or not infor-

Figure 2.6. Repetition Effects on Evaluation

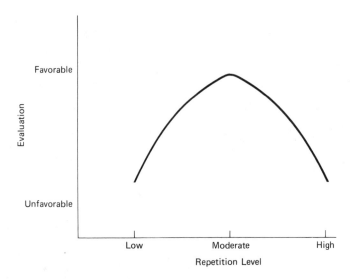

mation redundancy is nonmonotonically (inverted U) related to evaluations using theory testing procedures. However, the number of message repetitions required to yield the optimal evaluation cannot be determined.

These features distinguish theory research from the policy-oriented research discussed earlier. In policy research, participants are chosen to represent the target of interest. Since policy research frequently is intended to provide parameter estimates from tests of information processing theory, the manager learns that increasing the amount of advertising is a viable means of stimulating demand for full-size cars. The manager is also informed that the amount of advertising can be overdone. On the basis of this knowledge, several different repetition levels can be tested using true experimental or quasi-experimental approaches. This latter research will indicate the number of repetitions needed to optimize evaluation in the situation of interest.

SUMMARY

Consumer research provides a basis for understanding consumption behavior and for designing strategies to influence consumer demand. Specifically, three types of research are useful for this purpose. Descriptive research, which is based on archives, surveys, or observation provides details about the consumption activity. This information includes a demographic profile of product category and brand users, geographic areas of product and brand strengths and weaknesses, product characteristics important to choice and aggregate product demand. Explanatory research supplies information about how consumers view the consumption decision. Thus it puts the manager in touch with the market. It also is useful in identifying consumers' underlying motivations in making purchase decisions. By interpreting qualitative research findings in theoretical terms, strategies are suggested which are useful in influencing consumer demand. For this purpose theories that have withstood rigorous falsification attempts are most appropriate. Finally, strategies based on the theoretical analysis that are deemed appropriate to the manager's goals are subjected to evaluative research procedures. The most rigorous of these procedures is the true experiment. In instances where true experiments are not feasible, quasi-experiments may be used to assess strategy effectiveness.

In some firms, the manager may not have access to the complete arsenal of descriptive, explanatory, and evaluative research approaches outlined in this chapter. Nevertheless, a substantial number of these approaches can be employed as part of the everyday conduct of business. Sales records categorized by geographic areas should be available to all managers. These data are useful in establishing target objectives and evaluating strategy effectiveness. Firms of moderate size will have access to syndicated data useful in demographic targeting either by purchasing it directly or through their ad agency. Qualitative research needed to explain consumer behavior can be afforded by most firms.

QUESTIONS

1. Research data indicate the following BDIs for the three target competitors (A,B,C) in an industry and the CDI for the industry:

Geographic Area	BDI for Company			CDI
	A	B	C	
East	80	150	140	140
West	190	120	120	100
North	100	80	90	100
South	30	50	50	60

What region of the country is most attractive for Company A? Company B? Company C? Defend your selections.

2. Consider the following index numbers for soft drink consumption:

Age	Index #
18–24	120
25–39	100
40+	80

Income	
Under $10,000	80
$10,000–$19,999	120
$20,000 +	100

Number of children	
0	50
1	120
2	105
3	100
more than 3	125

Select a target for marketing soft drinks, making use of the index numbers shown.

3. Of what value is observation research? What advantages does observation research have in relation to other approaches to descriptive research?

4. Describe the research procedure you would use (a) to learn about consumers' thoughts about a brand of soft drink and (b) to identify the potential causes of consumers' brand choice among soft drinks.

5. What distinguishes a true experiment from a quasi-experiment?

6. Outline the advantages and disadvantages of a (a) true experiment (b) before-after study (c) time series study.

7. Of what value is theoretical consumer research to the marketing manager?

8. When is it appropriate to use students as research subjects?

9. Read the following case and determine whether the rebate was successful. Outline the reasons for your belief. Is it likely that Avery's modified rebate program will be effective?

> It is April 1980, and business in the auto industry is slow. So slow, in fact, that dealers are going out of business every month. To keep his General Motors operation viable, Kurt Avery planned a mid-year rebate program. Starting on April 1, he offered a one-hundred-dollar rebate and one month of free gasoline to purchasers of full-size Impalas. No rebate program is offered on the smaller size cars Avery sells. "This is a last ditch effort to keep my dealership going," Avery notes. "Why, just last week the Ford and American Motors operations in my region closed. They couldn't sell enough full-size or small cars."
>
> The table below shows Avery's monthly sales for Impala and smaller size cars. Avery considers his rebate program a success. He is considering using it again. But his previous experience indicates that it has eaten dramatically into profitability. Therefore, he plans to eliminate the free gasoline aspect of the rebate. Only the one-hundred-dollar rebate will be offered on the full-size Impala.

Avery Car Sales

		Full-size Impala	Small Cars
1979	Jan.	50	100
	Feb.	45	95
	March	60	110
	April	60	110
	May	60	115
	June	65	120
	July	70	115
	August	75	120
	Sept.	70	110
	Oct.	80	130
	Nov.	60	110
	Dec.	50	100
1980	Jan.	40	100
	Feb.	35	95
	March	30	105
	April	65	110
	May	75	110
	June	75	120

Part II

Consumer behavior as a field of inquiry is a relatively young discipline. Chapter Three sets it in historical perspective, starting with relatively simple models of consumer behavior developed several decades ago and ending with the most recent complex models. These models serve as a basis for the information processing model advanced in Chapter Four. This model organizes what is known about consumers' behavior and provides the structure for the remainder of the book.

Theory Development and Modeling Consumers' Behavior

Chapter 3

Theories of Consumer Behavior

Theory is the basis of consumer behavior inquiry. Theory directs research; it suggests the questions that the manager should pose to understand consumers' purchases. Theory is also useful in interpreting research findings and selecting strategies to influence behavior. Given the important role of theory, this chapter is devoted to a consideration of theory development in consumer behavior during the past several decades.

Interest in the development of theories to describe consumer decision making emerged after World War II. It was stimulated by dramatic changes in supply and demand that resulted from the war effort. On the supply side, there was a significant increase in the availability of goods and services. Firms that had been producing war material resumed production of peacetime goods. Technological advances spurred by the war effort resulted in more efficient operations. On the demand side, high wartime employment coupled with the lack of consumer goods during the war resulted in a mass market with financial stability. Furthermore, millions of Americans returned to civilian life with new interests, aspirations, and desires. These changes in the marketing environment resulted in the need to understand how diverse and sophisticated consumers made decisions. This was necessary to compete successfully with other producers for the consumers' dollar.

In response to this challenge, marketing academicians and practitioners attempted to explain and predict consumer behavior. On the basis of systematic inquiry they formulated theories, typically in the form of *models*. For our purposes, models are defined as simplified replicas of consumer decision-making phenomena. Models may incorporate one or more theories that provide an explanation for the phenomena of interest. As one might expect, initial attempts were based primarily on a single concept or a few concepts drawn from one discipline. These early models are called *monadic* models. Later, more complex models were suggested to explain and predict consumer behavior. These multiple variable models were interdisciplinary, reflecting the theoretical work done in psychology, sociology, and economics.

In this chapter, we examine some of the more prominent monadic and multiple variable models that have been developed to explain consumers' behavior. For each model considered, a description of how the model interprets consumer behavior is presented, the contribution of the model is identified, and its shortcomings are discussed. The aim of this analysis is to identify concepts that have contributed to an understanding of consumer behavior and to the development of effective marketing strategy.

MONADIC MODELS

Initial attempts to understand consumers' behavior relied on concepts from a single discipline. Monadic models developed by economists were first to attain prominence. In part, this was due to the existence of a well-developed microeconomic theory of consumer behavior, and in part to the fact that many marketers of the time were trained as economists. By the mid-1950s psychological models were competing for acceptance as explanations for consumers' behavior. Several monadic models are considered below.

Microeconomic Model

Microeconomic theory is based on the assumption that consumers attempt to maximize the utility of their purchases subject to some budget constraint. It is also assumed that consumers know what products and services they prefer, and have perfect knowledge about how to satisfy these preferences. Finally, it is assumed that consumers act in a consistent manner. One outgrowth of these assumptions is the prediction that consumers purchase less of an item as its price increases. This prediction is borne out in many real-world cases. In the mid 1970s coffee prices increased dramatically, and consumption of coffee dropped precipitously. There are numerous situations, however, in which the price-quantity relationship suggested by microeconomic theory is not substantiated. For products like health care items and alcoholic beverages, consumers often prefer the higher-priced brands. In situations such as these consumers are assuming that a higher price indicates better quality, and better quality is desired.

Several other problems emerge when the marketer attempts to employ the microeconomic model. One is that the model is normative. It states what consumers ought to do to maximize utility, rather than describing what they actually do. A second problem is that the model assumes that consumers have perfect knowledge. According to the microeconomic model, a consumer is aware of alternative brands, each of their prices, and their quality. When the price of a brand declines, it is assumed that consumers are aware of this change, and, other things being equal, will purchase the lower-priced item to maximize their utility. It should be noted, however, that even for frequently purchased items consumers may not retain a knowledge of specific prices or engage in comparison shopping (Craig, 1971). Rather, they may purchase a particular brand as long as it remains within an acceptable range of prices. Alternatively, they may select a store that they feel offers low prices, and once in the store make decisions on a nonprice basis. Thus, even the seemingly reasonable assumption that consumers are sensitive to price changes is subject to contradiction. A third problem with the microeconomic view is that its central construct, utility, is difficult to measure. A sensitive, reliable, and valid measure of utility has not been developed. When utility is measured it is generally after the fact. To know the utility consumers attribute to various goods and services, one must first observe the selection made. The marketing strategist, however, requires information concerning relative utility of alternatives before the consumers have made purchases if marketing strategies are to be planned, organized, and implemented to attract them.

Finally the microeconomic model fails to consider the psychological determinants of consumption behavior. It assumes that only economic factors guide consumer behavior. From the illustrative cases presented in Chapter One dealing with 7UP and Pringle's, it is clear that economic analysis is too restrictive.

Despite these shortcomings, microeconomic analysis makes an important contribution to the understanding of consumer behavior. Undoubtedly, utility is an important factor in consumer decision making. Curiously, recent models of consumer behavior have neglected economic factors as determinants of purchase and consumption activities.

Psychoanalytic Model

In the mid-1950s, the work of Sigmund Freud, Carl Rogers, and other personality theorists gained acceptance as a basis for understanding consumers' motivation for purchasing.[1] In contrast to the economic models of consumer behavior, which assumed consumer *rationality,* the psychoanalytic approach sought to explain *irrationality.* This view is expressed in the work of Sigmund Freud. He contended that two opposing forces guided behavior. One force, the id, impelled people to discharge psychic energy in instinctive ways that were often antagonistic to society's aims. The other force, the superego, was the desire to act in socially acceptable ways that people learned through socialization. The coordination of these forces by the ego, in "adjusted" individuals, involved establishing *defense mechanisms* that enable people to discharge psychic energy in a socially acceptable way.

The defense mechanism of greatest importance from a marketing perspective is one called sublimation. Instinctive needs are sublimated to form socially acceptable actions. Ernest Dichter (1964), a leading proponent of the psychoanalytic approach in marketing, employed the sublimation concept to explain a variety of behaviors. He contended that

---

[1]See Wells and Beard (1973) for a review of personality theories. Further discussion of this topic is presented in Chapter Nine.

TABLE 3.1. Qualitative Research Techniques

Focus Group - The focus group technique involves recruiting a group of people (usually six to eight) to express their ideas about some topic and to react to the opinion of others. (See Calder, 1977, for a detailed discussion of focus groups.)

Depth Interviewing - This technique entails having an interviewer pose questions to a respondent. The interviewer records the responses given and probes the respondent to insure detailed responses.

Sentence Completion - This technique involves presenting respondents with part of a sentence, which they are to complete with the first thought that comes to mind. For example, a respondent might be asked to complete the following sentence. The most important consideration in buying a car is _____.

Thematic Apperception Test (TAT) - This test was developed by Henry Murray (1938). Subjects are shown a picture and are asked to tell a story about it using their own motivation to fill in details. The process of apperception thus entails going beyond merely perceiving objects and events. It requires individuals to interpret a situation in terms of their own experience.

people like to eat corn flakes because it provides an acceptable way of discharging the need to crunch the enemy's bones in peacetime. According to Dichter, men bought convertible automobiles because it provided a socially acceptable way of sublimating the desire to have a mistress.

The psychoanalytic approach, sometimes referred to as motivational research, has made several important contributions to consumer behavior. Psychoanalytic principles and methods are useful in developing product strategies—whether the product category is ready-to-eat cereals, automobiles or some other good or service. Second, psychoanalytic analysis provides direction for communication strategies. The proposition that women baked cakes because it symbolized the act of giving birth could have been the basis for the campaign "Nothin' says lovin' like somethin' from the oven." Third, the techniques and measures used in psychoanalytic research have been adopted for use in qualitative analysis of consumer behavior. Indeed, focus group and depth interviewing research, which are widely used in marketing today, are adopted from psychoanalytic procedures. Less frequently used measures such as sentence completion and the thematic apperception test also have their origin in psychoanalytic methods (Table 3.1).

Despite these contributions, the psychoanalytic model is not an adequate theory of consumer behavior. It provides few actionable insights regarding how to stimulate the acquisition of information useful in making consumption choices. Rather, it provides a framework for anticipating and explaining consumers' reactions to products and services once they have acquired information about them.

Perceived Risk Model

A third approach to explain consumer purchase patterns was advanced in the mid-1960s, primarily by researchers at the Harvard Business School (Bauer, 1967; Cox, 1967.) They suggested that consumption is dependent upon an individual's perception of the risk inherent in a particular situation. In the purchase situation, risk is the product of two factors: uncertainty and consequences (Cox, 1967.) A consumer may be uncertain about what to buy, or whether an item considered for purchase will live up to expectations. In addition, the consumer's perception of the consequences of a wrong decision has an effect on the amount of risk perceived. According to the model, consumers select alternatives that minimize perceived risk.

Consider the purchase of an automobile. Consumers may narrow their selection to a choice between three makes. The brand purchased may be predicted by determining the uncertainty the consumer associates with each of the three brands. Consumers are asked how certain they are about the kind of car they should buy and how certain they are that each make will satisfy their needs. In Table 3.2 we have assumed that uncertainty or the probabilities that the various makes will be unsatisfactory are .2, .3, and .4, respectively. Furthermore, the consequence of a wrong decision is $8,000, $7,500 and $6,000. Thus, the perceived risk (uncertainty times consequences) is least for make A ($1,600) and greatest for make C ($2,400). If the consumer acts to minimize perceived risk, make A will be selected. Of course the consumer does not actually compute the perceived risk of each alternative considered; rather, the estimate is made intuitively.

The car-buying example illustrates several shortcomings of perceived risk as an explanation of consumer behavior. First, in the purchase of some products, for example salt, risk is not an important consideration. In other instances, the uncertainty and consequences are nearly identical for the various alternatives. When purchasing a home or car, individuals often decide between alternatives that involve about the same degree of uncertainty. Perceived risk is virtually the same for all alternatives, and the model's prediction is likely to be confirmed only at the chance level. Finally, the way in which the perception of risk is used by individuals in their decision making depends upon whether they are risk-seekers or risk-averters. Risk-averters act to minimize risk, whereas risk-seekers show a preference for a certain risk.

The notion of perceived risk is not a particularly useful means of predicting consumers' preferences among alternative brands. However, it does provide insight into consumer purchase behavior associated with certain classes of products. The greater the price of an item and the longer the consumer's commitment to using that product, the greater the perceived risk (Dommermuth, 1965). In turn, greater perceived risk is associated with more extensive information-seeking about a product (Arndt, 1967) and a greater degree of repeat purchase of a particular brand.

TABLE 3.2. Computation of Perceived Risk

Make of Car	Uncertainty	×	Consequences =	Perceived Risk
A	.2		$8,000	$1,600
B	.3		$7,500	$2,250
C	.4		$6,000	$2,400

MULTIPLE VARIABLE MODELS

Adequate theories of consumers' purchase and consumption activities cannot be achieved by a single concept. Economic, psychoanalytic, and perceived risk approaches represent only selected aspects of the consumer decision making process. This observation led marketing theorists to develop progressively more complex depictions of consumer behavior. Although we examine only three of these models, they are sufficient to represent the different approaches used to model consumer behavior.[2] The Engel-Kollat-Blackwell model (1968, 1973, 1978) is representative of the attempts to describe ultimate consumer behavior. The Webster-Wind (1972) model describes industrial buyer behavior. And, the Howard-Ostlund (1973) model attempts to capture the critical aspects of both ultimate consumer and industrial buyer behavior in one model. This discussion focuses on the identification of key concepts critical to an understanding of individuals' consumption behavior.

Engel-Kollat-Blackwell Model

A comprehensive model dealing with ultimate consumer's behavior was first published by Engel, Kollat, and Blackwell (EKB) in 1968 and later revised (1973 and 1978). As Figure 3.1 indicates, the 1978 version of the EKB model views consumer behavior as a five-stage decision process. Problem recognition occurs when an individual perceives a difference between the desired and actual state of affairs. Problem recognition initiates the search for information to resolve the problem. The information accumulated by searching one's own knowledge repertoire (internal search) and external sources is used to evaluate alternatives and make a choice. The consequences or outcomes of a choice, satisfaction and dissonance, are retained and used to guide subsequent decisions.

These five decision process stages constitute the core of the EKB model. The other factors depicted in Figure 3.1 serve only to amplify the decision process. Specifically, the factors labeled *information input* and *information processing* provide a detailed description of the activities involved in problem recognition and search. The *product brand evaluation* process describes factors affecting search and how alternative evaluation and choices are made. *General motivating influences* are individuals' dispositions that have their primary influence on product brand evaluations. And, *internalized environmental influences* have a predominant influence on the general motivating influences. Each of these factors is examined below.

EKB introduce the notion of information processing to describe the activities people engage in to recognize problems and evoke information search. The information people process depends on both the stimulus input and the thoughts held in active memory. The stimuli impinging upon consumers' senses result in exposure. Whether the information

---

[2]Models not discussed include ones developed by Andreasen (1965), Nicosia (1966), Hansen (1972), Britt (1978) and Bettman (1979).

Figure 3.1. The Engel-Kollat-Blackwell Model

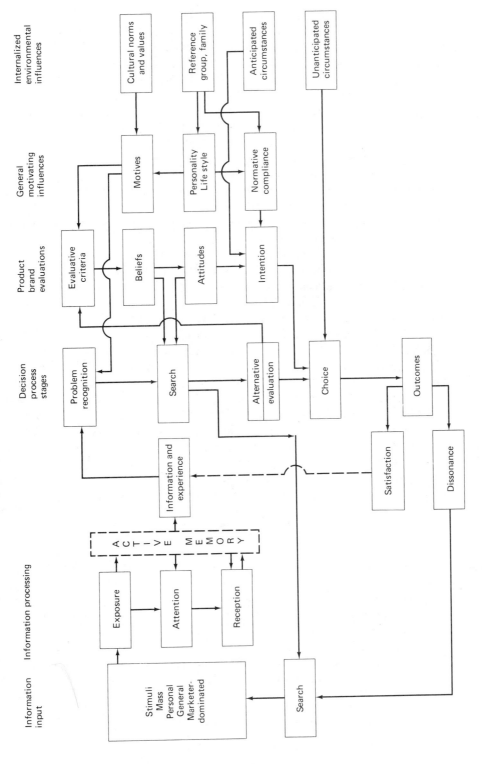

SOURCE: Engel, Blackwell, and Kollat, 1978.

to which people are exposed receives further processing (that is, reception) to be ultimately stored in memory as information and experience depends on the attention paid to it.

Once individuals have accumulated information about consumption choices via the search process, they undertake alternative evaluation. This involves what EKB term product brand evaluations. Depending on their motives or goals, people establish criteria for evaluating choice alternatives. By assessing the performance of choice alternatives on the evaluative criteria, people formulate beliefs about the alternatives which guide their attitudes, intentions, and ultimately their choice among alternatives.

A set of factors EKB term general motivating influences also affect the decision process stages. Specifically, an individual's personality and lifestyle affects his motives. Motives in turn influence problem recognition and choice via intentions. Personality and lifestyle also affect normative compliance—that is, the consumer's perceptions of the desires of others and their motivation to comply with these desires. Normative compliance affects people's choice by influencing their intentions.

A final set of factors, which EKB term internalized environmental influences, have their predominant effect on decision process stages by affecting general motivating influences and product brand evaluation. However, one internalized environment influence—unanticipated circumstances—does have a direct influence on the choice process.

The EKB model provides a comprehensive account of the factors that affect consumer behavior and the relationship among these factors. The model is a useful device for the purpose it was intended to achieve; it organizes the vast knowledge about consumer behavior. The EKB model is not, however, an adequate theory of consumer behavior. What is lacking is a specification of the preconditions under which certain outcomes will emerge. For example, it has been shown that increasing repetition from low to moderate levels increases the impact of a communication, whereas increasing repetition from moderate to high levels decreases a message impact. The EKB model allows the strategist to anticipate that message repetition will be related to consumers' response. But it does not allow anticipation of the conditions (low to moderate repetition versus moderate to high) that induce specific outcomes. Strategists are much more concerned with knowing whether the outcome under certain conditions will be positive or negative than knowing that there is a strategy-outcome relationship.

Webster-Wind Model

The Webster-Wind (1972) model focuses on industrial buyer behavior. The basic notion of their model is that " . . . buying is a decision-making process carried out by individuals, in interaction with other people, in the context of a formal organization." The organization, in turn, is influenced by a variety of forces in the environment.

Webster and Wind distinguish four classes of variables which determine industrial or organizational buying behavior: *environmental, organizational, social,* and *individual* (Figure 3.2). Within each class, there are two broad categories of variables, task and nontask. Examples of task and nontask influences are shown in Table 3.3.

The environmental influences denoted by Webster and Wind include the physical,

Figure 3.2. The Webster-Wind Model of Organizational Buying Behavior

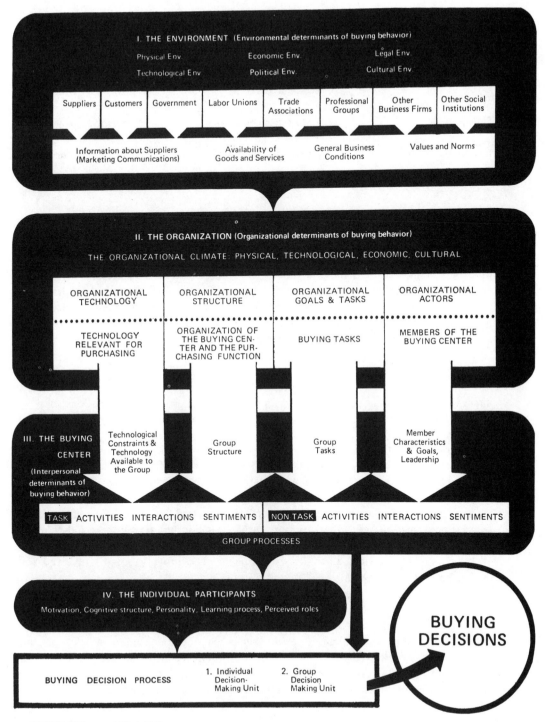

SOURCE: Webster and Wind, 1972.

TABLE 3.3. Classification and Examples of Variables Influencing Organizational Buying Decisions

	Task	Nontask
Individual	Desire to obtain lowest price	Personal values and needs
Social	Meetings to set specifications	Informal, off-the-job interactions
Organizational	Policy regarding local supplier preference	Methods of personal evaluation
Environmental	Anticipated changes in price	Political climate in an election year

SOURCE: Webster and Wind, 1972.

technological, economic, political, legal, and cultural forces exerted by government, trade associations, unions, and other business concerns. As Figure 3.2 indicates, environmental influences define the availability of goods, the general business conditions facing the organization, the values and norms guiding interpersonal relationships, and the flow of information concerning suppliers into the organization. The environmental influences provide a milieu in which the organization operates. Organizational influences are of four types: (1) Organizational technology: inventions for organization and managing work; (2) Organizational structure: subsystems of communication, authority, status, rewards, and work flow; (3) Organizational goals and tasks: the work to be performed to fulfill organizational objectives; and (4) Organizational actors: the people in the system. The interaction of these organizational influences delimits the information, expectations, goals, attitudes, and assumptions used by each of the individual actors in the organization to reach decisions.

To influence the organizational buying process one must understand not only the environmental and organizational milieu but also the behavior of the groups of individuals involved in the purchase decision. In an organizational setting, the buying center involves users, buyers, influencers, decision makers, and gatekeepers. Each of these roles is occupied by one or more members of an organization, and an individual member may occupy more than one role. Furthermore, the interrelationship among these individuals must be understood if their purchase behavior is to be predicted accurately. However, Webster and Wind do not elaborate the individual and group processes involved in decision-making in any detail.

The Webster-Wind model is an important contribution to knowledge about consumer behavior because it focuses on the much neglected organizational buyer behavior area. In so doing, it enumerates important environmental and group influences that aid in understanding both industrial and ultimate user purchase and consumption behavior. In the process, however, Webster and Wind have not articulated the manner in which buyers process and use information. Furthermore, the nature of the interaction between model components is described only in very general terms. Thus, it is unclear exactly how environmental and organizational factors impact on the decision-making process.

Howard-Ostlund Model

John Howard and his coworkers at Columbia University have pioneered the development of a comprehensive model of buyer behavior. Initial efforts by Howard (1963, 1965) were expanded and refined by Howard and Sheth (1969) and more recently by Howard and Ostlund (1973). Because the Howard-Ostlund model is purported to have greater predictive capability than the earlier models developed by Howard's group, it will be examined in the following discussion.

The Howard-Ostlund model (Figure 3.3) represents an effort to provide a theory of buyer behavior that is useful to theoreticians, researchers, and practitioners alike. Furthermore, it is intended to describe industrial, institutional, and ultimate consumer behavior.

For the purposes of discussion, the Howard-Ostlund model can be partitioned into three stages. The first to be considered are the *exogenous variables*. These include the institutional and societal environment as well as the buyer's personal characteristics. Suppose an individual is considering the purchase of an automobile. According to the Howard-Ostlund model, he or she may receive information from institutional sources that are commercial (for example, competing car manufacturers) or noncommercial (for example, *Consumer Reports*). The car purchaser's behavior may also be influenced by the societal environment, that is, time pressure, the societal/organizational setting, and culture. The model indicates that time pressure influences the amount of search and deliberation in which a consumer engages. The feelings of the buyer's family, the buyer's perceptions of what friends and relatives expect him or her to buy (that is, social/organizational setting) and the buyer's cultural background also influences behavior. Finally, personal characteristics are considered an exogenous factor comprised of a personality factor and a financial status factor. Personality affects individuals' confidence, while financial status influences their intentions.

A second stage of the Howard-Ostlund model pertains to *information processing*. It includes that portion of the model beginning with information sources and ending with information recalled (Figure 3.3). In purchasing a new car, information from various automobile manufacturers (marketer-dominated sources), *Consumer Reports* (neutral sources), and friends (interpersonal sources), as well as feedback from search behavior influence the consumer's media selection. Over time, an individual's media selection behavior yields stable media patterns. In turn, media patterns are determinants of the information to which the consumer will be exposed. Once consumers are exposed to information their perceptual bias may cause the distortion of that appeal. Bias is due to buyers' motives and brand comprehension. Whether the information to which buyers are exposed is distorted or not, some information will be recalled. This information will affect brand comprehension and attitudes.

The third stage of the buyer behavior model focuses on *cognitive and purchase processes*. It begins with motives and ends with purchase satisfaction (Figure 3.3). Two components of motives are distinguished: content and intensity. Content refers to the goals which the consumer is attempting to achieve and intensity to the relative importance of each goal. Motives involve feedback from personality, the societal environment, and

Figure 3.3. The Howard-Ostlund Model

Theory of Buyer Behavior

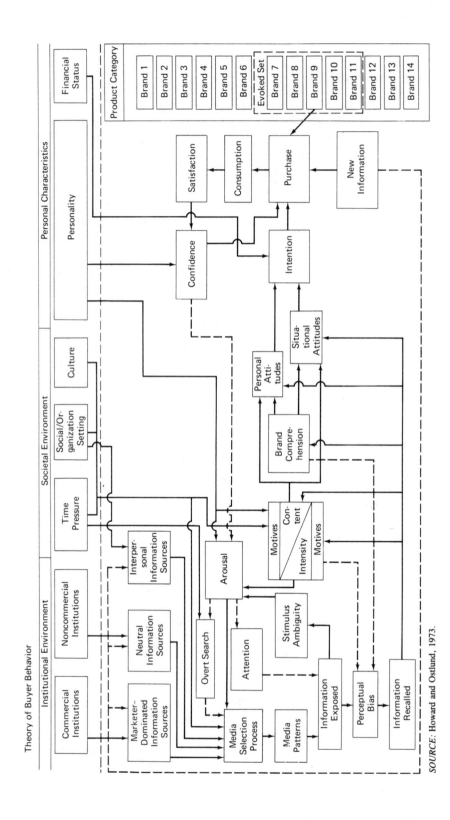

SOURCE: Howard and Ostlund, 1973.

information recalled. In turn, an individual's motives influence personal and situational attitudes (that is, attitudes of significant others.) Information recalled also feeds into personal and situational attitudes and brand comprehension. Brand comprehension, or the degree of knowledge about a brand, also influences attitudes.

The next link in the Howard and Ostlund buyer behavior model is intention. An individual's purchase intentions are determined by his or her attitudes and financial status. Intentions, confidence in judging a brand, and new information are conceived as the major determinants of purchase. Of course, a consumer might not know all the existing brands in a product category so that the purchase decision would be restricted to his or her evoked set (those with which the consumer is familiar). Having purchased a product, the consumer may then use it or consume it and derive some level of satisfaction from this activity. This information then affects an individual's confidence in the brand purchased, and ultimately the probability of repurchase.

The Howard-Ostlund model is an attempt to present a comprehensive depiction of consumer behavior processes. Although this goal may have been achieved, the model presents several difficulties for both users and students. Its complexity makes the Howard-Ostlund model as difficult to understand as it is to describe. This complexity may be justified if it is representative of how consumers actually behave in pursuing purchase and consumption activities. Whether this is the case is problematic. Many of the linkages specified appear to be supported either by intuition or by a very limited number of studies. For example, the justification for the relationship between arousal and media selection process and between motives and arousal resides in logic rather than empirical research. The conceptualization of the confidence variable as having a direct relationship to purchase and feedback to arousal is based on a few panel studies conducted by Howard and his co-investigators.

In this model, variables are operationalized at two different levels: a content level and a structural level. Content variables deal with *what* the consumer thinks. Brand comprehension, personal and situational attitudes, intention, and confidence are content variables. On the other hand, structural variables deal with *how* consumers think. Variables such as media selection process and perceptual bias are in this category. The problem caused by including structural variables is that it makes measurement difficult. Although content variables may be measured directly, structural variables require inferences to be made from observation and from questionnaires. Howard and Ostlund justify their approach by noting: "It should be recognized that at this stage in our knowledge securing these (operational) measures might better be regarded as a goal rather than an accomplishment." Yet, the admission that some variables have not been measured adequately questions whether these yet unmeasured variables should be included in the model.

THE RELATIONSHIP AMONG MULTIPLE VARIABLE MODELS

On cursory examination, the multiple variable models reviewed appear to have little in common. Models differ in the number of variables specified. Furthermore, some theorists have operationalized all model variables (Engel, Kollat, and Blackwell), while others have mixed conceptual and operational variables (Howard and Ostlund; Webster and Wind). Variables given the same label are often operationalized differently (Engel, Kollat, and Blackwell's versus Howard and Ostlund's definition of attention.) On closer examination, however, the models advanced to explain consumer behavior have several properties in common. They tend to be eclectic, drawing on findings from marketing as well as the behavioral sciences. Furthermore, consumer behavior typically is viewed as a multiple component system which includes information acquisition, decision making, and moderating factor components. In order to determine what consensus may exist between the Engel-Kollat-Blackwell, Webster-Wind, and Howard-Ostlund models, they are compared and contrasted.

Despite the seeming diversity in the way theorists have conceptualized the information acquisition component of consumer behavior, an underlying commonality appears to exist. As Table 3.4 shows, both the Engel-Kollat-Blackwell and the Howard-Ostlund models hypothesize the existence of an exposure variable. For the Webster-Wind model this and other information acquisition variables are implicit. Furthermore, attention, reception, brand comprehension, perceptual bias, and stimulus ambiguity all refer to human information reception processes. The attitude variable is given different labels such as evaluative criteria, beliefs, intention, or personal and situational attitudes, but it is usually measured in the same way regardless of how it is named. Similarly, the recall variable has been incorporated in two of the models (Table 3.4), though EKB provide a more detailed description of the recall process. Thus, information acquisition is generally viewed as being composed of four factors: exposure, reception, attitude, and retention. These factors constitute a hierarchy that describes how people acquire information to make purchase decisions. Specifically, exposure is necessary for reception which, in turn, is necessary for attitude formation and retention.

The multiple variable models examined also identify the decision-making process as an important determinant of consumer behavior. The decision-making component generally includes motivational, search, and choice factors. Webster and Wind conceive problem recognition as a motivational force guiding decision making. Howard and Ostlund term this variable "motives," and Engel, Kollat, and Blackwell use both of these terms. Furthermore, all of the models specify a search variable, although different descriptions like internal, external, and overt are used to characterize search. Choice is also similarly conceived in the models examined. All models indicate that the final decision whether or not to purchase involves a sequence of steps or processes. However, some theorists have postulated alternative evaluation which precedes the purchase act, while some have also distinguished variables which follow the act of purchase. These latter variables have been termed outcomes, satisfaction, and dissonance.

Several factors that moderate information acquisition and decision making are treated in the models reviewed. One is audience characteristics. Webster and Wind distinguish five types of audiences for marketing information. Howard and Ostlund denote personality and financial status and single out confidence as an important personality characteristic. Engel, Kollat, and Blackwell identify such audience characteristics as personality, lifestyle, and normative compliance. Finally, the source and channel moderators have been considered in all models reviewed.

TABLE 3.4. Comparison of Multiple Variable Models of Consumer Behavior

	Theorists		
Type of Variable	Webster-Wind (1972)	Engel-Kollat-Blackwell (1978)	Howard-Ostlund (1973)
INFORMATION ACQUISITION			
Exposure	—	Exposure	Information exposure
Reception	—	Attention Reception	Attention, perceptual bias, stimulus ambiguity, brand comprehension
Attitudes	—	Evaluative criteria Beliefs Attitude	Personal and situational attitudes Intention
Recall	—	Intention Active memory Information and experience	Information retained
DECISION MAKING			
Motivation	Problem recognition and assignment of buying authority	Problem recognition Motives	Motives
Search	Search	Internal and external Search Alternative Evaluation	Overt Search
Choice	Choice process	Choice outcomes satisfaction dissonance	Purchase Satisfaction
MODERATING PROCESSES			
Audience Characteristics	Users, Buyers Influencers, Deciders Gatekeepers	Personality Lifestyle Normative compliance	Personality confidence financial status
Communication Source and Channel	Individual group organizational environmental	Mass Personal General Marketer-dominated	Marketer-dominated Neutral Interpersonal

In sum, theorists have taken a variety of perspectives in attempting to explain consumption behaviors. Some theorists have emphasized ultimate consumer behavior (for example, Engel, Kollat, and Blackwell), others have focused on organizational buyer behavior (for example, Webster and Wind), while still others have integrated these two perspectives (Howard and Ostlund.) Despite these differences, there is an underlying commonality among the models. Characteristic of consumer behavior models is their inclusion of information acquisition, decision making, source, channel, and audience components. Moreover, there is substantial similarity in the way different models specify the process underlying each component. In Chapter Four, a framework for studying consumers is developed on the basis of the elements identified by previous investigators and shown in Table 3.4.

SUMMARY

In this chapter, two approaches to theorizing about consumers' behavior were identified. Monadic models which characterized the attempts to explain consumer behavior during the 1950s and 1960s relied on concepts from a single discipline such as economics or psychology. More recently, multiple variable models have been suggested. These models have employed concepts from a variety of disciplines to explain individuals' behavior. Some of these models have focused on ultimate buyer behavior, others have addressed organizational buyer behavior, while still others have attempted to explain both of these types of behavior. An analysis of representative models of each type revealed that they had many commonalities. All models included information acquisition, decision making, and moderating characteristics as important factors in accounting for buyer behavior. These factors serve as the foundation for the model of consumer behavior developed in the next chapter.

QUESTIONS

1. Theorists developing multiple variable models of consumer behavior have incorporated monadic models into their models. How have the economic and psychoanalytic models been incorporated in the Engel-Kollat-Blackwell model? How has the economic model been incorporated in the Howard-Ostlund model?

2. The Webster-Wind model includes an individual decision-making component, though the nature of this component is not elaborated on in their model. Describe how the Engel-Kollat-Blackwell model can be used to develop more adequately the individual decision-making component conceived by Webster and Wind.

3. Evaluate the Engel-Kollat-Blackwell model by attempting to match the data given about consumer's behavior in the Flex case (Chapter One), and the concepts provided in the model.

4. Develop a detailed scenario of a consumer's durable good purchase. To do this ask a consumer to relate all the events that led up to the purchase of a product, describe the actual purchase, and describe the outcomes related to that purchase. Take detailed notes or record your conversation. Probe the consumer to make sure all relevant details pertaining to the product purchase are described. Evaluate how well this purchase situation fits the Engel-Kollat-Blackwell Model, the Webster-Wind Model and the Howard-Ostlund Model. If necessary, develop your own model that captures the purchase behavior you have studied.

Chapter 4

A Framework for Analyzing Consumer Behavior

Consider the task of putting together a jigsaw puzzle. It might entail a number of steps. First, you must be certain that you have all the pieces necessary to complete the puzzle. Second, it is useful to devise a strategy for fitting the pieces together. You might sort puzzle pieces into different piles based on their color and then search within each commonly colored pile for pieces with complementary shapes. To help solve the puzzle you might also examine the picture of the completed puzzle appearing on the box. By analogy, this is what we have done in the previous chapter; we have identified the major puzzle pieces or concepts pertinent to consumer behavior. These included information acquistion, decision making, and moderating characteristics. In this chapter, we develop a framework called information processing that helps fit these puzzle pieces together. This framework provides an initial glimpse of how we go about analyzing consumers' behavior in the remainder of the book and provides a rationale for the structure of the text.

This chapter begins with a description of an iron purchase.[1] The scenario developed serves as a vehicle for highlighting important features of consumer decision making. It is also used to clarify the concepts that are necessary to explain, predict, and influence consumer behavior. In the final section of this chapter, we illustrate how the concepts can be measured.

---

[1]Edited from Williams (1976).

PURCHASING AN IRON

Teri Phillips is a twenty-three-year-old dental hygienist. Her husband is a student. Below she recounts her deliberations in purchasing an iron:

I'd been needing an iron for months because I had dropped this very expensive iron. I think it was around twenty-three to twenty-seven dollars. I bought it at Fields, and it had the see-through water gauge and all kinds of push-button steam and everything. But I dropped it twice, so everytime I plug it in and I fill it up with water it starts up fine, but then it sputters and spits, and the lights dim on and off as the current cuts on and off.

My husband will be in the other room studying and all of a sudden his light starts dimming and he knows I'm ironing. So, I was ironing my uniforms one morning, and I sort of felt somebody was behind me. I turned around and he pounced toward the cord, yanked the cord out of the socket, and with an evil look was pretending like he was cutting the cord with his scissors that he had in his hand, and so I thought, "No, no wait! Just let me finish my uniforms! Don't cut my cord and I'll promise to go out today and buy a new iron."

I always thought that when I was around and when I had the time I would buy an iron. But I just never did. All right, so today was the day. It was raining, and I had just had the car realigned, yet there was still a shimmy, so I had to take it back that day to the Goodyear place out in Skokie—all the way out there. Well, many months before I had been looking through a magazine and there was a discount coupon for an iron, a G.E. iron. I just clipped the coupon and slipped it into my purse, because I knew I was going to have to get an iron one of these days.

I went out to Goodyear to have the car realigned, and while he was doing that, checking it out, I looked across the way and there was one of those stores, True Value, or I can't even think of the name of the store now, but it was the same store that was on my coupon. So while he was fixing my car, I had this coupon in my purse. I walked the block through the rain to look for the store and to look for an iron. And, at the time I had enough money in my purse to buy an iron.

I reached the counter. There was one salesman and I said, "I'm looking for an iron." And there was a big display of irons stacked up, you know, how they do in discount stores. All different brands, all different kinds, some hold water, some were dry irons, some steam irons, some had shot of steam, every price from $7.99 to $30.00. So here I am standing thinking, "An iron. What iron to buy?" But that was all right because I had the time and I had enough money no matter what iron I decided to buy.

So the first thing I thought of was, sure, I'll buy this little iron over here. It's only $7.99 and it holds water for steam and it doesn't have a shot of steam or a Teflon coating. I definitely wanted a steam iron because a lot of times my uniforms are dry, and it is necessary to have steam in order to press them right because they are synthetic. I also wanted a brand I knew, and the $7.99 iron was made by General Electric.

Then I started looking at all these other irons, you know, to confuse the issue, all the way up to the $30.00 iron that has everything. Then I thought, I drop irons awfully easily. Right now we're poor and we don't have that kind of money to spend for an iron. When my husband is out working in a year or two, I can buy me one of these real super-duper ones, you know, the Cadillac-model iron. So that's what I did. After looking very carefully at all the irons, all the features, the price, I bought the $7.99 G.E. iron. I put the iron in my shopping cart, bought it, and was very satisfied with it. But, you know, I bet I'll have that iron for fifty years.

This episode describes how one consumer made an iron purchase. It may or may not be representative of how that consumer makes decisions regarding other products, or how other consumers make iron purchase decisions. Nevertheless, the description of the iron purchase is useful for making several observations about the nature of consumer decision behavior, and for demonstrating how an understanding of consumer behavior may be used to select a marketing strategy.

In developing an explanation of consumer behavior, the critical question is what causes consumers' behavior? In the case of the iron purchase, one might argue that Teri Phillips purchased the $7.99 General Electric iron because the one she owned was not working properly. Although this undoubtedly was a contributing factor, it does not provide a full account of why Teri selected the model she did. In fact, the malfunctioning iron is more directly linked to behaviors other than the actual purchase. Specifically, it motivated Teri to clip a coupon that would save her money if she eventually made an iron purchase at a True Value store. The malfunctioning iron also prompted her husband's antics. As Figure 4.1 shows, it was the coupon-clipping activity and her husband's antics that caused the consumer to take action and purchase an iron. In contrast, the selection of the True Value store in Skokie was serendipitous; it just happened to be near the Goodyear center where Teri had gone to realign her car.

Up to this point we have accounted for the causes of the product purchase and retail store selection, but not the specific brand of iron chosen. In part, the brand decision was constrained by the store selected; the consumer could only choose among the brands offered at the True Value store. In part too, the brand decision was motivated by the consumer's personal characteristics. The fact that she had a job requiring uniforms led her to select an iron that had steam. The fact that she perceived herself to be poor led her to select the cheapest brand having steam.

Figure 4.1.   Factors Related to Purchasing an Iron

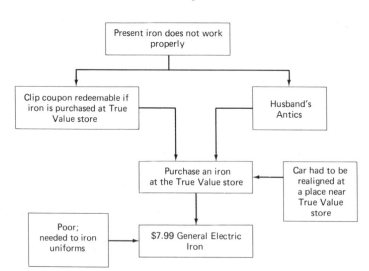

Our analysis of the iron purchase decision underscores the value of consumer behavior inquiry. It suggests that a knowledge of the process by which consumers make decisions helps guide the selection of appropriate marketing strategies. If there are a substantial number of consumers like Ms. Phillips, it is useful for the iron manufacturer to have the iron available in a great number of distribution outlets. Further, it would seem profitable to stimulate consumer purchase by using media-distributed coupons such as the one used by Ms. Phillips to purchase her G.E. iron. It would also be useful to familiarize people with a firm's brand of iron by using advertising and other marketing instruments.

The iron purchase illustration also highlights the limitations of consumer behavior analysis. It depicts consumer decision making as a complex multistage process. In fact, the complexity is such that even Ms. Phillips was not sure which iron she would buy or where she would buy it until she actually made the purchase. Thus, investigators of the consumer decision-making process cannot expect to have a complete understanding of how consumers make decisions. Rather, the aim is to gain some level of understanding that guides the development of more efficient marketing strategies than would be possible if such an understanding were absent.

Until now, we have focused on consumers' *overt physical* actions in making purchase decisions. As we have seen, a knowledge of these actions suggests strategies that are adaptive to consumers' behavior. It is important to also consider the *mental* processes that underlie consumers' overt physical actions. An understanding of these processes provides a further basis for strategies to influence consumers' behavior.

THE FRAMEWORK

The framework used to depict mental processes involved in purchase decisions emerges from the models of consumer behavior described in Chapter Three. The information acquisition aspect of consumer behavior discussed in Chapter Three is represented as two components in our model: (1) information acquisition from others and from one's own experience, and (2) information organization. What was termed decision making is discussed here under the heading of information utilization. The moderating characteristics identified in Chapter Three constitute the final element of our model. Collectively, these components comprise what we refer to as the information processing view. Here we examine information processing briefly, emphasizing the relationship between components. A more detailed analysis of each component is provided in Part III.

Information Acquisition from Others

How do consumers acquire the information they need to make decisions? One source of information is the people around them. In purchasing an iron, Teri Phillips may have acquired the information she needed from friends, salespeople, mass media advertising, or some other interpersonal source. An understanding of the process by which people acquire information from others is important because it suggests strategies the manager might employ to influence the information consumers use in decision making.

Our framework interprets the information acquired from others to be a function of a number of necessary but not sufficient factors. First, individuals must be exposed or physically present to acquire information. If they are exposed to information presented in a communication, there is some probability that they will receive or pay attention to that information. In turn the information received may stimulate message recipients to generate and rehearse thoughts relevant to those conveyed in a communication. If the information stimulates the generation and rehearsal of negative thoughts about the position advocated in a communication, message recipients will not be persuaded by the appeal. Their consumption choice thus is unlikely to be consistent with the choice advocated in the message. In contrast, if a communication stimulates positive thoughts about the position advocated, message recipients will accept the appeal as a basis for guiding subsequent behavior.

From a managerial standpoint, we are interested in the acquisition process because it provides information about why people have acquired the knowledge they have. If consumers do not have a favorable view of our product, we can determine whether it is because they have not been exposed to information about it, have not received that information, or have not responded to the information they received in a positive way. Further, by understanding what causes people to move from exposure to reception and ultimately to cognitive analysis, we can devise strategies to enhance the acquisition of information favorable to our product. To gain some insight into the process, we must examine the factors that move people from one acquisition stage to another.

Exposure to Information

Consumers exhibit a wide range of information exposure behaviors. In some cases, they are quite passive and nonselective. Teri Phillips just happened to be looking through a magazine when she saw an ad and coupon offer for irons at True Value stores. In many other instances exposure is an active and highly selective process. Given the large number of stimuli that are available to an individual at any one time, it is not surprising that exposure is selective; people must choose between competing stimuli. In such situations, exposure is determined by the perceived utility of the information obtained. Thus, Teri Phillips actively sought out a True Value store when purchasing an iron became relevant. This was the same store she had failed to see on her previous visit to the Goodyear dealer.

The fact that exposure to information can be passive as well as active has important implications for strategy. Passive exposure simply requires the manager to select the media that consumers use to obtain information. For example, if a disproportionately large number of consumers who are likely to purchase irons read *Ladies Home Journal,* information exposure may be achieved by placing advertising in it. When we have to motivate consumers to search actively for information, the utility of having that information must be stressed. This can be achieved by emphasizing the importance of a purchase decision to consumers' well-being and by questioning individuals' certainty about what they already know. Appeals, such as "If you think irons have not changed since you last bought one, then don't see ours," may be used to question certainty, while an appeal such as "You can pay a lot more for an iron, but you can't get a better one" or "Which iron you buy makes a difference in your family's appearance" addresses the importance of information exposure.

Information Reception

Even if people are physically present when information is being conveyed, they may or may not receive it. Information reception depends on arousal and attention. Arousal is analogous to the on-off switch of a radio; it energizes the central nervous system so that information can be processed. Arousal is optimal for processing information when it is at some moderate level (Figure 4.2). High levels of arousal severely limit the breadth of information that can be processed in any detail. Low levels of arousal enable greater breadth of information processing but limit the depth of processing; information tends to be processed superficially. Extending the radio analogy, attention is like the tuning knob of a radio; it focuses brain energy on a particular input (or station). The greater the attention paid to a communication, the greater the likelihood that information included in the message will be processed.

Like exposure, reception is selective. At a particular point in time, a person can only process information about a small number of the stimuli to which he or she is exposed. From a managerial perspective, we are interested in what determines which of the available stimuli people choose to receive. Two factors appear to underlie information reception. One is the strength of the message signal. The manager can control the strength of his or her signal by varying communication repetition. The other factor affecting

Figure 4.2.   Relationship between Arousal and Information Processed

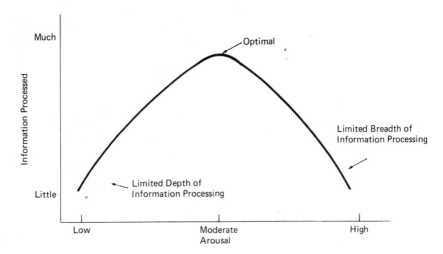

reception is the pertinence of the message. Reception is enhanced by increasing the pertinence of the information contained in an appeal.

To clarify how these strategies might be employed to enhance information reception, let us consider them in the context of Teri Phillips' iron purchase. One way to enhance the likelihood that she would purchase an iron at a True Value store is to repeat the message in several issues of a magazine she reads regularly or in several different media to which she is exposed. The probability of her purchasing an iron at True Value can be further enhanced by making the appeal salient. This might be achieved by offering a discount for purchasing an iron at True Value. By repeating the advertisement and increasing pertinence we are able to increase the likelihood of information reception.

Cognitive Analysis

Information that a consumer has been exposed to and has received is represented as thoughts or object-attribute associations in memory. For these thoughts to influence consumers' choices, further processing—which we call cognitive analysis—is required. First, the incoming information must be comprehended. Comprehension reflects the extent to which the meaning of incoming information inferred by a consumer is the one intended by the information source. For example, Teri Phillips comprehended the fact that the True Value coupon would save her money if she purchased the G.E. iron.

Once comprehension is achieved, a consumer may rehearse thoughts relevant to the object or issue in question. Rehearsal involves the active association of an object and attribute represented in memory. These thoughts may vary in valence. Thoughts may link a favorable attribute to an object, in which case they are termed support arguments or positive thoughts. Alternatively, thoughts may link an unfavorable attribute to an object, in which case they are termed counterarguments or negative thoughts. Furthermore, the support arguments and counterarguments a consumer chooses to rehearse can be distinguished in terms of their origin. They may be message thoughts, that is, more or less faithful representations of what is presented in incoming information. They also may be own thoughts, which are object-attribute associations that a person processed at some earlier point in time.

Cognitive analysis suggests that individuals' attitude toward a product, service, or some other object depends on the thoughts individuals rehearse in response to incoming information (Greenwald, 1968). Initially, incoming information is represented as message thoughts in memory. In most marketing contexts these message thoughts are likely to be positive thoughts because the information source is attempting to influence people to comply with the advocated position. The message thoughts represented in memory are likely to trigger the activation of own thoughts that consumers have previously processed about the object presented in incoming information. These own thoughts may be positive or negative. A consumer is more likely to adopt the view advocated in incoming information as the number of positive own thoughts activated in memory increases in relation to negative own thoughts. A person is likely to reject an advocated position when negative own thoughts are dominant in memory.

To illustrate the cognitive analysis process, consider the following situation. A newspaper ad for a G.E. iron enumerates several reasons for purchasing that brand. Specifically, it states that the G.E. iron was backed by a better warranty, was lighter, and required less servicing than competing brands. If the consumer were *initially favorably disposed* toward G.E. irons, he or she might rehearse these arguments, representing them as positive message thoughts in memory. In turn, these thoughts might stimulate the activation of positive thoughts that the consumer had stored previously (for example, I've always had good luck with G.E. products). Regardless of whether the positive thoughts are message thoughts or own thoughts, those thoughts that are rehearsed are likely to be retained, thus enhancing persuasion. Of course, the consumer may choose not to rehearse any arguments, in which case the consumer is unlikely to change his or her opinion about G.E. irons.

What happens if the consumer is *initially quite negative* about G.E. irons? In this case, the message thoughts represented in memory might stimulate the activation of negative own thoughts. For example, when the consumer reads that G.E. offers a better warranty, he or she may recall that *Consumer Reports* stated that the warranty period was too short and that consumers had encountered major problems with the iron shortly after the warranty expired. If this negative own thought were rehearsed, it is likely that it would be retained and the consumer would reject the persuasive attempt. However, if asked to recall the contents of the G.E. ad, the consumer would be able to do so by associating the negative own thought he or she rehearsed with the argument advanced in the message. Thus, even if a person is unfavorably predisposed to the position advocated in a communication, it may be remembered.

Individuals who are unfavorably predisposed to a persuasive message may employ a second approach to rejecting the arguments advanced. Rather than developing counterarguments, they may merely discount those presented without specifying any reasons, for example, "I don't believe it." Although this allows people to resist the persuasive attempt, it leaves them open to subsequent persuasion. New information is likely to persuade them because their initial opinions are not bolstered by a compelling rationale.

An important managerial implication of the cognitive analysis process is that initial focus should center on those who are favorably predisposed to the product or service. These people are likely to rehearse support arguments in response to an appeal and are therefore more readily influenced by it. In contrast, those consumers who are negatively predisposed to a product or service constitute less attractive targets for influence because they are likely to generate and rehearse counterarguments in response to a communication. Nevertheless, when the potential demand from those consumers who are favorably predisposed has been realized, it may be profitable to attempt to attract consumers who are initially negative. In this case, our notion of cognitive analysis suggests that emphasis be given to strategies that inhibit the generation and rehearsal of counterarguments.

In sum, the process by which individuals acquire information from others is conceived as a multistage process. For incoming information to be acquired individuals must be exposed to it, receive it, and perform cognitive analysis. As Figure 4.3 indicates, the product of processing information is the acquisition of an attitude, or set of beliefs about a product, service, or some other object. Attitudes are multidimensional; they may be

Figure 4.3. The Information Acquisition Process

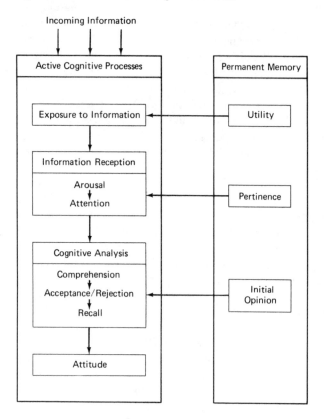

pro or con and they may range from weak to strong. Teri Phillips had a strong positive attitude toward buying the $7.99 G.E. iron. She also had a moderately negative attitude toward the more expensive irons.

Exposure, reception, and cognitive analysis that result in the acquisition of an attitude are referred to, for the time being, as *active cognitive processes*. This term is intended to reflect the fact that we are describing the processes involved in actively dealing with incoming information. In contrast, we shall use the term *permanent memory* to refer to the processes involved in using information that has previously been acquired and stored in memory. As Figure 4.3 indicates, the utility and pertinence of information as well as the information recipient's initial opinion are represented in permanent memory. According to our view, what is acquired from incoming information is affected by the information people already have acquired and stored. Consumers' response is thus influenced by incoming information as well as information acquired previously. But what if there is little or no information stored to facilitate the selection and interpretation of incoming information? In this instance, consumers may rely on their own behavior and the circumstances in which it occurs as a basis for attitude acquisition. We shall now consider information acquired from this source.

Acquisition of Attitudes from Behavior and Behavioral Circumstances

In situations where people are uncertain about their attitudes toward a product or service, they may engage in purchase behavior to determine their beliefs. If a consumer can only attribute a behavior to a personal reason, such as liking the product, then a positive attitude will be developed toward that behavior. Teri Phillips used this mode of information acquisition in purchasing an iron. Although she found an inexpensive iron that met her needs, she proceeded to consider more expensive models. In essence, she role-played a behavior, owning an expensive iron, as a basis of determining her attitude toward it. This role-playing behavior stimulated the generation of counterarguments; "I drop irons awfully easily. Right now we're poor and we don't have that kind of money to spend for an iron." In turn, the rehearsal of these counterarguments resulted in her rejection of the expensive models.

It is not only an individual's past behavior that guides the formation of an initial opinion. The circumstances in which that behavior occurred also constitutes an important determinant of the opinion formed. For example, suppose Ms. Phillips lost her $7.99 G.E. iron when moving to a new residence a short time after she had purchased it. When purchasing a new one she would consider her past behavior; that is how well she liked the iron. If it worked very well, she may have formed a positive attitude toward it, which would stimulate the generation and rehearsal of support arguments for purchasing it again. On the other hand, she may recall the fact that she bought the iron, in part, because she had a coupon that saved her money. As a result, she may be uncertain whether her previous purchase was due to the fact that she was pleased with the way the iron worked (that is, a product cause for behavior) or to the fact that it was available at a discount. Given these rival explanations for her past behavior, Teri is unlikely to generate a substantial number of support arguments for purchasing the iron she owned previously. Therefore, she is less likely to repurchase it than if the original purchase had not been stimulated by an incentive, unless the iron is again available at a discount.

To summarize to this point, we are suggesting that incoming information is processed via the active cognitive processes of exposure, reception, and cognitive analysis. Permanent memory, which represents thoughts acquired on the basis of past experience, can facilitate or inhibit exposure, reception, and cognitive analysis. In situations where the thoughts in permanent memory are not well-developed, people examine their behavior and the circumstances in which that behavior occurs to determine their thoughts. These thoughts are represented as initial opinions in permanent memory. They affect the acquisition of subsequent incoming information. These processes are represented schematically in Figure 4.4.

Information Organization

Whether information is acquired from interpersonal sources or on the basis of one's own behavior, it must be organized before it can be used to guide consumer decision making. Organization involves two processes. One is the combination or aggregation of bits of information. Teri Phillips had acquired information about the price and features of various models such as Teflon coating and steam. To select among alternative irons, it was necessary to combine these bits of information. Consumers may use a variety of strategies in aggregating the information they have acquired. They may evaluate each iron on important features and form a preference for the one that meets some minimum criteria on all attributes. This appears to be what Teri Phillips did. She exhibited a preference for the iron that met her needs with respect to price and features. An alternative approach to combining bits of information would have been to evaluate most highly the iron that dominated on a single factor, such as price.

The strategies for combining information we have examined constitute only two

Figure 4.4. The Role of Acquisition from One's Own Behavior in the Formation of Attitudes

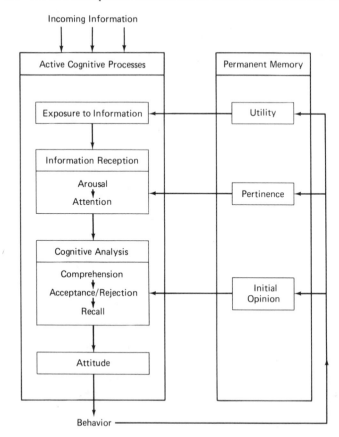

of the many different ways people aggregate bits of knowledge they have acquired. For now, the important point is that consumers combine various bits of information to facilitate making judgments about a product as an entity. A knowledge of the combination strategy consumers use provides the manager with guidelines for deciding what product features to develop and which to stress in communications aimed at potential consumers.

Organization not only includes the combination of bits of information but also the abstraction of that information. Abstraction involves using the physical cues of an object to infer its subjective characteristics. For example, the price of an iron, which is a physical cue, may be abstracted to evoke thoughts about the subjective characteristic economy. Characteristics of the retail outlet where the iron is sold, such as its location and the way merchandise is presented may also act as physical cues that serve as the basis for subjective evaluations of economy.

Consumers engage in abstraction because physical cues about a product such as its price, size, and color have little meaning *per se*. Indeed, the consumer typically makes judgments on the basis of subjective qualities such as economy, comfort, durability, and the like. Physical cues are most meaningful as a basis for inferring subjective qualities of a product. Once the subjective qualities are inferred, they may be aggregated to establish a preference among alternatives (Figure 4.5).

From the manager's perspective, the initial task is to identify the subjective factors which are important to consumers. Although the manager cannot affect subjective evaluations directly, he or she can develop product features (that is, physical cues) that will lead consumers to draw favorable inferences on subjective factors they use in evaluating alternatives.

The organization process is depicted schematically in Figure 4.5. Physical cues about a product are represented in memory in the form of physical attribute-object associations. These thoughts, singly or in combination, stimulate the activation of subjective attribute-object associations previously stored in memory. These latter thoughts are combined to determine preference.

Information Utilization

Information acquisition and organization processes result in the formation of an attitude. Interest in how individuals acquire and organize information stems from the fact that attitudes are important determinants of consumers' behavior. To specify how individuals' attitudes are related to their behavior, we need to distinguish three types of attitudes: *attitudes toward the object, personal normative beliefs,* and *social normative beliefs.* This distinction is useful because selection of the appropriate strategy to influence consumers' behavior depends upon the type of attitude that is guiding behavior.

Individuals' attitudes toward an object refer to their beliefs about it. Perceptions of how good, pleasant, or economical a product is constitute some of the attitudinal reactions people may have toward a product. In addition, personal normative beliefs may affect consumers' choice. This factor refers to individuals' perception of their moral obligation with regard to purchasing a product. In their roles as spouse, parent, or colleague, individuals perceive certain role obligations that guide their choice behavior. These personal normative beliefs may be independent and even contrary to people's attitude toward the object. Finally individuals' behavior may be guided by their perceptions of what others expect of them. These attitudes are called social normative beliefs.

To clarify the role of consumers' attitude toward the object, personal normative beliefs, and social normative beliefs, consider Teri Phillips' iron purchase behavior. She had developed a favorable attitude toward purchasing an iron because she felt her current iron made it difficult to do a proper job of ironing uniforms. The fact that she clipped a coupon from the newspaper also attests to Teri's favorable attitude toward purchasing a new iron. However, this positive attitude was not sufficient to stimulate purchase. A second motivating factor was her husband's antics. His evil looks and his pretending to cut the iron cord made clear his expectations with regard to buying a new iron. In this instance, Teri's social normative beliefs emerged by direct observation of her husband's behavior. In other cases, social normative beliefs may involve a person reflecting upon

Figure 4.5.   The Organization Process

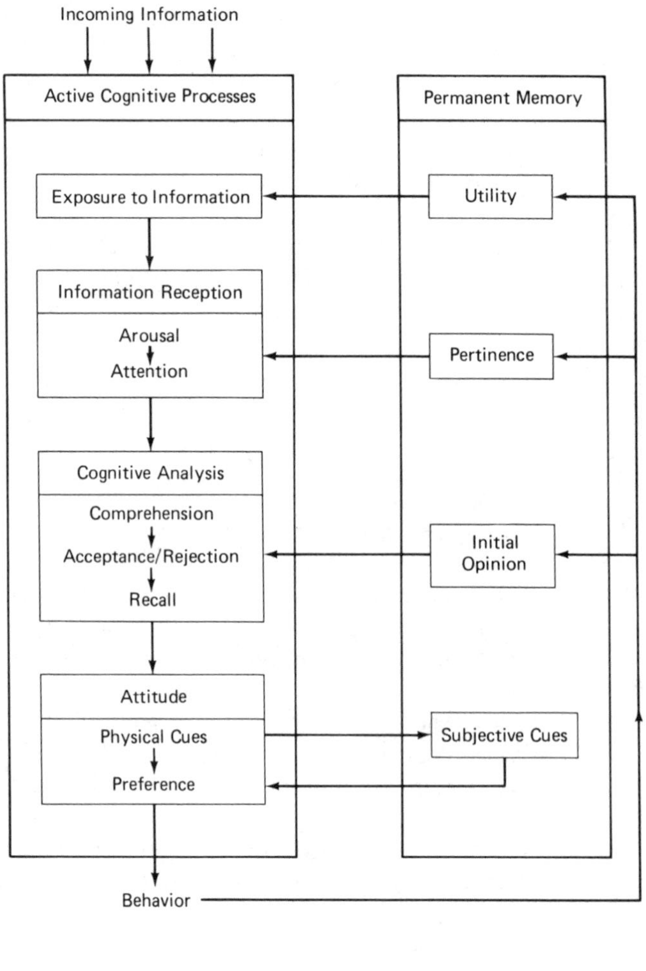

or anticipating the expectation of others. Mr. Phillips behavior also may have made Teri's personal normative beliefs salient. Given his displeasure, she may have felt that it was her obligation in her role as spouse to replace the defective iron.

A knowledge of consumers' attitudes toward the object, personal normative beliefs, and social normative beliefs enhances the manager's ability to predict behavior. However, even with a knowledge of consumers' reactions pertaining to these factors, we should not expect to predict their behavior with a high degree of accuracy. Consider the remarkable set of fortuitous events that led to Teri Phillips' purchase. She had to go back to the Goodyear store because the tires on her automobile were not aligned properly the first time. She also happened to see a store nearby that would honor the coupon. Luckily, too, she had the coupon and enough money to purchase an iron. In light of these events, which were not anticipated even by the consumer, it is not surprising that as researchers we cannot predict consumer behavior with a high degree of accuracy.

A measure called the *judged influence of extraneous events* has been devised to assess the behavioral impact of events beyond consumers' control. This refers to the extent people are motivated to perform some behavior in the face of inhibiting or facilitating events. While neither consumers nor researchers can foresee many of the situational factors that are likely to affect behavior, we can use consumers' judgments to evaluate the impact of unforeseen events on behavior. This is done by asking people how a change in weather, stockouts in a brand they intended to purchase, or some other unforeseen event would affect the likelihood of a behavior of interest.

It should be noted that information utilization does not require consumers to invoke all of the factors we have identified. In some instances, personal normative beliefs might be the critical determinant of behavior. This may be the situation when individuals decide whether or not to donate their hearts for transplant after their death. In other situations, such as the purchase of a car, an individual's attitude toward alternative brands and perceptions of the expectancies of others (that is, social normative beliefs) may guide choice behavior. Whether attitude toward the object, personal normative beliefs, social normative beliefs, or some combination of these factors affect behavior is an empirical question. The importance of each factor must be determined in the specific context of interest.

Individual Differences

Until now, we have emphasized the commonalities in consumers' decision making. All consumers engage in information acquisition, organization, and utilization as a basis for decision making. But consumers also differ from one another. They differ in *how* they process information as well as in *what* information they process. These differences are thought to be due to consumer differences in: (1) demographic characteristics, such as age and income, (2) personality characteristics, such as self-confidence and authoritarianism and (3) group affiliations, such as family composition and socio-economic class membership. We shall briefly consider how such individual differences affect what is processed.

To illustrate the role of individual differences in how information is processed, consider the effect of differences in education. Highly educated people are likely to comprehend incoming information, but may resist accepting the position advocated. In contrast, uneducated people are less likely to comprehend incoming information but are more likely to accept whatever information they understand. From a strategic standpoint, the manager must employ different strategies to enhance information acquisition between consumers differing in education. In a more general sense, the impact of individual differences on information processing is of interest because it guides the identification of viable strategies to attract specific consumer segments to the manager's product.

Individual differences also play an important role in what thoughts people process and use to make decisions. For example, individuals raised by parents who are affluent and well-educated are often socialized to value individuality. As adults, these people exhibit individuality by purchasing products that are unique. In effect, the distinctive thoughts held by certain segments of the population influence how they will react to various products.

Given the importance of consumer individual differences in determining how and what people process, it is useful to monitor the incidence of specific individual differences in the population. By knowing the size of a group possessing a particular characteristic, the strategist can determine the value of developing a strategy to attract people with that characteristic. The individual differences most rigorously monitored are demographic characteristics, such as age, income, marital status, and family size.

IMPLICATIONS OF THE FRAMEWORK

The framework for explaining, predicting, and influencing consumer behavior has two major implications for the marketing manager. First, it provides the manager with an approach to diagnose the reasons for the level of consumer response observed. By measuring each of the decision-making variables identified, it can be determined whether acquisition, organization, or utilization variables should be the focus of the manager's attention. In addition, the framework provides a starting point for developing strategies to rectify the problems identified. We shall consider only the diagnostic value of the framework here. The discussion of strategic implications is reserved for later chapters when we have examined acquisition, organization, utilization and individual difference factors more fully.

To demonstrate the diagnostic power of the framework we have developed, consider the purchase of hosiery. Suppose our firm has achieved a ten percent share of the market by offering one size that fits most women. Research is conducted using the decision-making framework to identify opportunities for growth. For illustrative purposes, we shall consider an abbreviated version of the framework. As Table 4.1 indicates, consumers' response is measured on five decision-making variables. Exposure to the brand is measured by stating the name of our brand to women in the target and asking what product category the brand belongs to. Those responding "hosiery" are considered to be exposed to our brand. Reception is determined by asking target women to list all the brands of hosiery they can think of. Consumers who mention our brand are considered to have brand reception. Attitude is measured by asking people to indicate their preference among alternative brands. Trial refers to whether the consumer purchased our brand at least once during the past year, while the repeat purchase measure refers to those who purchased our brand more than once during the past year. Note that attitude, trial, and repeat measures are administered only to people who have been exposed to our brand.

TABLE 4.1.　Illustrative Research Results

	Case 1	Case 2	Case 3	Case 4	Case 5
Number of consumers initially	*3,000*	*3,000*	*3,000*	*3,000*	*3,000*
Number of consumers for whom there was initial:					
Exposure to the brand	900	2,400	2,400	2,400	2,400
Reception of the brand	230	600	1,800	1,800	1,800
Preference for the brand	50	132	396	990	216
Trial behavior	10	26	79	198	130
Repeat purchase behavior	10	5	16	40	13

Five patterns of response are presented in Table 4.1. Each pattern is indicative of a different problem. In Case 1, exposure to our brand is low. This may be the reason performance is poor on the other consumer response measures. Thus, it suggests that the manager examine the media used. The critical question is: are the women in our target being reached? If not, a new media plan is required to deliver better exposure to our target market. The lack of exposure may also be attributable to the frequency of exposure. While we may be reaching most of our target, we may not be reaching the majority of them often enough. This would call for greater repetition of our communication.

Both the problems identified in Case 1 are communication problems. Suppose we respond by altering the media so that we reach our target and find the consumer pattern of response shown in Case 2. The lack of reception may be remedied by increasing the frequency of presenting our communications. If this is done and the pattern of response represented in Case 3 emerges, we are faced with a different type of communication problem. In contrast to Cases 1 and 2 where the problems were media-related, in Case 3 the content of the communication is the problem area. This may be rectified by changing the attributes stressed, so that the audience finds the product more attractive. Or, we may consider introducing a new product that caters to a substantial proportion of the target not attracted to our current product.

The framework developed can be used to diagnose problems beyond those related to communication strategy. In Case 4, response to our communications appears to be favorable, yet trial is low. This suggests two potential problems. One is distribution. The fact that many more consumers exhibit a preference for our brand than are purchasing it at least once per year suggests that our brand may not be distributed widely enough or that stockouts are frequent. Case 4 may also indicate a problem with price. While individuals prefer our brand, they are reluctant to purchase it because of its price.

Finally, the pattern of consumer response shown in Case 5 is indicative of a problem with the product. This inference emerges from the knowledge that although trial is high, repeat purchase is not. Apparently our marketing effort has been successful in stimulating trial, but once consumers have tried it they do not prefer it or buy it again. The pattern of response represented in Case 5 may also be one that occurs in response to an infrequent consumer promotion, such as cents off the marked price or a coupon distributed in the media. Such incentives are likely to stimulate trial, accounting for the sixty percent trial observed. However, the incentive may cause people to attribute the purchase of our brand to the promotional incentive. When the promotional incentive is withdrawn, so is a major reason for the purchase. As a consequence, preference for our brand and repeat purchase are low.

Although the cases examined do not fully show the diagnostic power of the complete conceptual framework, they are sufficient to indicate that the framework is useful in diagnosing all types of marketing mix problems. Once this diagnosis is completed, an understanding of consumer information acquisition, organization, and utilization may be used to generate strategies to rectify the deficiencies observed.

MEASURING CONSUMER RESPONSE

For the framework to be useful one must be able to measure the different components. In the hosiery example presented earlier, five different components of the framework were measured as part of the illustration. To develop this more fully, in this section approaches to measuring the framework components are presented. Some of the more common procedures are discussed, using the purchase of an iron and other common products to illustrate the measurement procedures.

Information Acquisition

Exposure. Exposure to information is measured by showing a person a product or a representation of a product (that is, an advertisement or a brand name) and asking them whether they are familiar with it. In responding to this question, some people may claim exposure when they have not been exposed. This response is motivated by a desire to appear informed or to help the researcher by giving what is perceived to be the expected response. To avoid false claiming, two procedures are often followed. Respondents should be informed that they may not have been exposed to one or more of the products being asked about. In addition, products that respondents could not have seen should be included in the questionnaire.

To assess exposure to advertising, an opportunity-to-see measure is often used. This involves determining, via a survey, the number of people who were exposed to the vehicle (for example, *Time* magazine, six o'clock news) in which advertising was presented. People who claim exposure to the vehicle are assumed to be people who were exposed to the advertising included in it. Although this assumption is questionable, it is widely used because direct measurement of exposure to the advertising of interest is often too expensive.

Reception. The most direct way to measure information reception entails using physiological instrumentation. An individual's level of arousal can be measured using the galvanic skin response (GSR). Electrodes are placed on the information recipient's ring and index finger. A small current is applied to one electrode, and the resistance the current meets in traveling to the second electrode is measured. A pen and paper device records the changes. When an individual is aroused, small amounts of sweat are secreted which reduces the resistance to the current resulting in an increase in response on the recording device.

Attention can be measured physiologically by using an instrument that measures pupil dilation. The pupil of the eye dilates in response to decreases in illumination. It also dilates as the information load being processed or attended is increased. By analogy, the pupil is like the meter that measures the aggregate demand for electrical energy. As the demand for electricity increases, the meter turns more quickly. Similarly, as the human organism demands more "brain energy" to attend a stimulus, the pupil dilates. One approach to measuring pupil dilation involves the use of a television camera equipped with an infrared light. This light is sensitive to edges and forms a crescent around the pupil. Changes in pupil size are detected by changes in the size of the crescent. These changes are transmitted by the television camera to a recording device, which traces the frequency, amplitude, and slope of pupil dilations.

Despite the interest shown by marketing researchers in using physiological instrumentation to measure information reception, it is not widely employed. Differences in physiological responses, even to very different marketing stimuli, tend to be small. Further, it is unclear whether the height, slope, or number of physiological responses (or some combination of these) constitutes the most appropriate measure of information receptivity. Finally, there are problems unique to each physiological instrument. Some people exhibit a highly stable GSR regardless of the stimulus. Instrumentation to measure pupil dilation often requires the information recipient to sit perfectly still and not blink if a continuous record of dilation is to be obtained. This requirement minimizes the variability in attention to different stimuli, the very response pupil dilation is intended to measure. Pupillary responses to visual stimuli are difficult to interpret because they may reflect both changes in attention and stimulus luminosity. Therefore, it is useful only for determining attention to auditory stimuli such as radio commercials.

A more promising approach to measuring information reception entails measuring physical responses. A procedure called Conjugately Programmed Analysis of Advertising (CONPAAD) has been developed for this purpose. Information recipients are seated in a laboratory and asked to watch and listen to some stimulus. They control the intensity of the visual and auditory signal by means of two foot pedals. The greater the frequency of pressing the visual foot pedal the clearer and brighter the image becomes. Similarly the greater the frequency of pressing the auditory foot pedal the greater the clarity and volume of the sound. If it is assumed that increases in the frequency of pressing the foot

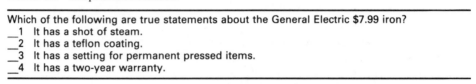

TABLE 4.2. Comprehension Measures

Which of the following are true statements about the General Electric $7.99 iron?
__1 It has a shot of steam.
__2 It has a teflon coating.
__3 It has a setting for permanent pressed items.
__4 It has a two-year warranty.

pedals reflects an increase in desire to pay attention to incoming information, CONPAAD can be used to track attention.

Cognitive Analysis. Several verbal measures are useful in evaluating recipients' cognitive analysis. Comprehension implies a congruity between the meaning of information inferred by the recipient and that intended by the source. Comprehension may be assessed by asking people to respond to a series of multiple choice questions, such as the ones shown in Table 4.2. This approach is selected because it permits a distinction between comprehension and recall. The extent of correct response on multiple choice items depends on understanding the information conveyed to a greater extent than it does on information recall.

The measurement of cognitive analysis also involves having information recipients generate the support arguments and counterarguments that are relevant to the stimulus object.[2] A procedure for eliciting and rating these thoughts is presented in Table 4.3. Responses to this type of questioning are generally used to construct indices. One index is support argumentation. This involves summing either the number of support thoughts (there are two in Table 4.3) or the scores for supporting thoughts (1 + 2 = 3). Similarly, an index of counterargumentation can be computed by summing the number of ratings of negative thoughts. A third score, net argumentation is computed by subtracting the number (or rating) of negative thoughts from the number of positive thoughts. Finally, a total thoughts score is obtained by adding the number (or ratings) on positive, neutral, and negative thoughts.

The thought-listing procedure outlined above differs from the recall measure commonly used in marketing research. Recall tests, such as the one presented in Table 4.4, measure the extent to which people have learned the incoming information. In contrast, the thought-listing measure reflects the outcome of learning. While some of the information presented in a communication may be represented in the thoughts people list, the thoughts may also be independent of the communication. Because these evaluative thoughts are more likely to guide decision making than message learning, the thought-listing approach is preferable to the more commonly used recall test.

Attitudes. The product of information acquisition is an attitudinal disposition. Attitudes are learned beliefs, feelings, and reaction tendencies. Beliefs are thoughts linking

---

[2]See Wright (1980) for a detailed discussion of the thought measurement issue.

TABLE 4.3. Thought-listing Procedure

Please write down all the thoughts that occur to you that are pertinent to the $7.99 G.E. iron.

A thought may consist of:

1. Information that is favorable or unfavorable about the iron.
2. Good or bad features of the iron.
3. Personal values of yours that are favorable or unfavorable toward the iron.

Use a new line for each thought

5 1 Looks cheap

2 2 A good value for the money

4 3 Weighs more than other irons

3 4 Comes in one color

1 5 It's quite versatile. Can do different jobs with it.

Now go back and rate each thought. Place your rating on the line to the left of each thought. Use the following scale.

__1 Very favorable thought about the iron
__2 Somewhat favorable thought about the iron
__3 Neither favorable or unfavorable thought about the iron
__4 Somewhat unfavorable thought about the iron
__5 Very unfavorable thought about the iron

an object to some feature or characteristic. Teri Phillips held the belief that the $7.99 G.E. iron was economical. Feelings refer to an emotional reaction associated with using some object. Using the G.E. iron might make Teri feel good, happy, or relieved. All of these reactions represent feelings. Reaction tendencies refer to a disposition toward action. Statements such as "I intend to buy a G.E. iron again" and "I'll keep my iron for many

TABLE 4.4. Recall Questions

1. What are the features of the $7.99 G.E. iron?

2. Where can a $7.99 G.E. iron be purchased?

3. What are the kinds of ironing jobs for which the $7.99 G.E. iron is particularly useful?

years" indicate reaction tendencies. Detailed attitude measurement procedures are discussed in Chapter Eight.

Normative Beliefs. We noted earlier that normative factors as well as attitudes toward an object guide people's behavior. Personal normative beliefs are measured by asking individuals what they perceive their moral obligation to be with respect to performing some behavior.

Social normative beliefs are determined by asking people to rate their perception of what "significant others" expect with regard to performing a behavior. Significant others may include a person's spouse, family, friends, or some other reference group whom the consumer considers important in making a decision. In developing social normative belief scales, it is necessary to know the relevant reference groups for the decision maker. Detailed measurement procedures for personal and social normative beliefs are discussed in Chapter Eight.

Extraneous Events. Judged influence of extraneous events is measured by presenting consumers with descriptions of unforeseen events and asking them to rate the likelihood that such events would affect their behavior. The unforeseen events chosen should be ones that *might* happen to all consumers. Otherwise, people are likely to respond simply by stating the unforeseen event is not relevant to them. Thus, in attempting to determine the judged influence of extraneous events on store choice it would be inappropriate to ask, "How likely is it that you would change the store you shop at if your car broke down?" For people who walk or take mass transit this question would be inappropriate. In addition, several extraneous events items should be used, reflecting levels of events ranging from unlikely to highly likely to affect consumers' behavior. Including a range of extraneous events increases the chances of being able to detect even small differences in people's motivation to perform a behavior.

Information Utilization

Choice Behavior. Choice behavior can be measured in several ways. The most frequently used procedure is to ask consumers to provide a report of their choice behavior. People are asked to indicate their choice when making their last purchase or the choice they make most frequently. When consumers are asked to keep diaries of their purchases, the researcher is able to track the proportion of purchases devoted to various alternatives. A problem with these self-reported measures is that consumers' responses may be influenced by social pressure or other motivations. For example, by summing American consumers' self-reports of their automobile gasoline consumption to the Internal Revenue Service, the estimates are frequently fifty percent greater than the amount of gasoline actually used in this country. In voting studies, it has been shown that about ten percent of those questioned state they have voted in an election when actual voting records indicate that they did not vote (Yalch, 1974).

To avoid the bias of self-reports, unobtrusive measures of behavior may be useful.

Rather than asking consumers about their behavior, the researcher observes it through direct observation. This involves monitoring people's behavior without them knowing it. For this purpose, the direct observation, and physical trace procedures described in Chapter Two are useful.

SUMMARY

Consumer decision making is a complex multistage process. Consumers acquire information from others as well as on the basis of their own experience. This entails exposure, reception, and cognitive analysis of incoming information. The bits of information acquired in this way are then organized. Organization entails the combination of bits of information relevant to decision making and the abstraction of physical cues to subjective ones. Once information is organized it is used to guide choice behavior. Consumers' behavior is also affected by personal normative beliefs, social normative beliefs, and situational contingencies.

Information acquisition, organization, and utilization are processes that occur in all consumer decisions. However, the specific nature of decision making is affected by the consumer's characteristics. Clustering people according to such individual differences as their past behavior, demographic profiles, and personality characteristics, guides the development of efficient marketing strategy.

The framework for analyzing consumer behavior outlined in this chapter is useful to the manager in two ways. First, it provides an approach for diagnosing the causes of consumer behavior. It also enables the manager to determine whether changes in the product price, channel, or promotional programs are most likely to improve his or her firm's competitive position. To apply the framework in this way requires measurement of the acquisition, organization, and utilization processes.

QUESTIONS

1. Go through the example of Bill Boggs' buying behavior at the end of Chapter One and relate it to the model (Figure 4.5) developed in this chapter. Compare it with the model you developed earlier.

2. What are some of the ways people resist being persuaded? Recommend some strategies for overcoming this resistance.

3. Most marketing strategies are aimed at influencing the information consumers acquire from others (for example, mass media approaches). How might the marketing manager influence consumers' acquisition of information from their own experience?

4. What are some important consumer individual differences? How do they influence how people process information? How might they be important in marketing and

advertising each of the following products: convenience foods; automobiles; stereos; and denture adhesives.

5. What are some of the problems with opportunity-to-see measures of exposure? What would be a better measure?

6. A leading manufacturer of baby food is thinking of coming out with a line of strained foods for elderly adults. Is this a sound idea? Using your knowledge of information processing, recommend a marketing strategy.

7. Reinterpret the Flex example given in Chapter One in terms of the model (Figure 4.5) presented in this chapter.

8. What are the differences between active cognitive processes and permanent memory processes?

9. Apply the model of consumer behavior presented in Figure 4.5 to the purchase of toothpaste, a new suit or dress, a television, and beer.

Part III

In Part III, we look at how consumers make decisions. In Chapter Five, we explore the way in which consumers acquire information from external sources. Chapter Six examines how consumers acquire information from their own experience. After consumers acquire information they must organize it in order for it to be useful in decision making. Organization of information is covered in Chapter Seven. With this as background, the ways in which consumers utilize information is treated in Chapter Eight.

Consumer Decision Making

Chapter 5

Information Acquisition

Marketing strategists tend to believe that persuasive communications have a positive effect on consumers' attitudes and purchase behavior. Advertisers spend over fifty-five billion dollars annually on media to proclaim their product's superiority. Political organizations devise elaborate and expensive campaigns to convince the electorate to vote for their candidates. Vast sums are spent to influence people to buckle their seat belts, stop littering, quit smoking, give blood, and get annual checkups.

The success of these and other persuasive communications is mixed. Marlboro cigarettes, using a strongly male western theme in their ads, has surged from a small seller twenty-five years ago to one of the leading brands in the United States. Miller beer had a relatively small share-of-market in the early 1970s. By using a heavy marketing investment strategy they have become a major challenger to Anheuser-Busch. In contrast, many products, such as the Edsel automobile, Cue mouthwash, and Revlon's supernatural hair spray, have failed despite considerable promotional efforts.

A similar pattern of market response is evident in the political and social cause arenas. Media expenditures by political parties influence voters, particularly those who are not committed to a particular party or candidate. Yet polls taken on voter preference at the outset and at the end of election campaigns indicate that less than ten percent of the people change their minds (Benham, 1965; Berelson, Lazersfeld, and McPhee, 1954; Lazersfeld, Berelson, and Gaudet, 1948). Campaigns relating smoking to lung cancer and urging drivers to wear seat belts have met with limited success. Less than five percent of the population routinely wear their seat belts for city driving, and consumption of cigarettes increases annually.

These illustrations suggest that providing consumers with information is not always sufficient. The first step in developing successful marketing strategies requires an understanding of how consumers process the information provided to them. In this chapter, we examine the information acquisition process. The factors underlying information exposure, information reception, and cognitive analysis are considered. For each factor, guidelines are identified for developing marketing programs that facilitate consumer information acquisition.

INFORMATION EXPOSURE

Consumers are constantly bombarded with marketing information. Advertisements in print and broadcast media alone provide several thousand messages daily, each vying for the consumer's attention. Given the human organism's limited capacity to process information, it is not surprising that consumers expose themselves to only a fraction of the communications presented. What is surprising is the apparent low level of exposure achieved for products, services, and issues that are presented frequently. In this section, we document low exposure, and indicate why it is a problem. Then we consider the factors that determine whether or not exposure to information occurs. On the basis of this analysis, strategies for enhancing the probability of exposure are developed.

The Case for Underexposure

Can you name the President of the United States, the Vice-President, or the Senators who represent your state? Studies indicate that almost everyone can correctly identify the President. However, only about two-thirds of the population can name the Vice-President and one-third knows both their Senators (Sears, 1969). Thus, despite considerable media exposure, the names and ideologies of many prominent political figures are virtually unknown to the general population.

Underexposure to marketers' appeals poses a critical problem. Although exposure is not sufficient to influence consumer purchases, without it there is no chance of persuasion. Moreover, relatively low levels of consumer exposure to the marketer's message may be worse than no exposure. In test markets, low levels of advertising for a brand have been found to stimulate primary demand. For example, scheduling a few commercials for a new mouthwash stimulates the demand for mouthwash, but not necessarily the brand advertised. Low levels of advertising by B.F. Goodrich stimulated demand for tires; however, consumers frequently purchased the better-known Goodyear tires than Goodrich tires in response to these ads.

Two approaches are useful in dealing with underexposure. One is to view consumers' exposure to information as a passive process. This approach is most appropriate when information exposure is achieved with mass media. In these instances, consumers are frequently exposed to information without engaging in a special effort to do so. They watch television and see commercials. They read magazines and newspapers and see ads. Exposure may be insured by selecting a media strategy that is adaptive to consumers' behavior. For example, Wilson, a manufacturer of sporting goods, may advertise its tennis racket line in *Sports Illustrated* because a large portion of its readers are potential customers for the product. If advertising is placed in *Sports Illustrated* with sufficient frequency, exposure to information about Wilson's rackets to a large number of readers is likely.

Viewing consumer exposure to information as a passive process is useful in situations where exposure is achieved with mass media. However, in situations where personal selling is an important aspect of the marketing program, a second approach is required. In such situations consumers typically seek out information. In industrial settings and door-to-door selling the sales person may initiate the contact, but even then the buyer is actively obtaining information. Thus, we need an approach that views information as an active process and that identifies factors that motivate consumers to seek out information. A knowledge of these factors serves as a guide to develop strategies that will influence consumers' active exposure to information. In developing an understanding of active exposure or information-seeking it is first necessary to describe the patterns of information exposer in which people engage.

Patterns of Exposure to Information

Frequently, those you would most like to persuade are the most difficult to reach. It is a common observation that Republicans are more likely to be exposed to Republican propaganda than Democrats, nonsmokers comprise the majority of the audience for anti-smoking appeals, and those with strong religious convictions are more likely to be exposed to proselytizing communications than individuals with weak or no religious convictions. Similar observations emerge from formal research. For example, Schramm and Carter (1959) conducted a survey shortly after Republican Senator Knowland had sponsored a twenty-nine-hour telethon in a last-minute effort to win the 1958 California gubernatorial race (Schramm and Carter, 1959). Respondents were asked if they had watched the telethon, how long they had watched it, and their political party affiliation. Republicans formed the greater percentage of the audience and watched for longer periods than did Democrats. Not surprisingly, Knowland lost the election by more than one million votes.[1]

Other investigations conducted in natural settings have obtained essentially the same result; a disproportionately high percentage of those exposed to a communication share the viewpoint being advanced (see Sears and Freedman, 1967). These findings provide strong evidence for the fact that information exposure is selective. Individuals behave in a systematic way, choosing the information to which they expose themselves. From a manager's perspective, these findings suggest the *selective exposure hypothesis* for explaining the causes of exposure. According to this hypothesis, individuals' initial opinions

---

[1]This example is adapted from Freedman, Carlsmith, and Sears (1970).

are important determinants of the information they will seek out. Specifically, people tend to seek information that is consistent with their initial opinion, and actively avoid information that conflicts with it.

The selective exposure hypothesis appears to explain the patterns of exposure exhibited by the voters we examined earlier. For example, Republicans watched Knowland's telethon because their initial opinion was favorable toward Republican candidates. In contrast, Democrats were likely to avoid the telethon because they had a negative opinion toward Republican propaganda. Despite the apparent ease with which the selective exposure hypothesis accounts for the findings described, other evidence indicates that it does not adequately explain consumers' patterns of information exposure.

This conclusion emerges in a series of experimental investigations conducted in laboratory settings. Subjects are asked to express their opinion about some issues. They are then given a choice of reading (or hearing) communications that either support or conflict with the opinion expressed. It is seen whether subjects choose supportive or nonsupportive information. To illustrate this approach consider the experiment reported by Mills, Aronson, and Robinson (1959). They told a class of undergraduate students that they were going to be given an exam. Students were asked to decide whether they would prefer an essay or multiple choice test. Once the students had made a decision, they were shown the titles of several articles. Some of the titles indicated that the articles favored multiple choice exams, while the remainder indicated that the articles provided support for essay exams. A questionnaire was then administered to all students to determine which article they wanted to read. Consistent with the selective exposure hypothesis, students who had earlier chosen an essay format exam preferred to read information supporting essay exams and students who had chosen a multiple choice exam indicated a preference for material supporting that decision.

Other studies employing a similar procedure have not always found a preference for exposure to supportive information. In fact, some have found that individuals prefer nonsupportive information. One such study is reported by Rosen (1961). He used essentially the same procedure employed by Mills and his coworkers. Subjects chose between an essay and multiple choice exam and then were given a choice of reading articles that supported or did not support their decision. However, in Rosen's study the nonsupportive article was titled, "Why Students Who Prefer a Multiple Choice Exam Should Have Chosen an Essay Exam." Students who had chosen multiple-choice exams exhibited a strong preference for the article favoring the essay exam. This preference for nonsupportive information, which is attributable to its provocative title, clearly is at odds with the selective exposure hypothesis.

A more compelling explanation for individuals' pattern of information-seeking and exposure involves interpreting it in terms of utility. Viewed from this perspective, Rosen's use of a provocative title for the nonsupportive article created the impression that it had greater utility than the supportive article. The provocative title may have led students to believe that they would learn more from the nonsupportive article than from one that supported their view. Or, they may have felt that they could strengthen their own view by reading and refuting a nonsupportive article. In contrast, when a cue indicating the utility of the nonsupportive information is absent, as is the case in the Mills, Aronson, and Robinson study, supportive information has greater utility and is therefore selected.

The contention that utility is a key determinant of information-seeking and exposure patterns also is supported in a study reported by Brock, Albert, and Becker (1970). People were found to prefer information that was unfamiliar but pertinent in making a decision to information that was familiar but not pertinent. Moreover, this preference was observed regardless of whether the information supported or contradicted individuals' initial opinions.

Despite the convincing evidence that utility guides exposure to information regardless of whether information supports or conflicts with an individual's initial opinion, it does not explain the differences in the patterns of exposure observed in laboratory and field settings. Why is it that in studies conducted in natural settings, such as the Knowland telethon study, people prefer supportive information, whereas in laboratory research their preferences vary? The answer to this question involves consideration of the procedural differences used in the two settings. In laboratory research, subjects are made aware of the alternative types of information available and are required to choose between these alternatives. In contrast, when studies are conducted in natural settings it is quite likely that individuals are not aware of all the information available. In fact, people tend to gravitate toward environments where a disproportionate amount of information is consistent with their initial opinion. Thus, the relatively small probability of being aware that nonsupportive information exists limits people's exposure to it.

Consider the case of students. They typically live in a community with other students, because that is what they can afford or because it caters to their lifestyle. They read the school newspaper, which reports on topics of interest to students and is produced by students. Thus, it is not surprising that students would not be present at hearings regarding landlord responsibility to tenants—even if it affected them. They may simply not be aware that these hearings were being conducted in the first place. Had they been informed, one might expect that exposure would be predicated on how useful students perceived the hearing to be. Similarly, business people who read the *Wall Street Journal* and *Business Week,* and associate predominantly with other business people, are unlikely to be aware of information that is anti-business.

Factors Related to Information Seeking

Given that consumers are aware of the availability of information, it appears that the extent to which it is sought depends upon its perceived utility. A logical question to ask is what determines the utility of information? In general, information utility is a function of *certainty* and *decision importance*. Each of these information-seeking factors is examined in greater depth.

Certainty. Consumers seek information when it has utility. One situation in which this occurs is when they are uncertain about which of several alternative courses of action to take. Consider a study conducted by Mills (1965). Students were told they were participating in a market research study. They were asked to rank the desirability of a large number of products and told they would be able to choose between two of them. Certainty was manipulated by offering subjects a choice between product alternatives they had previously ranked close together or far apart. Subjects randomly assigned to the *uncertain condition* were given a choice between two products which they had ranked close together. For one they read a print advertisement. The other was the one they had previously ranked immediately below the first in desirability. The remaining subjects were assigned to the *certain condition,* where the choice was between an advertised product and one they had ranked ten positions above it. The time spent reading the ad was the critical measure taken.

From the utility perspective, we expect people who are uncertain about a choice to expose themselves to information favoring one of the alternatives to a greater extent than those who are certain. After all, uncertain people are likely to perceive that the ad has greater utility in helping them decide which product to choose than it has for people who are certain about their choice. This is what Mills found. Subjects in the uncertain condition spent significantly longer periods exposing themselves to the advertisement than subjects who were initially certain.

Certainty about a decision seems to be consistent with the notion that utility affects information-seeking and patterns of exposure. We may next ask what are the specific factors that influence certainty? As might be expected, one factor is the amount of information the consumer already has accumulated about a product or service. The greater the amount of information they have, the less utility additional knowledge has. Consistent with this expectation, it has been found that information-seeking is likely to be greater among consumers who have accumulated relatively little knowledge rather than a lot (Heslin, Blake, and Rotton, 1972; Rotton, Heslin, and Blake, 1970).

A second factor affecting certainty is consumers' breadth and depth of experience. The longer consumers have purchased a brand, and the more brands purchased within a particular product category, the less they tend to seek further information (Hughes, Tinic, and Naert, 1969; Katona, 1964). Apparently, as the breadth and depth of experience with a brand and product category increases, the consumer's motivation to engage in more information-seeking and exposure diminishes. Interestingly, this findig is reported for both high priced items such as automobiles (Hughes, Tinic, and Naert, 1969) and lower priced goods and services (Katona, 1964).

A third factor that affects certainty is the individual's perception of the quality of existing information. Consumers engage in more search if the quality of their present information is perceived to be deficient because they have not recently purchased the product (Katona, 1964) or because prices, style, and the like have changed substantially since their previous purchase (Katona, 1951).

Finally, certainty is influenced by the consistency of previous information (Heslin, Blake, and Rotton, 1972; Rotton, Heslin, and Blake, 1970). Consistency refers to the degree of overlap between bits of information. To the extent that people have success with their consumption choices and are satisfied with them, it is unlikely that they will seek additional knowledge (Hempel, 1969; Katona, 1964).

Importance of the Decision. Uncertainty is one determinant of utility that influences consumers' information-seeking. The other major determinant is the importance of the decision. Importance may be interpreted in economic terms. As one might expect, as the price of a product increases, consumers engage in more information-seeking (Bucklin, 1966; Katona and Mueller, 1954). For example, Katona and Mueller (1954) observed that people sought more information when purchasing durable goods than they did in making sport shirt purchases. Equally apparent is the finding that when purchasers believe they will be committed to using a product for a prolonged period, the amount of information sought increases (Granbois, 1962; Katona and Mueller, 1954). What is surprising is that economic costs do not play a more pronounced role in guiding the extent to which consumers will actively seek information. For example, why is it that low income families do not seek as much product information as those with higher incomes? One would assume from an economic perspective that the utility of such information would be greater for low income families than for more affluent ones.

Clearly, the importance of a decision depends upon factors beyond economic ones. Specifically, the psychological and physical risk associated with a wrong decision may increase decision importance and therefore increase the probability of information-seeking. If the consumer's decision involves a conspicuous product, such as an automobile or suit, the decision assumes greater importance and is likely to induce more intensive information-seeking than for less visible products (Katona, 1964). In addition, if the product has potentially hazardous effects on the well-being of the purchaser or product user, greater importance is attached to purchase. The choice of medical products, for example, is often preceded by extensive information exposure.

The importance of a particular consumption decision varies with the perceived economic, psychological, and physical costs associated with a poor decision. Furthermore, the importance attached to a particular decision varies in accord with the consumer's lifestyle. In a study of information-seeking patterns related to the purchase of food items, Bucklin (1969) identified several individual difference factors that correlated with information-seeking. A family's wealth was positively associated with the amount of search-for-information related to food purchases. The role of the shopper in the family also had a pronounced effect on information-seeking. "Liberal women," defined as those who had a political interest but relatively little interest in "typically feminine chores at home" (Bucklin, 1969, p. 426), tended to expose themselves to relatively few sources of food-related information. Similarly, "traditionalists," women who based meal planning on what their parents had done, engaged in little information-seeking related to food purchases. In contrast, the "mother" type who was most concerned with taking care of her children and being a sexual companion to her spouse, engaged in extensive information seeking to satisfy her family's needs.

Another individual difference factor that Bucklin found to influence information-seeking was the social position of the family. For example, those who viewed themselves as transients in a community (that is, people who lived in rented quarters, were dissatisfied with their state, expected to leave the community, and were withdrawn), tended to do relatively little in the way of information-seeking. In contrast, the aging segment who perceived their past and present economic and social standing to be poor and expected their futures to be even more bleak, engaged in a significant amount of information search.

Bucklin's analysis underscores the fact that what consumers consider to be an important decision depends upon their lifestyles. Thus, strategies designed to stimulate information-seeking, which are based on decision importance, will differ for various consumer segments. For example, stressing how a product will help purchasers fulfill their role as caretakers for the family is appropriate for the mother segment, but is unlikely to affect the information-seeking patterns of traditionalists.

In summarizing our discussion of information acquisition, we have noted that exposure is selective. This is a descriptive fact, reflecting the human organism's limited processing capacity. More important is an understanding of how people select information for exposure. When information is presented via the mass media, exposure is frequently passive. In this case, consumers' exposure to information can be insured by appropriate media selection. In contrast, in many personal selling situations, consumers must actively search for information. Consumers gravitate to environments where a disproportionate amount of the information whose availability they are likely to be aware of, is consistent with their initial opinion. However, consumers will not seek information just because it is consistent with their beliefs, or avoid information simply because it is contrary to their opinion. Rather, when individuals are aware of the availability of information, exposure is a function of the perceived utility of information. In turn, utility is a function of consumers' certainty about their current store of information and the importance of a decision. A high degree of uncertainty and decision importance leads to the perception of information as useful, thus increasing the probability of information exposure.

The strategic implications of this view emerge from an understanding of the factors that affect individuals' perception of certainty and decision importance. Certainty may be reduced by questioning the breadth, depth, recency, and consistency of consumers' knowledge about a product or service. Importance is enhanced by stressing the economic, psychological, and physical risk associated with making a wrong decision.

Although these strategies to enhance the utility of information are most useful in stimulating consumers' information-seeking, they also can be employed when people engage in passive exposure. In this latter case, we may use utility enhancement strategies to gain further exposure to and reception of information. For instance, mass media communications begin their message with "If you think you know all about ---, then don't read (watch) this." This strategy is aimed at questioning message recipients' certainty about their current store of information and stimulating them to expose themselves to further information.

INFORMATION RECEPTION

Once an individual is physically present when information is being presented, there is some probability that the information will be received. The extent of information reception depends upon the impact of incoming information on the recipient's arousal and attention. Each of these components of reception is discussed in some detail.

Arousal

Incoming information is initially received by sense receptors. These receptors are sensitive to one of five types of input: auditory, visual, tactile (touch), olfactory (smell), and taste. We shall refer to these sensory systems as the sensory register. Information received by the sensory register is transmitted via a stream of impulses to the brain. Although we do not describe the process of sensing in any detail, it is important to understand several of its properties. First, the information transmitted by the sensory register does not have a one-to-one correspondence with incoming information. Some processing occurs even before information is transmitted from the sensory register to the brain. Second, when information is received by the sensory register, it transmits two types of information. One type is specific. It pertains to what is heard, seen, tasted, smelled, or felt. The sensory register can retain this information for a few seconds. If it is not transmitted for further processing during this time span, an information recipient will be unaware of its existence.

A second type of information transmitted by the sensory register is more general. The function of this more general information is to alert the brain so that the human organism is prepared to process specific information. Thus, the sensory register serves to energize individuals' processing systems so that they are sufficiently alert and oriented to absorb incoming information. As indicated in Chapter Four, some moderate level of arousal is usually optimal for this purpose. Very high levels of arousal may cause people to focus their attention on a small subset of incoming information. In an interesting demonstration of this phenomenon, experienced swimmers were placed in water over their heads. Their feet were tied and weight belts were secured around their waists. To prevent themselves from drowning, the swimmers had to unbuckle the weight belt. Without special training, most swimmers are unable to do so. Arousal was so high that they could concentrate on only one thing—pounding the water to keep their head above the surface. In contrast, very low levels of arousal are suboptimal because they inhibit detailed processing of incoming information. An everyday illustration of the effects of very low levels of arousal occurs when people misplace a wallet, coat, or purse. To find the misplaced object, people retrace their steps in the places they have been or look in the places where they typically leave the object. Even when it is found, people may have no remembrance of having put it there because a very low level of arousal was associated with this activity.

Although some moderate level of arousal is optimal for information reception, the specific level needed for effective processing depends on the task. When driving down a four-lane highway, for example, relatively little arousal is necessary to insure that you stay in your lane. If you are suddenly forced to pump the brakes and swerve to avoid an accident, the alertness needed to perform these activities increases. In decision making, too, the amount of arousal that is optimal depends on the nature of purchase. If the situation is routine, such as in the case of deciding which brand of butter to buy, or viewing a familiar commercial, relatively low levels of arousal are sufficient to process information. If incoming information is unfamiliar to the individual, a somewhat greater level of arousal is necessary to stimulate reception. Thus, individuals typically exhibit an increase in arousal when the stimulus is novel (Lynn, 1966).

Our description of arousal suggests that consumers should be provided with information that has a moderate arousal value. Further, it appears that communications with somewhat greater arousal-evoking power are appropriate when consumers are being presented with unfamiliar information than when it is familiar. Consistent with this view, advertisers often use television advertising to launch new products or to restage old ones.

Figure 5.1. High-Arousal Commercial

J. WALTER THOMPSON COMPANY

DATE: July, 1970
PRODUCER: Haboush Studios, California

CLIENT: The Seven-Up Company
PRODUCT: Seven-Up
FILM #/TITLE: 896R/"Thank You America" /:60
JOB #: 896R

1. (Music: Uncola song played by a high school marching band. Brief applause.)...

2. ...

3. (Music under, Anncr VO-- in style of country fair orator.) America, you're beautiful!

4. Why, did you know that since we... The Seven-Up Company...launched our Uncola campaign...

5. ...you have started to think...of us as an alternative to a cola.

6. And you are rapidly discovering...that 7UP does have a fresh, clean taste...

7. ...that never lets you down.

8. You are boldly going forth... finding out...that the uncola is great with food, friends and fun.

9. Some of you are even going so far as to order a hamburger and the Uncola.

10. Good for you. That's the old spirit.

11. Try it with Mom's apple pie.

12. Yes sir, America, you're doing fine.

13. Soon we'll have a carton... in every refrigerator...and a case in every pantry.

14. Seven-Up...from sea to shining sea!

15. (Music button)

Courtesy of The Seven-Up Company.

This medium provides the greatest opportunity to stimulate arousal. In addition, there is often much fanfare and action in an introductory ad campaign. This approach enhances stimulus novelty, increases arousal, and facilitates further information processing. Subsequent campaigns for the same brand often reduce the arousal value of the advertising to a level that is appropriate to facilitate processing of more familiar information. To illustrate this strategy consider the photoprints for two 7UP television commercials. The commercial shown in Figure 5.1 was part of a campaign used to restage the brand in 1967. Note the fanfare used to stimulate arousal. Three years later the "Uncola Nuts" commercial (Figure 1.2, in Chapter One) was aired. This ad has considerably less arousal value and is appropriate in light of consumers' familiarity with the brand.

Attention

As we noted earlier, information received by the sensory register is transmitted to the brain to alert the information recipient. The sensory register also transmits the content of incoming information. In order for this information to be processed, the information recipient must pay attention to it. Like exposure, attention is selective. Individuals cannot completely process all information that impinges on the sensory register. Either they completely process a small subset of the information in the sensory register or they superficially process a large amount of the sensory input. This tradeoff between the depth and breadth of processing is referred to as attention (Rumelhart, 1977).

To illustrate the attentional mechanism, consider a typical cocktail party.[2] You are engaged in a boring conversation about the weather with some acquaintances. Although you smile and pretend to be interested in your group's discussion, your attention is focused on a conversation of another group close by. If you are asked a question about the weather by a member of your group you will be able to respond to it in some appropriate manner. While you are responding, you will be unable to monitor the conversation of the nearby group. If, however, you are not called upon to participate in your group's conversation you will not have any recall of it even a few minutes later. In contrast, you are likely to have good recall of the interesting conversation that you were monitoring.

The cocktail party scenario underscores the balance between breadth and depth of processing. The attention mechanism that explains the reception described in the cocktail party example as well as other situations is described in Figure 5.2. Incoming information is processed first by the multiple channels of the sensory register. It then is processed by an attention device that attenuates all the signals so that they can pass through the limited capacity channel. More or less information from each channel gets through the limited capacity channel depending on the signal strength and the pertinence of the information contained in the channel. Strong signals containing pertinent information are registered more or less faithfully in short-term memory. In this event, information will be attended. Weak signals containing irrelevant information may be blocked by the limited capacity channel and, therefore, not registered in short-term memory. In this case, the information

---

[2]Adapted from Norman (1970).

Figure 5.2. The Attention Mechanism

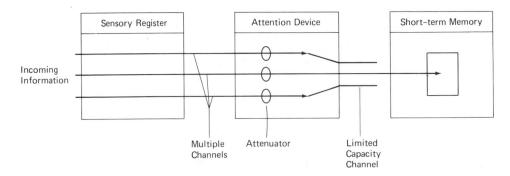

will not be attended. Information can be held in short-term memory only for a short period of time. Therefore, the information registered in short-term memory must receive further processing if it is to become part of an individual's permanent store of knowledge.[3]

The description of the attention mechanism accounts for the responses observed in the cocktail party situation. In that context, signals from the conversation in your own group as well as from the conversation nearby reach the limited capacity channel. Because the latter conversation is more interesting (that is, it has greater pertinence) more attentional resources are devoted to it than to the conversation in your own group. Nevertheless, you do devote enough attention to your group's conversation so that when called upon you can retrieve information from short-term memory and respond in a way that is consistent with the tenor of the discussion. Of course, while you are responding almost all of your attentional resources will be devoted to this task. As a result, little if any information from the overheard conversation will be attended during this time. If, however, you are not called upon to respond in your group, the information about that conversation registered in short-term memory will fade. You will have no recall of it even a short time later. In contrast, if the information registered in short-term memory about the overheard conversation had received further processing, it would have become part of your permanent store of knowledge.

More formal support for the attention mechanism we have described emerges from studies using the *shadowing* technique. This procedure requires research participants to repeat, or shadow, an auditory or visual message while being exposed to other irrelevant messages. In a series of experiments, Cherry (1953) had subjects repeat the messages they received in their right ear through ear phones. Subjects had little trouble with this task. While repeating messages received in the right ear, the input to the nonshadowed left ear was manipulated in various ways. At the beginning and end of each trial normal English was presented in the nonshadowed left ear. During the middle portions of a trial, subjects received a tone, German speech, and English spoken by a male or female. When

[3]A more detailed description of the short-term memory mechanism is developed in the next section.

subjects were questioned at the end of a trial about the nature and content of the message presented in the left (nonshadowed) ear, it was found that they noticed the change from speech to a tone. Often, too, participants observed changes in voice from male to female. In all instances, however, subjects were unable to identify the message content or the language presented in the left ear.

In a subsequent study, Moray (1959) confirmed Cherry's findings. Subjects repeated a message presented to one ear while receiving a short list of English words repeated thirty-five times in the other ear. When this task was completed, they were shown a series of words and asked to identify the ones that had been presented in the nonshadowed ear. Subjects were able to recognize the words presented in the nonshadowed ear only at a chance level, regardless of whether or not they were told about the recognition test beforehand.

Consistent with the attention mechanism described earlier, Cherry's and Moray's findings indicate that some properties of "unattended" messages are processed by higher brain centers. Thus, people recognize some aspect of the unattended stimulus but not all the details. This is probably because the shadowing task required most of the subjects' attentional resources. Very few resources could be devoted to attending the information being presented in the nonshadowed ear. If the shadowing task was less demanding, then enough attentional resources would be available for more detailed processing of the nonfocal information. Support for this contention is provided in a recent study by Shiffrin and his coworkers (1974). They found that subjects' ability to recognize a stimulus presented in a background of noise was similar whether subjects knew in which ear the stimulus would be presented, or whether they had to divide their attention between both ears. Apparently, this task is less demanding in terms of attentional resources than Cherry's or Moray's. As a consequence, subjects had enough attentional resources to divide them between ears.

Individuals' ability to divide attention is not confined to situations where the incoming information is undemanding. With practice, people can divide attention between complex tasks. For example, secretaries trained for an extended time period were able to take dictation and read simultaneously, tasks they were unable to do without the training. Apparently training makes one of the tasks automatic, so it requires almost no attentional resources. This frees the attentional resources that are necessary to perform the other task.

To summarize, when incoming information requires substantial attentional resources, few details of other signals are processed. In contrast, when few attentional resources are required, individuals can divide their attentional resources and process several inputs completely. This occurs when the processing tasks are not highly demanding or when through practice one of the tasks becomes automatic.

There is an additional factor that affects the extent to which nonfocal information is processed: the pertinence of incoming information. Using Cherry's shadowing procedure, Gray and Wedderburn (1960) had subjects shadow syllables presented in one ear and disregard syllables presented in the other ear. If a subject performed the shadowing task without error, he verbalized a string of nonsense syllables. On the other hand, if the subject attended syllables from both ears, and failed to shadow as instructed, he constructed meaningful words. For example, suppose subjects were asked to shadow syllables like *dic,* and *syll.* When *dic* was presented *tate* was simultaneously fed into the non-shadowed ear. Similarly when *syll* was being shadowed *able* was fed into the non-shadowed ear. If subjects followed the experimental instructions they would have verbalized *dic* and *syll.* In fact, what happened is that they verbalized words like dictate and syllable.[4]

Collectively, the studies described indicate that two factors guide attention. One is the strength of the signal. Strong signals, such as information presented to the shadowing ear, are usually attended. Second, the pertinence of information affects the extent to which it is attended. The extent to which weak signals and less pertinent information is attended depends on the resources that remain after focal information is processed. If the focal signal requires all of an individual's attentional resources, little information besides the focal signal will be processed, whereas if the focal signal requires few attentional resources, information from multiple channels can be attended simultaneously.

The view of attention described in this section has several implications for marketing strategy. Attention may be enhanced by using a strong signal. In marketing consumer package goods this may mean using frequent advertising, achieving concentrated distribution, and securing a substantial number of shelf facings in retail outlets. For industrial goods, signal strength can be achieved by increasing the number of salesperson contacts with customers and using heavy repetition advertising schedules. The description of the attentional process also suggests the importance of presenting pertinent information. Strategically, this entails developing products that incorporate characteristics important to buyers and stressing these characteristics in disseminating promotional information.

COGNITIVE ANALYSIS

Once people are exposed to and receive information, it is registered as thoughts in short-term memory. Whether it is processed further depends upon the cognitive analysis that occurs. Cognitive analysis requires some minimal level of comprehension of the information communicated. It also requires cognitive responding; that is, the acceptance or rejection of the information presented. These processes are examined below.

Comprehension

Comprehension refers to the extent to which the meaning intended by a communicator is the one that is understood by information recipients. Whether information registered in short-term memory is understood depends on message complexity. The more complex a message is, the more difficult it is to understand. But what determines complexity? One factor is substantive. To the extent that the concepts used in conveying information are unfamiliar to recipients, the message will be perceived as complex and

---

[4]For a more detailed description of the evidence pertaining to attention see Rumelhart (1977).

understanding will be poor. Consider the case of Frost 8/80 described in Chapter One. The product looked like vodka in that it was white, but it tasted like whiskey. Although consumers knew the appropriate uses for vodka and whiskey, they had difficulty in comprehending the appropriate way to use a hybrid of these products.

Complexity of information is also related to its presentation or execution. The greater the organization of the information conveyed, the greater comprehension is likely to be. Presenting conclusions at the outset of a presentation is one organizational device that enhances comprehension. Slowing the rate at which oral information is given may also serve to increase its comprehensibility (Foulke, 1968; Goldhaker, 1970). However, slowing the rate of delivery may cause as many problems as it resolves. Specifically, a slow-paced information presentation may adversely affect reception. A better solution to the problem of complexity is to allow information processing to be self-paced. This can be achieved by using a print appeal rather than an audio or audio-visual one. It has been shown that comprehension is greater when a message is read than when it is listened to (for example, Toussaint, 1960; Westover, 1958).

Message complexity is an important determinant of comprehension. However, even simple messages may not ensure comprehension. Consider the following description developed by Bransford and Johnson (1973):

> If the balloons popped the sound wouldn't be able to carry since everything would be too far away from the correct floor. A closed window would also prevent the sound from carrying, since most buildings tend to be well-insulated. Since the whole operation depends on a steady flow of electricity, a break in the middle of the wire would also cause problems. Of course, the fellow could shout, but the human voice is not strong enough to carry that far. An additional problem is that a string could break on the instrument. Then there could be no accompaniment to the message. It is clear that the best situation would involve less distance. Then there would be fewer potential problems. With face-to-face contact, the least number of things could go wrong.

Although this paragraph is quite simple and processing is self-paced, it is likely that you found it incomprehensible. However, if you study the picture in Figure 5.3, the paragraph becomes easy to comprehend.

This example illustrates the importance of the context in which information is presented. Information recipients will find it difficult to process communications unless they first have some understanding of the focal object being discussed. From a practical perspective, this suggests that marketers identify the product and brand before delivering an appeal advocating its purchase. Although this prescription seems obvious, it is not always followed. Advertisers sometimes defer product and brand identification until the end of their message. This strategy is typically motivated by the desire to minimize a negative reaction to a communication that results from early brand identification. However, late identification may adversely affect information comprehension.

Comprehension is necessary if people are to acquire attitudes about a product, service, or issue. However, in many cases individuals need not comprehend all that is said to acquire an attitude about the communicated issue. When a communication deals with familiar information, consumers need to comprehend only the gist of the appeal to

Figure 5.3. Context for Interpreting Bransford and Johnson's Balloon Passage

SOURCE: J. Bransford and M. Johnson, "Considerations of Some Problems of Comprehension," in *Visual Information Processing,* ed. E. Chase (New York: Academic Press, 1973).

be affected by it. Support for this contention emerges from studies using a time-compression technique. This procedure entails the systematic deletion of numerous but small portions of a tape-recorded speech. Suppose that a normal speech rate is 145 words per minute. Compressing this speech by 50 percent would entail cutting out small portions of the tape and splicing the remainder together so that speech rate is 290 words per minute. Using this technique, Wheeless (1971) examined the relationship between message comprehension and attitude change when speech was normal and compressed with parts of words missing throughout. Comprehension was significantly greater when the entire persuasive appeal was presented. Somewhat surprisingly, however, both the people who received the full and compressed version of the speech were persuaded to a substantial extent by the speech.

Advertiser's practice of using quick cuts also provides evidence for the assertion that complete comprehension is not necessary for attitude acquisition. Quick cuts involve rapid movement from one scene to another. For example, a commercial might show a parent scolding his or her children. Then there is a cut to the medicine chest where the parent is shown taking the analgesic being advertised. Again there is a cut to a scene occurring some time later where the parent is playing lovingly with the children. Quick cuts have been found to be effective despite the fact that cutting from one scene to another may reduce comprehension.

Why is full comprehension not always necessary in the acquisition of attitudes? Under what circumstances is full comprehension likely to be needed? Addressing these issues requires a description of cognitive responding, that is, how consumers go about accepting and rejecting persuasive information.[5]

Cognitive Response

Information from an incoming communication is registered in short-term memory. As we discussed above, further processing requires at least some minimal level of message understanding. Given the necessary level of comprehension, there is some probability of cognitive responding. In order to describe the cognitive response mechanism, a discussion of the structure of memory is required. Two constructs are necessary for this purpose: a short-term memory store and a long-term memory store. We shall first examine the properties of each of these stores and then consider the relationship between them.

Memory Stores. The short-term memory store is an individual's active memory. It temporarily holds information that is currently needed. The short-term memory store has two important properties. It has very limited capacity for storing information. Seven plus or minus two *chunks* of information can be stored in short-term memory at a time (Miller, 1956). A chunk is a unit of memory. As Table 5.1 shows, a chunk can be composed of, for example, two digits. By recording the digits, people can retain more digits, but still only seven chunks can be retained in short-term memory. In Table 5.1, the sixteen digits are recoded into four well-known dates that are highly memorable.

A second important property of short-term memory is that it can store information for only a limited time period before it fades. The more chunks, the shorter the time period a single stimulus can be held in short-term memory. However, even a single word is recalled for only a short while, if stored only in short-term memory. Murdock (1961) presented people with a word which they repeated. Immediately after repeating the word they counted backwards until a signal was given. This insured that research participants would not engage in deeper processing of the word. Murdock found that a single word was retained only eighty percent of the time after eighteen seconds. Three words were retained only twenty percent of the time after eighteen seconds.

TABLE 5.1. Chunking of Digits

8 Chunks composed of 2 digits	14	92	17	76	10	66	18	12
4 Chunks composed of 4 digits	1492	1776	1066	1812				

[5]A detailed discussion of cognitive response is provided by Petty, Ostrom, and Brock (1980).

Because short-term memory can store a limited amount of information for a limited time period, it is best viewed as a temporary store. It holds information so that it can receive further processing and permanent storage in long-term memory. Most, if not all, information a person has ever processed is stored in long-term or permanent memory. Long-term memory is thought to preserve two types of information. One type of information pertains to the meaning of objects. To store this type of information, long-term memory is thought to be organized in a hierarchical network (see Rumelhart, 1977).

To illustrate how information is stored in long-term memory, consider the concept *McDonald's restaurants*. As Figure 5.4 shows, McDonald's and other fast food restaurants are represented by nodes in memory. McDonald's is related by a directional pointer to the node fast food which, in turn, is related by a directional pointer to the node food. The directional pointer indicates that McDonald's is an instance of fast foods and that fast foods are an instance of food. Thus concepts are arranged in a hierarchy with a category concept (for example, food) at the top of the hierarchy and more specific exemplars of the category at the bottom. At each node in the hierarchy, the attributes specifically associated with the concept are represented. McDonald's is associated with fast service, good-tasting food, and clean surroundings. Fast food is associated with precooking, narrow assortment, and low prices. Food is associated with nutrition and edibility. An object (for example, McDonald's restaurants) and the attributes associated with it are referred to as an address in memory.

The hierarchical organization of long-term memory allows people to have access to what they know quickly. For example, to activate information about McDonald's,

Figure 5.4. The Memory for Meaning

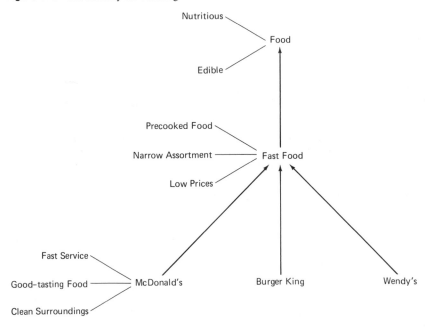

people first find the food address. Then via a directional pointer they are able to access their knowledge about fast food and ultimately McDonald's. In some instances, finding the relevant information is more difficult because it is stored at multiple addresses. The concept cardinal, for example, might be stored at the bird address, the church address, and the baseball address.

The hierarchical network provides a system for preserving the meaning of objects. But it does not indicate how people store event sequences. Yet we know that the human organism has this capability. To assure yourself of this fact, answer the following question: how many windows are there on the north side of the home you lived in three years ago? Most people are able to answer this question quite readily. They appear to be relying on pictorial representations activated from memory. These pictorial representations are believed to be the result of numerous thoughts (Kieras, 1978) that are linked to each other and that collectively form a pictorial representation of an event sequence.

Relationship between the Memory Stores.

Having described the features of short- and long-term memory, we turn to a consideration of how they are interrelated. Incoming information, represented as thoughts in short-term memory, is encoded in long-term memory by a process of retrieval and rehearsal. Initially, thoughts in short-term memory evoke a search of relevant addresses in long-term memory. The thoughts stored at one or more of the relevant addresses are activated and represented in short-term memory. The location of relevant addresses in long-term memory and the activation of thoughts associated with these addresses are termed retrieval. In the event that a person has no addresses relevant to incoming information represented in short-term memory, retrieval does not occur.

Retrieval serves to activate thoughts a person has had about some object. These thoughts as well as thoughts representing incoming information are the basis for evaluating an object. If an evaluation is to be made at some later point in time, the thoughts registered in short-term memory can be stored in long-term memory via a process of rehearsal. Rehearsal implies more than simply repeating a thought registered in short-term memory. Repetition of a thought only serves to maintain it in short-term memory. For effective thought storage, rehearsal must be elaborative (Craik and Lockhart, 1972). Elaboration involves linking new object-attribute associations to ones previously processed. The greater the extent of elaborative rehearsal, the greater the likelihood that thoughts will be stored in long-term memory, and the greater the likelihood of their availability for later retrieval.

The availability of thoughts depends not only on elaborative rehearsal but also the recency of processing. Memory appears to operate on a last-in, first-out principle. Thus, thoughts that are most recently retrieved and rehearsed are likely to be more available than thoughts that were less recently retrieved and rehearsed.

To illustrate the memorial process involved in decision making, consider a consumer who is inspecting automobiles in a showroom. He is uncertain about whether or not to buy the car he is examining. The price is right, and the car affords a lot of comfort, but he has heard that it is not fuel efficient. These thoughts are stored in the consumer's long-term memory store. For convenience we shall refer to them as initial opinion (Fig. 5.5).

Figure 5.5. Memorial Process Involved in Decision Making

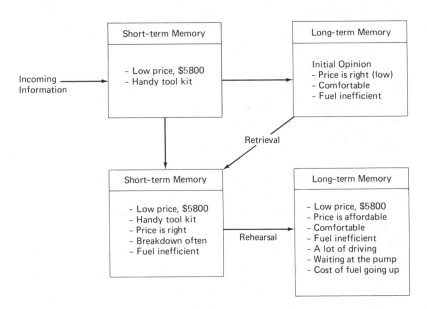

A salesperson comes up to the consumer and explains the features of the car. The salesperson informs the consumer of the low price, $5800, and points out that repairs can be done with an included tool kit. The consumer pays attention to this information, so it is registered in short-term memory (Figure 5.5). This information triggers the retrieval of thoughts from long-term memory and their registration in short-term memory. The salesperson's information about the price stimulates the consumer's own thoughts relevant to this issue.

At this point, the consumer is retaining both his or her own thoughts and thoughts presented in the salesperson's message in short-term memory. Those thoughts that the consumer chooses to rehearse will be stored in long-term memory as a new initial opinion that will affect his or her response to subsequent information. Suppose the consumer in our illustration rehearses thoughts pertaining to the buying price. The consumer thinks that $5800 will make the monthly finance charges affordable. Further, suppose the consumer thinks that the car's fuel inefficiency is a problem because he or she does a lot of driving, he or she hates waiting in line at the gas pump, and the price of fuel is likely to go up dramatically. This rehearsal of these thoughts enhances their storage in long-term memory. Because the consumer has multiple associations to the buying price and fuel efficiency these thoughts are likely to be available for later retrieval. Thoughts about the comfort afforded by the car also will be stored in long-term memory but will be less readily retrieved because they were less recently stored. Thoughts about the tool kit would not be available because they were not stored in long-term memory.

The description of the processes involved in cognitive analysis are useful in predicting the effects of persuasive messages on recipients' attitudes and recall. Suppose information recipients are negatively predisposed to a communication issue. In response to that communication they are likely to retrieve and rehearse counterarguments, that is, thoughts opposing the issue being presented. This will cause rejection of the message. However, recall will be substantial if the counterarguments rehearsed are related to arguments presented in the communication (Table 5.2). Alternatively, individuals who are negatively predisposed to a communication may merely *discount* the message arguments. Discounting is similar to counterargumentation in that it results in information rejection. But it differs from counterargumentation in that negative thoughts are not retrieved and rehearsed. The individual who discounts says, "I don't believe it," but does not bolster this position with counterarguments. The information recipient who discounts is more susceptible to subsequent influence than one who counterargues because counterarguing makes thoughts opposing a message available by virtue of their recency of processing whereas discounting does not. In addition, the lack of thought production when someone discounts is likely to result in poor recall of the communication or of related information (Table 5.2).

Cognitive response analysis can also be applied to situations where individuals have a favorable initial opinion toward the information conveyed in a communication. In this instance, information recipients are likely to retrieve and rehearse support arguments, thus increasing the likelihood that they will accept the position advocated in a communication. Moreover, they will exhibit good recall of the arguments rehearsed. If individuals merely say, "I believe it," in response to a communication without rehearsing support arguments, they will accept the position advocated, but they will be less resistant to counterpropaganda than if they engaged in support argumentation. The lack of thought rehearsal will also result in poor recall of message-related information.

Our analysis of memorial processes provides an explanation for the earlier observation that contextual cues have an important effect on comprehension. In effect, contextual cues represented in short-term memory facilitate the location of addresses relevant to the processing of incoming information. By activating the thoughts at relevant addresses, people are able to use their previously acquired knowledge in interpreting incoming information. Without appropriate contextual cues, individuals either will not rely on their previously acquired knowledge, or will activate irrelevant memory addresses.

TABLE 5.2. The Cognitive Response Mechanism

Initial Opinion Toward Communication Issue	Cognitive Response	Outcome Accept/Reject?	Recall
Negative	Rehearsal of counterarguments	Reject	Good
Negative	No rehearsal (discounting)	Reject	Poor
Positive	Rehearsal of support arguments	Accept	Good
Positive	No rehearsal	Accept	Poor

The cognitive response view also accounts for the fact that persuasion can occur even when a communication is not completely understood. Because much of persuasion entails the rehearsal of one's own thoughts, the message need be understood only to the point where it triggers these thoughts. When people are familiar with the message issue, even marginally understood appeals may be sufficient to trigger recipients' own thought repertoire. In contrast, when a communication deals with an unfamiliar topic, such as a new product, the message recipients may not have any of their own thoughts. If the appeal is not understood in this instance it will not evoke either message thoughts or the recipients' own thoughts and, therefore, will not be persuasive.

The description of information acquisition in terms of short- and long-term memory should not be taken literally. There are not separate areas in the human cortex that correspond to short- and long-term memory stores. Rather the two-store view should be conceived as a useful vehicle for understanding how people process information and for devising strategies to influence their behavior. Evidence supporting this view is presented in the next section.

Evidence for Cognitive Response

Evidence for the cognitive response mechanism focuses on two issues. First, evidence illustrating the importance of information retrieval and rehearsal in acquiring attitudes is presented. Then, the content of retrieval and rehearsal is examined in a variety of different circumstances. This discussion provides a rationale for the view of cognitive activity advanced. It also provides an elaboration of the cognitive response predictions in specific circumstances.

Importance of Retrieval and Rehearsal in Attitude Acquisition. The cognitive response view suggests that the rehearsal of information registered in short-term memory determines what is stored in long-term memory and what an individual's attitude will be. One type of evidence that supports this assertion is derived from studies where message recipients' ability to process information registered in short-term memory is experimentally controlled. For example, subjects are given a list of words to learn. They are then asked to recall the words. Typically, recall is a U-shaped function of the words' position in the list (Figure 5.6). (See Rummelhart, 1977.) The first words presented are better remembered than words in the middle of the list because subjects have more time to rehearse those early in the list. This is called the primacy effect. The last words are easily recalled because they are still registered in short-term memory. This is called the recency effect. When subjects are required to engage in a distracting task such as counting backwards by 4's (20, 16, 12 . . .) immediately after the list is presented, the recency effect disappears (Figure 5.6). The distracting task serves to clear short-term memory, forcing subjects to rely on long-term memory as a basis for recall. Because words at the end of a list were presented too late to permit rehearsal, they are not recalled after the distracting task. In effect, by preventing rehearsal learning is minimized.

A second type of study that indicates the importance of retrieval and rehearsal involves the use of physiological measures. Cacioppo (1977) measured subjects' heart

Figure 5.6. Effect of Position on Recall

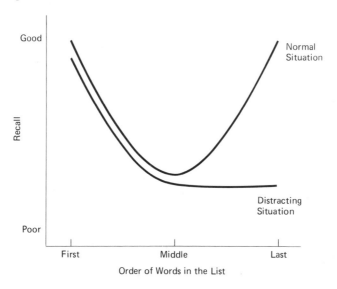

Figure 5.6. Effect of Position on Recall

rate and speech muscle activity (that is, lip, chin, and throat) while they were sitting quietly. This baseline response was compared to the heart rate and speech muscle activity that occurred when student subjects were asked to collect their thoughts about topics such as increasing tuition. It was found that there was greater speech muscle and heart activity during the thought collection period than during the period when subjects were sitting quietly. These data indicate that subvocal thought retrieval and rehearsal are part of message recipients' reaction to incoming information.

A third type of research that underscores the importance of retrieval and rehearsal in information acceptance and rejection is found in counterattitudinal role-playing studies. Counterattitudinal role-playing involves having subjects write an essay, deliver a speech, or in some other way act out a position that is counter to their initial opinion. Role-playing requires subjects to actively retrieve and rehearse arguments in support of a position, whereas passive receipt of information does not compel this cognitive activity. If the cognitive response view is correct, then role-playing, which requires active retrieval and rehearsal of thoughts, should induce more attitude change than passive receipt of information which does not require retrieval and rehearsal.

The findings in role-playing studies are equivocal (see Elms, 1967). Nevertheless, it seems clear that when people play counterattitudinal positions they accept that position to a greater extent than when they passively receive a persuasive message (Greenwald and Albert, 1968). It has also been observed that attitudes induced by counterattitudinal role playing persist to a greater extent than attitudes that are more passively acquired (Watts, 1967).

In sum, the evidence is congenial to the cognitive response view that retrieval and rehearsal are important determinants of acceptance or rejection. When retrieval and re-hearsal are inhibited or at least not motivated, the extent of learning, physiological response, and acceptance all decline. Given the importance of rehearsal in the influence process, we now turn to a consideration of retrieval and rehearsal content. This question is of prime importance to the manager. A knowledge of what people are likely to retrieve and rehearse in a particular situation provides guidance in developing strategies to affect the content of rehearsal.

Retrieval and Rehearsal Content.

According to the cognitive response view, retrieval and rehearsal content can take two forms—one's own thoughts and message thoughts. Furthermore, one's own thoughts can take the form of support arguments or counterarguments. Clearly, individuals will be more persuaded if they rehearse message thoughts or their own support arguments than if they rehearse counterarguments. The critical question is what stimulates the rehearsal of various types of thoughts?

A useful starting point in addressing this question involves considering situations where the attitude acquired depends primarily on the content of a message. These are situations where message recipients are unlikely to have well-formulated prior opinions about the position advocated. Individuals' own thoughts are likely to be closely related to message thoughts. A series of experiments conducted by Calder, Insko and Yandell (1974) fall into this category. They used a simulated jury trial in which research participants acted as jurors. They received arguments made by both the prosecution and defense. As the number of prosecution arguments presented was increased, subjects increased their perceptions of the defendant's guilt. In contrast, when the number of defense arguments presented were increased, subjects' perception of the defendant's innocence increased. The pattern of subjects'own thoughts was consistent with the number of prosecution and defense arguments made. Interestingly, the addition of arguments beyond seven did not affect thought production or attitude about guilt or innocence.

These findings are readily interpreted in terms of cognitive response. As the number of arguments favoring a particular advocacy are increased, more of these message thoughts are registered in short-term memory, at least up to a point. These message thoughts may also trigger the retrieval of individuals' own thoughts that are consistent with the message thoughts. Rehearsal of these thoughts permits their storage in long-term memory. Thus, the thoughts people have and their attitude will be more favorable toward some advocacy as the arguments for that position are increased. However, beyond a certain point, the limited capacity of short-term memory inhibits the rehearsal of additional arguments. For this reason, attitude change is not likely to increase when the number of arguments presented exceeds seven.

The experiment reported by Calder and his coworkers provides a description of how people process message information in a situation where their own thoughts are likely to be closely related to message thoughts. We shall now extend this analysis by considering a situation where two communications are presented. The first is similar to the one used in the Calder *et al.* study in that: (a) it provides arguments favoring an advocated position, and (b) the message issue is one toward which individuals do not have many highly salient thoughts of their own. The second communication advances a position that is contrary to the one expressed in the first communication. Investigations involving *cultural truisms* reported by McGuire (1964) fall into this category. Cultural truisms are beliefs that are so widely held that most people would not have heard them attacked or believe that they are susceptible to attack (McGuire, 1964). For example, one truism commonly used is the contention that "Everyone should visit his doctor at least once a year for a routine physical checkup."

Of particular interest here are studies in which supportive or refutational messages pertaining to a truism have been used. Supportive messages give arguments that bolster an individual's reasons for accepting the truism (for example, brush your teeth twice a day to avoid cavities and keep your gums healthy). Refutational arguments first demonstrate that the truism is susceptible to attack and then provide ways to defend against such an attack (for example, some people may argue that brushing your teeth twice a day will cause the enamel to wear away. But this is not the case if you use a soft brush and a nonabrasive toothpaste). After receiving one of these messages, individuals are exposed to a communication that opposes the truism. Using this procedure, it has been found that: (a) exposing people to either supportive or refutational arguments first, caused a second communication that attacked a belief to be less effective than when no prior exposure was given (McGuire and Papageorgis, 1961); (b) providing people with supportive arguments was the most effective way to strengthen an individual's attitude. However, refutational defenses were more effective in making individuals resistant to subsequent persuasive attacks on their beliefs (McGuire, 1961; McGuire and Papageorgis, 1961). This relationship held whether or not the defenses presented were ones used in a subsequent attack (Papageorgis and McGuire, 1961).

These findings provide evidence consistent with the cognitive response view that stresses the importance of initial opinion as a determinant of persuasion. In effect, exposure to a supportive message provides the recipient with support arguments. These arguments are stored in long-term memory, resulting in a strongly positive initial opinion. When message recipients are later presented with a second message that opposes their views, these arguments are registered in short-term memory. They stimulate the retrieval of arguments previously stored in memory. As a consequence, both message arguments that oppose information recipients' views and their own thoughts supporting their views are registered in short-term memory. Both message and own thoughts are likely to be rehearsed, resulting in a weaker attitude than was held prior to the opposing message.

In contrast, when the initial message is refutational, recipients are not only provided with arguments to support their view but also are alerted to the fact that their position is susceptible to attack. This stimulates the formation of counterarguments against opposing views. Later exposure to a message opposing their view stimulates the retrieval of the information recipient's counterarguments as well as arguments favoring their own position. As a result, the opposing message has little impact on message recipients' attitude.

The cultural truism studies conducted by McGuire and his associates indicate that attitude acquisition is a function of the message thoughts and the recipients' own thoughts that are rehearsed. But what determines the extent to which each of these thought types is rehearsed? This question is of interest because knowledge of the factors that direct thought selection in response to a communication helps guide the development of strategy. Specifically, the manager will want to incorporate factors in a communication that stimulate the rehearsal of message thoughts and recipients' support arguments but not their counterarguments.

Recent research suggests that message-related cues are important determinants of the thoughts selected for rehearsal. One such factor is the source's credibility; that is, how trustworthy and expert a communicator is perceived to be. In an experiment addressing this issue, Sternthal, Dholakia, and Leavitt (1978) categorized subjects on the basis of their initial opinion toward establishing a consumer protection agency. Those who indicated that they favored government protection of consumers were classified as having a positive initial opinion toward the establishment of the agency, whereas those who viewed such government protection in an unfavorable light were classified as having a negative initial opinion. Five weeks later, both groups were exposed to a message advocating the establishment of a consumer protection agency. For half of those with favorable initial opinions and half of those with unfavorable initial opinions the message was attributed to a highly credible Harvard-trained lawyer. The remaining participants were exposed to the same message, but it was attributed to a less credible individual. The results indicate that the highly credible source was more persuasive for those individuals with a negative initial opinion. The less credible source was more persuasive for those individuals with a favorable disposition toward the communication issue.

These findings suggest the following interpretation. When individuals have a negative predisposition toward a message issue, they are likely to have a greater number of counterarguments stored in long-term memory than support arguments. When a message is attributed to a highly credible source, people are not motivated to check the veracity of message assertions. In effect, a highly credible communicator facilitates the retrieval and rehearsal of message thoughts and inhibits the retrieval and rehearsal of the message recipient's own thoughts. Because the recipient's own thoughts are largely composed of counterarguments, these thoughts are particularly inhibited by a highly credible source. When the source is less credible, people are motivated to check the accuracy of the source's assertions. To do this, message recipients retrieve and rehearse their own thoughts, which are largely composed of counterarguments. Because a highly credible source stimulates the rehearsal of message thoughts and a less credible source stimulates the rehearsal of counterarguments, a highly credible source induces greater persuasion.

A similar line of reasoning can be used to explain the impact of source credibility when message recipients have an initially favorable opinion about the communication's advocacy. In this situation, recipients' own thoughts are composed largely of support arguments. In response to a proattitudinal message attributed to a highly credible source, individuals are likely to rehearse message thoughts, if anything. In contrast, when the source is less credible, message recipients are likely to be motivated to rehearse their own thoughts, presumably to bolster the position they favor. Because own thoughts are primarily support arguments, a less credible source is more persuasive than a highly credible source.

A variety of other message-related variables stimulate either message thoughts or own thoughts. Among them are the extent to which a person is distracted while receiving a communication and the number of message repetitions presented. It is useful to consider briefly the effects of message repetition to illustrate the generality of the model. A detailed discussion of distraction and message repetition is deferred until Chapter Thirteen.

In response to initial message exposures, one would expect people to rehearse the thoughts presented in the appeal if they have utility. However, as exposures continue to mount, the message content becomes redundant and it loses its information value. Thus, people are likely to rehearse more of their own thoughts and fewer message thoughts. These thoughts will likely be composed of not only support arguments but also counterarguments. As a result it is expected that agreement with a message will increase in response to initial exposures and then drop as exposures continue to mount. This pattern of response, known as wearout, has been observed for repeated exposure to print ads (Craig, Sternthal, and Leavitt, 1976) and television commercials (Calder and Sternthal, 1980).

Implications of Cognitive Response

To summarize, in response to the presentation of information, individuals may rehearse message thoughts as well as their own thoughts. Which of these thoughts predominate depends on message-related cues such as source credibility and redundancy as well as the individual's current store of support arguments and counterarguments. This depiction of cognitive response is useful to the manager because it permits anticipation of consumer reactions to various marketing strategies. As such it provides an approach to understanding and influencing consumer behavior. The implications of the cognitive response view are amplified in the next section. Perhaps most important are the implications for positioning, attribute selection, market segmentation, and measuring communication effectiveness.

Positioning and Attribute Selection. From a cognitive analysis perspective, positioning refers to the category address in memory with which a brand is associated. Although one might think that thoughts about brands in a particular product category are stored at the same address, this is not necessarily the case. For example, in the early 1960s, colas were typically associated with the soft drink address, whereas noncolas were associated with the mixer address. In the alcoholic beverages category, beers are positioned so they are associated with everyday beverage consumption or with special occasion consumption.

In selecting a position, it is useful to start by identifying the various positions that a brand with particular attributes might reasonably assume. Next, the potential demand for each of the positions identified is estimated. Finally, an estimate is made of the firm's ability to attract the potential demand associated with various positions. A viable position is one where a firm dominates similarly positioned competitors on attributes important to consumers. A viable position is also one that does not adversely affect the demand for other products a firm produces.

To illustrate the development of a position, consider a new product concept developed by General Foods. This product was an ice cream soda that consumers would serve at home. To make this soda required the addition of water. Consumers were given a description of this product and were asked to evaluate its appropriateness for various occasions. Consumers indicated that the ice cream soda was most appropriate for special occasions such as parties. It was also viewed as appropriate for dessert and as a snack. Many consumers noted that it was unlike other snacks because it would appeal to the entire family; it was a way to foster family sociability. Finally, consumers agreed that the General Foods product could be a substitute for soda fountain sodas, but it could not match the sociability of going out to a soda fountain.

The four positions identified vary in their viability. Positioning the new product to compete with soda fountain products is least attractive because the new product cannot match competition in sociability. The dessert position is somewhat more attractive, but may be ruled out because it is likely to cannibalize a dessert already marketed by General Foods, Jello. Cannibalism *per se* is not to be avoided. Cannibalism is desirable if failure to cannibalize would result in competitors stealing share from a firm. It also is acceptable to cannibalize when a new product affords a greater profit margin than an existing product. Because these conditions were not present in the case of General Foods' ice cream soda, the dessert position is not attractive.

The choice between the two remaining positions involves a tradeoff. The special occasion position is seen as more appropriate by consumers than the snack position. The special occasion position also is likely to attract less competition than the snack position. However, a special occasions position severely limits frequency of use and therefore demand. For this reason, the snack position might be considered superior. But to pursue the snack position, General Foods' ice cream soda must be distinguished from other snacks on attributes important to the consumer. This appears to be possible by stressing the family sociability attribute.

The ice cream soda example illustrates the development of strategy for a new product. This entails selecting a position and choosing attributes that will differentiate a product from similarly positioned competitive products on dimensions important to consumers. In contrast, when dealing with an existing product, positioning is already established. If management is dissatisfied with product demand, the first resort is to change the attributes used to promote a product. A more costly repositioning strategy is considered when it is clear that changing attributes for a given position is likely to be ineffective.

The strategy pursued by Schaeffer beer illustrates a successful attribute change strategy. Schaeffer is a regional beer sold in the Northeastern part of the United States. In promoting their beer, Schaeffer stressed the premium attribute: "What do you hear in the best of circles? Schaeffer all around." Sales for Schaeffer languished behind those for Budweiser, a nationally distributed beer, and several regional beers, including Rheingold and Ballantine. To remedy this situation, research was conducted. It was found that fifteen percent of the population consumed eighty-five percent of the beer in areas where Schaeffer was sold. Further, these heavy users of the product did not like the taste of their beer after they had several glasses. To meet the needs of heavy users, Schaeffer changed the attribute stressed in promoting their brand. This entailed changing the communications. Advertising presented Schaeffer as "The one beer to have when you're having more than one." Sales response to this position was excellent. Schaeffer surpassed Rheingold and Ballantine and approached Budweiser as the leading beer in the Northeast.

The Schaeffer strategy illustrates the value of focusing on attributes that are not only important to consumers, but also provide a point of difference in relation to competition. Whereas Schaeffer's former emphasis on quality may have evoked support arguments from consumers, these thoughts are likely to have been linked to the better known and more prestigious Budweiser brand. In contrast, by stressing an attribute important to heavy beer drinkers, Schaeffer elicited support arguments that were uniquely associated with the Schaeffer brand.

Schaeffer's success was achieved without altering its positioning as a beer. Rather the success was due to a change in the attribute stressed in advertising. In selecting an attribute to stimulate demand, Schaeffer chose one that was important to consumers and one that differentiated Schaeffer from other beers. Marketing failures often are due to the fact that the attribute selected does not conform to these criteria.

The consequences of the failure to select an attribute important to consumers is exemplified in the marketing of Duractin. This brand of analgesic was promoted as one that gave sustained pain relief. In contrast, most consumers wanted an analgesic that gave fast relief. From a cognitive response perspective, by positioning an analgesic as long-lasting few support arguments were generated. Moreover, long-lasting may have implied Duractin was slow to act, which would stimulate the generation of counterarguments and rejection of the brand. In light of these considerations, it is not surprising that Duractin failed to capture a significant share of the analgesic market.

Although an understanding of consumer wants is necessary to select the appropriate attribute, it is not sufficient. Competitive action also must be anticipated. Two questions should be asked with regard to competition. One question is: Will the attribute selected distinguish a brand from those of competitors assuming the same position? If the answer to this question is yes, the attribute is likely to be appropriate. For example, Harris Bank, which is positioned as a full-service financial institution, distinguished itself from competitors by promoting the fact that it offered customers a personal banker to handle all customer financial needs. This strategy was successful because the personal banker attribute was important to customers and distinguished Harris from other banks positioned as full-service financial institutions.

If the attribute selected does not distinguish a firm from competitors assuming the same position, a second question should be asked: Does a firm have adequate resources to insure that the attribute will be associated with that firm? If the answer to this question is affirmative, the attribute may be appropriate despite the fact that it is not distinctive. Continental Bank promotes its retail financial services by stressing interest rates, premiums for saving deposits, and other nondistinctive attributes. This strategy is successful because the largest bank in the Chicago area, Continental Bank, has sufficient resources to outshout competitors in the marketplace. By outspending competitors in advertising, nondistinctive attributes are associated with Continental.

In situations where a firm does not have an attribute that distinguishes it from competitors and cannot dominate competition on attributes common to several firms, product failure is likely to result. The almost simultaneous introduction of Fact, Vote, Cue, and Reef mouthwashes is estimated to have resulted in cumulative losses in excess of forty million dollars (Kollat, Blackwell, and Robeson, 1972). All of these brands were positioned as mouthwashes and all stressed the bacteria-killing and good flavor attributes.

Although these attributes are important to consumers, with so many brands competing, the demand for any one brand was not sufficient to make it viable.

When a firm cannot distinguish its brand by selecting a unique attribute or by outshouting competition on a common attribute, it is appropriate to consider repositioning a brand. The idea in repositioning is to find an address in memory where competitive brands are not represented. To illustrate a repositioning strategy, consider the case of Pepsi-Cola. A decade ago, soft drink sales were dominated by Coca-Cola. For every ten bottles of Coke sold, only four bottles of Pepsi were sold. Both brands were positioned as soft drinks and both emphasized the refreshment attribute. Coke dominated Pepsi because it had greater resources to devote to advertising and distribution.

To remedy this situation, Pepsi promoted its brand in a series of campaigns that emphasized people rather than soft drinks. In the early 1970s, Pepsi-Cola advertising centered on the theme "You've got a lot to live. Pepsi's got a lot to give." In 1973 this theme was replaced by "Join the Pepsi people, feeling free." The objective was to focus on the needs of the self-oriented "me" generation. In 1977, "Have a Pepsi day" was introduced, stressing the idea that good times were worth preserving. And in 1980, Pepsi launched the "Drink it in" campaign, which emphasized Pepsi's role in sharing memorable moments.

All of these campaigns served to reposition Pepsi-Cola. Rather than being represented at the soft drink address, Pepsi was represented at an address where thoughts about personal aspirations and personal relationships were stored. Because people have many thoughts about themselves and their relationships, associating Pepsi with this address made Pepsi advertising highly memorable. Moreover, the repositioning distinguished Pepsi from Coca-Cola, which maintained the soft drink position throughout the 1970s. In a succession of campaigns, Coke used themes such as "Things go better with Coke," "The real thing," and "Coke adds life." These campaigns presented Coke as the hero in situations where soft drinks were appropriate.

Pepsi-Cola's repositioning has been highly successful. This brand has grown at an average rate of about six percent during the past several years, three times the industry growth rate. In 1980, Pepsi's food store sales exceeded those for Coke. Nevertheless, Coke has maintained sales leadership by virtue of its domination in fountain sales, where it has more than a sixty percent share-of-market.

Pepsi's strategy illustrates one situation when it is appropriate to reposition a brand to distinguish a brand from a dominant competitor. Another instance when repositioning is appropriate occurs when there is a reduction in the demand for the brands assuming a particular position. The repositioning of Head and Shoulders shampoo illustrates this situation. Head and Shoulders emerged as the leading shampoo by assuming a medicinal position that emphasized dandruff control. Its medicinal smell gave integrity to this positioning and attribute strategy and helped distinguish it from shampoos assuming the cosmetic position, which had a pleasant fragrance. In the early 1970s, consumers began to wash their hair more frequently, and at the same time reduced their use of Head and Shoulders and other medicinal shampoos. Apparently consumers believed that a medicinal shampoo would damage hair if used frequently.

To stop the decline in demand for medicinal shampoos, Head and Shoulders employed an attribute change strategy. Advertising emphasized how manageable Head and Shoulders left hair and how well it controlled dandruff. In essence, the attempt was to maintain Head and Shoulder's consumer franchise by reinstating the dandruff control claim and at the same time limit the generation of arguments that it would damage hair. This strategy was less than successful; Johnson and Johnson's baby shampoo surpassed Head and Shoulders as the leading shampoo. Apparently, merely telling consumers that Head and Shoulders left hair in a manageable condition was not very convincing because the brand was still positioned as a medicinal shampoo. To halt the decline in Head and Shoulders's market share required a repositioning. The new positioning attempted to represent Head and Shoulders as a cosmetic shampoo that left hair manageable and dandruff-free. This positioning and attribute strategy was made convincing by modifying the product so that it had a pleasant fragrance. As a result, the decline in the Head and Shoulders brand was halted.

To summarize, the development of a strategy for an existing brand begins with the selection of one or more attributes that are important to consumers and that allows a firm to differentiate itself from competitors who are positioned similarly. When this is not possible, it is appropriate to attempt a brand repositioning so that it is stored at a different memorial address than dominant competitors. Repositioning also is appropriate when demand for a position is diminishing.

Segmentation. The cognitive response view has important implications for market segmentation. It suggests that initial focus center on consumers who are favorably disposed toward a firm's brand. These individuals are likely to rehearse their own repertoire of support arguments, in effect persuading themselves to purchase the brand. Operationally, this strategy entails targeting consumers with the same demographic profile as current brand users. We shall call this strategy *dollars to sales,* reflecting the fact that the marketing effort is spent against those targets from whom sales were previously generated.

Pursuit of a dollars to sales strategy is most viable early in a product's life cycle. Beyond this point, demand among current users becomes saturated. Continued brand growth may or may not require maintenance of the dollars to sales strategy to protect the brand franchise, but it does require a *dollars to opportunity* strategy to attract new brand users. These are individuals who purchase the product category, but not the firm's brand (that is, nonbrand users) or do not purchase the category (that is, product nonusers). Which of these two segments constitutes the more attractive segment varies from situation to situation. It depends on how well a firm's brand meets nonbrand users' and product nonusers' needs in relation to competition. However, both nonbrand users and product nonusers are likely to have counterarguments against purchasing the firm's brand. Nonbrand users' counterarguments will be directed toward the brand, and product nonusers' counterarguments will be directed at the product category.

From a cognitive response view, influencing opportunity requires strategies that reduce counterargumentation. There are a wide variety of approaches useful for this purpose. They will be described in detail when we consider message, source, and channel strategies in Part V of the book. Here we shall describe two strategies to clarify how counterargumentation may be inhibited. As we noted earlier, a highly credible source inhibits the generation of counterargumentation. Perhaps this is why E.F. Hutton recruited John Paul Getty to present an appeal favoring the use of their financial services. The use of evidence that is unfamiliar to consumers to support an assertion may also inhibit counterargumentation. Schick used clinical tests showing that their brand of electric razor, Flexmatic, shaved closer than competing brands. The use of unfamiliar evidence and heavy advertising expenditures was largely responsible for propelling Flexmatic's share of market from eight to sixteen percent.

An important conclusion emerging from the discussion of targeting is that it is closely related to positioning. The target selected helps define the appropriate position. For example, prior to the early 1970s Miller beer was positioned as a premium beer—it was the champagne of bottled beer. Advertising featured dress-up party scenes. When Phillip Morris acquired the brand, they noted that Miller was attracting upscale individuals who were relatively light beer drinkers. To stimulate demand for Miller, Phillip Morris changed the target to a slightly downscale segment. This change in target required an alteration in the brand's position from one of special occasions to one featuring reward for hard work. Miller was positioned as the beer to have when you've put in a hard day's work and want to relax with the guys.

Measuring Communication Effectiveness. The predominant approach to measuring the effectiveness of a communication entails asking people for verbatim recall of the message content. For example, television commercials are often assessed using a day-after-recall procedure. People are contacted by telephone one day after a commercial has aired and are asked to describe what the commercial showed and said. The higher the percent of people in the target who recall the commercial, the more effective it is judged to be.

Cognitive response theory questions the appropriateness of message recall as a measure of communication effectiveness. According to the cognitive response view, people will exhibit good recall of the thoughts they rehearse. If people rehearse counterarguments in response to a message, they are likely to recall the message by associating their own negative thoughts to the message information. For example, in response to a message stating that a particular make of automobile comes equipped with a tool kit, people may rehearse the counterargument that a tool kit is needed because the car breaks down frequently. Recall of the message will be good because people will remember the counterargument they rehearsed (the car breaks down frequently) and readily associate it with the message information (a tool kit is provided). In effect, by using communication recall as the criterion for judging message effectiveness, it is possible to infer that an appeal is very effective when in actuality people reject the arguments advanced. It also follows from cognitive response that a communication can be highly persuasive by evoking recipients' favorable own thoughts and yet be poorly recalled.

A more compelling approach to measuring communication effectiveness is suggested by cognitive response theory. It involves administering the thoughts measure described in Chapter Four. Although this measure reflects communication recipients' recall, it is not recall of the message. Rather, the recall pertains to the thoughts people have about a product. A knowledge of these thoughts is useful as a basis for identifying the causes of people's consumption behavior. In addition, communication effectiveness can be measured by administering the attitude measures discussed in Chapter Four. A comparison of the attitudes held by those exposed to a communication in relation to those not exposed would indicate the persuasive effect of a message.

SUMMARY

In this chapter, we have presented a description of the information acquisition process. The information consumers acquire from others is viewed as an active process. Acquisition depends not only on consumers' exposure, reception, and cognitive analysis of a communication, but also on consumers' reactions at each of these stages. Consumers' reactions are based on thoughts, which we have referred to in various ways depending on the processing stage being discussed. They were termed evaluations of utility when determinants of exposure were described, pertinence for reception, and initial opinions in developing the cognitive analysis mechanism. While such a distinction was a useful pedagogical device for describing the acquisition process, it should be noted that utility, pertinence, and initial opinions all refer to thoughts stored in long-term memory.

A schematic diagram of the acquisition process is shown in Figure 5.7. By simultaneously considering message cues and consumer reactions, we are able to derive guidelines for enhancing information acquisition at each stage of the acquisition process. When information exposure is passive, it can be enhanced by appropriate selection of media and repetition schedules. In situations where exposure is predicated on information-seeking, the perceived utility of information determines exposure. In essence, utility is determined by thoughts (that is, initial opinions) stored in long-term memory. Knowledge of the availability of information triggers the retrieval of one's own thoughts from long-term memory (arrow labeled 1 in Figure 5.7) and their registration in short-term memory (arrow labeled 2 in Figure 5.7). Rehearsal of these thoughts determines the thoughts stored in long-term memory (arrow labeled 3 in Figure 5.7) and the likelihood of information exposure. To the extent that the decision is important and consumers are uncertain

Figure 5.7. Schematic of the Information Acquisition Process

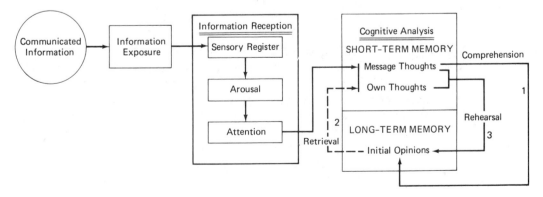

about the veracity of their current store of knowledge the retrieval and rehearsal processes lead to information-seeking.

Like exposure, information reception depends upon both message cues and consumers' reactions. The arousal induced by stimuli impinging on the sensory register depends on such factors as their novelty. In turn, novelty is a function of the properties of the stimulus message as well as consumers' familiarity with it. Attention, too, depends on a message factor, signal strength, and a consumer reaction factor, the evaluation of information pertinence. Both familiarity and pertinence are a function of initial opinions stored in long-term memory. The presentation of a communication stimulates the retrieval of these thoughts and their registration in short-term memory. Optimal reception occurs when arousal is at some moderate level, the signal strength is substantial (for example achieved by use of repetition) and the message is pertinent to the consumer.

Finally, cognitive analysis entails the processing of both the cues presented in a communication and the message recipient's own reactions. Comprehension is influenced by message factors such as the complexity of an appeal and the context in which it is presented. Equally important determinants of comprehension are recipient factors such as familiarity with the communication issue and intelligence. Cognitive response is affected by communication cues such as the speaker's credibility and information redundancy. It also depends on the recipients' pool of support arguments and counterarguments stored in long-term memory. Acceptance of the position prescribed in a communication is enhanced by achieving at least some minimal level of message comprehension by focusing on market segments that have a positive initial opinion toward the communication issue and by employing message cues that inhibit the generation of counterarguments among those with a negative disposition.

In sum, information acquisition is interpreted to be a process that depends on incoming information and consumers' reactions based on their current knowledge. This view suggests a variety of strategies that are useful in facilitating information exposure and reception. It also provides guidelines for developing positioning and segmentation strategies. Nevertheless, the description of information acquisition presented in this chapter is not complete. It fails to consider an important source of information acquisition: the consumers' own experience. In the next chapter we shall extend our view of the information acquisition process to incorporate this source of information.

QUESTIONS

1. A new appliance which slices, dices, and blends food has been developed. Initial sales for this product are well below projected sales. Research is conducted, revealing several factors that might account for the sluggish sales. Specifically, it is found that a substantial number of potential buyers have never heard of the product, despite the extensive use of media advertising. In addition, there are a substantial number of people who exhibit awareness of the advertising for the product, but who claim that they cannot see the advantages of the new appliance in relation to competitive ones. For this reason they have not sought out demonstrations of the new appliance in retail

stores. Outline strategies you would use to enhance consumers' exposure to the new appliance.

2. Two ads are being considered to persuade people not to smoke. Ad 1 is fear-arousing. It focuses on the consequences of smoking; shorter life-expectancy, disability, and children growing up without their parents. Ad 2 is less fear-arousing. It tells people how to stop smoking and outlines a series of steps to follow. Which ad would you choose to insure information reception?

3. Outline strategies you would consider to enhance the attention consumers paid to a communication.

4. Two commercials are being considered to promote a product. Commercial 1 presents the sales message alone. Reasons for using the brand are specified. Commercial 2 presents the same sales message. However, an unrelated humorous and interesting event is occurring in the background for Commercial 2. Which commercial would you select to insure reception of the sales message?

5. Outline strategies you would consider if it were found that consumers could not understand a communication.

6. What accounts for the effectiveness of quick cuts?

7. "Recall of the message content is a poor measure of advertising effectiveness." Defend or refute this contention drawing upon your knowledge of cognitive responding to support your position.

8. Explain why highly credible sources are less persuasive than ones lower in credibility when message recipients favor the communication advocacy.

Chapter 6

Information Acquisition from One's Own Experiences

How do consumers know whether or not they liked a particular movie? How do students determine whether a professor is an effective instructor? Once people have tried a brand, how do they decide whether or not to purchase it again? In brief, how do consumers know what they know?

As we have seen in Chapter Five, individuals' acquisition of knowledge entails active processing of the information presented by commercial institutions, family, friends, and other interpersonal sources. In part, our evaluation of movies, instructors, and brands is based on the information acquired from others. An equally important way of acquiring information involves consumers' interpretation of their own experience. The process of this interpretation is called *self-perception*. An understanding of the self-perception process enables us to anticipate the attitudes individuals acquire as a result of their own behavior. It provides some insight into the likelihood of repeating a behavior. It also suggests strategies to affect consumers' interpretation of their behaviors and the actions they take.

This chapter begins with an overview of the self-perception process. First, we describe how people employ their own behavior to acquire information that guides subsequent decision making. Next, we depict the relationship between the acquisition of information from interpersonal sources and from one's own behavior in terms of a single process. The integrity of this view is evaluated by comparing it to a multiple processes theory that has become popular during the past decade. In the final section of this chapter, the strategic implications emerging from our analysis of the self-perception process are discussed.

THE SELF-PERCEPTION PROCESS

Self-perception theory describes the process by which individuals use their own experience as a basis for acquiring attitudes and guiding subsequent action.[1] According to this theory, people come to know their attitudes partially by inferring them from their own *behavior* and the *circumstances* in which that behavior occurs (Bem, 1972). In essence, this proposition suggests that consumers who are uncertain learn what they think by observing what they do. It also implies that attitudes derived from observing one's own behavior guide subsequent action.

In this section, we describe in detail a number of studies pertaining to self-perception theory. The complete description of these studies is warranted for three reasons. First, the study descriptions document the fact that individuals' behavior is influenced by their prior actions and the circumstances in which those actions occur. Second, they help identify the process by which actions and circumstances influence subsequent behavior. Finally, the detailed description of studies pertaining to self-perception theory suggests the conditions necessary to develop effective influence strategies.

The Effect of One's Own Behavior on Decision Making

The effect of consumers' own behavior on decision making has been studied intensively using the so-called *foot-in-the-door technique*.[2] This approach entails gaining compliance with a small request in the hope that it will increase the likelihood of compliance with a subsequent large request. Frequently, insurance salespeople offer to discuss potential clients' insurance needs at no charge. They hope that the customers compliance with this request will make them more likely to buy a policy at some later point in time. Similarly, door-to-door salespeople of cosmetics and household products attempt to get initial purchase of a low priced item in the hope that it will facilitate the sale of more expensive items in the product line.

In a seminal study, Freedman and Fraser (1966) systematically investigated the effectiveness of the foot-in-the-door technique. Initially, they asked people to comply with a small request: either to sign a petition or to place a small sign in their window to show their support for one of two issues, keeping California beautiful or promoting safe driving. Virtually all those asked complied with this request. Two weeks later, a different experimenter returned to these people and asked them to place a large sign supporting the safe driving issue on their front lawn. Substantially more people complied with this

---

[1]Kelley (1973) provides a detailed description of attribution theory of which self-perception is a part. For a review of the self-perception literature relevant to marketing, see Scott (1975).

[2]For a detailed review of foot-in-the-door studies, see De Jong (1979).

large request when they had been previously contacted than when they were cold-called and merely asked to comply with the large request.

Self-perception theory provides an explanation for Freedman and Fraser's finding. When asked to comply with a large request, people were likely to have been uncertain about their attitudes toward it. This uncertainty may have caused people who had previously signed a petition or placed a small sign in their window to examine their own behavior as a basis for determining their attitudes. Because they had complied with the initial request, it is likely that they viewed themselves as socially concerned citizens. As a result, they exhibited a strong tendency to comply with the large request. In contrast, those people who were not asked to comply with the small request had no basis for developing a self-perception as concerned citizens. Thus, they were less likely to comply with the large request than people who had previously agreed to comply with the small request.

The Freedman and Fraser study provides support for the self-perception proposition that people's own behavior is an important cue in guiding subsequent decision making. Nevertheless, several questions remain unanswered. Although Freedman and Fraser demonstrate that compliance with a small request influences *intentions* to comply with a large request, whether it also affects *actual* compliance is not addressed. Freedman and Fraser never actually placed the large sign on people's lawns, they only received research participants' consent to do so. Furthermore, Freedman and Fraser used different solicitors for the small and large request. At issue is whether the foot-in-the-door is effective in the typical marketing situation where the same solicitor makes both requests. Finally, whether the foot-in-the-door affects the magnitude of compliance as well as compliance per se requires investigation.

To address these issues, Pliner and her associates (1974) asked people to comply with a small request. This involved wearing a lapel pin in support of an upcoming cancer fund drive. The following day, the same requester returned and asked the person originally contacted to donate money to the cancer fund. It was found that people who had been previously contacted were more likely to make a donation than those who were merely asked to donate without prior contact (that is, cold-called). Thus, the foot-in-the-door technique is effective as a means of enhancing both intention and behavior whether the same or different people make the small and large request. Pliner *et al.* also examined the amount of money given by those who donated. They found that the average contribution made by people in the foot-in-the-door condition was greater than the donation made by people who were cold-called. But this was because more people in the foot-in-the-door condition donated money. When only donors were examined, there was no difference in the contribution made by those who had previously been contacted and those who were cold-called. This finding suggests that the foot-in-the-door technique enhances the probability of action (that is, donation) but not the magnitude of the action taken (that is, the amount donated).

The effectiveness of the foot-in-the-door technique in the studies examined is consistent with self-perception theory. People who agree to a small request come to view themselves as the kind of people who favor that behavior. They are, therefore, more likely to comply with a subsequent larger request than people who had no salient behavior as a basis for inferring their attitude. If this reasoning is correct, then one would expect that people who reject an initial request would be more likely to reject a second smaller request than those asked only to comply with the small request. In self-perception terms, people who reject an initial request will view themselves as the kind of people who have a negative disposition toward the requested behavior. They are, therefore, less likely to comply with a subsequent request than people who did not have a salient prior behavior as a basis for discerning their attitude.

To test these self-perception predictions, Snyder and Cunningham (1975) used a *door-in-the-face* procedure. This entails asking people to comply with a large request and when it is rejected, asking for compliance with a more modest request. People were phoned and asked to participate in a survey by answering fifty questions. Most people refused this request. Two days after this large request was administered, a second interviewer recontacted participants and asked them to comply with a smaller request—answering thirty questions over the phone. Consistent with self-perception theory, it was observed that people who had previously rejected the large request were more likely to refuse the request to answer thirty questions than those who were cold-called and asked only to respond to thirty questions.

Until now, the foot-in-the-door studies examined have involved a time interval between the first and second request ranging from a day to several weeks. Cann and his co-investigators (1975) examined the foot-in-the-door technique in a context where the second request immediately followed the first. Research participants first answered three questions and then were asked to devote two hours to perform a second task. As was found in previous foot-in-the-door investigations, compliance was greater when the large request followed the small request than when only the large request was made. This finding suggests that the timing of the second request is of little importance; the foot-in-the-door strategy is effective whether the second request follows the first immediately or after some delay. However, this conclusion is questioned in a study reported by Cialdini and Ascani (1976). They asked people to display a small card showing the logo of the local blood services organization. Immediately after research participants had agreed to this small request, they were asked to donate a pint of blood. It was found that compliance with the small request was no more effective in gaining compliance with the request to donate a pint of blood than merely asking people to donate a pint of blood.

What accounts for the disparity in the results obtained in the Cann *et al.* study and the Cialdini and Ascani study? Why do Cann *et al.* obtain evidence for the effectiveness of the foot-in-the-door when the two requests are made in close temporal proximity whereas Cialdini and Ascani find it to be ineffective in a similar situation? The key to resolving this discrepancy is likely to be found by examining the small initial requests made in the two studies. In the Cann *et al.* study, complying with the small request entailed answering three questions. Requiring people to engage in this behavior caused them to focus on it and attribute it to a favorable attitude toward the issue. As a result, they were more likely to comply with the large request than those asked only to comply with the large request. In contrast, Cialdini and Ascani asked people to agree to the small request. This may have made individuals' own behavior less salient than if they had to perform the behavior requested in the initial solicitation. Moreover, by requiring only agreement with the initial request, the requester's behavior may have become relatively more available than the research participants' own behavior. Thus, participants may have reacted to the inequity of the exchange. "I already agreed to one request and now I'm being asked for compliance with an even greater request." This type of reaction may have accounted for Cialdini and Ascani's failure to observe the foot-in-the-door effect.

The conclusion emerging from this analysis is that the effect of one's own behavior on subsequent action depends uponthe availability of a cue. When people's own behavior is the most available cue, it is used to determine attitudes and guide subsequent action. When people's own behavior is made more available by requiring performance of the requested behavior, people focus on their own behavior and the foot-in-the-door technique is effective (Table 6.1). In contrast, when there is no delay between requests and when the availability of thoughts about one's own behavior is overshadowed by the inequity in the requester's demands, the foot-in-the-door approach is ineffective.

In essence, our analysis of foot-in-the-door studies interprets the self-perception process in terms of the information processing view described in the preceding chapter. More specifically, in situations where people engage in behavior in response to a small request, for example, this action is stored as a thought memory. If people are uncertain about the appropriate action to take with regard to a subsequent request, thoughts about their previous behavior are retrieved and registered in short-term memory. These thoughts trigger the retrieval of other thoughts supporting the behavior from long-term memory. To the extent that they are rehearsed, they result in the acquisition of a favorable attitude and an increased likelihood of repeating similar behaviors. However, if thoughts about one's own behavior are less available than thoughts regarding other people's behavior, as appears to be the case in the Cialdini and Ascani study, then thoughts about one's own behavior are unlikely to be retrieved and represented in the short-term memory store. Rather, thoughts about other people's behavior are likely to be retrieved and registered in short-term memory. When this behavior is viewed as inequitable, it triggers the retrieval of negative thoughts about the requested behavior. To the extent that these counterarguments are rehearsed people reject the second request.

TABLE 6.1.   Conditions Affecting the Effectiveness of the Foot-in-the-Door Technique

	Small Initial Request		Delay Between Requests		
Outcome	*Agreed to*	*Performed*	*No*	*Yes*	*Researchers*
Foot-in-the Door Effective	x			x	Freedman and Fraser
	x			x	Pliner *et al.*
		x	x		Cann *et al.*
Foot-in-the Door Ineffective					Cialdini and Ascani
	x		x		

Own versus Others' Behavior as Determinants of Decision Making

In describing how individuals' employ their own behavior to acquire attitudes and to guide their subsequent action, we noted that other people's behavior may also play a role in decision making. We shall examine the effects of one's own behavior and others' behavior more closely. This is achieved by considering more fully investigations that have tested the door-in-the-face technique. Although an explanation of the door-in-the-face effect requires a discussion of acquisition processes beyond the one encompassed by self-perception theory, it is introduced here because it will help us identify the situations in which one's own behavior is likely to guide attitude acquisition.

As you will recall from the previous section, the door-in-the-face approach entails asking for compliance with a large request, having it rejected, and then asking for compliance with a smaller request. You will probably recognize this strategy as one that is used in a courting relationship:

"Will you marry me?"

"Ah . . . No."

"Well, how about getting engaged?"

A formal study examining the door-in-the-face technique was conducted by Snyder and Cunningham (1975). As we already noted, they found that people were more likely to reject a second small request several days after they had rejected a large request that was made by a different requester than if only the small request were made. This outcome is readily interpretable in terms of self-perception theory. Rejection of a large request caused people to view themselves as the kind of individuals who do not favor the behavior. Therefore, they reject even small requests pertaining to the same behavior.

From a practical perspective this suggests that the door-in-the-face strategy is not useful as an influence device. However, a recent study by Cialdini and his coworkers (1975) qualifies this conclusion. They asked people to comply with a large request: working with delinquent children for several years. All people asked to comply with this request refused. Immediately after this rejection, the *same* requester asked for compliance with a smaller request (spend two hours with delinquent children). This door-in-the-face procedure was found to be significantly more persuasive than merely asking for compliance with a small request. But this finding emerged only if the same requester made the second request immediately after the first. When *different* people made the two requests, compliance with the second was no greater than if people were cold-called and asked to comply with the second request. Apparently, the door-in-the-face strategy is effective because the individual of whom a large request is made feels the need to reciprocate in order to be *equitable* when the requester makes a concession. The thinking might be, "This person made a concession in the size of his request. To be equitable, I should also make a concession by changing my refusal to an acceptance."

The door-in-the-face studies can be interpreted in terms of the information processing view. Consider the situation investigated by Cialdini and his coworkers (1975) where the same individual makes a large request and immediately follows it with a smaller request. The recipients have little time to reflect on their own behavior in this situation. Moreover, the fact that the requester is making a concession causes the request recipient to perceive the second request as equitable. This triggers the retrieval and rehearsal of thoughts that support the behavior, resulting in the effectiveness of the door-in-the-face.

The same line of reasoning can be used to explain Cialdini *et al.'s* door-in-the-face finding when the two requests are made in close temporal proximity by different people. In this situation, request recipients are unlikely to focus on either the requester's behavior or their own behavior. The immediacy of the second request makes it difficult to reflect on the reasons for rejecting the first request. Furthermore, because different people make the two requests, thoughts about the equity of the requester's behavior are not highly available. If thoughts are retrieved and rehearsed, they are likely to be composed of both support arguments and counterarguments. Thus, the door-in-the-face approach is likely to be no more effective than cold-calling. This is what Cialdini *et al.* found.

Finally, in the situation investigated by Snyder and Cunningham, where there is considerable delay between the large and small requests, each made by different people, recipients focus on their own behavior. The time interval between requests allows recipients to analyze the causes of their own behavior. Because the two requests are made by different people, thoughts about the requester's behavior are not highly available. As a result, rejection of the large request stimulates the retrieval and rehearsal of thoughts opposing the behavior. In turn, this causes people to reject the smaller request to a greater extent when it follows the large request than when the smaller request is presented alone.

Our analysis of both the foot-in-the-door and door-in-the-face investigations underscores the fact that circumstances in which behaviors occur have an important influence on the attitudes acquired and the action taken. The foot-in-the-door technique is effective in situations where the recipient interprets compliance with a small request as an indicator of positive feelings toward that action. This occurs in circumstances where recipients are given enough time to reflect on the reasons for compliance or when thoughts about their own behavior are highly available. The door-in-the-face procedure is effective in circumstances where thoughts about the requester's behavior are available and are interpreted as equitable. This may be achieved by eliminating the time necessary to reflect on the cause of one's own behavior and by employing the same requester to make thoughts about the requester's behavior available.

Clearly, the circumstances in which behavior occurs affect whether acquisition will occur from one's own behavior or that of others. Although circumstances have been viewed up to this point as the action of other people, circumstances have a more general meaning. They refer to behavior-related cues that may help explain the cause of a person's actions.

The Effect of Circumstances on Self-Perception

Suppose a friend asks you if a particular instructor that you had for a course was good. Although you may know you liked the instructor, you may be uncertain about the reasons for this feeling. It may be due to the fact that the instructor was interesting and effective, or it may be due to circumstances. If the course dealt with issues that you were interested in, or if the class was offered at a particularly convenient time, it is likely that you would be hesitant to endorse the instructor strongly. The reason for this uncertainty is that there are multiple explanations for your feelings about the instructor. Your evaluation may be based on the fact that the instructor was good or it may result from circumstances such as when the course was offered, or the nature of the material covered. In contrast, if you felt positively about the instructor despite the fact that the class covered topics of little interest and was held at an inconvenient time, you are likely to endorse the instructor strongly.

The point of this illustration is that circumstantial factors may affect the thoughts individuals have about their own behavior. The fact that the instructor's course was offered at a convenient time and dealt with interesting material constitute circumstantial cues that cause you to *discount* the instructor's effectiveness as the sole reason for your positive feeling about him or her. Circumstances that cause discounting are ones that provide an alternative explanation for feelings or behavior. Thus, you are uncertain about the causes of your reactions and a strong attitude is not acquired. In contrast, circumstances may *augment* the attribution of feelings and behaviors to certain causes, reducing uncertainty and causing the formation of a strong attitude. The fact that a class deals with a subject of little interest or is held at an inconvenient time are circumstantial cues that augment the attribution of a positive feeling about an instructor to the fact that he or she is good. Despite these negative circumstances, you are favorable.

To illustrate the mechanism by which circumstantial cues can influence the acquisition of information from one's own behavior, let us consider a study conducted by Lepper, Greene, and Nisbett (1973) in which children were asked to draw pictures. One group of children was promised a reward for drawing; another was not promised a reward, but given one unexpectedly after they had performed the behavior. A third group received no reward for the drawing activity. Some time later all children were given a second opportunity to use drawing materials, but no mention was made of a reward. The children who had previously been given an unexpected reward for drawing engaged in the activity significantly more than those whose previous drawing was perceived to be reward contingent and slightly more than those not receiving a reward. Thus it is not the reward per se, but the perceived contingency of reward upon behavior that causes reward to serve as a discounting cue.

The circumstantial cues examined to this point have been rewards or incentives. While this type of circumstantial cue is the one that has been investigated most intensely, other factors may produce a similar effect. In fact, any cue that has the potential of facilitating or inhibiting the attribution of the cause for a behavior can be considered a circumstantial cue. To illustrate this point, consider a study reported by Dholakia and Sternthal (1977). Research participants were presented a communication requesting that they support the then-pending Consumer Protection Agency bill by signing a petition which would be sent to their congressional representative in Washington. Half the participants received the appeal from a highly trustworthy and expert communicator and half from a source who had less of these attributes of character. After reading the communication, all subjects were given the opportunity to sign the petition. Finally, research participants' attitudes toward the Consumer Protection Agency bill were determined.

In the Dholakia-Sternthal study, the trustworthiness and expertise of the source served as the circumstantial cue. For those who complied with the request of the highly trustworthy and expert source, two factors could explain their behavior: either they signed the petition because they favored the issue or because the source was trustworthy and expert. The source's characteristics are expected to result in the discounting of personal reasons as the cause of their behavior. Thus, their attitude toward the bill should not be very positive. In contrast, individuals who complied with the less trustworthy and expert source can only attribute their behavior to a favorable attitude toward the bill. This source augments the perception that behavior was caused by personal reasons. The prediction emerging from this analysis is that the less trustworthy and expert source would induce a more favorable attitude than a communicator with more of these attributes. Dholakia and Sternthal's data are consistent with this expectation.

In sum, there is substantial evidence that the circumstances in which behavior occurs serve as a cue people use to determine the cause of their actions. If the circumstantial cue is one that facilitates behavior, individuals will be uncertain as to the cause of their behavior. They will not acquire a strongly positive attitude toward that behavior and the likelihood of repeating it or performing similar behavior is low. In contrast, if the circumstantial cue is one that normally inhibits the performance of a behavior, but does not do so in a particular instance, individuals will be more certain about the cause of their behavior. It will be attributed to personal reasons, causing the acquisition of a strong attitude toward the behavior and a substantial likelihood of repeating the behavior or performing similar actions in the future.

SELF-PERCEPTION AND INFORMATION PROCESSING

We have described the process by which individuals acquire information from their own experience in terms of self-perception theory. When people are uncertain, they come to know their attitudes, in part, by examining their behavior and the circumstances in which that behavior occurs. As we have already noted at several points in this chapter, self-perception can be interpreted readily in terms of information processing. Here, we shall present a detailed description that elaborates this perspective. Two objectives are accomplished by this analysis. First, it indicates how information acquired from others and information acquired on the basis of one's own behavior can be described in terms of a single process. Second, it provides the background necessary to evaluate the usefulness of a multiple processes view that has become popular in the last decade.

The Single Process View

The view advanced in this text is that a single process is adequate to explain information acquisition. According to this view, once individuals are exposed to incoming information, its content is processed by a sensory register. Whether this information receives further processing depends on its signal strength and its pertinence to the recipient.

Strong signals that are pertinent to the information recipient are attended and therefore registered in short-term memory. In turn, the information in short-term memory may trigger the retrieval of thoughts from long-term memory that are relevant to the incoming information. Those thoughts retrieved from long-term memory are registered in short-term memory. The thoughts now in short-term memory that are rehearsed are stored in long-term memory and used to guide decision making.

You will recognize this description as the one presented in Chapter Five. We have already shown that it provides a convincing explanation for how individuals acquire information from others. Here, we shall describe how it accounts for the acquisition of information from one's own behavior and the circumstances in which that behavior occurs.

An individual's own behavior can be viewed as a cue that is processed in a manner similar to incoming information from external sources. First, past behavior, which is stored in long-term memory, is processed by the sensory register (Figure 6.1, line labeled 1). If that behavior is pertinent to making a subsequent decision and has sufficient signal strength, it will be represented in short-term memory. When the consumer is uncertain about his or her attitude toward the product, the representation of past behavior triggers the retrieval of thoughts from long-term memory (Figure 6.1, lines labeled 2 and 3). If circumstantial factors do not account for past behavior, the thoughts retrieved are likely to be favorable. Rehearsal of these thoughts results in the acquisition of a positive attitude and a high probability of repeating that behavior or similar behaviors (Figure 6.1, line labeled 4). This outcome was observed in foot-in-the-door studies when an individual's own behavior is made salient.

What happens if circumstantial factors such as incentives or the communicator's characteristics are plausible explanations for past behavior? In this case, both past behavior and the circumstances in which it occurred are registered in short-term memory. When

Figure 6.1. Schematic of Information Acquisition from One's Own Behavior

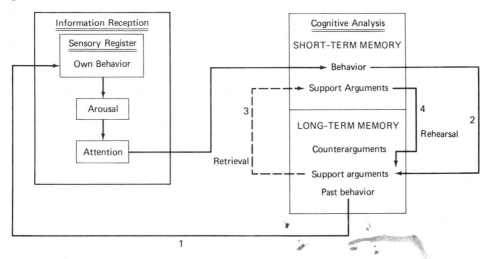

the circumstances constitute discounting cues, they are likely to trigger both support arguments and counterarguments about the behavior. As a result, a strongly positive attitude toward the product is not acquired and the likelihood of repurchase is relatively low unless the circumstances are again present at the time of repurchase. This outcome was observed in studies where incentives were the circumstantial cues, and in foot-in-the-door investigations where thoughts about the requester's behavior were likely to be highly available and viewed as inequitable. In contrast, if the circumstances constitute augmenting cues, support arguments are triggered and there is a substantial probability of repurchase.

To illustrate the explanatory power of the single process view, a recent study conducted by Tybout and Scott (1978) is described. These investigators offered research participants a choice between two soft drinks. To help them make a decision, some product information was given. The information was biased so that virtually all the women chose a particular brand. This procedure was used rather than just giving participants a brand so that they would perceive that the choice was made of their own volition. Half the participants were given an incentive (fifty-cent coupon) for making their choice, while the remainder were given no incentive for doing so. Next all subjects were given two pieces of information about the brand of soft drink they had chosen. One was given an opportunity to taste the soft drink. The other was given information about how others had evaluated the brand. The order in which these pieces of information were presented was varied so that some research participants tasted the brand and then received information about the opinion of others, while for the remainder of the participants the order was reversed. Finally, subjects rated the soft drink they had chosen.

The results are shown in Figure 6.2. When information regarding the opinion of others about the soft drink was given first, people were made uncertain about how to evaluate the product. This uncertainty presumably emerged because research participants did not know how representative the opinions of others would be of their own opinion. This uncertainty caused people to assess their behavior and the circumstances in which it occurred. When no reward was present, people could only retrieve positive insights about the soft drink they had chosen. For those who were given an incentive for choosing the soft drink, both their choice and the incentive were relevant cues. The incentive caused people to retrieve counterarguments about the brand. Thus their evaluation was quite negative.

Those who got an opportunity to taste the product before being presented with the opinion of others had greater certainty regarding how they felt about the soft drink they had chosen. As a result of this certainty, they did not feel it was necessary to engage in the extensive cognitive work that uncertain people had apparently felt obliged to do. They considered a reward as but another positive characteristic of the soft drink. Thus the presence of an incentive resulted in a more positive evaluation of the soft drink than its absence.

The Tybout-Scott study provides strong evidence favoring the single framework view. It demonstrates that a single conception of how information is acquired handles situations where individuals' behavior and the circumstances in which it occurs can be interpreted in terms of information processing. Nevertheless, proponents of the multiple

Figure 6.2. Results of the Tybout-Scott Study

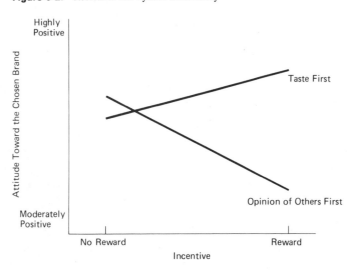

processes view have had substantial impact on current thinking about how individuals acquire information. In the next section, we shall describe and evaluate one such multiple processes view.

The Multiple Processes View

The development of multiple processes to account for how people acquire information was based on the conviction that the learning of mass media advertising, particularly television advertising, differed from the learning of other materials.[3] Krugman (1965) suggested that the major point of difference is the level of audience involvement, where involvement is defined as the "number of conscious 'bridging experiences,' connections, or personal references per minute that the viewer made between his own life and the stimulus" (Krugman, 1965). Krugman contended that for most commercials, audience involvement was likely to be low.

The motivation for distinguishing between low and high involvement situations was that each involved different processes. In high involvement situations, the attitude acquired by processing a communication guides the action taken, that is, attitude acquisition precedes behavior. In contrast, low involvement situations are ones in which there are "gradual shifts in perceptual structure, aided by repetition, activated by behavioral-choice situations, and followed at some time by attitude change" (Krugman, 1965). In essence, Krugman is suggesting that there are two mechanisms for information processing; one

[3]In this section, Krugman's multiple processes view is described. An alternative multiple processes view is provided by Ray (1973).

is a high involvement process where attitudes precede behavior, while the other is a low involvement process where reception leads to behavior and then attitude formation.

In his more recent work, Krugman (1972, 1977) has elaborated the mechanism by which people learn. He contends that three exposures may be enough to stimulate purchase. Exposure refers solely to the opportunity to see and does not necessarily mean reception of the information presented. According to Krugman, the first exposure yields the response, "what is it?" Individuals are attempting to understand the nature of the information presented. The second exposure yields a more evaluative response, "what of it?" Here message recipients are attempting to evaluate the personal relevance of the appeal. While a "what is it" reaction may occur in response to a first exposure, this is unlikely when information is externally paced as it is when advertising is presented on television. The third exposure serves to remind people if they have not executed behaviors that are consistent with previous evaluations of the message information. The third exposure also initiates the withdrawal of attention from a completed task.

Krugman's dual process view does not constitute a radical departure from the single process view we described earlier. In fact, it is quite similar. The "what is it" stage is conceptually similar to the process we have labeled *reception* and "what of it" is similar to what we have called *cognitive analysis*. Furthermore, both low involvement and self-perception address situations in which behavior precedes the acquisition of attitude.

Despite these similarities the single process view provides a more compelling explanation of the information acquisition process. Low involvement emphasizes the *fact* that behavior precedes attitudes. The single process elaborates the *mechanism* by which this occurs. As we have demonstrated in this chapter, the single process yields accurate predictions of outcomes when behavior and the circumstances in which behavior occurs constitute persuasive cues. Krugman's low involvement theory cannot order these findings.

The superior explanatory and predictive power of the single process view suggests that the central factors in information acquisition from one's own behavior are uncertainty and cue availability, and not involvement, as Krugman contends. It is uncertainty that stimulates message recipients to use behavioral and circumstantial cues to make attitude judgments. The specific cues used for this purpose depend on their availability. This is not to imply that involvement has no effect on processing. It does. Following Krugman's definition, involvement is viewed as a function of the number of own thoughts in memory. Because high involvement implies that own thoughts are highly available, it is expected that object evaluation will depend on these thoughts under conditions of high involvement. In contrast, thoughts representative of incoming information are more likely to dominate object evaluations made under conditions of low involvement where own thoughts are less available. To the extent that message thoughts are more favorable than own thoughts, the single process view predicts that low involvement will yield greater persuasion than high involvement.

In sum, the single process appears to provide an adequate explanation of how individuals acquire information. The process has strong predictive power. In contrast, Krugman's dual processes explanation provides few details of the processing mechanism and has very limited predictive power. Thus, despite the popularity of the Krugman view, analysis of information acquisition will be based on the single process view throughout this text.

INFORMATION ACQUISITION FROM ONE'S OWN BEHAVIOR AND MARKETING STRATEGY

The description of how individuals acquire information from their own behavior and the circumstances in which that behavior occurs suggests a variety of strategies to influence consumers' purchase decisions. In this section, we shall present guidelines for using the foot-in-the-door technique that are based on current understanding of the self-perception process. Also considered are influence strategies that are useful if the foot-in-the-door approach fails.

Guidelines for Using the Foot-in-the-Door Technique

The foot-in-the-door technique is a useful approach to influencing consumers' behavior when individuals are uncertain about their attitudes. In using this approach, it is first necessary to gain compliance with a small request. Research suggests that this is most readily achieved by face-to-face solicitations. Indeed, it has been found that there is less than full compliance, even with very small requests, if the solicitation is made by telephone rather than in person (see Reingen and Kernan, 1977; Scott, 1976; Snyder and Cunningham, 1975).

If the foot-in-the-door technique is to be effective, it is not only important to gain compliance with a small request, but also to insure that individuals have thoughts available about their compliance. Availability may be achieved in several ways. One way is to allow enough time between requests so that individuals reflect on their own behavior and not on the behavior of the requester. Alternatively, thoughts about one's own behavior may be made available by requiring people actually to comply with a small request, rather than merely agreeing to comply with it. Finally, the availability of thoughts about one's own behavior can be increased by enlarging the initial request. In fact, the larger the initial request that yields a high degree of compliance, the greater the likelihood of compliance with a subsequent request (Seligman, Bush, and Kirsch, 1976).

The effectiveness of the foot-in-the-door procedure depends on the extent to which compliance with an initial request is attributed to personal reasons. Operationally, this means avoiding cues such as incentives which may cause people to discount personal reasons as the cause of their behavior. To the extent that individuals attribute compliance to an initial request to reasons other than their attitude toward that action, the likelihood of repeating that behavior at some later date is reduced, unless the other reasons are again present. For example, getting people to try a brand by using an incentive may reduce their repeat purchase of the brand unless the incentive is continued.

By avoiding circumstantial cues, the probability that behavior will be attributed to personal reasons is increased. However, a strategy that avoids circumstantial cues such as incentives, may also result in low compliance, even with a small request. To resolve this dilemma, the incentive or other circumstantial cue must be strong enough to stimulate trial behavior, but weak enough so that the trial behavior is not attributed to the circumstances. This optimal level of the circumstantial cue must be determined by trial and error.

When Foot-in-the-Door Fails

In formal research much pretesting is often necessary to determine the size of initial request that is likely to yield substantial compliance. In practical settings, the manager may not have the time or money to determine what constitutes a small request. Or, it may be that people will not comply with small requests. In either event, the foot-in-the-door technique is unlikely to be effective. One way to overcome this problem is to institute a door-in-the-face strategy. If consumers reject an initial request, it should be considered a large request. By having the same requester immediately ask for compliance with a smaller request the likelihood of compliance with the smaller request is high, at least in relation to just asking for compliance with the smaller request. However, even if this approach is successful, it is likely to result in low levels of reward for the requester. The problem with the door-in-the-face technique is that people are likely to comply only with the small request. To gain compliance with more substantial requests, it is useful to follow up the door-in-the-face strategy with the foot-in-the-door technique.

SUMMARY

An important source of information on which consumers base decisions is their own behavior. When individuals are uncertain about their attitude, they examine their past behavior and the situations in which this behavior occurred as a basis for deciding on attitudes and action. By considering this self-perception process within the context of information processing, a single process is developed that accounts for both the acquisition of information from one's own behavior and the behavior of others. The single process view provides an explanation of how consumers use attitudinal judgments to guide behavior as well as the process by which behaviors influence the acquisition of attitudes.

From a practical perspective, the description of the process by which consumers use their own behaviors and circumstantial cues to acquire attitudes is useful in developing face-to-face influence strategies. Specifically, it suggests the use of the foot-in-the-door strategy. This entails gaining compliance with a small request in the hope of gaining acceptance of subsequent larger requests. In using the foot-in-the-door technique it is important to: (1) gain substantial compliance with the initial request, (2) insure that consumers' compliance with an initial request is salient to them, and (3) minimize the circumstantial cues that may cause people to discount personal reasons as the cause of their behavior.

If it is not possible to gain substantial compliance with an initial request, then door-in-the-face procedure may be used. To execute this strategy effectively, the requester makes a smaller request immediately after the consumer has rejected the initial request. If this is successful, the requester may then solicit compliance with a more substantial request, in effect, using a foot-in-the-door procedure.

QUESTIONS

1. Define the following:

    a. foot-in-the-door technique

    b. door-in-the-face technique

    c. discounting cue

    d. augmenting cue

2. Why is it likely that the foot-in-the-door technique will be more effective in face-to-face influence situations than in more indirect solicitations (such as telephone or mass media)?

3. Explain why the foot-in-the-door technique works, using the single framework view and Krugman's multiple framework view.

4. Outline the procedures you would institute to enhance the effectiveness of the foot-in-the-door technique.

5. Under what circumstances is it appropriate to use the door-in-the-face technique? Outline the procedures you would institute to enhance its effectiveness.

6. Evaluate the validity of the following statements using your understanding of self-perception theory to defend your position:

    a. Incentives should never be used to gain consumer trial of a product because they will undermine the probability of repurchase.

    b. An individual's attitude toward a product is always highly related to his or her purchase choices.

Chapter 7

Organization of Information for Decision Making

Bill recently purchased a new Mustang. He recounts the deliberations that led to this choice:

> . . . I wanted a car that was economical to run. With the high price of gasoline and repair work, not to mention my limited budget, economy was very important to me. Still I wanted a sporty car—I'm still young and this may be my last chance to get something sporty. I also wanted a car with plenty of headroom—I'm six-foot-one and I need a car where my head doesn't touch the ceiling.
>
> I narrowed my selection down between a Mustang and a Fiat sedan. I chose the Mustang. The Fiat had about as much headroom as the Mustang—and it gave better gas mileage; but I was worried about the high cost of repairs that I heard were charged for foreign cars. Besides, the Fiat wasn't as easy to handle as the Mustang—it was definitely boxier in appearance . . .

Bill's description of his automobile purchase indicates the importance of information acquisition for decision making. He acquired information from others about anticipated repair cost. He used his own experience to evaluate such features as handling, size, headroom, and appearance. He got information about fuel consumption from the Environmental Protection Agency (EPA) mileage estimates. However, in order to make a decision about which car to buy, Bill had to organize the information he acquired. Information organization entails two processes, *abstraction* and *aggregation*. The abstraction process involves using the physical attributes of an object to infer its intangible or subjective attributes. As Figure 7.1 shows, Bill used two physical attributes, handling and size, to infer a subjective attribute—a car's sportiness. Consumers engage in abstraction because their evaluation of products is typically based on a product's intangible qualities. Physical attributes provide the input for inferring these intangible qualities.

The aggregation process involves combining the pieces of information that a consumer has acquired about a product. It may entail combining either two or more physical attributes or two or more subjective attributes. Bill combined information he had acquired about two physical attributes, size and headroom, in order to evaluate the roominess of alternative cars (Figure 7.1). In addition, the subjective attributes of sportiness, roominess, and economy were aggregated in such a way that the Mustang dominated the Fiat sedan. Consumers aggregate information because it provides an efficient means of considering the various pieces of information they have acquired to evaluate choice alternatives.

In this chapter, the way consumers abstract and aggregate information is described. Conceptually, consideration of information organization processes adds precision to our description of how people formulate attitudinal dispositions to evaluate alternatives. Specifically, information organization is conceived of as the process by which the various pieces of information acquired from one's own behavior and external sources are readied for utilization. Viewed from this standpoint, organization is an inherent part of the information retrieval and rehearsal process.

From a strategic perspective, a knowledge of the organization process guides the development of marketing programs. An understanding of how decision makers abstract

Figure 7.1.   The Information Organization Process

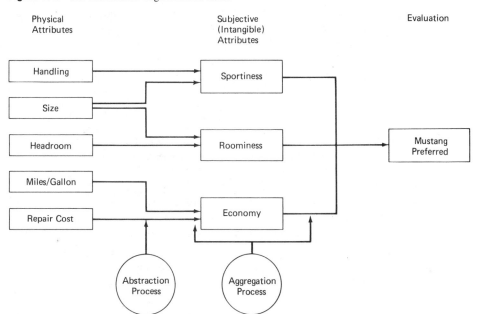

information allows the manager to anticipate how a particular physical feature of a product is likely to affect perceptions and evaluations of a product. By varying the physical attributes of a product, or by emphasizing certain physical attributes in promoting a product, a manager may influence these perceptions and evaluations. An understanding of the aggregation process is important to the strategist because it helps him or her identify those attributes that are primarily responsible for a consumer's evaluation. In turn, this knowledge may be used to develop or modify product offerings and guide the selection of attributes stressed in persuasive communications.

The chapter begins with a discussion of the abstraction process. The physical cues that people use to infer such common subjective attributes as a product's masculinity/ femininity and product performance are identified. Next, some of the frequently used aggregation strategies are described and the situations in which particular strategies are likely to be used are indicated. In the final section of this chapter, the strategic implications of the analysis are reviewed.

THE ABSTRACTION PROCESS

Consumers engage in abstraction as a means of organizing the information they have acquired. The physical cues of a product such as its color, size, shape, and noise level are rarely used directly by consumers to evaluate their product and brand preferences. Rather, these and other physical attributes are surrogates, used to infer subjective attributes such as economy, performance, and masculinity or femininity of a product.

From an information processing perspective, we can view abstraction as follows. A product's physical cues are represented in short-term memory. These cues activate the retrieval and rehearsal of thoughts related to the physical cues. These thoughts may be ones that link a tangible or physical attribute to an object. These thoughts may also be ones linking a subjective or intangible attribute to an object.

It should be noted that the abstraction process often is not subject to conscious awareness. People learn to associate physical attributes with specific subjective attributes throughout their development. In the adult, these associations are sufficiently strong that they do not require attention to evoke. Thus people rely on these strong associations to state the subjective attributes represented by a stimulus. But they may not be able to identify the physical attributes that caused this inference because the abstraction was done without devoting attention to it.

To illustrate the abstraction process, consider consumers' reaction to Pringle's potato chips, which was briefly discussed in Chapter One. Prior to introduction, consumers were asked to compare the taste of Pringle's and other potato chips in a blind test (that is, the brands tested were not identified). Response indicated that Pringle's tasted as good as competitive brands. Yet, after Pringle's were introduced, a very substantial number of consumers changed their opinion, contending that Pringle's had an artificial taste. What accounted for this change in consumers' evaluation of Pringle's? In large measure, it was probably attributable to the way consumers abstracted the physical cues associated with the product. Specifically, Pringle's potato chips were uniform in shape and, at the time of introduction, contained additives to lengthen shelf life. In addition, the chips were not broken, greasy, or burned. The uniformity of Pringle's chips on these physical attributes probably led consumers to infer that they had an artificial taste. The additives in Pringle's served to heighten this perception. Because artificiality is a subjective attribute and has a negative connotation, Pringle's were not positively evaluated. In contrast, in the blind tests consumers did not have sufficient evidence of the brand's uniformity to infer taste. As a result, few mentions were made about artificial taste by participants in this test.

The abstraction process appears to account for consumers' change in evaluation of Pringle's potato chips. For this process to be useful to the manager, a knowledge of how consumers abstract physical cues must also suggest strategies to enhance consumers' demand. Assuming that the explanation we have offered for consumers' evaluation of Pringle's potato chips is correct, what action should be taken? One approach would be to minimize the physical cues that imply uniformity. This could be achieved by having some chips broken, greasy, or burned. However, this strategy is likely to minimize the differences between Pringle's and its competitors, making Pringles's a "me too" product. A more compelling approach, and one pursued by Pringle's, was to introduce a ruffled chip. This strategy reduced the strength of the uniformity cue without diminishing the points-of-difference between Pringle's and its competitors. In addition, the preservatives were removed from the product so that it contained all natural ingredients.

In this section, we shall consider how some of the more common abstractions are made. Although there are no hard and fast rules regarding the subjective attributes consumers infer from particular physical cues, sufficient research has been conducted to suggest some guidelines. This discussion also underscores the importance of researching the relationship between physical attributes, which the manager controls, and subjective attributes, which consumers use to evaluate alternatives.

Masculinity-Femininity

Although many products are intended for use by both males and females, certain brands are targeted toward one sex. Generally, this is achieved both in product design and the way in which the product is promoted. Consider, for example, two different brands of cigarettes—Kool and Marlboro. Examination of the ads in Figures 7.2 and 7.3 leads most individuals to believe that Marlboro is a man's cigarette and Kool is for women. In part, this is attributable to the fact that the focal person in the Kool ad is a woman, while the central figure in the Marlboro ad is a man. Beyond this rather obvious cue, more subtle symbols frequently are used to imply masculinity or femininity. Marlboro advertising is dominated by browns. It has been found that brown is a cue that suggests dryness and aridity, which individuals associate with males. On the other hand, the Kool package contains green and advertising for Kool typically is cast in a setting dominated by a green color. These symbols connote moistness, an attribute that is typically associated with femininity.

Thus, a variety of physical attributes presented in an ad, such as the colors employed and the amount of action depicted, are used by consumers to infer subjective attributes such as aridity and moistness. In turn, these subjective attributes lead to inferences about the appropriateness of a brand for men and women. Consumers can then decide how

Figure 7.2. Marlboro Ad

SOURCE: Philip Morris

Figure 7.3. Kool Ad

compatible the brand is with their needs. Of course, this evaluation is influenced by the product *per se* as well as by product promotion. For example, strong-tasting cigarettes will be perceived as masculine while milder ones will be perceived as feminine. Long slender cigarettes connote a daintiness associated with women, while cigarettes that are short and wide convey a masculine image.

In sum, consumers abstract physical cues to determine the appropriateness of a brand for males and females. Among the cues that connote masculinity are those that give a feeling of aridity and action. On the other hand, cues suggesting moistness, daintiness, and tranquility connote femininity. Selection of those cues that are consistent with the sex of the target audience facilitate acceptance of the brand.

Social Class

Cues regarding social class are also conveyed by a product and its advertising. Consumers make inferences from the available social class cues to ascertain whether a brand is compatible with their lifestyle. In advertising, the type of people shown, how they relate to one another, and the setting in which the product is cast all convey information relevant to inferring the social class for which a brand is appropriate.

In Figure 7.4, a variety of physical cues are presented to convey the compatibility of Lane Furniture with middle-class values. The furniture is well-coordinated, unlike the mixture of pieces one often finds in working class homes. Furthermore, it is not as lavish as one would expect in an upper-class home. The paintings and ornaments also reflect middle-class values. In contrast, lower-class individuals are likely to have trophies and religious objects as well as a television prominently placed in their living room, whereas upper-class living rooms are typically more formal than the one depicted in Figure 7.4. Finally, the way the people in the ad are dressed and their positioning is identifiable with the middle class.

Performance

Consumers employ a variety of physical attributes to infer how a product is likely to perform. For example, performance may be inferred from the noise made by a product. A lawnmower manufacturer produced a model that made much less noise than competitor's brands. The motivation for this innovation was consumers' complaints that their current mower made too much noise. Yet the quieter mower did not sell very well. Consumers contended that it did not have as much power as conventional models. Apparently, noise was used as an indicator of power. Interestingly, consumers did not make the same inference when asked to judge the power of an almost silent battery-operated mower. In this case, it appears that when the power source is changed from gasoline to batteries people do not use noise level to infer power.

Color is another cue consumers use to judge product performance. Consider the role of color in marketing mouthwashes. Listerine is yellow, Lavoris is a vivid red, and Scope is green. These colors are physical cues that reinforce the distinguishing feature of each brand. Listerine is promoted as the brand that "kills germs on contact." This claim

Figure 7.4. Lane Furniture Ad

We make furniture for lovers

Lovers of the good earth. Of joys as simple as the smell of clean, crisp country air and farm fresh eggs in the frying pan. Even if your home is sixteen floors up in a high rise, our "Honeyshuck Farm" collection creates a delightfully warm retreat from the hassles of the day. Charming country inspired pieces for living room, bedroom and dining room. All in knotty pine and ash veneers, hand-rubbed to a light, smokey finish. Handsome upholstery shown is by Pearson, a division of Lane. For folders showing "Honeyshuck Farm" and other Lane furniture send 25¢ to The Lane Company, Inc., Dept. 000, Altavista, Va. 24517.

Lane
The Love Chest People

For a "Honeyshuck Farm" dealer, telephone free: 800-243-6000. (In Conn., 1-800-882-6500).

SOURCE: Lane Furniture

Figure 7.5. Continental Airlines Ad

After-dinner liqueur on the Golden Jet: *transatlantic touch number 5*

You're on a Continental Airlines Golden Jet, non-stop from Chicago to Los Angeles. Dinner in First Class is Transatlantic Touch No. 1. Our Belgian chef, Lucien Dekeyser, sees to that. From lobster cocktail in fire-and-brimstone sauce to judiciously aged tenderloin, it's quite a feast. The choice of wines with your entree is Touch No. 2. The subsequent array of French pastry is No. 3 and the champagne with it is a sparkling Touch No. 4.

Now, as you sip your coffee, the liqueur cart arrives (5). Spot of brandy? Benedictine, perhaps? You decide on some creme de menthe. Having made that hard choice, you face another. To kibitz the cribbage across the aisle or to watch TV (6) in the First Class lounge. You solve this quandary by dozing off.

Your next business trip, vacation while you fly. Get "jet-to-Europe" treatment within the U. S. A.—and at standard jet fares. Both Luxury First Class and Club Coach on every Golden Jet.

Fly Golden Jets to
CHICAGO • LOS ANGELES
DENVER • KANSAS CITY
HOUSTON • EL PASO

CONTINENTAL AIRLINES

MOST EXPERIENCED **JETLINE IN THE WEST**

SOURCE: Continental Airlines

is reinforced by Listerine's antiseptic yellow color. Scope is promoted as a mouthwash that leaves your breath fresh, an attribute that is consistent with its green color. Lavoris' red color reinforces its refreshing active mouthwash claim.

Multiple Abstractions

In using an understanding of the abstraction process to evaluate marketing strategy, the manager is often faced with the problem of assessing the impact of a large number of physical cues. Consider the print ad for Continental Airlines shown in Figure 7.5.[1] Although the ad shown in Figure 7.5 is black and white, the original ad is in color. The central male figure in the ad is dressed in a brown suit. The passengers' seats also are brown. The interior of the plane is gold, and the woman seated beside the central male character is dressed in purple. Is this ad appropriate for a male or female target? Is this ad appropriate for a middle-class audience or is it more appropriate for an upscale target?

There are several cues that suggest the ad will have stronger appeal to men than to women. As we noted earlier, the predominance of browns conveys a feeling of masculinity. The relationship of the focal man to the women around him also implies a masculine orientation. The stewardess and the woman passenger seated on his right (who is probably not his wife because she has no ring on her prominently-placed left hand) are both catering to him. Moreover, in the background a man with a ring is conversing with a woman who is across the aisle, suggesting that Continental is the swinging airline.

Social class is conveyed by a number of cues. The snob appeal of transatlantic travel presented in the headline is likely to appeal to upper-class individuals. In addition, the colors of royalty, gold and purple, the style of the clothing worn by the focal people in the ad, and the exotic beverages being served are suggestive of the upper class. Finally, the plane's interior is drawn to reflect the comfort and coordination of an upper-class living room.

Research examining consumers' responses to the Continental Airlines ad indicated that it appealed to men. In addition, middle-class individuals did not view Continental as compatible with their lifestyle. They preferred less comfort, less service, beer rather than fine wine, and a lower price. Interestingly, recent promotion by Continental has sought to accomodate these preferences.

THE AGGREGATION PROCESS

In order to make a decision, individuals must combine the bits of information they have acquired. This aggregation can be achieved in a number of different ways.[2] To illustrate some of the more common aggregation strategies, we shall consider a situation where

[1]This illustration was developed by Levy (1978).

[2]The authors are grateful for comments made by Ruby Dholakia on this section. For a discussion of the marketing issues relative to the aggregation process, see Cohen (1972), Cohen, Fishbein and Ahtola (1972), and Lutz (1975).

a jogger, Chuck, is buying a new pair of running shoes. For our purposes, it will be assumed that four attributes affect his decision: fair price, light weight, high degree of cushioning, and a durable sole. In practice, the salient attributes are typically determined by asking consumers to enumerate the attributes that affect their selection and by considering the four or five most often cited as the key determinants of choice.[3]

Linear Model

The vast majority of the investigations dealing with the aggregation process have focused on determining the extent to which the linear model predicts preference. Although variants of the linear model have been proposed (for example Fishbein, 1967; Rosenberg, 1956), basic to all linear models are two components that are thought to account for judgment: (1) a belief that an alternative possesses some attribute and, (2) an evaluation of that attribute. Algebraically, this model can be expressed as follows (Slovic and Lichtenstein, 1971):

$$J(X) = b_i X_i + \ldots + b_k X_k, \ i = 1, 2, \ldots k$$

$J(X)$ = overall judgment of an alternative, X

X_i = amount of attribute i possessed by an alternative

b_i = weight of the ith attribute

To clarify the linear model, consider how a consumer, Chuck, would aggregate information in selecting running shoes. First, the weights are determined for each attribute: fair price, light weight, high degree of cushioning, and a durable sole. In Fishbein's version of the linear model, this is achieved by having Chuck rate the *consequences* of each attribute on say a seven point scale ranging from positive to negative. Alternatively, the weights may be determined by having Chuck rate the *importance* of each attribute, on a seven point scale ranging from important to unimportant. Whatever the procedure used to obtain attribute weights, let us assume that the weights shown in Table 7.1 have been obtained. Next, each of the four running shoes being considered is evaluated on each of the attributes. This may be done on a seven point scale ranging from one (does not meet requirements at all) to seven (fully meets requirements). As can be seen from Table 7.1, Puma was perceived as meeting the requirement of price and weight attributes quite well (six and five respectively) and was perceived to be less adequate on the cushioning and durability attributes (two and four respectively). Chuck's evaluation of the other three running shoes on the four attributes is also shown in Table 7.1.

Given the data presented in Table 7.1, the use of linear models leads to the selection of Puma. This conclusion is derived by multiplying each attribute weight by Chuck's evaluation of a particular running shoe on that attribute and summing over all four

[3]See Fishbein and Ajzen (1975), Chapter Eight, for a discussion of the attribute selection procedure.

TABLE 7.1. The Aggregation Process

Attributes	Attribute Weight	Decision Alternatives			
		Puma	*Adidas*	*New Balance*	*Nike*
Fair Price	4	6	4	6	6
Light Weight	2	5	5	2	1
High Degree of Cushioning	1	2	5	7	1
Durable Sole	3	4	4	2	5

Puma	$48 = (4)(6) + (2)(5) + (1)(2) + (3)(4)$
Adidas	$43 = (4)(4) + (2)(5) + (1)(5) + (3)(4)$
New Balance	$41 = (4)(6) + (2)(2) + (1)(7) + (3)(2)$
Nike	$42 = (4)(6) + (2)(1) + (1)(1) + (3)(5)$

attributes. Puma achieved a score of 48, whereas the next closest running shoe, Adidas, achieved a score of 43 (Table 7.1).

A basic feature of the linear model is that decision making is viewed as a *compensatory* process; that is, a particular alternative may be selected despite relatively poor performance on a particular attribute, if that poor performance is compensated by relatively good performance on some other attribute. For example, Puma is judged to be superior to Adidas even though Adidas is judged to fulfill the cushioning requirement much better than Puma. In essence, Puma's relatively poor performance on the cushioning attribute is compensated by performance that is superior to that of Adidas on the more important price attribute.

The linear model we have examined to this point is an *additive* linear model. Overall, judgment is determined by adding the weighted evaluation on each attribute. An alternative form of the linear model involves *averaging* (Anderson, 1965). This is achieved by summing the weighted evaluation on each attribute and dividing by the number of attributes. Using the data in Table 7.1, the averaging model would yield a score of 12 (48 ÷ 4) for Puma; 10.75 (43 ÷ 4) for Adidas; 10.25 (41 ÷ 4) for New Balance; and 10.50 (42 ÷ 4) for Nike.

The distinction between additive and averaging linear models is important because these models often have different implications for the strategists who plan to influence and modify the consumer's evaluations of alternatives. If a linear-additive model represents the process by which aggregation occurs, then the evaluation of an alternative can be enhanced by the addition of attributes.[4] A competitor can, therefore, try to obtain a more favorable evaluation of his product by introducing or making salient attributes other than the ones currently taken into consideration by the decision maker. However, this

[4]This contention may not hold if the weights and evaluations of previously considered attributes change when a new attribute is considered.

conclusion may be invalid if an averaging model is the true representation of how information is aggregated.

To illustrate this point, consider the running shoe selection example. Let us assume that the evaluation is currently based on just the two most heavily weighted attributes: fair price and sole durability. Then Nike will be selected on the basis of *both* the linear-additive and the averaging models. The makers of Puma, which is rated second, might decide to introduce into the decision process a third attribute, weight, on which it performs quite well. According to the linear additive model, all running shoes will be more favorably evaluated (Table 7.2). However, the averaging model shows that the change will be negative for all but Adidas; that is, the addition of attributes will not automatically enhance the evaluation of an alternative. In this case, if Nike does not provide any information on its light weight and consumers have to rely on its two known attributes—price and sole durability—then Nike will continue to be evaluated more favorably despite the addition of attributes by Puma. Only if Puma touted its superiority on the new attribute *and* highlighted the deficiency in Nike's performance on it, could a favorable evaluation of Puma be expected.

A substantial number of investigations have examined the extent to which the linear model predicts consumers' preferences. The consistent finding is that the linear model provides a reasonably accurate *prediction,* whether an additive or averaging version of the linear model is used (see Slovic and Lichtenstein (1971), and Wilkie and Pessemier (1973), for a review of this literature). Nevertheless, there are several reasons for questioning whether the linear model *describes* the way individuals actually aggregate information. First, by having individuals verbalize the procedures they use to arrive at a judgment, it has been found that information organization often does not proceed in accordance with the linear model (Bettman, 1970; Einhorn, 1971). In addition, when decision makers were asked to compare the linear model and other aggregation strategies they reported that the linear strategy was one that was difficult to implement and one that they used infrequently (Wright, 1975).

TABLE 7.2. Additive vs. Averaging Linear Model

Attribute	Attribute Weight	Puma	Adidas	New Balance	Nike
Price	4	6	4	6	6
Durable Sole	3	4	4	2	5
Linear-Additive		36	28	30	39
Averaging		5.14	4.00	4.29	5.57

Decision: Choose Nike.

Addition of:	Attribute Weight	Puma	Adidas	New Balance	Nike
Light Weight	2	5	5	2	1
Linear-Additive		46	38	34	41
Averaging		5.11	4.22	3.78	4.56

Decision: Choose Puma only if Nike's performance on weight is known and taken into account.

Figure 7.6a. Relationship between Weight of Running Shoe and Evaluation

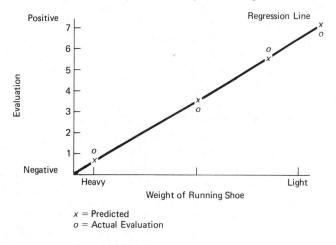

x = Predicted
o = Actual Evaluation

Figure 7.6b. Relationship between Actual and Predicted Evaluation

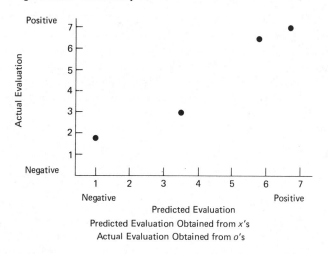

Predicted Evaluation Obtained from x's
Actual Evaluation Obtained from o's

If the linear model does not describe the way people organize information, then how can we account for its substantial power in predicting decision makers' evaluations? In large measure, the predictive power of the linear model reported in many studies is due to the fact that the attributes investigated have an ever-increasing relationship to overall judgment (Dawes and Corrigan, 1974). In our example, the lower the price, the more positive the judgment; the lighter the weight, the more favorable the judgment. In such cases, it is not surprising that the correlation between Chuck's evaluation on specific attributes and overall judgment are high. To illustrate this point, consider the relationship between weight and evaluation of a running shoe. As Figure 7.6a illustrates, the correlation between weight and evaluation is highly positive; as weight decreases, the evaluation of the supplier becomes more favorable. For this reason, the correlation between the actual and predicted evaluation (derived from the regression line) is high (Figure 7.6b). Adding other attributes, which enhance evaluation as they increase, would also yield high correlations between predicted and actual evaluations. Thus, the linear model is a good predictor of individuals' evaluations in cases where the attribute has an ever-increasing (or ever-decreasing) relationship to evaluation, whether or not people actually aggregate information in this way.

A second condition must be present in order for the linear model to provide a *valid* and *accurate* description of how decision makers organize information. Specifically, the situation must be one where the decision maker uses relatively few attributes in evaluating alternatives. This is because the organization task would be unwieldy with many attributes. In fact, there are a considerable number of consumption situations in which only a few attributes are used. For example, Katona and Mueller (1955) found that twenty-seven percent of their respondents used only price and brand reputation in making durable goods purchase decisions; an additional thirty-four percent considered only three attributes, while the remaining thirty-nine percent based their decision on more than three product attributes.

If consumers use a linear model to evaluate their preferences, then it is appropriate to develop strategies that enhance individual's perception of a firm's brand on those attributes that contribute most to the overall evaluation. Or, the manager might attempt to change attribute importance, or add an attribute, depending on the type of linear model being used. In our running shoe purchase example, one might focus on the low price and high quality of a firm's brand because these attributes are likely to contribute most to overall judgment. Alternatively, one might attempt to insure that a firm's brand is evaluated in a relatively favorable manner on most or all of the attributes.

Lexicographic Model

In light of the great degree of mental activity that is required to combine bits of information using a linear model, it is likely that consumers use strategies that are less taxing than the linear model to evaluate their preferences, particularly in complex decision-making situations. One such simplifying strategy is the lexicographic model. Using this model involves sequential evaluation. The decision maker must first order the attributes in terms of their importance. Once this is achieved, the choice alternatives are compared on the single most important attribute. If one of the alternatives is superior on this attribute, it is selected. If, however, the consumer cannot discriminate between alternatives on the most important attribute, those alternatives which are comparable are evaluated on the second most important attribute. Thus, the lexicographic model entails evaluating alternatives, one attribute at a time, until one alternative emerges as superior.

In the running shoe example, a consumer would first order the importance of the attributes. Suppose the descending order of importance is price , sole durability, weight, and cushioning. Next, the four running shoes would be evaluated on the price attribute. As Table 7.1 indicates, the decision maker would not be able to discriminate between Puma, New Balance, and Nike on this attribute; all three receive a score of six. Thus, the decision maker proceeds to evaluate these shoes on the second most important attribute, sole durability. On the basis of this evaluation, Nike would be chosen because it obtained a higher score than Puma or New Balance.

In contrast to the linear model, which involves evaluation of the choice alternatives across all relevant attributes, the lexicographic model entails evaluation of an alternative on a specific attribute. Furthermore, poor performance on an important attribute cannot be compensated for by superior performance on some other less important attribute. In essence, the decision maker who uses a lexicographic model is attempting to insure that the chosen alternative outperforms other alternatives on the important attributes.

Few investigations have focused on determining the extent to which individuals employ a lexicographic model in making consumption choices. Nevertheless, it does appear that individuals use a sequencing strategy like the one described by the lexicographic model. Russ (1971) reported that in about half of the eighty choice situations he examined, individuals requested the most important information first. Also consistent with the lexicographic model is the observation that people evaluated the alternatives sequentially—one attribute at a time—and eliminated alternatives on the basis of their performance on specific attributes (Payne, 1976).[5]

Despite the evidence that aggregation involves sequential processing, there is little evidence to indicate that evaluation proceeds by considering the attributes in the strict order of their importance. Thus, some individuals may choose the second most important attribute to evaluate alternatives after they have been unable to make a decision on the basis of considering the most important attribute. Other people may select the third most important attribute dimension when unable to discriminate on the most important attribute.

One reason that decision makers may not consider attributes in the strict order of their importance is that certain attributes, though important, are perceived as being unlikely to facilitate discrimination between alternatives. This lack of discrimination power is probably due to the fact that beyond a certain standard, people are indifferent about the degree to which a choice alternative possesses a particular attribute. For example, although sole durability is an important attribute, it may not be used to evaluate alternatives because it is perceived that the alternatives are of acceptable quality. Instead, the decision maker considers a somewhat less important attribute, such as weight, that is more likely to discriminate between choice alternatives. In essence, this variant of the lexicographic model views the decision maker as attempting to *satisfice* (Simon, 1955) rather than optimize, as is the case in the basic lexicographic model. In the one study that has examined the representativeness of these two models, the satisficing lexicographic model has been found to be superior in explaining choice decisions. It accounted for about seventy-five percent of the eighty choice situations examined, whereas the basic lexi-

[5]Investigations reported by Alexis, Haines, and Simon (1968), Kleinmuntz (1968), Montgomery (1975), and Swinth *et al.* (1975) also provide evidence for sequential evaluation.

cographic model only accounted for about half of the choices made (Russ, 1971).

From a strategic perspective, the basic lexicographic model suggests that the decision maker focuses on identifying the most important attribute and insuring that his brand is superior on that attribute. If superiority cannot be achieved on the most important attribute, but there is equity with other alternatives on this attribute, then an attempt should be made to insure superiority on the second most important attribute. In contrast, the satisficing lexicographic model implies that the strategist should insure that his brand is equal to or exceeds some standard of performance established by the decision maker as the minimum on important attributes.

Conjunctive Model

Closely related to the satisficing lexicographic model is the conjunctive model (Dawes, 1964). This model conceives the decision maker's strategy as one aimed at insuring that the alternative selected is satisfactory on *all* attributes. In using this model, the decision maker evaluates performance on important attributes. This enhances the likelihood that a consumer selects the preferred choice regardless of whether the final choice entails a linear or lexicographic mode of information aggregation.

Disjunctive Model

An alternative to the conjunctive model, which is likely to be used to reduce the number of choice alternatives to a manageable size, is the disjunctive model. This mode of information aggregation entails establishing a cutoff standard on each attribute, and selecting the alternative or alternatives that surpass the cutoff on any attribute.

Consider the evaluations of the four running shoes presented in Table 7.1. Suppose a consumer sets a cutoff at 6.5 on all attributes. In this case, only New Balance would be acceptable. This running shoe surpasses the cutoff on one attribute, cushioning, whereas the other three running shoes do not surpass the cutoff on any attribute. Alternatively, suppose the cutoff on all attributes is 5.8. In this case, Puma, New Balance, and Nike are acceptable because they surpass the cutoff on at least one attribute. In effect, the disjunctive model with a cutoff standard set at 5.8 serves to reduce the number of alternatives requiring further consideration from 4 to 3.

Although few investigators have examined the representativeness of the disjunctive model, the limited research that has been done suggests that it is used by at least some decision makers as a basis for choice (Einhorn, 1971, 1972; Einhorn and Komorita, 1972). Moreover, there are many everyday situations in which it seems likely that a disjunctive model is employed. Consider, for example, the football coach's selection of players for his team. In choosing players, the coach is likely to select individuals who meet a certain standard in running or catching or blocking ability. If he finds that two or more players are equally proficient in running, he may then use a conjunctive or linear model to make a decision about which player to keep (Dawes, 1964).

If consumers are using a disjunctive model as their aggregation strategy, it would seem appropriate for the manager to maximize performance on some attributes, and ignore performance on other attributes. This strategy is somewhat risky if the consumer is using the disjunctive model primarily to reduce the choice set. Maximizing performance on some attributes at the expense of performance on other attributes may insure passing an initial screening when a disjunctive model is used. However, it may also increase the likelihood of rejecting this alternative in subsequent evaluation when a lexicographic, conjunctive, or linear model is used.

To summarize our discussion to this point, the vast majority of the investigations dealing with how individuals combine the bits of information they have acquired to make a decision have focused on the linear model. These studies indicate that the linear model provides a relatively accurate prediction of choice. It is equally evident, however, that the linear model does not describe the way people go about making their decisions unless a decision is made on the basis of a few attributes that have an ever-increasing (or decreasing) relationship to overall evaluation. When these conditions are not present, nonlinear models such as the disjunctive and conjunctive models are used in the initial stages of decision making to reduce the choice set to a manageable number of alternatives. More specifically, a disjunctive model may be employed to reduce the alternatives being considered to ones that are acceptable on one or more relevant attributes. Next, a conjunctive model may be used to reduce the alternatives to those that attain some minimum level of acceptability on all attributes. Finally, a lexicographic and/or linear model may be applied to make a final decision among the remaining alternatives.

This scenario of the aggregation process is but one of the many strategies available to the decision maker. Implicit in the above situation is the assumption that the decision is complex and involves a substantial amount of risk; that is, the consumer is concerned enough to go through detailed aggregation. Clearly then, in different situations, other approaches may be used to evaluate alternatives. We shall now examine the effects of the decision situation on the way people choose to aggregate information.

Situational Effects on Information Aggregation

It is apparent that the decision maker may use a linear model, lexicographic model, conjunctive model, disjunctive model or some other mode of aggregation to make a choice. The issue is not which model describes the aggregation process most accurately, but rather under what circumstances are the various models used. Answers to this question are still at a stage of speculation. Nevertheless, the available data improve the strategists' ability to influence product choice.

Decision Complexity. One factor that is likely to affect the mode of information aggregation is the complexity of the decision to be made. Complexity increases with a corresponding increase in the number of viable decision alternatives, the number of attribute dimensions on which a decision is predicated, or the novelty of the situation. It is generally acknowledged that as a decision becomes more complex, the decision maker will increasingly seek ways to simplify the evaluation process (Bruner, Goodnow, and Austin, 1956). This can be achieved by using models such as the lexicographic, conjunctive, or disjunctive, rather than a linear model.

Several recent studies provide support for the assertion that decision complexity leads to increased use of simplifying strategies. In a study conducted by Wright (1975), decision-makers reported that the difficulty in using linear and lexicographic models increased as the number of decision alternatives increased. Moreover, subjects reported using the conjunctive model most frequently when the number of alternatives was large (for example, ten), suggesting that this model may be a useful screening device in complex situations. Jacoby and his coworkers (Jacoby, Speller, and Berning, 1974; Jacoby, Speller, and Kohn, 1974) observed that the number of decision maker choices predicted by a linear model decreased as the number of decision alternatives increased. Apparently when a decision is complex, simplification in decision making occurs, making the linear model too arduous.[6]

Complexity of a decision has also been found to affect the time required to make a decision. Specifically, as the complexity of a decision increases, the time required to make a choice increases (Jacoby, Speller, and Berning, 1974). If it is assumed that the use of multiple aggregation strategies requires more time than a single strategy, then the Jacoby *et al.* finding may be viewed as evidence for the decision maker's reliance on multiple aggregation strategies when the selection task is complex.

Perceived Risk. Another factor that affects the way people combine information is the risk they perceive to be associated with a wrong decision. Perceived risk is related to the economic, physical, and social consequences of a wrong decision. It might be anticipated that an individual is more likely to use a comprehensive mode of evaluation such as the conjunctive model when risk is high rather than low. Under conditions of high risk, the decision maker's use of a conjunctive model insures that the selected alternative will at least be satisfactory on all attributes. Consistent with this expectation, it has been found that the conjunctive model predicted choice more accurately than other models when people were asked to evaluate high risk decisions such as job alternatives (Einhorn, 1971).

Let us consider this finding in terms of the running shoe selection decision discussed earlier. If the selection of a running shoe is perceived to be risky, the consumer may reduce risk by selecting that running shoe that passes the cutoff for price, weight, cushioning, and sole durability, that is, by using the conjunctive model. This assumes that there is an approximately equal risk associated with each of these attributes. If this is not the case, and risk is associated with only one or two attributes—say price and weight—then the consumer is likely to use the lexicographic model. By so doing, the consumer would be assured of selecting the alternative that maximizes those attributes that are of critical importance. Consistent with this line of reasoning, Russ (1971) found that women used a lexicographic model in selecting home appliances, which were viewed as high risk product decisions.

[6]See Russo (1974) for an alternative interpretation of the Jacoby *et al.* studies.

In situations where risk is low, the decision maker is likely to adopt a disjunctive strategy. Given the low level of risk associated with a wrong decision, the benefits accruing from using a more complex aggregation model are not worth the effort required to use it. Thus, Einhorn (1971) observed that subjects used a disjunctive model when evaluating graduate school applications, which was perceived to be a low risk decision.

Information Format. Implicit in our description of the various aggregation models is a distinction between two approaches to combining information. One approach is to process information on all attributes for one alternative and then to repeat this procedure for a second alternative. In the running shoe example, this *alternative bias* would involve evaluating Puma on price, weight, cushioning, and sole durability and then repeating this aggregation for other brands of running shoes. This approach is assumed to be the one consumers use in using the linear, conjunctive, and disjunctive models. A second approach entails evaluating all the alternatives on one attribute before proceeding to evaluate them on a second attribute. In the running shoe illustration, this *attribute bias* would involve evaluating all shoes on the price attribute, for example, followed by their evaluation on weight and so on. This approach to aggregation is assumed when consumers use the lexicographic model.

Investigations pertaining to consumers' preference for alternative bias and attribute bias approaches are equivocal. Some studies indicate a preference for aggregating information on the alternatives on one attribute at a time (Russ, 1971; Russo and Dosher, 1975; Russo and Rosen, 1975), while others have reported that consumers aggregate by considering all attributes on one alternative at a time (Svenson, 1974; Van Raaij, 1976). Bettman and Kakkar (1977) suggest that this inconsistency may be due to systematic differences in the information format used in various studies. To test this hypothesis, research participants were asked to select a brand of ready-to-eat cereal from among eleven brands. For each brand, there was information on thirteen attributes to help individuals make a choice. Some participants were given information that was formulated so that it would favor an attribute bias. Operationally, this was achieved by preparing thirteen booklets, one for each attribute. In each booklet, there was information on one attribute for all alternatives. Subjects provided with information in this way tended to favor the attribute bias approach. In contrast, those given eleven booklets each containing information about one of the brands on all thirteen attributes, used an alternative bias strategy. The conclusion emerging from this analysis is that consumers will select the aggregation strategy that is easiest to use for a given information format.

SUMMARY AND STRATEGIC IMPLICATIONS

An understanding of how consumers organize information has several strategic implications for the marketing manager. A knowledge of the abstraction process allows managers to anticipate how a product's physical attributes, which they can control, will be subjectively evaluated by consumers. This knowledge suggests the physical attributes that should be incorporated in designing a product and emphasized in promoting it. Of equal importance is an understanding of how individuals aggregate the bits of information they have acquired as a basis for evaluating decision alternatives. Such knowledge is basic to identifying the attributes on which a decision is predicated. As the running shoe purchase example illustrates, consumers may use a variety of strategies to aggregate information, and for each strategy the decision is based on different sets of attributes.

Beyond these rather general implications are ones that are quite specific to advertising practice. The information organization literature questions the premise that the greater the amount of information conveyed to consumers and other decision makers the more effective the appeal. Indeed, when time to process information is short or when the risk involved of making a wrong decision is low, individuals simplify the aggregation process; as the amount of information presented is increased, the amount processed initially increases and then declines. Advertisers have used this fact in developing television advertising campaigns that typically focus on one or two attributes. For example, "Anacin gives you fast relief," "M&Ms melt in your mouth, not on your hands," and "Nyquil is the nighttime colds medicine" are all single attribute campaigns.

In some situations more information is better. When the risk involved in making a wrong decision is high and when consumers have sufficient time to process information, a very substantial amount of information can be organized. In this situation, print advertising is probably most appropriate. It enables people to process a substantial amount of information because processing is self-paced.

To illustrate how the manager might apply the principles of information organization we have outlined, consider the experience of a major retailer in its home furniture division. Traditionally, this firm used television advertising to promote their sofas, chairs, dressers, and other furniture. Media choice was predicated on the fact that television was more efficient than other media in reaching the target audience; it cost less to reach each prospective buyer than print, radio, and the like. Moreover, most competitors used magazine advertising to promote their furniture, so the firm was faced with little direct competitive advertising. When the firm's sales began to stagnate, advertising was switched to women's magazines. Sales response to this strategy was impressive. Although potential buyers were not reached as efficiently with print as they had been with television, the use of print enabled the presentation of far more product information. Because furniture purchases are usually high-risk decisions, consumers responded positively to the print campaign that provided them with detailed information about a choice alternative.

An understanding of the information organization process is also useful to those charged with the responsibility of regulating marketing practices. Yet, this knowledge has been frequently ignored by regulators in designing product-related information environments. Consider for example, a Federal Trade Commission (FTC) proposal pertaining to foods with nutrient labels (FTC, 1974).[7] An important aspect of their proposal is that for commercials of thirty seconds duration or less, at least six seconds of the *video* portion be devoted to providing nutritional information. From the perspective of information organization and processing there are several weaknesses in the FTC plan. First, by only requiring video transmission of nutrient information, the likelihood of information

---

[7]See Bettman (1975) for a detailed discussion of the nutrient information issue.

reception is undermined. The audio portion that accompanies the video presentation of nutrient information may be sufficiently distracting so that the nutrient information is not processed. Second, even if the information is processed, it may not be useful to consumers in making brand choices. The proposed nutrient information will be presented by brand. Thus, consumers interested in selecting a brand with the highest nutritional content are required to commit to memory nutritional information for alternative brands, and then aggregate the bits of information they have acquired for the various brands. The arduousness of this task makes it unlikely that consumers will be affected by nutrient information on television commercials.

The point of this analysis is not to disparage the attempt to regulate the consumer's information environment. Quite the contrary, we are assuming that such regulation is needed. The criticism pertains to the design of the regulatory program. A more compelling approach entails providing information that compares the nutrient value of the advertised brand and competitive brands. This format conforms to the way consumers are likely to aggregate information. Moreover, both the visual and audio portion should focus on the nutrient information in order to reduce the chance of information reception deficits.

QUESTIONS

1. Why is it important for the manager to understand how consumers abstract information?

2. Using your understanding of the abstraction process, identify the potential problems with each of the following strategies: a blender that makes no noise when it is in operation; a cake mix that requires very little effort to use; and an analgesic that is much less expensive than other brands.

3. Research has indicated that women between ages twenty-one and forty-nine purchase fifty percent of the beer sold and consume twenty-five percent of the beer sold. Furthermore, no major beer producers target their brand at the women's market. On the basis of this evidence, you decide to develop a brand targeted at the women's market. Outline the product package strategy you would use to appeal to this segment.

4. A consumer is attempting to decide which brand of soft drink to purchase. The attributes on which evaluation of brand alternatives is based are shown in the table. Attribute weights and brand evaluations are also presented in the table. (Note: Higher numbers indicate a more favorable evaluation).

		Brand Alternative		
Attribute	Weight	Pepsi-Cola	7UP	Dr. Pepper
Highly carbonated	2	4	5	2
Good taste	4	5	5	7
Very refreshing	3	7	5	2

    a. Which brand will the consumer select if a linear additive model is used?

    b. Which brand will the consumer select if a conjunctive model is used with the cutoff set at five?

    c. Which brand will the consumer select if a lexicographic model is used?

    d. Which brand will the consumer select if an alternative bias is observed?

5. Regulators have instituted a unit pricing program. Unit pricing involves listing the price charged per unit (say a pound or gallon). It is intended to facilitate price comparisons between brands. Two procedures are being considered for making consumers aware of unit prices in supermarkets. One involves posting the unit price on the shelf just below each brand. The other procedure entails posting a list that ranks the brands on the basis of their unit price and indicates the unit price for each brand. Which procedure would you adopt? Why?

6. Indicate how the information organization process is related to the process by which individuals acquire information from others and their own behavior.

Chapter 8

Explaining and Predicting Consumers' Behavior

In the preceding chapters, we described how consumers acquire and organize the information they use to make decisions. These processes are of interest to the marketing manager because they provide a means of explaining consumers' overt actions or behavior. In the present chapter, we examine the relationship between the attitudes people acquire and organize and their subsequent behavior. Because attitudes are the beliefs and feelings individuals have about some product or service, we expect them to be good predictors of behavior. As we shall see, this expectation is borne out by research, although in many situations attitudes are not the only predictors of behavior, or even the most important predictors. Other factors such as consumers' perception of what others expect and consumers' sense of moral obligation may also guide behavior.

This chapter begins with a review of studies that have looked at the attitude-behavior relationship. On the basis of this analysis, strategies for improving the prediction of behavior from attitudes are suggested. Considered next are factors beyond attitude that account for consumers' overt action. The model for explaining and predicting behavior emerging from this analysis is then employed to assess the extent to which people's behavior can be influenced without their knowledge. In the final section of this chapter, a procedure is developed to predict consumer behavior occurring in the distant future.

Figure 8.1. The Relationship between Group Attitudes and Behavior

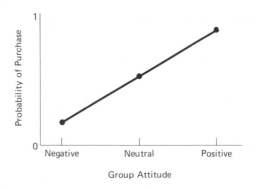

THE PREDICTION OF BEHAVIOR FROM ATTITUDES

From our everyday experience, it seems apparent that individuals' attitudes toward a product or service are closely related to their purchase behavior.[1] People who have strong positive beliefs about religion seem to attend church more often than those who do not. Those who have a favorable attitude toward our political system appear to vote more often than those who are cynical about it. Consumers who value a varied menu and subdued lighting seem to patronize restaurants that have these attributes to a greater extent than consumers who do not value these characteristics.

The assumption that individuals' attitudes are accurate predictors of their behavior appears to be so compelling that marketing strategists often use consumers' attitudinal responses as a proxy measure for their behavior. The demand for new products is estimated frequently on the basis of consumers' attitudes toward alternative product concepts. The effectiveness of advertising is often evaluated by examining the change in consumers' attitudes toward a product as a result of exposure to a campaign. Political pollsters use measures of constituent attitudes to predict the outcome of elections.

Despite the intuitive appeal and widespread acceptance of the premise that consumers' attitudes guide their behavior, it requires qualification. There is strong evidence that *groups* that differ in attitude differ in their behavioral responses (Day, 1970). As Figure 8.1 shows, groups of consumers who have a negative attitude toward a product exhibit lower purchase probabilities than those who have a more favorable attitude. However, when an individual rather than a group is the unit of analysis, there is less attitude-behavior consistency. Some people with positive attitudes engage in purchase, while others with equally positive attitudes do not. Similarly, some people with negative attitudes do not purchase whereas others with negative attitudes do purchase (Figure 8.2).

[1]A comprehensive review of the prediction of behavior literature is provided by Wicker (1969) and Fishbein and Ajzen (1975). An excellent analysis of the prediction issues from a consumer behavior perspective is due to Ryan and Bonfield (1975). An empirical test is reported by Lutz (1977).

Figure 8.2. The Relationship between Individual's Attitudes and Behavior

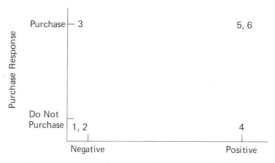

Individual's Attitude (numbers indicate individuals)

We shall consider representative studies from the literature reporting different degrees of attitude-behavior consistency. The motivation for this analysis is to determine the circumstances in which attitudes are likely to be powerful predictors of behavior.

The seminal investigation of the relationship between individuals' attitudes and their behavior was conducted by Richard LaPiere in 1930. Accompanied by a Chinese student and the student's wife, LaPiere drove 10,000 miles up and down the Pacific coast of the United States. Unknown to his companions, LaPiere studied the reception they received at the hotels, tourist camps, restaurants, and cafes they frequented on their journey. In many instances he lingered behind the Chinese couple when they requested service in order to observe how they were treated. Of the 251 times it was necessary to request food or lodging, only once was the party refused service. This result surprised LaPiere. As he stated:

> . . . Knowing the general "attitude" of Americans towards Chinese as indicated by the "social distance" studies which have been made, it was with considerable trepidation that I first approached a hotel clerk in their (that is, the Chinese couple's) company. Perhaps the clerk's eyebrows lifted slightly, but he accommodated us without a show of hesitation. And this in the "best" hotel in a small town noted for its narrow and bigoted "attitude" toward Orientals . . . (LaPiere, 1934).

When LaPiere returned from his travels, he wrote the hotels and restaurants they had previously visited, as well as other establishments they had not frequented, requesting service for himself and the Chinese couple. LaPiere found that over ninety percent of the establishments refused to accommodate the Chinese. This finding led LaPiere to conclude that individuals' attitudes (as indicated by the response to his written request for service) were not always consistent with their behavior (as exemplified by the entrepreneurs actual willingness to serve Chinese).

The LaPiere investigation typifies an approach to testing the attitude-behavior relationship that usually results in a low association between these variables. The probable reason for this low association is that attitudes and behavior are measured in different situations. In LaPiere's study, the behavior measure was a face-to-face interaction where the social pressure to accept the Chinese couple's request was great. Thus entrepreneurs complied. In contrast, the social pressure was likely to have been minimal when the Chinese couple's request was made in writing. As a result, entrepreneurs felt free to express a negative attitude.

The implication emerging from this analysis is that individuals' attitudes are unlikely to be powerful predictors of their behavior when these measures are administered in situations differing in social pressure. However, even if this factor is controlled to some extent, attitudes may still not be a good predictor of behavior. Consider studies pertaining to job attitudes and performance. Individuals' attitudes toward their job are measured and correlated with performance measures such as productivity and absenteeism (see Vroom, 1964, for a review of this literature). It would seem logical that positive attitudes towards one's job would be associated with good performance, whereas a negative attitude would be associated with poor performance. Yet, the predominant finding is that a knowledge of people's attitude improves the prediction of behavior by less than ten percent relative to not having information about people's attitudes.

Why are attitudes toward one's job not more closely aligned with performance? One reason is that behavior is guided by dispositions other than people's attitudes toward their jobs. It may be that persons with a negative attitude toward their jobs perform well because they have a strongly positive attitude toward providing for their families; performance is related to attitude toward providing for the family and not attitude toward the job. Stated more generally, the lack of attitude-behavior consistency may be due to differences in the specificity of the attitude and behavior measures; a general attitude is a poor predictor of a specific behavior.

In sum, low correlations between attitude and behavior emerge when these measures are not matched in social pressure, as is the case in the LaPiere study, or when attitude and behavior measures are not matched in specificity, as is the case in job attitude-performance studies. These observations suggest that attitude may be a powerful predictor of behavior if these measures are matched in terms of the conditions in which they are administered, and in terms of their specificity. Given comparable conditions for attitude and behavior measurement, a general attitude is expected to predict accurately a general behavior, and a specific attitude is expected to predict a specific behavior.

Support for the contention that a general measure of attitude is a powerful predictor of behavior is provided by Fishbein and Ajzen (1974). They had people indicate their attitude toward being religious on a series of scales. These composed a general measure of attitude in that individuals' beliefs about an object, religion, were being assessed. In addition, research participants stated whether or not they intended to perform each of one hundred behaviors dealing with religion.[2] This behavioral measure included activities such as giving a donation to a religious institution and taking a religion course for credit. Respondents' behavioral responses were summed to yield a behavioral index. This index

---

[2]Some researchers contend that behavioral intention is a good proxy measure for actual behavior if certain conditions are met (Ajzen and Fishbein, 1969). We shall make this assumption for the present and examine its veracity later.

was a general measure of behavior because it reflected individuals' tendency to engage in religious behaviors, whereas each item comprising the index (for example, donating money to a religious institution) was a specific behavior measure.

Fishbein and Ajzen found that their general measure of attitude was a good predictor of a general behavior measure represented by the behavioral index. In contrast, the general attitude measure afforded poor predictions of the specific behaviors. Individuals' attitudes toward religion did not provide a powerful predictor of intention to donate money to a religious institution or to take a religious course for credit.

The Fishbein and Ajzen study indicates that a general measure of attitude is useful in predicting a general behavioral response but not a specific behavior. Other investigations suggest that the prediction of a specific behavior requires a specific measure of attitude. For example, Tittle and Hill (1967) found a substantial relationship between students' attitude toward "personal participation in student political activity" and whether or not they voted in a subsequent student body election. A more detailed consideration of the strategies for improving the prediction of behavior is provided in the following section.

IMPROVING THE PREDICTION OF BEHAVIOR FROM ATTITUDES

Our analysis of studies pertaining to the attitude-behavior link suggests two strategies for improving the prediction of behavior from attitudes. One is to employ a specific measure of attitude to predict a specific behavior. The other is to employ a general behavioral measure when prediction is based on a general attitude. We shall illustrate how each of these strategies is implemented, using toothpaste purchase as the vehicle. Then, we shall consider the situations in which the manager might want to employ each strategy.

Selecting the Attitude Measure

The traditional approach to measuring attitudes in studies attempting to predict behavior entails using a general attitude measure. This measure is termed attitude toward the object (Ao). If we are interested in determining consumers' attitude toward Crest toothpaste, the scales shown in Table 8.1 might be employed. Consumer A's responses on these scales are represented by the letter O. As Table 8.1 indicates, Consumer A finds Crest toothpaste good ($+1$), pleasant ($+1$), and quite refreshing ($+2$). If we assume that these three attributes have equal weight, Consumer A's attitude score is 4 (that is, $1+1+2$). Consumer B, whose attitude toward the object Crest is denoted by the letter X, has a negative attitude toward the brand. This individual's attitude score is 13 (that is, $4+5+4$).

As we have already noted, when the aim is to predict a specific behavior, such as whether a consumer will purchase Crest, Ao is not an appropriate way to measure attitude. What is needed is a specific measure of attitude. One such measure is termed attitude toward the act (Aact). Aact is defined as a "person's attitude toward performing a particular act in a given situation with respect to a given object" (Ajzen and Fishbein, 1973). In

TABLE 8.1. Attitude toward the Object Crest

Crest toothpaste:		
good	$\dfrac{0}{1}\ \dfrac{}{2}\ \dfrac{}{3}\ \dfrac{x}{4}\ \dfrac{}{5}$	bad
pleasant	$\dfrac{0}{1}\ \dfrac{}{2}\ \dfrac{}{3}\ \dfrac{}{4}\ \dfrac{x}{5}$	unpleasant
refreshing	$\dfrac{}{1}\ \dfrac{0}{2}\ \dfrac{x}{3}\ \dfrac{}{4}\ \dfrac{}{5}$	not refreshing

Consumer A's responses denoted by 0

Consumer B's responses denoted by x

the context of toothpaste purchase, Aact may be operationalized as follows: "Purchasing Crest toothpaste the next time I buy this product at the drugstore is . . ." Responses are measured on scales such as good-bad.

Notice that the Aact is specific in relation to several criteria. It is specific with respect to behavior. In our example, the attitude measure specifies purchasing Crest. Aact is also specific with regard to situation. Thus we ask the respondent about purchasing Crest at the drugstore. Finally, Aact is specific with respect to time. In our example, the time specified is the next time toothpaste is purchased. Studies in which the Aact measure is employed indicate that it is a good predictor of individuals' behavioral intention (Ajzen and Fishbein, 1969, 1970, 1972; Brislin and Olmstead, 1973; Schwartz and Tessler, 1972; Wilson, Mathews, and Harvey, 1975).

From a managerial perspective, this suggests that Aact is the appropriate measure of attitude when the specific behavior, situation, and time of interest can be identified. This is the case in our illustration of Aact with regard to Crest. But what if there is difficulty in specifying behavior, situation, and time? This problem may arise because the manager is interested not only in the behavior of using Crest, but also the behavior of purchasing it. Or, it may arise because interest is in knowing consumers' attitude toward purchasing Crest in places other than drugstores. Finally, specifying the time may be difficult if purchases beyond the next one are of interest. When these problems in specification occur, the Ao measure is appropriate. In using Ao to predict behavior, a general measure of behavior is needed. Approaches to developing specific and general behavior measures are discussed in the next section.

Before considering the behavior measurement issue, it is useful to point out the pivotal role of Ao and Aact in predicting and explaining consumers' behavior. Because Ao and Aact are frequently good predictors of behavior, they allow the manager to estimate demand. In addition, because Ao and Aact are the product of the information acquisition and organization processes discussed earlier, they are instrumental in demand modification. Suppose consumers' attitudes toward Crest are determined by its decay prevention and whitening abilities. By modifying perceptions of Crest's performance on these attributes, individuals' attitudes toward Crest can be altered. In turn, a change in attitude guides consumers' demand. This pivotal role of attitudes is shown in Figure 8.3.

Figure 8.3. The Pivotal Role of Ao and Aact

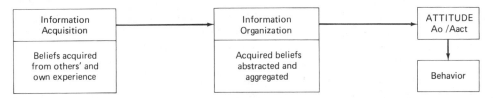

The Behavior Measure

Specific Behavior. When the manager's objective is to predict a specific behavior, several approaches are available. One is to use a *single act* criterion. The single act may be a dichotomous measure. For example, "voted in an election, did not vote in an election" is a dichotomous criterion. Alternatively, the single act may involve three or more behavioral responses: "purchased Crest, purchased Colgate, purchased Gleem, or did not purchase toothpaste." The defining characteristic of the single act measure of behavior is that it partitions a single behavior into two or more response categories.

The single act criterion is an appropriate way to measure a specific behavior that occurs infrequently. Thus it is useful when the behavior in question involves the purchase of durables or voting in a presidential election. The single act criterion is less useful when behavior involves a frequently purchased item such as cigarettes, margarine, or ketchup. In this context, the manager is interested in repeat purchase, which is likely to generate most of the demand for a brand. The single act behavior measure gives no indication of consumers' repeat purchase tendencies. Moreover, it tends to be unstable; that is, the single act may be influenced by infrequently occurring events. For example, a consumer may have a highly favorable attitude toward Crest and purchase it regularly. However, at the point in time when behavior was measured the consumer switched brands because the store was out of stock, or because he wanted to reaffirm his favorable attitude toward Crest by trying another brand, or because a competitive brand was on sale.

To overcome these problems with the single act criterion, a *repeated measures* behavioral criterion can be employed. This entails obtaining information about a sequence of purchases. For example, the proportion of times a consumer purchased Crest in his last ten purchases of toothpaste is a repeated act measure. These data may be obtained from consumer panels where panel participants record their brand purchases on a continuing basis.

In sum, the repeated measures approach to measuring behavior has several advantages in relation to the single act measure. It is less sensitive to infrequently occurring events. Thus, it is likely to be more closely related to consumers' attitudes than the single act criterion. Furthermore, from the marketing strategist's perspective, multiple observations of behavior are preferable to a single observation when a brand's market share depends on repurchase over time rather than on one-time purchase.

General Behavior. As we have already noted, a general measure of behavior is appropriate when the manager cannot pin down the specific behavior or the situation and time when behavior will occur. Measuring a general behavior is also appropriate when interest centers in consumers' reactions to a product line rather than a specific product. For example, the manager may be interested in women's attitudes toward Cover Girl cosmetics and the relationship between these attitudes and the purchase of lipstick, eye shadow, mascara, blusher and other products in the line.

When a general behavior is of interest, a *multiple act* criterion is an appropriate measure. This entails determining whether a set of behaviors related to some object were performed, and developing an overall index on the basis of these responses. For Cover Girl, consumers might be asked whether they purchased Cover Girl lipstick, eye shadow, and blusher. Responses for each of these items would be scored 1 if the respondent had purchased them and 0 if they had not. Thus, if a consumer had purchased all three Cover Girl products, her behavior index would be 3, whereas it would be 0 if she had purchased none of them.

The strategy underlying the use of the multiple act criterion is to examine consumers' behavioral response for a series of different but related objects. This strategy avoids the problem of specifying the behavior, situation, and time (which are requirements in using a single act or repeated measure behavioral criterion) by including different behaviors, situations, and times. One can then examine the relationship between a general attitude, Ao (for example, Cover Girl) and behavior. Furthermore, by evaluating the correlation between Ao and each of the behaviors included in the multiple act measure, it may be possible to isolate the specific behaviors that are most closely related to consumers' attitudes.

Procedures for Measuring Behavior.   Whether one is interested in specific or general behavior, several procedures are available to measure these responses. Consumers may be asked to provide self-reports of their behavior. This entails having people state what products and brands they purchased. In using self-reports one should be sensitive to the fact that consumers may have a hidden agenda. They may misrepresent their behavior in order to make themselves appear to be smart, or ethical, or display some other attribute. Thus, consumers may overstate their purchase of certain products such as deodorants and nutritious foods and understate the purchase of others such as adult magazines. In essence, the problem with self-reports of behavior is that individuals may engage in image management rather than state their actual behavioral responses. This problem is less severe when self-reports are collected from a panel of consumers over an extended time period. The biases related to image management stabilize quickly. Once this occurs, the extent of bias can be determined by comparing the consumption estimated on the basis of self-reports and actual consumption determined by sales audits. The discrepancy between these measures is then used to adjust future projections made on the basis of self-reports from panel members.

The use of a panel increases the accuracy of a self-reported behavior measure. Nevertheless, self-reports are not as accurate as actual measures of behavior. The reason they are used in lieu of an actual behavior measure is largely a matter of practicality. Consider, for example, the difficulty and cost in monitoring ten purchases of toothpaste. Therefore, the use of actual behavior as a criterion is typically restricted to situations where a single act occurs in a limited time period at a given location. Yalch (1974) examined voting records to ascertain the behavior (that is, voted, did not vote) of constituents who had previously been administered scales measuring their attitude toward voting. Kapferer (1975) sent people a persuasive communication by mail urging them to have their blood pressure checked and unobtrusively monitored who actually showed up at the clinic for a checkup. Scott (1976) solicited subscriptions for a weekly community newspaper and identified subscribers. Tybout (1978) offered indigents a new health care plan and identified those who switched from their current health plan. In addition, it is sometimes possible to monitor unobtrusively behavior for an extended period of time. Craig and McCann (1978) mailed consumers appeals to conserve electrical energy and monitored their electric bills over a several month period.

Other Variables To Improve the Prediction of Behavior

We have reviewed several measurement strategies for improving the prediction of people's behavior from a knowledge of their attitudes. Even if these strategies are implemented, individuals' attitudes are frequently not powerful predictors of their behavior. Thus, we might ask what variables other than individuals' attitudes account for their behavior? In answering this question, we shall be guided by two considerations. First, the number of other variables should be small enough so that they are manageable. In addition, the other variables should have explanatory power; they should suggest strategies to alter consumers' behavior.

Normative Beliefs

Consumers' behavior may be affected by factors other than their attitude. One such factor is *social normative beliefs* (NBs).[3] NBs refer to an individual's perception of the behavior expected by "significant others." Significant others may be one's spouse, family, friends, or anyone else the individual considers important in deciding whether or not to engage in a behavior. NBs may be acquired directly as is the case when significant others state their expectations to the consumer. For example, family members may tell the purchaser of toothpaste which brand they prefer. NBs may also be acquired when the purchaser makes inferences from observations of significant others' behavior. The purchaser of toothpaste might infer that family members do not like the brand purchased by observing that they bought some other brand.

Social normative beliefs can be measured using scales such as:

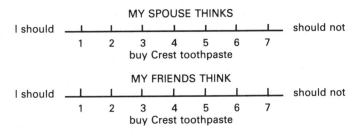

---

[3] The normative belief factors discussed in this section are due to Fishbein (1967).

By measuring NBs, the consumers' perceptions of what significant others want can be determined. However, this knowledge is not adequate to predict behavior because the decision maker is not motivated to comply with the perceived expectations of significant others. To address this issue, consumers must be asked to indicate their motivation to comply (MC) with each one's NBs. This is achieved by scales such as:

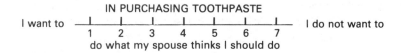

Individuals' scores on each NBs item are then multiplied by the score on the MC item to form adjusted scores. If multiple items are used to measure NBs and MC, the adjusted scores on each item are summed to yield an overall score.

Social normative beliefs are likely to be important determinants of behavior when a consumer's purchase will be used by others. The food products and brands purchased for family use are likely to be guided to a great extent by the purchaser's perception of other family members' expectations. Gift purchases will be determined in part by the buyer's perception of the recipient's expectations. Social normative beliefs are also likely to be important determinants of behavior when the product is perceived to reflect some personal consumer attribute. Choice of automobiles, appliances, and certain clothing items are likely to be affected by NBs. Finally, NBs may be important predictors of behavior when people are uncertain about their attitude. Because objective criteria are not available for many consumer decisions, people are uncertain about the quality of their judgments. In such cases, consumers are likely to check their perceptions of what significant others would do in the situation as a means of solidifying their own attitude about the appropriateness of a purchase.

If NBs are important determinants of behavior, what steps can the strategist take to influence NBs and ultimately behavior? Suppose a consumer is purchasing Aim toothpaste because her children like the flavor of that brand. As a brand manager for Crest, you might alter social normative beliefs by suggesting to the consumer that she has misperceived the expectations of others; that is, children like the taste of Crest as well as that of Aim. Or, you might attempt to change the people who constitute significant others for the consumer by noting that the consumer's spouse or dentist has the expectancy that Crest will be purchased.

In sum, in situations where: (1) the purchaser and user are different people, (2) the product reflects on the kind of person the consumer is, or (3) the consumer is uncertain about what to do, NBs are likely to be important determinants of behavior. If this is the case, then NBs can be altered by changing consumers' referent or changing consumers' view of what the referent expects them to do.

A second normative belief factor that may influence behavior is *personal normative beliefs* (NBp). NBp refers to individuals' perception of the behavior they feel morally obligated to perform (Schwartz and Tessler, 1972). They can be measured by using scales such as:

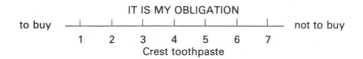

IT IS MY OBLIGATION

to buy   1   2   3   4   5   6   7   not to buy

Crest toothpaste

NBp are acquired through the socialization process. Starting early in childhood, people are taught the duties and obligations required by the various roles they perform. Children are socialized to comply with the requests of their parents and teachers. Parents have been socialized to support their families and protect their children. Employees are socialized to give an honest day's work for their pay. NBp are also acquired as the values of society change. It is only recently that our society has recognized the moral obligation of citizens to preserve scarce energy resources and to reduce environmental pollution.

The most frequently used NBp strategy involves associating some product attribute with a consumer's role obligation. For example, if a particular brand of margarine is low in cholesterol, one might link this attribute to homemakers' moral obligation to provide their families with healthful foods. This NBp strategy will be effective to the extent that message recipients perceive the brand in question to be low in cholesterol, view the purchase of low cholesterol food as a moral obligation, and believe that using low cholesterol margarine discharges this obligation.

Judged Influence of Extraneous Events

By measuring consumers' attitudes and normative beliefs, we are able to obtain a fairly accurate prediction of their *behavioral intentions* (Fishbein and Ajzen, 1975), that is, what people state they will do. However, attitudes and normative beliefs may be less accurate as predictors of actual behavior. This is because new information, changing aspirations, or other unforeseen events may negate the conversion of an intention into an actual behavior. What is needed is a way to determine the extent to which people's likelihood of performing a behavior is affected by unforeseen situational contingencies that occur between the statement of their attitudes and normative beliefs and the performance of an act.

A measure that satisfies this need is termed the *judged influence of extraneous events* (EE). For example, to predict people's church attendance, Wicker (1971) asked individuals the following EE question: "What effect on your church attendance would weekend guests who did not attend church regularly have?" Four responses were available: (a) the event would almost certainly not influence the behavior (scored 4); (b) the event probably would not influence the behavior (scored 3); (c) the event would probably influence behavior (scored 2); (d) the event almost certainly would influence behavior (scored 1). Subjects with a score of 4 are ones who are highly motivated to attend church, while those who scored 1 have much less motivation. Similarly if focus centered on predicting the consumer's likelihood of purchasing Crest toothpaste, an appropriate EE question might be: "Suppose the store where you shop for toothpaste is out of Crest. How likely is this to affect the brand of toothpaste you purchase?" If subjects' brand choice is unaffected by this unforeseen event, they would be considered to be highly likely to purchase Crest, while those whose behavior is affected by situational contingencies are conceived as having lower probability of purchasing Crest.

In the two studies in which the EE measure has been used to predict behavior, it was found to account for between fifteen and twenty percent of the variation in behavior (Brislin and Olmstead, 1973; Wicker, 1971). In these same studies, measures of normative beliefs and attitudes were much less powerful predictors of behavior, generally accounting for less than ten percent of the variance.

If the extraneous events measure is an important predictor of behavior, what strategies are available to influence behavior? It may be argued that an attempt should be made to eliminate those events that disrupt the conversion of intentions to behavior. While it is important to facilitate the conditions on which behavior is predicated, the EE measure gives little direction about what the barriers to performing a behavior will be. For example, if people who have a positive attitude toward attending church indicate that they are unlikely to go if they have weekend guests who do not normally attend, there is little to be done in terms of removing this barrier. Indeed, the event "having weekend guests who do not normally go to church" may never occur. Consequently, if EE is the critical determinant of behavior, focus should center on increasing individuals' motivation so that they will strive to perform the behavior despite any barriers that may inhibit it. One way to achieve this aim entails strengthening attitudes and normative beliefs.

EVALUATION OF THE BEHAVIORAL PREDICTION MODEL

The model developed in this chapter to predict and explain behavior can be represented as follows:

$$BI = f(A, NBs \times MC, NBp)$$

$$B = f(BI, EE)$$

where B = Behavior

A = Attitude

NBs = Social Normative Beliefs

MC = Motivation to Comply

NBp = Personal Normative Beliefs

BI = Behavior Intention

EE = Judged Influence of Extraneous Events

The model implies that behavioral intention can be predicted from a knowledge of consumers' attitudes, social normative beliefs multiplied by the motivation to comply with those beliefs, and personal normative beliefs. Behavior is predicted from a knowledge of behavioral intentions and the judged influence of extraneous events.

The model is useful in dealing with two types of predictive tasks. When interest is in predicting a specific behavior, such as purchase of Crest, then Aact should be used. In addition, NBs and NBp specific to the behavior in question are appropriate. In contrast, when a general behavioral response is to be predicted, such as purchase of products in the Cover Girl line, Ao as well as general NBs and NBp measures are appropriate. In both instances inclusion of EE is likely to improve the prediction of behavior.

By incorporating the model variables specified, behavior can be predicted far more accurately than would be the case if the manager were simply to guess at behavioral response. In fact, it has been shown that the model can account for as much as fifty percent of the variation in behavior (Brislin and Olmstead, 1973; Wicker, 1971). Moreover, by including only a small number of predictors the model is easy for the strategist to employ. Because each of the predictors suggests strategies to modify behavior, the strategist is given specific direction regarding how to influence behavioral response.[4]

Several features of the model require further elaboration. First, it should be noted that a distinction has been made among three dispositions—attitude, NBs, and NBp—despite the fact that these dispositions are acquired by the same process; that is, information from one's own experience and external sources is processed by the sensory register and the short-term memory store and ultimately stored in long-term memory. Why is a distinction among attitudes, NBs, and NBp necessary given their common mode of acquisition? First, the distinction is appropriate because it has been demonstrated statistically that A, NBs and NBp are independent of each other (Bagozzi *et al.*, 1979).[5] For example, a consumer may have a favorable attitude toward buying a Mercedes-Benz automobile; he likes its styling and handling. However, NBs are negative in that he perceives that other family members object to such an extravagant expenditure. NBp do not affect his decision. Second, it is useful to distinguish the three predictors because, as we have seen, each suggests a unique set of strategies to influence behavior.

A second issue emerging from our description of the model pertains to how it can be used strategically. Given that several factors may influence behavior, how is the strategist to decide whether to channel resources into modifying attitudes, NBs or NBp? To determine these priorities, a statistical analysis (that is, multiple regression) may be employed. This analysis indicates the relative importance of A, NBs, and NBp in predicting behavioral intention. For example, if the task involved predicting the brand of salt the consumer intended to purchase, NBp and NBs might be unimportant predictors of brand choice. To change consumers' behavior strategies to alter A would be appropriate. In contrast, if the task involved predicting the donation of a kidney, NBs and NBp are likely to be important determinants of behavior. In this instance, the NBs and NBp strategies discussed earlier would be focal points in attempting to modify behavior.

The third issue pertains to the role of variables not specified in the model. Our description appears to suggest that consumers' demographic profile (for example, age,

---

[4]A more detailed discussion of strategies to influence behavioral response is presented in Part V of the text.

[5]Statistical independence has not always been observed. See Miniard and Cohen (1979) and Ryan and Bonfield (1975).

income, education) and personality traits (for example, self-confidence, authoritarianism) have no effect on their behavior. This is not the case. Indeed, non-model factors can influence behavior in two ways. They can affect the evaluation of attitudinal and normative factors, and they can influence the relative importance of A, NBs and NBp. Thus, young and old adults may differ on their evaluations of A, NBs and NBp with respect to automobile choice. Moreover, for younger adults NBs may be the most important determinant of choice, whereas A may be most important for older adults.

THE EFFECT OF SUBLIMINAL STIMULI ON BEHAVIOR

The scenario we have developed to describe the consumer decision-making process depicts consumers as active processors and users of information. Consumers may not be receptive to information if the signal strength is weak or the information conveyed is not pertinent. Information that is registered in short-term memory triggers the retrieval of consumers' own repertoire of thoughts, and these thoughts as well as those included in the incoming information determine individuals' evaluations. In addition, consumers abstract and aggregate the information they process to determine their product references. Finally, they often consider their moral obligations and the expectations of others as well as their attitudes in making choices.

Despite the evidence for viewing decision making as an active process, there are some who contend that decision making also can be passive. Specifically, it is argued that if a persuasive appeal is presented just below a person's threshold of awareness (that is, subliminally) it will bypass the active processing stages we have described and affect behavior.

The belief that subliminal presentation of information directly affects individuals' behavior without their knowledge has been fostered by a study reported in 1957. While patrons of a Fort Lee, New Jersey theatre were watching a movie, the words "Drink Coke" and "Eat Popcorn" were flashed on the screen at subliminal levels. Although the details of the procedure were not reported, subliminal presentations are typically executed using a tachistoscope. This apparatus is like a slide projector. However, it allows for much faster shutter speeds than are available on most slide projectors. The idea is to present the stimulus for a sufficiently short period of time (approximately one-fiftieth of a second) so that people are unaware of it, but for a sufficiently long period of time so that people process the subliminal information. Using this type of procedure, Subliminal Project Company reported that popcorn sales increased by more than fifty seven percent and Coca-Cola sales by eighteen percent after presentation of subliminal messages regarding these products. Apparently, even though people watching the movie were unaware of the subliminal appeals saying "Eat Popcorn" and "Drink Coke," their behavior was affected by these messages.

There are several reasons to question the integrity of these findings. First, because people differ in their perceptual thresholds, it is extremely difficult to select the appropriate length of exposure. If it is very short, it will be subliminal for all people. However, for a substantial number of individuals, the exposure will be too brief to register at all. On the other hand, if the exposure time is sufficiently long so that all people can process it, the stimulus will be clearly visible or supraliminal for at least some of the audience. This is what happened several years ago when a television advertiser attempted to use a subliminal message that said "Get it" while a commercial was being aired. Many people could readily see what was supposed to be subliminal, complained about it, and the commercial was taken off the air. Another problem is that there is no evidence to indicate whether subliminal information is more effective in stimulating behavior than supraliminal appeals (that is, ones that are clearly visible). Indeed, the Subliminal Project study does not rule out the possibility that no information about Coke or Popcorn would have been as effective as the subliminal presentation. A particularly hot night, a scary movie, or some other unknown factor may well have accounted for the increase in consumption observed. Given the ethical question of using subliminal advertising, the difficulty in selecting the appropriate length of exposure, and the unreliability of existing data regarding the efficiency of subliminal advertising, it has been discredited as a persuasive vehicle.

Despite this view, there is some research indicating that people can process information without being aware of it. In a seminal study, McGinnis (1949) presented swear words (that is, four letter words) to subjects subliminally, using a tachistoscope, while monitoring their galvanic skin response. It was found that subjects were unable to verbalize words even though their galvanic skin response indicated discrimination or reception. This result was considered as evidence for discrimination (that is, GSR response) without awareness (that is, verbal response).

This evidence is less than compelling. Consider yourself as a subject in McGinnis' study. A word is flashed tachistoscopically, and you are relatively sure you know what it is. This discrimination leads to a GSR response. However, you do not verbalize the word because you will be very embarrassed if you are wrong; verbalizing a swear word is socially unacceptable, particularly in the company of an experimenter who is a stranger to you. You might give the researcher a clue that you are aware of the word and still avoid embarrassment by saying something like "Is it *shot?*"

In a more rigorous follow-up study (Lazarus and McCleary, 1951), subjects were shocked when shown experimental nonsense words but not for control nonsense words. Subsequently, subjects were presented both experimental and control words tachistoscopically. In this part of the study none of the words were accompanied by shock. It was found that people gave GSR's to the previously shocked experimental nonsense words even though they were unaware of what the word being flashed was. For the control nonsense words, subjects showed no GSR (discrimination) or awareness. Interpreted from an information processing standpoint, this finding suggests that information can be processed by the sensory register and perhaps be represented in the short-term memory store without recipients being aware of it.

More recent evidence suggests that subliminal information represented in short-term memory can influence subsequent evaluation. In a demonstration of this phenomenon, subjects were asked to shadow information presented in one ear while several melodies were played five times each in the unshadowed ear (Wilson, 1975). After completing this task, subjects were played the melodies that were played during the shadowing task as well as new ones. Subjects were able to identify the melodies they had heard previously only at the chance level. Yet they evaluated these melodies more favorably than the new ones.

These data imply that at least for some stimuli, evaluation can be affected by a subliminal presentation without people having stimulus thoughts available in memory. However, caution is needed in accepting this conclusion. It may be that asking people to indicate whether or not they heard ten melodies may not be a sufficiently sensitive measure to detect thoughts weakly stored in memory. A more convincing measure to document the fact that thoughts about the preferred melodies were not stored would entail presenting a previously presented melody and a new one, and then asking subjects to identify the one they had heard before. But even without such evidence, it appears that subliminal presentations affect evaluation.

Practitioners also have examined the use of subliminal presentations. In fact, Key (1974) claims the use of subliminal advertising is widespread. As testimony for this claim, he analyzed the cues in advertments such as that for Gilbey's gin. The ad depicts a bottle of Gilbey's, a cork, and a glass filled with ice cubes and gin, all on a table. The ice cubes are vertically arranged in the glass. Close examination of an ice cube near the top of the glass reveals what appears to be the letter *s* embedded in the ice. The ice cubes just below appear to have the letters *e* and *x* embedded in them. Thus the word *sex* is spelled out by the ice cubes. Further, the reflection cast by the gin bottle and the cork on the table gives the appearance of a man's legs and genitals. There is a bead of moisture just below the reflection of the cork suggesting that "Feelings after Sex" is an appropriate title for the ad.

When individuals are asked to list the thoughts that pop into their minds after seeing the Gilbey's ad, they say things such as: cool, refreshing, inviting, summer and sex. This response may have been stimulated by the subliminal cues which appear to be present in the ad. However, this is not necessarily the case. It may be that the Gilbey's ad without the subliminal cues would have yielded similar responses. What is needed is an investigation that compares the responses generated from ads differing only in the presence or absence of subliminal information.

In sum, there is evidence that information can be processed at the level of the sensory register and short-term memory store without people being aware of it. There also is evidence that subliminal presentations affect evaluation. But there are no data indicating that subliminal presentations are as effective or more effective than ones that are supraliminal.[6]

PREDICTING LONG-TERM BEHAVIOR

The model developed in this chapter provides a relatively powerful approach to predicting behavior and, at the same time, suggests strategies for influencing behavior. However, the model is only likely to be useful in predicting and explaining behaviors that occur

---

[6]For a detailed discussion of this and other subliminal ads, see Key (1974). For a theoretical discussion of subliminal perception, see Dixon (1971).

within several weeks or months of the time when the verbal predictor measure was administered. It is of little value in predicting behaviors that will occur several years or decades in the future. To do so requires the consideration of technological, political, social, and legal changes that will occur in the future and the present model considers these factors to be constant.

In the last decade there has been a growing interest in developing an approach to predicting the long-term future. Much of this interest is attributable to the staggering costs firms have paid because of their inability to anticipate future consumption patterns. Gerber boasted "Babies are our business . . . our only business" at a time when fertility rates in the United States were rapidly declining. Although Gerber broadened its baby product line, developed single-serving brands to attract a growing singles market, and changed their motto to "babies are our business," the change took place only after earnings had declined sharply. In cases like these, keeping current with the changing demographic profile of the population would have allowed the problem to have been largely avoided.

In other instances, anticipation of future trends is much more difficult. In the late 1960s Gillette introduced a series of products for women including *Look of Nature, Magic Moment,* and *Innocent Color* to compete in the lucrative hair coloring market dominated by Clairol. These brands were unsuccessful because they were introduced at a time when women were becoming interested in a natural look. In essence, the lack of product acceptance was attributable to poor monitoring of women's changing values.

Even more difficult to predict are changes in the political environment. Unlike changes in demography and values which emerge gradually over time, changes in the political climate are often sudden and dramatic. The Arab oil embargo in October 1973 suddenly caused a severe shortage of gasoline. As a result, the availability of gasoline declined, its price rose, and consumers demand for small gas-efficient automobiles increased dramatically. Although auto manufacturers reacted to this turn of events by increasing their production of smaller cars, none had adequately anticipated these events beforehand. It might be argued that it was virtually impossible to anticipate the shortage in oil supply. Yet some corporations reacted more quickly than others. Hertz, for example, modified its fleet of rental cars so that at the height of the gasoline shortage, the bulk of their fleet was comprised of compact cars.

Given the importance of being able to assess the long-term future, many major corporations such as Gillette, AT&T, Shell, and General Electric have hired futurists to predict long-term behavioral trends and identify product and service opportunities. Although the details in approach differ from corporation to corporation, a general strategy for predicting the distant future is emerging. Futurists read magazines, newspapers, and professional journals as well as examine the results of polls to determine changing values in the society. On the basis of these data, inferences are made about the criteria people will use in the future to make consumption decisions. The changing technology is also closely monitored—not only the technology pertaining to the products and services produced by the corporation, but also the technology in areas that may ultimately affect the corporation's product. Finally, the changing demographic profile of the American public is examined. Each of these inputs is ultimately assessed in terms of the threats and opportunities it presents to the corporation.

Using the approach outlined above, the futurist at Gillette made the following recommendations. Given the trends towards increased utilization of services, the major opportunity for Gillette was in the service area. Based on this recommendation, Gillette purchased Welcome Wagon International in 1971 and Jafra Cosmetic, an in-home cosmetic service in 1973. Furthermore, because a growing proportion of the population is over fifty-five years of age (more than twenty percent of the population in 1974), it was recommended that Gillette place more emphasis on products and services for the elderly. Similarly, General Electric, having observed the trend toward increased concern for energy conservation is responding with the development of products to be offered to the public in the 1980s that will consume less energy than present ones.

From the above illustrations, it is apparent that long-term prediction of behavior involves essentially two types of forecast. One must be able to predict what the consumption environment will be like. A scenario is needed of the social, political, and legal environments of the future. In addition, forecasts must be made to determine feasible technologies that conform to the environmental requirements and that are profitable for the firm.

In this section, we shall examine the procedures available for developing environmental and technological forecasts. As we shall see, all the techniques involve the extrapolation of past events into the future. However, for many of them, past events are tempered by subjective judgments of what will occur in the future.

Environmental Forecasting

Accurate environmental forecasts broaden the alternatives available to management in coping with its environment. As the history of the last several decades illustrates, corporate failure to react quickly to societal expectations leads to a politicizing of these expectations, legislation, and ultimately litigation (Wilson, 1975). As the issue moves from the stage of societal expectation to the stage of litigation, the alternative courses of action open to business become more and more limited. Thus it is important from a corporate perspective to recognize emerging issues while they are still societal expectations.

Consider the evolution of the environmental protection issue (Table 8.2). By 1970, environmental protection had become a persuasive societal expectation. Indeed, it was in that year that Americans held the first "Earth Day" to dramatize their desire for a pollution-free environment. Business enterprises failed to react sufficiently to this societal concern and environmental protection became a political issue. Former President Nixon proposed a program to protect the environment in his 1970 State of the Union message, Congress killed proposals to produce supersonic transports (SST), and the construction of the Alaska pipeline was delayed. This politicizing was followed by a series of legislative responses including the establishment of the Environmental Protection Agency (EPA), congressional legislation, and court rulings that regulated environmental pollution. As a result, the number of environmental protection cases before the courts almost doubled between 1970 and 1972 (adapted from Wilson, 1975). At each of these stages, the recourses open to business become progressively fewer.

TABLE 8.2. The Sequence of Environmental Events

	Environmental Protection	Business Options
Societal Expectations	Environmental Protection: Earth Day 1970	Many
Politicizing of Issues	State of the Union Message 1970, SST, Alaska Pipeline	Defensive
Legislation	1970 EPA established	Compliance
Litigation	1972 268 Environmental Cases before the Courts	Pay Penalties

SOURCE: Adapted from Wilson, 1975

The most often-used technique for identifying those societal expectations that are likely to affect the conduct of business by a particular firm is the Delphi method. This procedure entails forming a committee composed of individuals with expertise regarding the issue in question. Unlike other committees, however, when Delphi is used, committee members do not know who else is serving on the committee. This anonymity permits individuals to consider issues on their merits rather than having committee members make judgments on the basis of group pressure. Committee members get feedback regarding the opinions of others. However, the feedback is controlled. An individual designated as the director gleans the opinions relevant to the issue and disseminates them to individual committee members. The feedback is presented in statistical form so that committee members know the proportion of the members making specific forecasts. In addition, the statistical reporting procedure preserves the forecasts made by all members, rather than requiring group consensus as is usually the case in decisions by committees.

Given this overview of the Delphi method, let us now consider the specifics of the procedure. To make this description concrete, we shall focus on forecasting environmental factors related to the development of a mass transit vehicle.

Step 1: *Identification of Consumer Demand.* Members of the committee are asked to identify the demands consumers will make regarding mass transit. The director edits this list so that redundancies

TABLE 8.3. Consumer Demands Regarding Mass Transit

Demand	Definition
Preserves individuality	Service allows the individual to travel without being disrupted or impeded by others.
Short waiting time	Service is highly available.
Safe	Service is free from accidents.
Fast	Service gets the traveller from point of departure to destination quickly.
Nonpolluting	Service does not emit pollutants.
Preserves environment	Service does not require the construction of permanent structures that detract from the aesthetic quality of the landscape.

and irrelevant demands are eliminated. On this basis, a list of consumer demands like the one presented in Table 8.3 is developed.

Step 2:   *Assessment of Cross-Impact of Consumer Demands.* The edited list of demands is presented to committee members. They are asked to assess the impact of each demand on every other demand. As Table 8.4 illustrates, the demands have little cross impact. The exception is the cross impact between the demand for a fast transit mode and a safe one. Members anticipate that as the demand for a fast transit system becomes increasingly satisfied, the probability of having a safe system is reduced (represented by a minus [−] in Table 8.4). Committee members are alerted to the tradeoffs between speed and safety and are asked to keep them in mind in making subsequent judgments.

Step 3:   *Determination of the Impact of Emerging Societal Trends on Consumer Demands.* This requires committee members to identify societal trends and to assess the impact of these trends on consumer demands regarding mass transit. In Table 8.5, four such trends are identified. Committee members then evaluate the extent to which each of these trends will affect customers' demands regarding mass transit. For illustrative purposes, Table 8.5 shows how one committee member might use a ten point scale to evaluate the impact of the four trends on consumers' five demands. By summing each committee member's ratings across all trends for each demand, a score is obtained indicating the extent to which each demand will be "in tune with the times."

If the evaluation depicted in Table 8.5 is representative, then it can be concluded that in light of the major environmental trends identified, consumers' demands will be for a safe transit mode that is nonpolluting and that preserves individuality as well as the environment. Furthermore, consumers will be less concerned with the speed and waiting time involved in using the transit system.

Step 4:   *Determination of the Impact of Pressure Groups on Consumer Demands.* This entails having committee members identify relevant pressure groups and assess the impact of each group on demand. The pressure groups might include corporate stockholders, consumers, environmental protection groups, unions, and the like. By summing the evaluations of the impact of the various pressure groups on each demand, the demands can be ordered in accord with the extent to which they are likely to be supported.

On the basis of these analyses, a matrix can be developed to identify the priority of consumer demands. One dimension of such an environmental matrix is the extent to which the demand is in tune with societal trends. The other dimension is the extent to

TABLE 8.4.   Assessment of Cross Impact on Consumer Demand

	Preserves environment	Nonpolluting	Fast	Safe	Waiting time
Preserves individuality	0	0	0	0	0
Short waiting time	0	0	0	0	
Safe	0	0	−		
Fast	0	0			
Nonpolluting	0				

0 = no cross impact

− = negative cross impact

TABLE 8.5. Evaluation of the Effect of Trends on Consumer Demands

Consumer Demand	Trend				
	Increasing service orientation	*Growing leisure time relative to work time*	*Increasing emphasis on quality of life*	*Increasing affluence*	Total Score
Preserves individuality	9	5	10	7	31
Short waiting time	10	7	2	3	22
Safe	10	5	8	7	30
Fast	8	2	3	4	17
Nonpolluting	4	7	10	7	28
Preserves environment	4	8	10	7	29

Response Scale

Trend has

```
   1    2    3    4    5    6    7    8    9    10
  No effect                         Great effect
 on consumer                        on consumer
   demand                             demand
```

which a demand is likely to receive wide public support. As Figure 8.4 indicates, safe, nonpolluting mass transit vehicles are of top priority, because these demands will be in tune with the times and will receive broad public support. Somewhat less focus will center on short waiting time and environmental preservation because these demands are only high on one of the two dimensions. Finally, there will be relatively little management concern for a fast system because this demand will not be in tune with the times or achieve widespread public support.

Figure 8.4. The Environmental Matrix

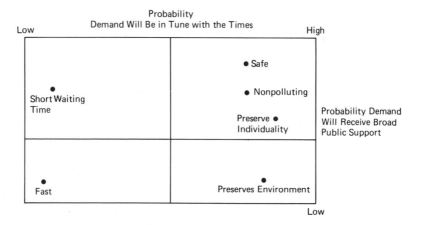

Technological Forecast

Once the major consumer demands that will impinge upon the corporation have been identified, attempts to forecast the feasibility of developing the technology needed to satisfy consumer demands can be initiated. As was the case for environmental forecasting, technological forecasting may involve the Delphi method or any of several other approaches that are commonly used to predict future technology.

Growth and Trend Curves. In situations where the forecaster is interested in predicting the rate at which a particular technical approach will change in efficiency, the use of *growth curves* is appropriate. This procedure involves plotting the changes in performance of a technical approach over time and fitting a curve to it. By projecting the curve into the future, one can forecast the future performance of a technical approach. For example, the solid line in Figure 8.5 shows the growth for mercury-vapor fluorescent

Figure 8.5. Growth Curve

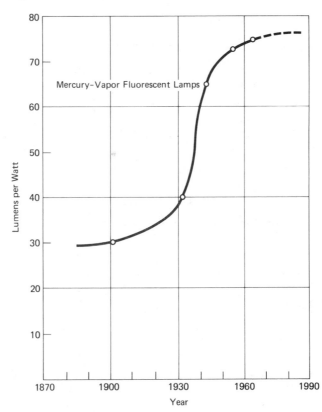

SOURCE: Martino, 1970

lamps. It was developed using historical data regarding the lumens per watt provided by fluorescent lamps at different points in time. By extrapolating this curve into the future, predictions are made about the lumens per watt that will be available from fluorescent lamps in the future.

The major drawback in using the growth curves approach to forecast technological change is that it does not consider the possibility that entirely new technologies will be developed that surpass the performance of the technology being forecasted. Without this consideration, the forecast may be erroneous. For example, it was predicted in 1865 that New York City would never have a population of more than three million people. This prediction was based on the fact that the space needed to house the horses required by

Figure 8.6.   Trend Curve

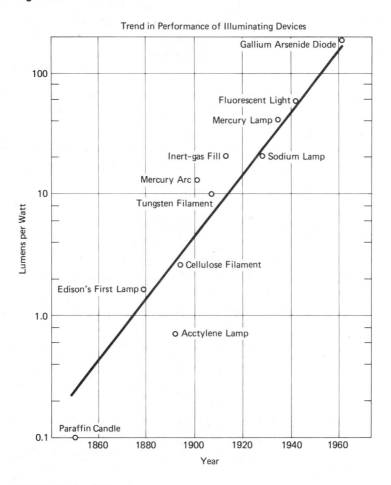

Trend in Performance of Illuminating Devices

SOURCE: Martino, 1970

three million people would leave little room for expansions beyond that number of people. Clearly, this forecast failed to consider the development of the automobile and mass transit. Indeed, without these technological developments, New York would now either be a much smaller city or knee-deep in horse manure.

The erroneous forecasts caused by focusing on the future growth of a single technological approach may be overcome by using *trend curves*. A trend curve is developed by plotting performance of a variety of technical approaches that have been introduced over time. On the basis of this historical data, extrapolations to future performance can be made. Figure 8.6 shows how a trend curve can be used to forecast the lumens per watt that will be available in the next several decades.

Correlation. Both the growth curve and trend curve procedures are exploratory technological forecasting methods. Exploratory forecasts use historical data to identify the technology that is likely to be available in the future (Martino, 1970). However, they do not indicate the technology that will be needed. To address this issue, a normative forecasting procedure is required. Normative forecasting involves identifying the technology needed given that certain changes in the environment will occur. One approach to normative forecasting is correlation.

The correlational approach entails identifying those environmental factors that are associated with technological change. This may be achieved by using historical data. Next, the values for the environmental factors must be forecasted, perhaps using the Delphi method outlined earlier. By knowing the correlation between environmental factors and technology, and by estimating the nature of the environment in the future, one can forecast the technology needed.

To illustrate the correlation method, suppose it has been determined that the average income and age of the population is positively related to the demand for luxury automobiles; as the population gets older and more affluent, demand for luxury automobiles increases. Using census data, one can forecast the average age and income of the population in, for example, 1985 or 1990. This forecast and a knowledge of the correlation between age, income, and demand for automobiles permits forecasting of the needed transportation technology.

Caution is required in using correlation for forecasting purposes, particularly when age of the population is used to predict behavior. Among other things, age represents position in the life cycle, and a set of dispositions associated with growing up in a particular generation. Thus, observing that the current generation of older people prefer luxury cars and that the population is growing older does not necessarily imply that the demand for luxury cars will increase. It may be that as people move into certain stages of their life, they demand more luxury. If this is the case, age represents a life cycle stage and should predict future demand. In contrast, it may be that the current generation of older people grew up at a time (for example, the depression) that causes them to value luxury cars. If this is the case, age represents a generational factor that is not expected to predict future demand unless subsequent generations experience the same environmental forces.

An Integrated Approach to Predicting Long-Term Behavior

Although we have discussed environmental and technological forecasting procedures separately, they are actually employed sequentially to identify new product and service opportunities. As Figure 8.7 illustrates, environmental forecasts are developed to identify consumer demands in the distant future. This information serves as input for a normative technological forecast that determines the technology needed to satisfy consumer demands. In turn, normative technological forecasts serve as the basis for exploratory technological forecasts to determine whether the technology needed is feasible. If it is not feasible, then alternative technologies for satisfying consumer demand must be determined. Once a feasible technology is identified, experimental versions of the product or service are developed and the extent to which they satisfy consumer needs is determined. Consumer feedback is then used to refine the product and service. This procedure is repeated many times, often over a period of many years.

To illustrate the sequence of procedures involved in forecasting future behavior, consider the following example. A group of transportation experts outlined the following scenario regarding mass transit.

1. The emergence of universities, malls, and city shopping areas closed to automobile traffic.
2. A growing disenchantment with the air and noise pollution associated with the automobile and mass transit.
3. A negative attitude toward waiting for mass transit vehicles.
4. A disenchantment with the way mass transit reorganizes the use of space. For example, rapid transit vehicles now require tracks that render the space they occupy useless for other purposes even when transit cars are not in use.

These demands raised many technological questions. Could a nonpolluting and noiseless vehicle be made at reasonable cost? What technology would be needed to reduce

Figure 8.7. The Stages in Predicting Long-Term Demands and Ways of Satisfying Those Demands

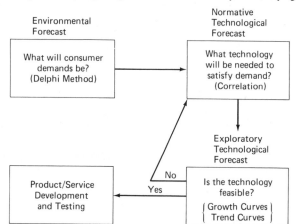

the waiting time for the mass transit vehicle and at the same time not require a prohibitive number of individuals to operate the vehicles? How could the vehicle be powered so that it would not deface the environment in which it is operated?

After substantial technological forecasting, futurists at a large manufacturing firm developed a free-access transit system. Vehicles holding about thirty people would move along a single track buried in the concrete at two miles per hour. No driver would be needed; a computerized system would stop the vehicle if some object passed in front of it; otherwise it would proceed at two miles per hour, which easily enables people to get on and off the moving vehicle. The vehicles would be silent and consume relatively little electricity. By programming a series of these vehicles for a particular route and time of day, the system could be made to conform very closely to a predetermined schedule.

The proposed vehicle takes into account all of the environmental factors mentioned earlier. First, there will be substantial demand for the vehicle because of the growing number of settings in which there is no adequate means of transportation—malls, universities and the like. In addition, consistent with consumer desires, the vehicle does not cause noise and air pollution, minimizes waiting time, and does not affect the use of space when the vehicle is absent.

Although environmental and technological forecasts do not guarantee that a firm will be adequately prepared to compete in the future, the systematic assessment of the environment and technology serves to reduce the likelihood of being caught totally unprepared. Indeed, the activities involved in forecast development force management to consider seriously the contingency plans necessary to cope with a changing environment.

SUMMARY

This chapter describes a model to explain and predict consumers' behavior. According to this view, behavior can be predicted from a knowledge of three factors. One is attitude. When the task is to predict a specific behavior, Aact is a useful measure of individuals' attitudes, whereas Ao is a more appropriate measure when predicting a general behavior or class of behaviors. Normative beliefs may also increase the extent to which behavior can be predicted. People's perceptions of what others expect (that is, NBs) and their own sense of moral obligation (that is, NBp) frequently guide the actions they take. Finally, by measuring the judged influence of extraneous events, the extent to which people are motivated to convert their dispositions into actions can be assessed.

The behavioral prediction model has several attractive features. It enables the manager to focus on a relatively small number of factors in estimating demand. It suggests strategies to modify demand. Finally, although the model is most powerful when formal research is conducted to assess attitudes, normative beliefs, and extraneous events, it is also instructive when research is not feasible. The model provides the manager with a set of different strategies that might be considered in influencing consumers' response— ones pertaining to attitude, NBs and NBp.

The model developed in this chapter underscores the active nature of consumer decision making. Thus, it questions the effectiveness of subliminal information presentation as a device for stimulating behavior. Although evidence pertaining to subliminal presentations offers some support for the fact that such presentations influence people's evaluations, there is no evidence that subliminal presentations are as effective or more effective that supraliminal presentations.

The behavioral prediction model is a useful device for managing consumers' short-term response. It is not suited to the prediction of behaviors that will occur in the distant future. For the latter purpose, environmental and technological forecasts are required. These forecasts are based on expert judgment and statistical procedures. By using them, the manager is better able to anticipate the long-term viability of current strategies and to identify the course of action required in the distant future.

QUESTIONS

1. Define the following terms: Ao; Aact; NBs; MC; NBp; EE; single act; repeated measures; multiple act; Delphi Method; and subliminal presentations.

2. Why are individuals' attitudes toward voting in an election likely to be better predictors of actual voting than are attitudes toward a brand in predicting brand choice?

3. Consumers' attitudes toward Burger King fast-food products are determined by having respondents' rate Burger King on the following scales that are known to be important in fast-food restaurant choice:

good						bad
	1	2	3	4	5	
wise						foolish
	1	2	3	4	5	
enjoyable						unenjoyable
	1	2	3	4	5	
economical						not economical
	1	2	3	4	5	

   a. Will the prediction of behavior from these scales be more accurate if a single act behavioral criterion is used or if a repeated measures behavioral criterion is used?

   b. What procedure would you use to measure behavior? Evaluate self-reports from a survey, panel self-reports, and unobtrusive monitoring of actual behavior. In defending your selection enumerate the advantages and disadvantages of each alternative.

4. An attitude survey is conducted to predict industrial buyers' purchase of the line of IBM business machines. What measure of behavior is most appropriate? Provide a rationale for your decision.

5. The manufacturer of Heat & Serve Stuffing has found it difficult to gain frequent use of its product. Housewives consider Heat & Serve appropriate for special occasions but not for the typical meal. Housewives indicate for everyday meals they prefer potatoes. Potatoes, they claim, are easy to fix, inexpensive and are liked by their children. The manager of the Heat & Serve brand has noted that the cost per serving is somewhat higher for his product than potatoes, but that Heat & Serve can be made much more quickly than potatoes. Furthermore, the manager noted that research has consistently indicated that men prefer stuffing to potatoes. Devise attitude NBs, and NBp strategies to increase the use of Heat & Serve.

6. In each of the following situations, decide whether attitude, NBs, or NBp (or some combination) is likely to be the most important determinant of behavior. Justify your choice.

   a. which brand of sugar to be purchased

   b. whether to purchase sugar or a sugar substitute

   c. whether to donate a kidney to a close relative

   d. whether to give your eyes to the eye bank when you die

   e. whether to buy a grey or blue suit

7. Why is it that a subliminal presentation is unlikely to be an effective means of persuasion?

8. Why is the model for predicting short-term behaviors (that is, $B = f$ (A, NBs, MC, NBp, EE) inappropriate for predicting behaviors that will occur in the distant future?

9. The Delphi method is often used to develop environmental forecasts. What are the procedures involved in using this method? What factors may cause this method to be inaccurate?

10. Outline procedures for developing technological forecasts.

Part IV

Consumers act as individuals in making consumption choices. These choices differ depending on the individual. To examine this, individual differences in decision making are treated in Chapter Nine. Although individual actions are important, it is frequently more useful to consider groups of consumers. This is first looked at in Chapter Ten where the impact of changing demographic trends on consumption is considered. Finally, Chapter Eleven covers the ways consumers are influenced by the groups to which they belong.

Consumers as Individuals and Groups

Chapter 9

Consumer Individual Differences

Consumers come in all different sizes and shapes. Some are young, others are old. Some have postgraduate degrees, others lack a high school education. Some have very high incomes, others live on welfare and food stamps. The diversity of consumers is evident any time one goes into a supermarket or other retail establishment. The patrons will be quite heterogeneous. Some will appear very much like yourself, while others will appear to be quite different. Marketers have long been intrigued by these differences. The fundamental question they ask is this: given that consumers differ on readily identifiable characteristics (such as demographics) and less apparent characteristics (such as person-ality) do these factors influence consumption choices? In attempting to answer this question, marketing strategists have tried to identify individual differences that are useful in predicting and explaining consumers' behavior. Initial focus centered on using demo-graphic characteristics such as age, income, and education to predict consumers' behavior. Although these characteristics were useful in selecting target markets they were not totally adequate. Demographic analysis did not provide highly accurate predictions of behavior or the detailed description of consumers necessary for strategy development.

After World War II, marketers actively searched for individual differences that would supplement demographic analysis. This led to qualitative and quantitative inquiry regarding the value of individuals' psychological characteristics, or personalities, to ex-plain behavior. The qualitative analysis was heavily influenced by Freud's psychoanalytic theory which provided a rich description of the consumer. This was useful in designing marketing strategy. Nevertheless, this approach was viewed as inadequate by a large segment of the marketing research community because success depended on the interpretive ability of the particular researcher. To address this concern, quantitative analysis of the relationship between personality and behavior was undertaken. It entailed correlating scores on standardized personality inventories with consumers' responses. The results of these analyses suggested that standard personality inventories were hardly more useful than no information at all in predicting consumers' behavior (Advertising Research Foundation, 1964; Kassarjian, 1971).

Two conclusions emerged from the failure of standardized personality measures. First, personality measures and demographic characteristics are inadequate predictors of behavior. What is needed are measures tailored specifically to consumers' behavior.[1] In essence, this involves quantifying the qualitative approach used by those following the psychoanalytic tradition. Second, standardized personality measures and demographic characteristics might influence how individuals process information, rather than affecting behavior per se. This observation suggests that personality traits and demographic characteristics might be of value if viewed in terms of their effect on information acquisition and their use in decision making.

In this chapter, several approaches to consumer individual difference analysis that are useful in explaining and predicting consumer behavior are reviewed. To illustrate a qualitative approach to determining the role of individual differences in guiding behavior, Freud's psychoanalytic theory is reviewed. This is followed by a discussion of a tailored personality measurement approach to individual differences called psychographics. The final section examines the effect of selected personality and demographic measures on consumer information processing.

FREUD'S PSYCHOANALYTIC THEORY

Two aspects of Freud's psychoanalytic theory are of particular relevance in understanding the impact of individual differences on consumers' behavior.[2] One deals with the structure of personality which provides insight into the process underlying individuals' reactions to certain product and message symbols. The other aspect of psychoanalytic theory relevant to understanding consumer behavior deals with the development of personality characteristics. This description amplifies our understanding of how people acquire and use the dispositions that guide decision making. By integrating the psychoanalytic descriptions of personality structure and personality development, we shall be able to provide a description of how personality factors influence consumers' behavior.

Personality Structure

Freud viewed personality in terms of three interactive psychological systems. The *id* is the reservoir of psychic energy that people inherit and have at birth. Increases in

---

[1] See Cohen (1967) for an example of a personality inventory tailored to consumers' behavior.

[2] See Hall and Lindzey (1978) for a detailed description of psychoanalytic theory.

psychic energy due to hunger, thirst, sex, and other basic drives induce a tension that the id seeks to discharge immediately so as to maximize pleasure. The id pursues any available means of tension reduction without regard to its social acceptability. The *superego* acts as a moral arbiter. It attempts to inhibit the selection of tension-reducing behaviors that are contrary to the values and moral standards of society. The superego strives for perfection rather than pleasure maximization. The *ego* serves a control function. It selects the tensions that are to be reduced and the means of tension reduction. The ego obeys a reality principle, seeking an appropriate means of tension reduction. In so doing, it seeks to mediate the demands of the id for pleasure maximization and the demands of the superego for morality.

Freud identified several mechanisms that an individual uses to resolve conflicts between the id and superego. Of greatest interest to students of consumer behavior is the sublimation mechanism. This mechanism allows people to express socially unacceptable motives in acceptable ways. Consider a cylindrical-shaped deodorant bottle. What motives might this package design be sublimating? To answer this question, one needs to consider the symbolic meaning that Freud attributed to certain stimuli; that is, how individuals abstract physical cues (see Chapter Seven). Elongated objects, such as the deodorant bottle, represent the penis. Cavities such as underarms may represent a woman's sexual organs. Viewed from Freud's perspective, a phallic-shaped bottle may serve to sublimate individuals' desire for sex.

Personality Development

Freud's view of personality structure describes the process by which personality affects behavior. It does not deal with the specific content on which personality structure operates. Consumers' choice of a phallic-shaped deodorant bottle is interpreted as a process involving a realistic compromise between the pleasure sought by the id and the morality sought by the superego. But personality structure yields little insight about why people focus on specific sexual desires to begin with. This issue is addressed in Freud's description of personality development.

Freud's theory of personality development is based on the premise that children's experiences during the first five years of life have a major effect on their psychological makeup. In this time period, children pass through three developmental stages, each associated with the achievement of sexual pleasure via a specific part of the body. During the first stage, called the oral stage, the mouth is the primary source of pleasure. The infant initially achieves pleasure by sucking, and later by biting and chewing. In the anal stage, which emerges during the second year of life, the child achieves pleasure by relieving tensions through the expulsion of feces. With the initiation of toilet training, which usually occurs during this stage, the child learns to postpone the pleasure of anal tension reduction in order to please his parents. The anal stage is followed by a phallic stage which lasts until the child is four or five. During the phallic stage, the child focuses on pleasure associated with the genital organs. In this stage, the sex organs are a source of pride and personal pleasure. It is characterized by a sexual desire for the parent of the opposite sex and a hostility toward the parent of the same sex.

The phallic stage is followed by a period of latency, when sexual motivations do not play an important role. At puberty, however, the adolescent enters the genital stage. This stage is characterized by altruistic love of others rather than the self-love that characterizes the three pregenital stages. The adolescent begins to achieve gratification by entering relationships with people of the opposite sex.

The four developmental stages are of interest because they help explain the specific content of an adult's psychological makeup. According to Freud, each developmental stage creates frustrations and anxieties. To the extent that these are not overcome satisfactorily during childhood, the person may remain fixated at an early developmental stage. In the adult, the fixation is rarely complete. Rather, people exhibit both mature and immature forms of behavior. Individuals with an oral fixation may exhibit their oral aggression by being sarcastic or argumentative. Alternatively, an oral fixation may manifest itself in terms of gullability; they "swallow" almost everything they are told. Individuals with an anal fixation may develop a retentive makeup characterized by obstinence and stinginess or by disorderliness and cruelty. These traits are thought to emerge as a result of strict and repressive methods of toilet training. In contrast, toilet training characterized by rewarding a child's bowel movements with praise is associated with creativity and productivity in the adult. Having examined Freud's theory of personality structure and theory of personality separately, we shall consider how these theories are related. In doing so, we shall present Freud's view of how personality affects behavior.

The psychoanalytic view of personality structure addresses how individuals go about making decisions. People discharge psychic tensions in a realistic way that is more or less socially acceptable. Freud's theory of personality development extends the structural view by specifying the psychic tensions that are likely to emerge and suggests how they are likely to be discharged. Specifically, Freud contends that individuals' success in overcoming early life frustrations and anxieties determines the tensions that will emerge later and directs how they will be discharged. To the extent that individuals do not successfully deal with frustrations and anxieties associated with some developmental stage, they become fixated at that stage. The tensions that emerge will be related to the stage of fixation. Processing strategies and behaviors that reduce this tension in a socially acceptable way are likely to be pursued.

To illustrate the applicability of the integrated psychoanalytic view, consider individuals who are fixated at the phallic stage. They may reduce psychic tension by publicly exhibiting their sex organs or masturbating. Because these means of tension reduction are socially unacceptable, they are often sublimated. Such people are likely to be influenced by communications which indicate how a product or service can be employed as a means of sublimation. For example, an advertisement for Bic disposable blade razors which emphasizes the fact that you get "stroked" with a Bic is likely to be effective in influencing people with a phallic fixation to purchase that brand.

Freud's theory of personality structure and development is particularly noteworthy because it extends our understanding of information processing. In describing information acquisition, we noted that pertinent information is likely to be processed and stored in memory. But what determines whether or not information is pertinent? Freud addresses this issue by noting that in the process of development, individuals face anxieties and frustrations that are not completely resolved. We may speculate that the failure to resolve frustrations causes people to store multiple thoughts about those frustrations in memory, making these thoughts highly available. Thus information is pertinent to the extent that it relates to unsuccessfully resolved frustrations or anxieties. For example, an orally fixated individual may find information about cigarettes, cigars, or coffee pertinent because they have many thoughts available related to oral gratification.

Freud's theory also extends our view of information processing by specifying the different processing strategies that people might use. Individuals with an oral fixation characterized by gullibility are likely to make evaluations primarily on the basis of incoming information, whereas those with an oral fixation characterized by obstinence may base evaluations on their own repertoire of previously stored thoughts. In this way, information retrieval and rehearsal strategies are linked to personality development.

CONSUMPTION-TAILORED PERSONALITY MEASURES

The psychoanalytic approach was useful in gaining insight about the motivations that direct consumers' behavior. But many researchers were uncomfortable with the approach because it was not quantitative; its success depended on the researcher's interpretative skill. For this reason, interest grew in using standardized personality measures such as the California Psychological Inventory, Edwards Personal Preference Schedule and the Minnesota Multiphasic Personality Inventory. These measures were reliable and valid psychological indices but did not predict consumers' behavior. Wells and Beard (1973) have identified no less than forty-nine personality traits whose relationship to consumers' preferences and purchases were studied in more than ninety studies. The results in these inquiries were almost always the same. Personality traits typically improved prediction by ten percent or less (Bem and Allen, 1974; Mischel, 1973).

By the early 1960s marketing researchers began to devise instruments that would combine the rigor of standardized personality inventories with the detailed descriptive information afforded by psychoanalytic procedures. The result was an approach that has variously been called psychographics, lifestyles, and AIO (activities, interests and opinions).[3] Psychographic analysis involves measuring individuals' consumption-related activities, interests, and opinions. Table 9.1 lists the elements in each of the lifestyle dimensions. Activities refer to how an individual spends his or her time, interests refer to an individual's preferences, and opinions reflect a person's feeling about some object or issue (Plummer, 1974).

Psychographic analysis usually involves more than just measures of activities, interests, and opinions. Consumers' demographic characteristics, product use, and media preferences are also determined. This allows the strategist to segment consumers by product use, describe user segments in demographic and psychographic terms, and identify the media used by various segments.

To illustrate this approach, consider a study pertaining to the use of eye makeup

---

[3]See Wells (1975) for a comprehensive review and critique of psychographics.

TABLE 9.1. Elements of Lifestyle Dimensions

Activities	Interests	Opinions
Work	Family	Themselves
Hobbies	Home	Social Issues
Social Events	Job	Politics
Vacations	Community	Business
Entertainment	Recreation	Economics
Club Membership	Fashion	Education
Community	Food	Products
Shopping	Media	Future
Sports	Achievements	Culture

SOURCE: Plummer, 1974.

(Wells and Beard, 1973). Consumers were initially segmented by the extent to which they used eye makeup. A demographic analysis of the heavy eye makeup users indicated that they were young, well-educated women who lived in metropolitan areas. An analysis of product use revealed that heavy eye makeup users were also heavy users of face makeup, lipstick, hair spray, perfume, and cigarettes. The picture emerging from this analysis suggests that the major market for eye makeup is the young, well-appointed city woman.

Psychographic analysis provides further insights about what the heavy eye makeup user is like. A large number of AIO statements were administered to a group of women. The women rated their degree of agreement with each statement. Statements on which heavy eye makeup users agreed more than average are shown in Table 9.2. These data indicate that the heavy users of eye makeup are highly concerned about personal appearance—their skin, hair, and clothing. They enjoy social activities such as parties and

TABLE 9.2. Activities, Interests, and Opinions for Heavy Eye Makeup User

Heavier users agreed more than average with:
  I often try the latest hairdo styles when they change.
  I usually have one or more outfits that are the very latest style.
  An important part of my life and activities is dressing smartly.
  I comb my hair and put on my lipstick first thing in the morning.
  I take good care of my skin.
  I like ballet.
  I like parties where there is lots of music and talk.
  I do more things socially than do most of my friends.

Heavier users disagreed more than average with:
  I am a homebody.
  I like grocery shopping.
  I enjoy most forms of housework.
  I try to arrange my home for my children's convenience.

SOURCE: Plummer, 1974.

ballet, which probably motivates their concern for personal appearance. They are more interested in activities outside the home than those within the home.

The psychographic analysis of the heavy eye makeup user fills in descriptive details that would not be available on the basis of demographic analysis alone. These descriptive details provide the strategist with information useful in developing products to attract the heavy eye makeup user. It is also useful in deciding the product characteristics that should be emphasized in eye makeup advertising.

Thus, an important application of psychographics is in brand positioning. To illustrate this application, consider the positioning of Schlitz beer in the late 1960s (Plummer, 1974). At the time, Schlitz was positioned as an upscale beverage. It appealed most to men in professional and managerial occupations with college educations and incomes over $15,000. This target was composed primarily of light beer drinkers. Schlitz was less successful in attracting the high school educated, middle income, blue-collar people who composed the heavy beer drinking segment.

Psychographic analysis was conducted to determine how Schlitz could reposition the brand so as to attract the heavy beer drinker. Statements on which the heavy beer drinker differed in agreement from the nondrinker are shown in Table 9.3. Heavy beer drinkers viewed themselves more as risk takers and pleasure seekers than the nondrinkers. They also expressed a greater preference for a physical male-oriented existence than the nondrinkers.

This analysis guided the development of an advertising campaign for Schlitz which featured the lifestyle of men who earned their living at sea. This lifestyle was depicted as being risky, pleasurable, and physical. They lived their lives with gusto and wanted gusto in their beer. Judging by awareness and sales studies this campaign was highly effective (Plummer, 1974).

Psychographic analysis can also be used to determine how a particular brand is related to an individual's lifestyle. An excellent example of this application is the psychographic analysis done for Ford Pinto (Young, 1971). When Pinto was launched in the

TABLE 9.3. Activities, Interest, and Opinions of Heavy Beer Drinker

---

Heavy beer drinker agreed with:
  I like to take chances.
  I like danger.
  I sometimes bet money at the races.
  I smoke too much.
  If I had my way I would own a convertible.
  I would do better than average in a fistfight.
  I like war stories.
  Men should not do the dishes.

Heavy beer drinkers disagreed with:
  Spiritual values are more important than material things.
  I would rather spend a quiet evening at home than go out to a party.
  I am careful what I eat to keep my weight under control.

SOURCE: Plummer, 1974.

early 1970s, the plan was to position it against imported small cars. It was to be carefree, small, and romantic. But as the introduction proceeded, psychographic analysis disclosed that this positioning was inappropriate. Potential Pinto buyers were more interested in a car that was functional and economic than one that was carefree and romantic. They agreed with statements such as "I am more practical in car selection," and "I wish I could depend on my car more." They rejected statements like "The kind of car you have is important as to how people see you" and "Taking care of a car is too much trouble" (Young, 1971).

On the basis of this analysis, Pinto was repositioned. It was depicted as an economical and functional car. This position was not only congenial with potential Pinto owners' wants, it was also believable. Ford had a tradition of building economical and functional transportation dating back to the Model A. Sales of Pinto indicated the wisdom of the repositioning, although the change in positioning is unlikely to have been the only reason for Pinto's success.

In sum, psychographic analysis provides the strategist with a detailed picture of how consumers relate to a product or brand. This information is a useful input in describing markets and in developing product positioning strategies. When psychographic studies are repeated over time, the data are useful in monitoring trends in consumer lifestyles. In turn, this information is helpful in anticipating the types of products and services that will be in demand in the future.

Despite these uses of psychographic analysis, it should be employed with caution. Lifestyle constructs are not highly accurate predictors of consumers' behavior. Individual lifestyle measures typically improve the manager's ability to predict behavior by less than ten percent. When all relevant measures are linked together, the manager's ability to predict behavior is usually increased by less than thirty percent (Wells, 1975).

Another reason for exercising caution in using psychographics is that there has been no test of its superiority in relation to other approaches (that is, demographic analysis). Such a test would entail comparing the consumer response to a psychographically-based strategy with the response to a strategy based on some other approach. In the absence of such a test, it can only be concluded that psychographic analysis is one of the approaches to be considered in describing markets and positioning products.

THE IMPACT OF INDIVIDUAL DIFFERENCES ON CONSUMER INFORMATION PROCESSING

In the past several years, there have been attempts to revitalize personality individual difference measures as predictors of consumers' behavior. One approach, suggested by Bem and Allen (1974), is based on the premise that individual differences (that is, personality inventories) are useful in predicting only some of the people's behavior some of the time. To identify those people whose behavior could be predicted from a knowledge of their personality, Bem and Allen asked individuals to rate themselves on some personality trait and to indicate how variable they were on this trait from one situation to another. For example, a person might be asked to rate his or her self-esteem and to indicate how much self-esteem varied from one situation to another. It was found that behavior could be accurately predicted for people who indicated they did not vary much from situation to situation. Predictions were inaccurate for those who rated themselves as variable. Presumably in this latter case some situational factor or other personality trait predicts behavior.

Although it may appear that predicting some people's behavior some of the time on the basis of personality traits represents progress in the use of personality inventories, Bem and Allen's approach has a glaring weakness. It does not explain why people vary in their perceptions of the effects of situations on the use of some personality trait. It merely states that low variability affords good prediction. In effect, Bem and Allen have developed good predictions at the expense of explanation. This observation becomes evident when it is recognized that their approach gives us little insight about how one might predict the behavior of people who view their personality dispositions as variable from situation to situation.

A second approach to revitalizing individual differences as predictors of consumers' response is based on the assumption that personality and demographic characteristics have an impact on how individuals acquire and use information. Viewed from this perspective, individual differences do not affect behavior directly, but affect the information people use in making decisions. To illustrate this process, we shall consider one personality variable, self-esteem, and one demographic variable, consumers' age.

Personality Characteristics

The impact of personality characteristics on information processing is illustrated by considering the self-esteem (or self-confidence) variable. Self-esteem refers to the "value an individual attributes to various facets of his person" (Cohen, 1959). It has typically been measured by a twenty-three-item *feelings of inadequacy* questionnaire developed by Janis and Field (1959). All of these items are shown in Table 9.4. The self-esteem personality variable is chosen to illustrate the value of personality because a substantial number of marketing and psychology studies have investigated its effect on information processing. Self-esteem is also selected because it has been viewed as an important determinant of consumer behavior (Howard and Sheth, 1969).

The effects of self-esteem on the acquisition of information from others is typically studied by categorizing research participants on the basis of their responses to a self-esteem measure and presenting all participants with a persuasive appeal. From an information processing perspective, it is expected that low self-esteem people will be more persuaded by a message than people with high self-esteem. Individuals' low self-esteem inhibits them from generating thoughts that oppose those presented in an appeal. Their attitude toward the message issue is therefore determined by the message arguments they process. In contrast, high self-esteem individuals are motivated to retrieve their own repertoire of message-related thoughts and ignore thoughts developed in the message. Because their own thoughts are likely to be less favorable than message thoughts, people with high self-esteem are less likely to be persuaded than people with low self-esteem.

TABLE 9.4. Measures of Self-Esteem

The following twenty-three statements are evaluated on a five-point scale. Most questions are answered on the scale ranging from very often (score 1) to not at all (scored 5):

1. How often do you feel inferior to most of the people you know?
2. Do you ever think that you are a worthless individual?
3. How confident do you feel that some day the people you know will look up to you and respect you?
4. How often do you feel to blame for your mistakes?
5. Do you ever feel so discouraged with yourself that you wonder whether anything is worth while?
6. How often do you feel that you dislike yourself?
7. In general, how confident do you feel about your abilities?
8. How often do you have the feeling that there is nothing you can do well?
9. How much do you worry about how well you get along with other people?
10. How often do you worry about criticism that might be made of your work by whoever is responsible for checking up on your work?
11. Do you ever feel afraid or anxious when you are going into a room by yourself where other people have already gathered and are talking?
12. How often do you feel self-conscious?
13. When you have to talk in front of a class or a group of people your own age, how afraid or worried do you usually feel?
14. When you are trying to win in a game or sport and you know that other people are watching you, how rattled or flustered do you usually get?
15. How much do you worry about whether other people will regard you as a success or a failure in your job or career?
16. When in a group of people, do you have trouble thinking of the right things to talk about?
17. When you have made an embarrassing mistake or have done something that makes you look foolish, how long do you usually keep on worrying about it?
18. Do you find it hard to make talk when you meet new people?
19. How often do you worry about whether other people like to be with you?
20. How often are you troubled with shyness?
21. When you are trying to convince other people who disagree with your ideas, how worried do you usually feel about the impression you are making?
22. When you think about the possibility that some of your friends or acquaintances might *not* have a good opinion of you, how concerned or worried do you feel about it?
23. How often do you feel worried or bothered about what other people think of you?

SOURCE: Janis and Field, 1959

Information processing theory predicts that people low in self-esteem will be more persuaded than high self-esteem people. But, it is important to note that this result is expected only in situations where high self-esteem people are motivated to retrieve counterarguments; such situations are likely to occur when the message arguments lack convincing facts and sound logic (Skolnick and Heslin, 1971). If, however, the message arguments are compelling, they are likely to be processed by those of high self-esteem. Evaluation will therefore be based on the message thoughts as well as the message recipients' own thoughts that are consistent with the appeal. Low self-esteem people are unaffected by the quality of message arguments. Their low self-esteem inhibits them from generating their own thoughts whether the message is compelling or not. As a result,

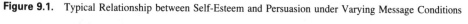

Figure 9.1. Typical Relationship between Self-Esteem and Persuasion under Varying Message Conditions

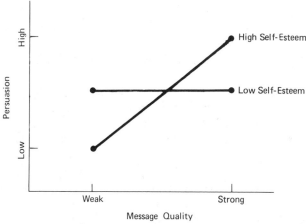

high self-esteem individuals are expected to be more persuaded than low self-esteem people when message arguments are compelling and less persuaded when they are not compelling.

The information processing predictions are borne out by research findings. Skolnick and Heslin (1971) have shown that high self-esteem individuals are more persuaded when the message is compelling than when it is not (Figure 9.1). They have also shown that people low in self-esteem are equally persuaded by messages of high and low quality. Thus, low self-esteem people are more persuaded than high self-esteem people when the message is not convincing and the reverse occurs when the message is compelling (Figure 9.1).

To reiterate, the discussion of the self-esteem-persuasion relationship illustrates the value of personality traits in understanding consumer behavior. It underscores the fact that the way consumers use their ability to store and retrieve information depends, in part, on their personal characteristics. Thus, individuals high in self-esteem are likely to evaluate a communication on the basis of the thoughts provided in the message, as well as on their own thoughts. When message thoughts are weak, high self-esteem individuals retrieve and use their own repertoire of counterarguments and therefore reject the message. Compelling messages stimulate the retrieval of support arguments and message acceptance results. Low self-esteem individuals, on the other hand, do not have the confidence to use their own thoughts. They process and use message thoughts as a basis for evaluation—whether those thoughts are compelling or not.

Demographic Characteristics

Consumers' demographic characteristics, like standardized personality measures, are not accurate predictors of behavior. Yet, like personality measures, demographic characteristics are useful in understanding how consumers process information. Perhaps the most important demographic characteristic is the consumer's age. In this section, we focus on the age variable to illustrate how demographic characteristics are related to consumers' responses. This entails examining how children of different ages and elderly adults respond to marketing stimuli. The knowledge gained is useful for developing strategies to influence children's and elderly adults' behavior, as well as for assessing how age-related factors, in general, affect consumers' information processing.

Children's Responses. Inquiry pertaining to age differences in children's responses has centered primarily on their reaction to television commercials.[4] The evidence indicates that younger children have less ability to discriminate between programs and commercials, less understanding of advertising's persuasive intent, and less suspicion about the truthfulness of advertising than older children (Blatt, Spencer, and Ward, 1972; Robertson and Rossiter, 1974; Ward, Reale, and Levinson, 1972; Ward, Wackman, and Wartella, 1977). Younger children also exhibit poorer recall of message information than older children (Blatt *et al.*, 1972; Ward *et al.*, 1972; Ward *et al.*, 1977).

To understand why these age differences in children's responses to television advertising occur and to develop strategies for overcoming younger children's response limitations, we shall consider how children of different ages store and retrieve information. This analysis suggests that children can be segmented into three groups: *strategic* processors (aged ten and older), *cued* processors (aged six to nine), and *limited* processors (below age six).

Strategic processors' response to incoming information is similar to that of adults. These children are able to select the information that is central for understanding communications. Strategic processors have the ability to rehearse incoming information spontaneously and to store it in memory. Their product evaluation is enhanced by their ability to retrieve stored information that may include thoughts expressed in an appeal as well as their own thoughts. Strategic processors can resist influence attempts to the extent that their own thoughts oppose those stated in a communication. Given their considerable processing skills, strategies other than those used in communicating with adults are not required.

Cued processors have about the same ability to store and retrieve information as strategic processors. However, cued processors frequently do not use these abilities unless specifically prompted (or cued) to do so. They do not spontaneously distinguish between the central and peripheral aspects of incoming information or spontaneously rehearse information presented in an appeal. Cued processors do not spontaneously locate memory addresses where pertinent information has been stored or exhaustively retrieve the information from memory once it has been located.

There are a variety of strategies available to help cued processors overcome their deficiencies in using the information storage and retrieval abilities they possess. One is aided learning, informing cued processors about what constitutes the central aspects of product appeals. A second strategy is to use repetition. It may serve not only to enhance message comprehension, but also to activate the rehearsal necessary for information storage in long-term memory. Finally, retrieval may be improved if product information

---

[4]See Roedder (in press) for a review of the children's information processing literature.

about one attribute is presented completely before another attribute is considered, and if each attribute is labeled by concepts familiar to children (for example, cost and flavor). In effect, these approaches will help cued processors locate relevant memory addresses and exhaustively search each address.

Limited processors exhibit difficulties similar to those of cued processors. But unlike cued processors, limited processors do not have storage and retrieval strategies available. Thus, prompts to evoke efficient information processing have no effect on limited processors. In effect, limited processors' inability to store and retrieve communicated information serves as a self-protecting mechanism that limits the extent to which they can be influenced.

The analysis of strategic, cued, and limited processors indicates that a child's cognitive development, which is reflected in age, has an important effect on the information they can acquire and use to make decisions. Children under six are difficult to influence because they are highly limited in their ability to store and retrieve information. Children between ages six and nine are subject to influence providing that approaches to stimulate information storage and retrieval are employed. Children aged ten or older spontaneously use storage and retrieval strategies. Influence depends on the extent to which they generate and rehearse thoughts that support a persuasive appeal.

Elderly Adults' Responses. The effects of age on individuals' responses are also made evident by comparing elderly adults and their younger adult counterparts.[5] This analysis reveals that older people differ from younger adults in terms of the information to which they are likely to be exposed, ability to process that information and influenceability. As we examine each of these response differences, it should be noted that there are at least two causes that may contribute to age differences. One is the biological process involved in aging. The other is the generation in which particular groups were born and raised. Thus, the observation that elderly adults are more cautious than younger adults may be related to the aging process, or to the fact that in their earlier years today's elderly lived in an environment that fostered cautiousness (for example, the Great Depression). For many of the age differences we examine below, it is not possible to distinguish between biological and generational causes of age differences.

Between the ages of sixty and sixty-five, there begins a change in the sources of information to which an individual is exposed. In large measure, this change is caused by a reduction in the roles one assumes. With advancing age one retires, which results in the loss of such roles as employee and colleague. The death of one's spouse and the marriage of one's children also cause role reduction. The loss of contact with persons because of role attrition is compensated for by greater reliance on the mass media, the extended family (particularly one's daughter) and friends who live nearby.

Advancing age also affects individuals' ability to process information. It is thought that starting at about age forty-five, individuals exhibit a reduction in ability to learn. This deficit can be offset by pacing the rate of presentation so that information is readily processed, or by allowing the older person to self-pace (that is, by using print media). This learning deficit can also be minimized by avoiding inclusion of irrelevant information

[5]This section is adapted from Phillips and Sternthal (1977).

that frequently distracts elderly people from processing the central content of a communication. Even if these precautions are instituted, the elderly person's ability to learn unfamiliar information is likely to be poorer than that of younger adults. Thus information about a new product is likely to be processed less completely by an older individual than by a younger counterpart.

In most situations, elderly individuals are no more influenceable than younger adults. An exception occurs when elderly people perceive that they lack the competence necessary to make a decision. In this instance, they are more easily persuaded than younger people. Older adults are likely to perceive themselves as incompetent when performing roles that are acquired at an advanced age. They find the new roles difficult to learn and thus question their ability to make appropriate decisions in these situations. For example, an elderly widow may feel incompetent in deciding how to invest her money because this role was only acquired after her husband's death. Consequently, she is easily influenced by those she perceives as more competent in financial matters.

The analysis of elderly people's decision-making in relation to that of younger people has several strategic implications. In attempting to reach elderly individuals with marketing communications it is useful to target their extended family (that is, their spouse and children's families). Elderly people not only have substantial contact with their extended family, but they rely on them for information. Attention should also be given to reaching the older consumer directly. This approach is particularly efficient in communities where there is a high proportion of older people because elderly individuals rely on their peers as sources of information.

In selecting media to disseminate new information to elderly consumers, emphasis should be given to newspapers. Aged people are heavy users of this medium and consider it their most important source of information. Moreover, newspapers allow older adults to process information at their own pace, thus enhancing the acquisition of message information.

Communications to elderly people that are disseminated on television should avoid the use of distracting devices such as humor and quick cuts (that is, rapid movement from one scene to another). Although low levels of distraction enhance persuasion in younger adults, the elderly's inability to ignore irrelevant information makes it likely that even mild distractions will inhibit the processing of message information.

As we have seen, a consumer's age is an individual difference that affects how information is used in decision making. An understanding of the relationship between age and information processing enables the strategist to anticipate problems that particular age segments will have in processing communications; it also guides the development of strategies to overcome these problems.

SUMMARY

The approaches to investigating consumer individual differences considered in this chapter make important contributions to our understanding of consumer decision-making. Freud's psychoanalytic theory extends our understanding of information processing. It suggests that early life experiences are represented in memory and influence the processing and interpretation of subsequent events. Moreover, the psychoanalytic view provides an explanation for individual differences in storing and retrieving information, and interpreting these differences in terms of a child's experiences during cognitive development. The description of personality and demographic differences reaffirms the importance of storage and retrieval in information processing. When storage abilities are limited such as they are in young children or in elderly adults who are faced with an unfamiliar issue, information acquisition is limited; when storage is not limited, acquisition is extensive. When retrieval of thoughts is not extensive, as is the case for low self-esteem people, resistance to a persuasive message is weak. But when retrieval of thoughts is extensive, for example with high self-esteem individuals, resistance to uncompelling messages is substantial.

The analysis of individual differences described in this chapter is also useful in devising marketing strategy. Freud's psychoanalytical theory provides a qualitative approach to devising product and communication strategies that will stimulate demand among specific targets. Psychographic analysis provides a less detailed but quantifiable approach for the same purpose. And a knowledge of the impact of personality traits and demographic characteristics on information processing is a basis for developing effective communication strategy.

QUESTIONS

1. Of what value is Freud's view of personality structure in understanding consumer behavior?

2. What contribution does Freud's theory of personality development make to our understanding of consumer information processing?

3. Using the data described in Table 9.2, develop a product and communication strategy for an eye makeup brand.

4. What are the limitations of psychographic analysis?

5. Of what value is an understanding of the relationship between personality traits and consumer information processing?

6. What effect does an individual's self-esteem have on his persuadibility? How is this relationship explained?

7. What communication strategies are appropriate to influence (a) children age eight and (b) elderly adults?

Chapter 10

Demographic Trends and Consumption

Demographic analysis is of value in planning short- and long-term marketing strategy. In the short-run, concern centers primarily on how a brand fares in relation to competitive offerings. As we described in Chapter Nine, an analysis of demographic and other individual difference variables is useful in developing brand strategies. In planning for the longer term, more attention is given to product category demand because the viability of a brand ultimately depends on category demand. An analysis of demographic trends provides a basis for anticipating category consumption.

Gerber's experience illustrates the dramatic effect demographic trends in the American population can have on consumer demand. For many years, Gerber's has been a leading firm in the baby food industry. In the early 1970s, it controlled sixty-five percent of this market. Yet Gerber's outlook was not bright. Sales had leveled off and earnings fell. In response, Gerber introduced a line of non-food items for babies including babywear, bottle sterilizers, and disposable bottles. They dropped the slogan "Babies are our business . . . our only business" and introduced a line of single serving adult food with the slogan, "We were good for you then and we are good for you now."

The erosion of demand for baby food can be traced directly to the decline in fertility rates (the average number of children born to a woman during her lifetime), which began in the mid-1960s. Although this trend had its initial impact on the producers of baby products, its ultimate effects are more far-reaching. By the mid 1980s the soft drink industry will experience a sharp decline in its main market, people thirteen to twenty-six years of age. And by 1990, firms will be hard-pressed to find management talent for entry level positions.

In this chapter, several of the major demographic trends that affect consumers' behavior are described. They include trends in fertility, household composition, women in the labor force, social class factors, and migration. These trends are of interest because they allow the manager to predict long-term demand for various product categories and to plan strategies that will sustain a firm's viability. To demonstrate this point, examples of the potential impact of each trend on consumption behavior are presented.

FERTILITY RATES

The rate of fertility in the American population provides the marketing manager with important information for long-term planning. Because death rates and migration are relatively static, fertility provides a basis for estimating the future size of the population. And a changing rate of fertility alerts the manager to the fact that some age segments will grow, while others will experience attrition.

In the last twenty-five years, fertility rates in the United States population have fluctuated dramatically. Between the years 1946 and 1964, there was a baby boom. As Figure 10.1 shows, the number of babies born annually increased from about 2.9 million in 1945 to 4.3 million in 1957. Between 1954 and 1964, the number of children born annually exceeded 4 million. Since 1964 there has been a steady decline in annual births. Fertility rates, which had been as high as 3.8 (that is, an average of 3.8 children per woman during her lifetime), dropped well under 2—the rate needed to sustain a stable population.

These historical fertility data help explain why Gerber's, and other companies catering to the young, experienced a decline in demand during the 1970s. But to anticipate the long-range implications of fertility, one must also be able to estimate the fertility rates of future generations.[1] Population experts hold contradictory views on this issue. One view is that there will be an upswing in fertility (Easterlin and Wachter, 1979). This prediction is based on the following scenario. As children born during the post 1964 low fertility period become adults, they will enter the labor force in smaller numbers than earlier generations. As a result, they will view their prospects as more promising than those of the baby boom generation, marry earlier, and have more children.

Evidence for this view emerges from correlational data indicating a negative relationship between the size of the population of a particular age and the fertility of that group. For example, the relatively small number of people born in the 1930s is related to their high fertility rate in the 1950s, and the large number of people born in the 1950s

[1] See Bagozzi and Van Loo (1978) for a review of fertility theory.

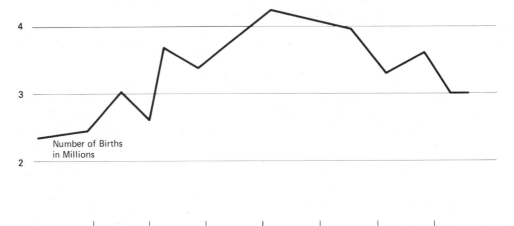

Figure 10.1. Baby Boom and Baby Bust

Number of Births
in Millions

SOURCE: Taeuber, 1979.

is related to their low fertility rate in the 1970s. If this trend continues, the relatively small number of people born in the 1970s will exhibit a high fertility rate and create another baby boom.

Critics of this view contend that dramatic changes in the environment make it unlikely that history will repeat itself (Butz and Ward, 1979). Perhaps the most crucial of these changes are ones related to the rising income of women. Since 1970, women's wages have risen dramatically (Figure 10.2) Thus the opportunity cost of having children has also risen, causing women to enter the workforce in ever-increasing numbers (Figure 10.2). In fact, the number of women entering the labor force has doubled since 1970. During this time period, there has also been a steady decline in the proportion of women who marry between the ages of twenty and twenty-four. Presumably, the increase in women's wages has caused the opportunity cost of marriage to become high. These trends suggest there will be a larger number of young and single entrants into the labor market than in earlier generations. In turn, this supply of labor is expected to reduce optimism among young marrieds regarding their economic prospects and, therefore, keep fertility rates low.

At present, there is no definitive evidence that would allow us to choose between the models of fertility examined. Nevertheless, we shall focus on the implications of a sustained low fertility rate because its occurrence will require a more dramatic change from current marketing strategy than will an increase in fertility rate.

A fertility rate sustained at the present level will significantly reduce the population growth in future decades. Table 10.1 shows projections of population size assuming the following fertility rates: the replacement level of 2.1 or the current fertility rate of 1.7. In the 1980s, the population will grow quite rapidly even with low fertility rates because

Figure 10.2. Fertility, Women's Income, and Women's Employment

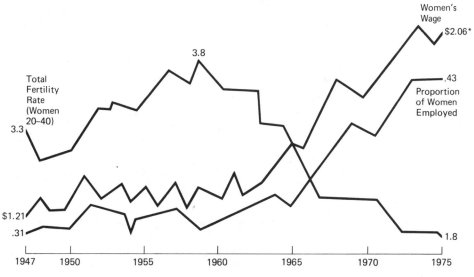

* in constant 1964 dollars

SOURCE: Butz and Ward, 1979.

of the large number of people (a product of the baby boom) who are in their reproductive years. By 1990, the population growth will slow dramatically and fall thereafter. The slow long-term growth in the population, particularly at the fertility rate of 1.7, suggests that aggregate demand will not grow at the rate it has in the past. A firm's growth will therefore be achieved at the expense of competitors rather than by attracting new consumers into the marketplace.

The fertility rates of the past few decades will have an even more noticeable effect on the age composition of the population than it will on population growth. As the postwar baby grows up, the average age of the population will grow older. The average age

TABLE 10.1. Projections of Population Size (Millions)

	Fertility Rate			
	1.7		*2.1*	
	number of people	*% increase*	*number of people*	*% increase*
1980	220.7	3.4	222.2	4.1
1985	228.9	3.7	232.9	4.8
1990	236.3	3.2	243.5	4.4
1995	242.0	2.4	252.8	3.8
2000	245.9	1.6	260.4	3.0

SOURCE: Department of Commerce.

of the American population in the 1980s is expected to be about thirty years old, and by the year 2000 it is expected to be thirty-five years old. In the last quarter of this century, there will be a ripple effect through various age segments. As Figure 10.3 shows, between 1975 and 1985 there will be a decline in the five to thirteen year old segments. The most rapidly increasing segment during this time period will be the twenty-five to forty-four group. And, during the last twenty-five years of this century the population over sixty-five will experience rapid growth. By the year 2000 one person in eight will be sixty-five or older—about forty percent more than there were in 1980.

The changing size of various age segments in the population constitutes a threat to some industries. Firms that produce soft drinks, snack foods, and records will be faced with a decline in their major markets—those aged thirteen to twenty-four. They will have to look for other opportunities to sustain growth. Soft drink producers, for example, have attempted to meet the impending decline in their prime target with approaches that stimulate category demand and induce brand switching. Pepsi-Cola has gained entry into the lucrative Soviet Union market and Coca-Cola has captured much of the soda fountain market through sales at fast food restaurants like McDonald's (*Business Week,* May 23, 1977).

The changing size of age segments is an opportunity for firms whose primary target is elderly people. The over-sixty-five population comprises a substantial proportion of

Figure 10.3.   The Effect of the Baby Boom on Age Segments

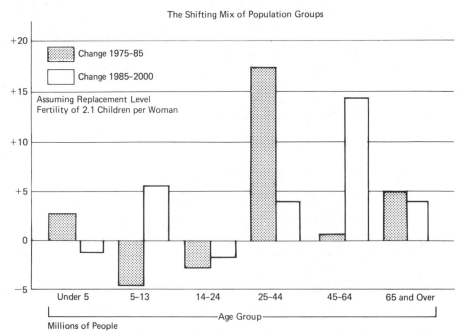

SOURCE: Census Bureau.

the consumers for travel services, recreational activities, retirement housing, health care products, and single-portion food packaging (Blum, 1977). The growth of the twenty-five to forty-four year old group augurs well for a wide variety of discretionary consumer goods producers. This segment spends heavily on travel, entertainment, personal care, and luxury items (Blum, 1977).

To summarize, changes in the fertility rate have a significant impact on aggregate demand as well as the demand emerging from different age segments of the population. If the current low rate of fertility persists, aggregate demand will grow slowly and at a decreasing rate. However, persistence of the current low fertility trend will increase the size and, therefore, the attractiveness of the older age segments in the population. Given the impact of fertility on demand, it seems useful to examine the trends in factors that affect fertility. Two such factors, household formation and composition, and women in the workforce, are considered in the following sections.

HOUSEHOLDS

Americans have traditionally married in their early twenties, and spent the remainder of their lives as members of a family. Many elements of this basic pattern remain today. The number of households in the United States has continued to grow over this century and is expected to reach 80 million in the 1980s. There are, however, several features characterizing the current trend of household formation that make it of special interest to marketing strategists.

The rate of household formation over the last decade is substantially greater than the increase in population. This outcome is due to the fact that households are smaller than they were in previous generations. The trend for most families is to have one or two children. Thus, the number of first and second children born annually has remained fairly stable (Table 10.2). This trend reflects, in part, the postponement of marriage and an increase of women in the workforce noted earlier.

During the past several decades, there has been a rapid increase in the number of one-person households. In 1980, twenty-three percent of households were one person, an increase of eight percent from 1960. In large measure, this is due to the fact that elderly people in general, and elderly women in particular are living alone rather than with their extended family or in institutions for the elderly. In fact, forty-three percent of one-person households are people sixty-five years of age or older, and about two-thirds of these people are women.

Although one might expect that a reduction in marriages also accounts for the growth of one-person households, it is not apparent in the data. Despite the trend of postponing marriage, the number of marriages has increased substantially in the last two decades (Table 10.3). These contradictory findings are explained by the high incidence of remarriage. According to Paul Glick, a leading demographer, thirty-eight percent of women aged twenty-five to twenty-nine will have their first marriage end in divorce. Three-fourths of these divorcees will remarry and about forty-five percent of these re-marriages will end in divorce. Thus, while more people are postponing marriage, this

TABLE 10.2. Birth Order

	Thousands			
Year	First Child	Second Child	Third Child	Fourth Child and Over
1945	961	763	446	688
1946	1,291	935	487	699
1947	1,574	1,019	524	700
1948	1,343	1,047	545	701
1949	1,235	1,093	584	737
1950	1,140	1,097	630	764
1951	1,195	1,116	666	826
1952	1,169	1,122	733	889
1953	1,150	1,120	753	942
1954	1,160	1,119	785	1,014
1955	1,138	1,104	800	1,063
1956	1,166	1,109	821	1,122
1957	1,180	1,111	838	1,179
1958	1,140	1,085	826	1,203
1959	1,124	1,066	821	1,232
1960	1,122	1,053	820	1,263
1961	1,132	1,032	813	1,292
1962	1,118	1,002	782	1,265
1963	1,131	987	752	1,228
1964	1,167	965	721	1,175
1965	1,159	911	647	1,043
1966	1,226	888	585	908
1967	1,238	908	560	815
1968	1,312	919	539	731
1969	1,365	973	560	703
1970	1,450	1,025	579	677
1971	1,396	1,007	544	610
1972	1,329	956	473	500
1973	1,307	956	445	430
1974	1,336	995	442	387
1975	1,337	997	446	364

SOURCE: Department of Health, Education and Welfare.

trend is not detectable in the annual marriage rate because of the substantial number of people getting remarried annually.

The high incidence of divorce in America has inflated not only marriage statistics, but also has changed the composition of the household. At the end of the 1970s, there were about 7.5 million families with a woman head of household and no husband. This group is at a substantial economic disadvantage, earning an average of $7,210 annually. In contrast, families composed of a husband and a wife have a median income of $16,200.

TABLE 10.3. Marriages and Marriage Rates

Year	Marriages (Thousands)	Marriage Rate[1]
1920	1,274	92.0
1930	1,127	67.6
1940	1,596	82.8
1945	1,613	83.6
1946	2,291	118.1
1947	1,992	106.2
1948	1,811	98.5
1949	1,580	86.7
1950	1,667	90.2
1951	1,595	86.6
1952	1,539	83.2
1953	1,546	83.7
1954	1,490	79.8
1955	1,531	80.9
1956	1,585	82.4
1957	1,518	78.0
1958	1,451	72.0
1959	1,494	73.6
1960	1,523	73.5
1961	1,548	72.2
1962	1,577	71.2
1963	1,654	73.4
1964	1,725	74.6
1965	1,800	75.0
1966	1,857	75.6
1967	1,927	76.4
1968	2,069	79.1
1969	2,145	80.0
1970	2,159	76.5
1971	2,190	76.2
1972	2,282	77.9
1973	2,284	76.0
1974	2,230	72.0
1975	2,153	66.9
1976p	2,133	n.a.

[1]Rate per 1,000 unmarried females aged 15 years and over

n.a.—Not available

p—Preliminary

SOURCE: Department of Health, Education and Welfare

The trends in household development have important implications for consumption behavior. They suggest that demand in the 1980s will not be as limited as one would expect on the basis of fertility alone. For example, the reduction in family size will not appreciably affect the total demand for housing in the next decade. But the type of housing demanded will be affected. There will be an increase in the demand for apartments, condominiums, and smaller homes and a reduced demand for large homes. Similarly, the reduction in fertility, which might be expected to restrict the growth in the number of households, will not have this effect because of the rapid growth in one person households. This growth suggests that demand will continue to be strong for such items as home furnishings, small appliances, and household cleaners. Each household requires such products whether it is composed of one or several people. Finally, stability in the number of first and second born children is likely to keep the demand strong for such baby products as cribs and toys. Families often purchase these products when the first born arrives and use them for all subsequent family additions.

The changing composition of the household also is likely to increase the polarity of consumption behavior. There will be a segment who is able and willing to pay for quality. As we noted earlier, this group will be composed of husband-wife families who earn more than $16,000. There will also be a segment that demands low-priced products. This segment will be comprised of the financially limited households headed by women, who typically earn less than $8,000. The polarity of these segments has already been felt in the marketplace. There is now substantial demand for products at both ends of the price spectrum. While there is still significant demand for $25 Timex watches, impressive demand has also emerged for $1,500 Cartier watches. Although demand for low priced subcompact cars has grown in the past few years, so has the demand for such luxury cars as the Cadillac Seville and Mercedes Benz. The polarity in family income is manifested in a polarity in purchase behavior.

WOMEN IN THE WORK FORCE

In the period since World War II, there has been a dramatic increase in women's participation in the labor force. Women currently account for more than forty percent of the labor force, compared to thirty percent after World War II. This trend seems to be only marginally affected by marriage or the establishment of families. Over half of the married women aged twenty to forty-four are employed. One-third of all women with children under three, and more than fifty percent of those with children between six and seventeen are in the labor force.

More significant than the growing incidence of women in the labor force is the substantial increase in the number of women in professional positions. Wives who work full time account for about forty percent of the family's income. And, in over half of the families with incomes greater than $25,000, there are husband-wife incomes. Further, these trends are not limited to the United States (Douglas, 1976).

The trend for women to work after marriage and the birth of children has several ramifications for consumption. It stimulates demand for convenience items such as quick-prepared foods and microwave ovens. It affects the distribution of products. Fast food chains, which have traditionally been located in the suburbs, are now locating in shopping malls and the center city. It has been found that women frequent fast-food restaurants in conjunction with other activities. Quality hosiery, which was traditionally sold in department stores and specialty shops, is now being sold at drugstores and supermarkets. The inroads made by the latter outlets indicate the rewards for catering to working women's needs.

The high incidence of women in the work force also affects promotional strategy. Homemakers are not as readily reached by daytime television advertising as they were ten years ago. Magazines, especially those that have broadened their homemaker scope, have become effective vehicles for reaching working women.

Personal selling has also undergone considerable change. For example, Avon historically relied on homemakers to serve as door-to-door salespeople for their line of cosmetics. Today, these homemakers are in the fulltime work force. Thus, the pool of salespeople available to Avon is limited, as is the number of women consumers for Avon products who might be found at home during the day.

MOBILITY AND MIGRATION

The American population is highly mobile. About twenty-five percent of Americans live outside the state in which they were born. During the course of a year, about seventeen percent of Americans change residences. About two-thirds of these are to new residences in the same county. The remainder are divided almost equally between moves to different counties in the same state and moves to different states. The most mobile Americans are between eighteen and thirty-four years of age and are college-educated.

Historically, Americans have migrated to the northeastern and north central states. Recent migration trends, however, diverge from historical patterns (Taeuber, 1979). Since 1970 people have been moving south and west (Figure 10.4). In effect, people are moving out of the "Frost Belt" and into the "Sun Belt." In the early 1970s the West attracted the majority of migrants, whereas more recently there has been a greater rate of migration to southern states. Much of this migration has come from the northeastern quadrant of the country. In fact, the migration has been so great in New York, Pennsylvania, Rhode Island, and the District of Columbia that total population has declined in these areas. Such population declines are infrequent because migration out of a state is usually offset by the fact that more people are born each year than die. The fact that four areas have experienced a net population decline underscores the extent of migration from these areas.

Changes have also occurred in Americans' choice between metropolitan and nonmetropolitan areas. During the early 1970s there was a substantial migration out of the eight largest cities in the United States (Table 10.4). With the emergence of a movement back to nature in the early 1970s, it was thought that nonmetropolitan areas would be the main beneficiaries of this out-migration. But this prediction has failed to materialize. Nonmetropolitan areas experienced substantial growth only in 1970 and 1971. Since then, growth has slowed. In major metropolitan areas, the rate of out-migration has slowed.

Figure 10.4. Migration between 1970–1977

Migration

Since 1970, Americans have been moving South and West.

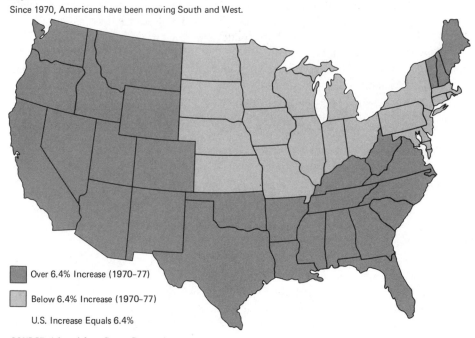

Over 6.4% Increase (1970–77)

Below 6.4% Increase (1970–77)

U.S. Increase Equals 6.4%

SOURCE: Adapted from Census Bureau data.

Chicago, for example, has reduced average annual out-migration from a rate of 3.51 percent in 1970–73 to 2.75 in 1976–77. Thus, the population of cities appears to have entered a period of stability.

The trends in mobility and migration have important implications for consumption behavior. Americans' frequent relocation enhances the demand for home furnishings. The migration to the sun belt changes the mix of goods that are required. Specifically, there will be greater demand for such products as outdoor furniture and lightweight clothing, and less demand for products such as snow tires and winter coats. The migration to the less densely populated southern and western regions will result in more consumer travel. This is because the opportunities for leisure activity are typically located much closer to where people live in the Northeast than in other parts of the country. More subtle changes in demand are expected if migrants assume the consumption habits of the region to which they move. For example, the migration from the Northeast to the Southwest will cause greater consumption of brandy, bourbon, black coffee, and milk, but less consumption of blended whiskey, soft drinks, and coffee with cream and sweeteners. Finally, the migration patterns suggest that the South will emerge as a more important market area for a variety of products than it was in the 1970s.

TABLE 10.4. Average Annual Migration Rates of Selected Cities

City	1970–73	1973–75	1975–76	1976–77
New York City	−2.85%	−2.92%	−2.47%	−2.72%
Chicago	−3.51	−3.20	−2.62	−2.75
Los Angeles	−2.76	−2.49	−2.29	−2.43
Philadelphia	−2.53	−2.06	−1.59	−1.93
Houston	−0.16	0.54	0.71	−0.57
Detroit	−4.05	−3.81	−4.19	−4.47
Dallas	−2.00	−1.61	−1.70	−0.94
Baltimore	−2.14	−2.38	−2.12	−2.05
San Diego	1.88	1.02	0.17	−0.31
San Antonio	0.19	−0.62	−0.66	−0.52
Washington, D.C.	−3.02	−3.80	−2.65	−3.24
Phoenix	2.18	0.75	−0.21	0.77
San Francisco	−3.20	−2.90	−2.30	−3.04
Cleveland	−4.26	−3.42	−3.05	−3.06
Boston	−3.11	−3.57	−3.84	−4.09
New Orleans	−2.75	−2.49	−1.29	−1.54
San Jose	1.87	2.00	0.60	0.59
Jacksonville	0.31	0.62	−0.64	−0.90
St. Louis	−4.90	−3.54	−2.93	−2.75
Seattle	−3.59	−1.30	−1.59	−1.94
Denver	−0.72	−2.81	−2.03	−1.51
Kansas City, Missouri	−2.06	−2.20	−2.42	−1.81
Pittsburgh	−2.78	−2.28	−1.56	−1.90
Atlanta	−4.23	−3.81	−3.55	−2.91
Cincinnati	−2.75	−2.15	−2.16	−2.04

EDUCATION, INCOME, AND OCCUPATION

An individual's education, income, and occupation are often combined to represent his or her social class. We shall examine the effect of social class on consumption in the next chapter. Here the trend for the components of social class are assessed individually.

Over the past several decades the American population has become better educated. By 1985, about thirty-one percent of the population (forty-four million people) over twenty-five years of age will have attended or graduated from college. This represents an increase from 1970, when twenty-one percent of the population (or twenty-three million people) had at least some college experience. Despite this trend toward greater education, thirty percent of the 1985 population will not have completed high school.

In the decade of the eighties, there will also be a continued growth of white collar occupations. By 1985, about fifty-three percent of the population is expected to be employed in professional, managerial, clerical, sales and other white-collar occupations. This represents an increase of ten million white-collar workers from 1975. The percentage of workers involved in blue-collar occupations will be reduced slightly and there will be a significant decline in the percentage of people engaged in farm work.

Finally, in the 1980s there will be a larger affluent segment than ever before (Figure 10.5). More than one-third of the population will earn $15,000 or more (based on 1973 dollars) by 1985. The majority of affluent people will be twenty-five to fifty-four years of age with college and postgraduate degrees, and with professional, managerial, or sales jobs. Despite this affluence, there will be a substantial percentage of the population living on incomes under $10,000. This group will be composed of elderly adults, racial minorities, and households with female heads-of-family.

The trends in education, occupation, and income are related to the population trends examined earlier. As education increases, the quality of jobs available improves and thus family income increases. Women's opportunity cost of having children becomes high. Fertility is reduced and women enter the workforce. Even women who have children limit the number they have and reenter the workforce. Higher education often provides an opportunity to learn about different geographical areas of the country and, therefore, enhances mobility.

The trends in education, occupation, and income have several implications for marketing strategy. One is that the marketplace of the 1980s will be highly polarized. There will be a segment of poorly educated and low income individuals whose purchases will be guided primarily by price considerations. There will also be a substantial group of college educated white collar workers with incomes over $15,000 (based on 1973 dollars). These individuals will constitute a strong market for high quality branded products. They will be reached most efficiently by upscale magazines and late fringe (after the late news) television.

The emergence of a substantial well-educated, high income, white collar group will also mean greater diversity in product demand. As we shall see in Chapter Eleven, people

Figure 10.5. Families by Income Class (1973 dollars).

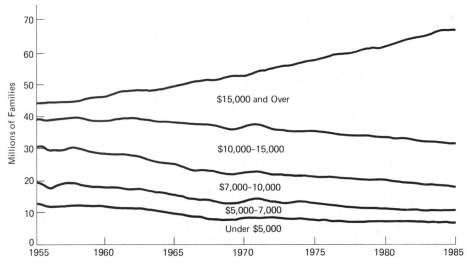

SOURCE: Adapted from Census Bureau data.

with these characteristics highly value individuality. This orientation implies that to meet demand, product proliferation will be required. And as products proliferate, the market share of a particular brand is likely to fall. For many product categories such as shampoos and beer, one can expect successful new brand entrants to achieve market shares on the order of two or three percent, rather than the ten or fifteen percent market shares customary a decade ago.

SUMMARY AND CONCLUSIONS

The analysis of population trends suggests that the 1980s will be characterized by slowed population growth and the presence of diverse consumer segments. For consumer products, people aged twenty-five to forty-four will be important targets, as will those over sixty-five. Single person households will constitute an important segment, as will three and four person households. Those earning over $15,000 will be substantial targets, as will people earning less than $10,000. Working women will require special consideration, as will homemakers. College-educated people will comprise about one-third of the population, as will people with less than a high school education. The northeastern and central states will be major markets, but so will the South and West.

The diversity of segments has major implications for product, distribution, price, and promotion strategy.[2] It suggests that firms will have to produce multiple products and services to meet the unique desires of each segment. Thus, the number of brands of a particular product will proliferate and the market share of each brand is likely to be small. We have already witnessed this outcome in several industries. In the cigarette industry, for example, the heavily promoted Barclay brand has made what are considered significant inroads, yet it has around a one percent share. Similarly, a flood of hair shampoos for every kind of hair has been introduced, and each brand typically has achieved only a two percent share of market.

The proliferation of brands to meet diverse consumer segments has distribution implications. As the number of brands increases more shelf space is required to keep each brand in stock. As a result, retail outlets such as supermarkets have become much larger. Whereas supermarkets stocked about 8,000 items ten years ago and about 10,000 items five years ago, they now stock more than 12,000 items. An increase in the number of brands also means increasing inventory costs. This has created a risk that retailers have been reluctant to bear. Manufacturers who are willing to bear inventory costs have made significant inroads in retail outlets. For example, L'eggs hosiery gained entry into drugstores and supermarkets in large measure because of their willingness to sell on consignment.

Diversity in consumer segments also has implications for pricing strategy. It suggests polarity in pricing. Some consumers will gravitate to low-priced products with acceptable performance characteristics, while others will pay a high price for superior product

---

[2] This analysis was suggested by M. Lawrence Light, Batten, Barton, Durstine and Osborne. Personal communication, November 1978.

performance. This outcome will emerge, in part, to attract low-income families who primarily use a low price strategy and upper income families who primarily use high quality as the criterion for purchase. In part, too, polarity pricing will cater to upper income families using a low price strategy in purchasing some products so that they can use a high quality strategy in purchasing others. Families who are purchasers of low priced generic brands may also be purchasers of expensive Cartier watches. In effect, this trend will squeeze out moderately priced products.

Finally, the population trends will affect promotional strategy. The diversity of consumers will make network television advertising less popular than it was in the 1970s. The strategist attempting to reach a narrow segment of the population will find network television wasteful, because it reaches many nontarget consumers. Further, the emergence of a substantial college educated white-collar segment will increase the popularity of print media, in particular upscale magazines.

QUESTIONS

1. What are the implications of the fertility trends for universities in the 1980s; high schools in the 1980s; Upjohn, manufacturer of contraceptives; and Mattel, producer of children's toys?

2. What are the implications of trends concerning women in the labor force and household competition on marketing by Avon, a door-to-door cosmetic marketing firm; the demand for low price grocery products; and the demand for high quality restaurants?

3. What implications do migration trends have on Sears' marketing strategy?

4. What impact do the current marriage and fertility trends have on housing developer strategies?

5. Demand for many products will not decrease by as much as one would predict on the basis of fertility rates. Explain.

6. What effect will the trend toward a better educated population have on the effectiveness of television advertising?

7. On the basis of your analysis of United States population trends, do you feel market segmentation will be a more or less important strategy in the 1980s than it was in the 1970s? Defend your position.

8. Our analysis of population trends indicates that there will be many women over sixty-five living in one person households. There will also be a large percentage of households with young women who work. What business opportunities do these observations suggest?

Chapter 11

The Impact of Groups on Consumer Behavior

Our analysis of how consumers make decisions has proceeded from the perspective of a single individual. By assuming this perspective, we are able to describe how people acquire, organize, and use information to make decisions. Incoming information, as well as thoughts previously stored in memory are abstracted and aggregated to determine one's choice. The specific thoughts activated in response to incoming information are determined by individual differences in demography and personality.

Although this description is useful in explaining and predicting consumers' behavior, it does not provide a detailed account of the factors influencing choice. Specifically, it does not consider the role of group influences in decision making. In this chapter, two types of group influences are considered. One is social stratification. Social strata are composed of people with similar demographic profiles who have similar thoughts about objects of consumption. Understanding the thoughts held by different strata in our society allows us to anticipate the kinds of consumption activities in which they are likely to engage. The other group influence is the family. By describing the consumption role of husbands, wives, and children we shall have a more complete view of how individuals' evaluations, preferences, and choices evolve.

SOCIAL STRATIFICATION[1]

Thelma is a thirty-five-year-old wife of a plumber. She spends considerable time cooking for her husband and children, so she enjoys having the latest kitchen appliances. She likes to shop at places where she is known. She sticks to brands she has used before. When she gets a long-distance call her first thought is that some relative has died. When asked about the use of sex to sell toothpaste Thelma says, "The good Lord gave us teeth to chew with not to have sex with." (Bernstein, 1978).

Mary is married to a lawyer. She enjoys preparing food for dinner parties. She likes to shop at places she has not been before and to try new things. On an impulse she will call a college friend who has moved to another city. Mary will try a toothpaste that promises to make her more attractive.

These profiles are useful in illustrating several important features of the social stratification concept. Individuals can be classified hierarchically in groups reflecting their position in society. Their demographic characteristics are helpful for this purpose. Thelma represents a lower class stratum or social class, in part, because she is married to a person whose occupation is viewed as being of relatively low status. Mary belongs to a more upscale stratum, in part, by virtue of her husband's occupation as a lawyer.

Although demography helps us to classify people in terms of social class, it does not tell the whole story. Occupation and income *per se* cannot account for the consumption behaviors typically associated with each social stratum. What is needed is an understanding of the thoughts people in particular social classes have acquired through socialization. These thoughts reflect the kind of activity that is valued and the type of person that is to be emulated. As we shall see, the thoughts acquired about these issues differ among social classes and determine a wide range of consumption practices.

In discussing social stratification, we first consider demographic variables useful in identifying social class membership. Then we describe the thought patterns and associated consumption behaviors for three critical strata: upper middle class, lower middle class, and upper lower class. This characterization enables us to anticipate how different groups are likely to respond to marketing communications, product offerings, and other marketing instruments. The emphasis is on how various social strata differ in thoughts and actions, and not on evaluating the relative value of their respective contribution to society. In fact, our view is that each stratum makes an important, though different, contribution.

Demographic Classification of Social Class

To investigate the relationship between social class and consumption, criteria for classifying people's social class membership are needed. The criteria typically used are demographic factors such as occupation and income. These characteristics have intuitive

[1]This discussion is based in large part on discussions with Sidney J. Levy and his writings on social stratification (Levy, 1978). Also see Zaltman and Wallendorf (1979) for a detailed treatment of sociological perspectives in consumer behavior.

appeal. It seems reasonable to assume that people's jobs and financial resources represent their social position, which in turn affects their views about themselves and the objects around them. Demography also has the virtue of being practical. The statistical data necessary for demographic classification of social class membership is readily available from the census, as well as from private industry surveys. Thus potential demand from various social class groups is easily estimated. It should be noted, however, that a demographic basis for social class categorization is not without liability. Demography provides only a rough and sometimes misleading set of social class categories.

To illustrate the value and limitations of demography as a basis for identifying social class, we shall consider two of the more frequently used characteristics: occupation and income. These have sometimes been used individually as the basis for classifying social position. More often they are combined with other demographic characteristics to compose an index of social class.

Occupation. Occupation is the most frequently used demographic criterion for determining social class. Table 11.1 presents the results of a study examining the prestige or status associated with a broad spectrum of occupations. These ratings are not readily explained in terms of income or education. Scientists are rated higher in status than airline pilots, though the latter are likely to have higher incomes. A Supreme Court Justice is rated higher than a county judge, though they are likely to have similar educational backgrounds.

A more compelling way to explain these status ratings is in terms of the societal functions performed by those engaged in different occupations. In many spheres of society such as law, commerce, and physical production, three functions are typically performed: initiation or creation of knowledge, the application of such knowledge to defined problems, and the physical or manual activity involved in implementing principles (Levy, 1978). From Table 11.1 it appears that the highest status is conferred on those whose occupations entail initiating knowledge, the next most status to those whose occupations involve applying principles, and the least status to those engaging in physical or manual activity. Thus in the sphere of law, United States Supreme Court Justices have higher status than lawyers, and lawyers have higher status than policemen. Similarly in the commerce sphere, a member of a board of directors has greater status than an accountant, who in turn has greater status than a store clerk.

Our analysis of the social status associated with various occupations has several important implications. First, it suggests that whatever the sphere of societal activity, status is highest for those who initiate knowledge and least for those who physically implement it. Second, within a sphere, say commerce, an individual has status mobility. For example, in marketing, an entry level assistant brand manager who collects facts can become a brand manager who applies strategies and eventually a group product manager who initiates strategy. Third, not all spheres of societal activity are equally valued. From Table 11.1, it appears that those who initiate legal knowledge (for example, Supreme Court Justices) are conferred greater status than those engaging in the same function in the business sphere (for example, member of a board of directors). Apparently, society confers greater status to the legal sphere of activity than it does to the commercial sphere.

TABLE 11.1. Status Ratings for Various Occupations

Occupations	Scores
U.S. Supreme Court Justice	94
Physician	93
Nuclear physicist	92
Scientist	92
Government scientist	91
State governor	91
Cabinet member in federal government	90
College professor	90
U.S. representative in Congress	90
Chemist	89
Lawyer	89
Diplomat in the U.S. Foreign Service	89
Dentist	88
Architect	88
County judge	88
Psychologist	87
Minister	87
Member of the board of directors of a large corporation	87
Mayor of a large city	87
Priest	86
Head of a department in a state government	86
Civil engineer	86
Airline pilot	86
Banker	85
Biologist	85
Sociologist	83
Instructor in public schools	82
Captain in the regular army	82
Accountant for a large business	81
Public school teacher	81
Owner of a factory that employs about 100 people	80
Building contractor	80
Artist who paints pictures that are exhibited in galleries	78
Musician in a symphony orchestra	78
Author of novels	78
Economist	78
Official of international labor union	77
Railroad engineer	76
Electrician	76
County agricultural agent	76
Owner-operator of a printing shop	75
Trained machinist	75
Farm owner and operator	74
Undertaker	74
Welfare worker for a city government	74
Newspaper columnist	73
Policeman	72
Reporter on a daily newspaper	71
Radio announcer	70
Bookkeeper	70
Tenant farmer—one who owns livestock and machinery and manages the farm	69
Insurance agent	69

TABLE 11.1 *(Continued)*

Occupations	Scores
Carpenter	68
Manager of a small store in a city	67
A local official of a labor union	67
Mail carrier	66
Railroad conductor	66
Traveling salesman for a wholesale concern	66
Plumber	65
Automobile repairman	64
Playground director	63
Barber	63
Machine operator in a factory	63
Owner-operator of a lunch stand	63
Corporal in the regular army	62
Garage mechanic	62
Truck driver	59
Fisherman who owns his own boat	58
Clerk in a store	56
Milk route man	56
Streetcar motorman	56
Lumberjack	55
Restaurant cook	55
Singer in a nightclub	54
Filling station attendant	51
Dockworker	50
Railroad section hand	50
Night watchman	50
Coal miner	50
Restaurant waiter	49
Taxi driver	49
Farm hand	48
Janitor	48
Bartender	48
Clothes presser in a laundry	45
Soda fountain clerk	44
Sharecropper—one who owns no livestock or equipment and does not manage farm	42
Garbage collector	39
Street sweeper	36
Shoe shiner	34

SOURCE: Hodges, Siegel and Rossi (1966)

In the remainder of our discussion about social stratification, we shall be concerned with three social class groups. Those initiating knowledge will be referred to as upper middle class. Those applying principles will be referred to as lower middle class. And those engaging in physical activity will be designated upper lower class. Other strata such as the upper class and lower lower class will not be discussed. The upper class is thought to represent a very small proportion of the population (about three percent, McCann, 1957) and do not constitute an important market for most products. The lower lower class is substantial, comprising about twenty percent of the population, but it is not discussed here because their consumption behaviors have not been thoroughly investigated. This lack of information reflects the difficulty in querying lower lower class people and their marginal importance in the overall demand for many products and services.

Income.   Income is a second characteristic that has been used frequently to identify social class membership. Proponents of this measure contend that income yields as good or better predictions of whether or not people will buy a product than social class indices (composed by aggregating measures such as occupation, education and household possessions).[2] There is some evidence to bear out this contention. It has been found that income is equal or superior to social class indices in predicting whether people will buy such household products as toiletries and detergents, as well as whether they will purchase durables such as appliances and furniture (Myers and Mount, 1973; Myers, Stanton, and Haug, 1971). But other research indicates that social class indices are superior to income in predicting the *frequency* of purchase (Hisrich and Peters, 1974).

The implication emerging from these studies is that income is a necessary factor in making consumption decisions. Some minimal income level is required to purchase a product. But once this threshold is exceeded, the extent of consumption is associated with other factors such as occupation and household characteristics. Consistent with this view is the finding that a social class index yields better predictions than income for consumption activities such as going to an art gallery, attending a bridge club, and participating in multiple service organizations (Myers and Gutman, 1974). For these consumption activities, the minimal income requirement is surpassed by the vast majority of the population. Income is, therefore, not a factor in determining consumption.

It appears that income is a necessary but not sufficient criterion for predicting consumer behavior. Consumers' financial resources must exceed some threshold level if they are to purchase a product. Moreover, it should be recognized that the threshold income is not an absolute sum of money. Rather, the threshold income necessary for purchase depends on the income available in relation to others in the same social stratum. Individuals with more income than others in their stratum are termed *overprivileged* whereas those with less income than others in their class are termed *underprivileged*. Viewed from this perspective, one would expect privilege to predict consumption, but absolute income would not. This prediction is supported in studies of automobile purchases, where overprivileged people from various social strata were disproportionately represented in ownership of full-sized cars and underprivileged individuals overrepresented in ownership of compacts (Coleman, 1961; Peters, 1970). Absolute income does not predict consumption patterns in this case.

Apparently relative income plays an important role in consumption choices. Those with more discretionary income than others in their social class, the overprivileged, often exhibit similar consumption behaviors. Those with less discretionary income than others in their social class, the underprivileged, also make similar choices. These observations

---

[2]Social class indicies are discussed later in this chapter.

suggest that for some products social class differences do not necessarily imply different consumption patterns.

Social Class Indices. Although single variables such as occupation and income provide a starting point for identifying social class membership, indices that combine these and other demographic characteristics are thought to provide a more accurate basis for classification. The best known of these composite indices is Warner's ISC (1960). It involves four demographic characteristics, each of which is weighted for its importance in the overall index. Occupation (weighted four) and income (weighted three) have already been discussed. It should be noted, however, that Warner judged income with regard to its source (that is, inherited wealth, earned wealth, profits and fees, salary and so on) rather than with regard to amount. The two other ISC characteristics pertain to housing and are both weighted three. *House type* refers to the quality of a person's home and *dwelling area* reflects the quality of the area where the home is located.

Other indices have been developed to simplify or extend Warner's ISC. Haug (1977) included only occupation and education in her index of social position. Coleman and Neugarten (1971) developed a six factor index that included housing questions similar to Warner's as well as church affiliation, community associations, occupation, and wife's education. Coleman and Neugarten included education of the wife in their index because it correlated more highly with income and social class than did the husband's education. These indices, other variants of Warner's ISC, and Warner's original concept are the classifications of social class most frequently used in investigations pertaining to the social class-consumption relationship.

Social Class and Consumption

Interest in identifying social class groups stems from the belief that there are unique behaviors associated with social class membership. Starting at an early age, children are socialized to view themselves, others around them, and products in ways determined by their family's social class—its occupational activity, income, dwelling type and location (Levy, 1978). For example, as early as in elementary school, children's ranking of various occupations are very similar to those given by adults (Simmons and Rosenberg, 1971). These socialized views or thoughts often have a profound effect on consumption decisions made later in life. In examining the relationship between social class and consumption, we shall consider the typical thoughts associated with the three social strata mentioned earlier: upper middle, lower middle, and upper lower. The thoughts that are unique to each of these social classes are identified, and their impact on consumption behavior is examined.

Upper Middle Class. Upper middle class individuals are socialized to value individuality and achievement. These values are reflected in upper middle class consumption choices. They select careers involving the initiation of knowledge: judges, business owners, scientists, and the like. In choosing spouses, they are attracted to people who are viewed as good companions—people who can reinforce their individuality and facilitate their achievement. As parents, upper middle class individuals want their children to be bright, active, and precocious. These characteristics serve as the basis for later achievement and individuality. They buy products for their children that develop and reinforce these qualities.

Achievement and individuality also guide the upper middle classes' consumption of economic goods and advertising communications. Upscale women shop more frequently and in a broader variety of stores than their downscale counterparts (Rich and Jain, 1968). They prefer stores with exciting displays. Although they are generally skeptical of advertising, they can be appealed to by themes that have a unique tone. Presumably these dispositions reflect the upper middle class desire for individuality. It should be noted, however, than when shopping for products perceived to involve a high degree of social risk (for example, men's dress shirts, handbags, wall decorations), upper middle class women resist such desires by purchasing at more conventional outlets such as department stores and speciality stores (Prasad, 1976).

Upper middle class men's consumption choices also reflect the desire to express individuality. They are more likely than lower status men to be self-expressive by using cologne and wearing highly styled underwear (Levy, 1978). These behaviors are fostered by the belief that masculinity means cleanliness and good grooming, a belief that is quite consistent with their achievement orientation.

Lower Middle Class. Lower middle class individuals are guided by morality and respectability. In light of these values, they tend to take a pragmatic view. In choosing jobs they exhibit a preference for jobs that allow them to apply principles as a means of achieving respectability. They are lawyers, accountants, and engineers. In choosing a spouse, they look for someone who is efficient at applying procedures, whether in the home or at work. In raising children, they attempt to instill control and conformity, teaching their children to be orderly, neat, and polite (Levy, 1978). In essence, this prepares children from lower middle class families to be oriented toward achieving respectability.

The lower middle classes' product choices reflect their orderliness and moral orientation. In contrast to upper middle class individuals, who like to experiment in furnishing their homes, lower middle class people prefer coordinated furniture groupings. They want their homes to be organized, neat, and pretty. To illustrate these differences in social class orientation, consider the ads for David & Dash (Figure 11.1) and Henredon (Figure 11.2). The David & Dash ad is likely to appeal primarily to lower middle class individuals. The illustration emphasizes coordination and neatness. In contrast, the Henredon ad is likely to appeal to upper middle class members. The illustration depicts both elegance and distinctiveness.

Lower middle class men tend to satisfy their "macho" urges in ways that conform to this sense of morality. They are customers for phallic-shaped grooming products. They can be appealed to by advertising such as getting "stroked" with Bic's razor blade.

Upper Lower Class. Members of the upper lower class share the belief that luck has much to do with the events occurring in their lives. They have a physical orientation,

Figure 11.1. David & Dash Ad

SOURCE: From the Design Studios of David & Dash, Miami, FL.

Figure 11.2. Henredon Ad

SOURCE: Henredon.

believing that it is important to be adept at manual tasks. They take jobs that involve the use of manual skills, such as construction, plumbing, and carpentry. Their choice of spouse is guided, in part, by his or her ability to accomplish physical tasks. For women, men who are competent at some physical task such as police work, truck driving, or one of the trades are viewed as attractive mates. Men are usually drawn to women who are proficient at cooking, cleaning, and raising children.

The physical orientation of the upper lower class accounts for their product purchases. Upper lower class expenditures are substantial for kitchen and other appliances that facilitate the performance of the cooking and cleaning tasks. In contrast, expenditures tend to be small for living room and bedroom furniture. Unlike lower middle class people, the upper lower class family often has pieces of furniture that are uncoordinated.

The belief that luck determines outcomes, accounts for many upper lower class consumption behaviors. They shop at places where they are known. They seek immediate gratification of their needs, so as to take advantage of their luck before it turns bad. This orientation is reflected in short planning horizons for purchases. Upper lower class members buy for today's event, whereas upscale people typically develop more extended planning horizons.

Summary and Conclusions

Social class membership has profound implications for consumer behavior. Various social strata have unique orientations that guide their choice of spouse, occupation, products, and other objects. Upper middle class members stress achievement and value individuality. Lower middle class individuals emphasize morality and an orderly life. Upper lower class people depend on luck and gravitate to manual/physical activities.

This characterization of social strata contributes to our understanding of consumer information processing. It implies that from an early age, children are socialized to accept their family's views about social objects. These views are stored as thoughts in memory. They affect an individual's educational and occupational aspirations, the choice of spouse, the rearing of children and product choices.

The above description suggests how social class affects the development of personality, discussed in Chapter Nine. A family's social class determines the kinds of behavior a child is taught to value. This teaching instills the family's social class orientation in the child. For example, upper middle class parents are likely to reward a child with praise for initiating appropriate toilet training behavior. Such a parental response instills a desire to be productive and creative—an orientation consistent with upper middle class membership. In contrast, lower middle class parents are likely to emphasize neatness and control in teaching toilet training, instilling a sense of orderliness in their children.

Finally, our characterization of social strata helps to explain the diverse product demands we described in Chapter Ten. As the population becomes better educated, people gravitate to more upscale occupations.[3] In performing these jobs they are socialized to

---

[3]See Sorensen (1975) for a detailed discussion of the structure of intergenerational mobility.

acquire the upscale orientation of achievement and individuality. Individuality, in turn, stimulates the consumption of a diverse array of products. Hence, the emergence of brands that appeal to a very limited portion of the population, and the proliferation of brands that accomodate various small segments appears to have its roots in the migration to more upscale strata.

FAMILY DECISION MAKING

In describing the relationship between social class and consumption, it was noted that the roles and behaviors of various family members depended heavily on class membership. We shall now consider in greater detail the influence of individuals' families on their consumption behaviors.

It seems apparent that consumers' decision making is influenced by the opinions and behavior of their families. A housewife's choice of food products and brands is guided, in part, by the likes and dislikes of other family members. A husband's choice of automobile is frequently influenced by the needs and preferences of his wife and children. The choice of personal use products such as clothing and cosmetics is affected by the anticipated reactions from family members.

The influence of family members on individuals' consumption decisions was represented in terms of social normative beliefs in Chapter Eight. As you will recall, social normative beliefs refer to consumers' perceptions of what significant others (such as family members) want them to do in a specific situation. Here we shall extend this discussion by examining the family as a decision-making unit. This entails identifying the roles that are performed in making purchase decisions, and describing how these roles are divided among the various family members. It also entails examining how a family's stage in the life cycle influences its purchase decisions.

Family Consumption Roles

The family acts as a buying center in making consumption decisions.[4] A buying center performs the roles required for market transactions. These roles are shown in Figure 11.3. The decision to purchase a product and the selection of a brand is made by a *decider*. The choices made by a decider are affected by an *influencer*, who has some stake or expertise regarding the purchase in question. The decider may also be influenced by a *gatekeeper*, who is typically the family financial officer. Once the decider has chosen an alternative, its purchase is made by a *buyer* and consumed by a *user*.

Although the five buying center roles identified in Figure 11.3 are performed whenever a purchase is made, the individuals performing each role may vary from purchase

---

[4]See Webster and Wind (1972) for a discussion of the buying center concept.

Figure 11.3. The Buying Center

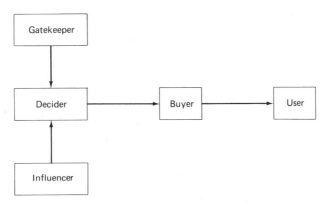

to purchase and family to family. For example, in the purchase of household cleaning products, a single person may perform all buying center roles. In contrast, in purchasing ready-to-eat cereal, the mother may act as the decider and buyer, her children as influencers and users, and her husband as the gatekeeper.

The value of treating the family as a buying center is illustrated by describing what happens when it is not. For example, several years ago a product called *Koogle* was introduced. Koogle was a peanut butter-like product, but it was sweeter than peanut butter, more expensive, and came in several flavors (banana, chocolate, vanilla). The brand was positioned as a snack and targeted to children. Advertising featured a cartoon character named Barney Koogle. Children reacted positively to Koogle, and stimulated considerable trial by influencing their mothers to purchase it. Repeat purchase, however, was very disappointing. Apparently mothers were unwilling to repurchase Koogle because it was more expensive than peanut butter and because children did not seem to have a strong preference for Koogle in relation to peanut butter. To overcome this resistance, a second advertising campaign was developed and aimed at mothers. It addressed mothers' resistance to the brand directly ("Don't say no, say Koogle") and stressed the benefits of the brand. This campaign was not effective, and Koogle was eventually withdrawn from the market.

The Koogle vignette suggests the value of the buying center concept. Initially, Koogle targeted only the product user and influencer in promoting the brand. This approach failed to consider the mother who served as the decider, gatekeeper, and buyer. By the time Koogle management decided to target mothers, they had decided not to repurchase the brand. A consideration of buying center roles would have made it evident at the outset that both children and mothers had to be informed about Koogle when it was introduced. Although this realization would not have necessarily guaranteed the success of Koogle, it would have alerted management sooner to the importance of overcoming mothers' resistance.

Division of Buying Roles

Because of the importance of knowing the buying center roles assumed by various family members in order to develop marketing strategy, considerable research has addressed this issue. Inquiry has focused primarily on the roles of husbands and wives in the selection of products. The research involves asking husbands or wives or both to indicate the influence they exert in the decision to purchase various products. Responses are categorized according to whether the wife is the dominant influence, the husband is the dominant influence, the husband and wife share the influence (called syncratic), or either the husband or wife is completely autonomous in making a consumption decision (called autonomic).

Investigations using this approach have been successful in classifying husband and wife roles in making decisions. For example, Woodside (1972) found that wives were the dominant influence when the purchase involved products used in the home, especially if they were related to traditional women's roles. Thus, the choice of detergents and appliances would be wife-dominated. In contrast, purchase decisions about products used outside the home, and particularly mechanically complex products, (such as lawnmowers) were typically husband-dominated. Other investigations have indicated that the choice of housing, schools, and vacations are typically syncratic decisions.

The role of husbands and wives in decision making depends not only on the type of product they are thinking about purchasing, but also the stage in the decision process. Hempel (1974), for example, reported that husbands are usually the ones to initiate the home buying process. Once this process is initiated, however, the wife identifies and screens the choice alternatives. She is primarily responsible for selecting the neighborhood and style of the house. The husband then assumes responsibility for deciding about the price, mortgage, and timing of the purchase. Similarly, in the purchase of automobiles, the husband typically has more influence in the decision about when to buy a car, where to buy it, how much to spend, and what make to buy (Davis, 1970). Model and color decisions appear to be made jointly.

The analysis of husband-wife roles in decision making is useful in that it underscores the fact that the key members of the buying center differ depending on the product and the decision-making stage. But it goes little beyond establishing this fact. Current research has not addressed why the husband or wife dominates. As a result, there is no formal approach that allows the manager to anticipate who will perform various buying center roles.

The value of research pertaining to husbands' and wives' roles is also questionable because of the choice of informants. Studies typically have used wives as informants. The problem with this approach is that wives' perceptions of decision-making influence may not be veridical. Studies in which both husbands and wives are respondents indicate that there is not necessarily a consensus in their perceptions of influence (Davis, 1976). This does not imply that wives' perceptions are wrong, but it does suggest that multiple informants are required to ascertain influence. Moreover it implies that in studies using single informants, we cannot be confident about what roles husbands and wives play.

Buying center participation is not confined to husbands and wives. Children, too, play an important role in influencing product choice. Younger children make frequent requests for a variety of different products. As Table 11.2 shows they often attempt to influence the purchase of breakfast cereal, snack foods, candy, and soft drinks. Older children make fewer requests of their parents (Table 11.2). Nevertheless, they have considerable influence on their parents' consumption choices by using *passive dictation* (Reynolds and Wells, 1977). This entails refusing to consume products that they do not like. Frequently passive dictation is effective in causing parents to adjust their purchases so as to accommodate their children.

Table 11.2 also suggests that mothers are selective in their choice of the requests to which they will yield. They frequently accommodate their children's request for food products that will be used primarily by their children. These items include products such as breakfast cereal, snack food, candy, and soft drinks. Children's requests for inexpensive products such as toys also are accommodated frequently. Mothers are less yielding to children's requests for products that will be used by the entire family (for example, bread, shampoo) or that are used by children but are expensive (for example, bicycle, camera).

The view emerging from our analysis is that consumption choices are frequently the product of joint decision making. Although the housewife may be the primary purchaser for most products and services, her selections are influenced by her husband and children. Family influence involves not only overt requests for a particular brand, but also passive dictation of consumption choices.

One way for the purchaser to accommodate the brand requests of family members is to purchase multiple brands. This strategy is used frequently. The result manifests itself as frequent brand switching. For example, the average American family purchases about ten different ready-to-eat cereals annually. Although this reflects the fact that consumers are not loyal to a particular brand, it probably overstates disloyalty. Each family member may have favorite brands to which they are loyal. But because family members prefer different brands, it appears as though the household engages in frequent brand switching.

The Family Life Cycle

The structure of a family changes over time. The bachelor marries and has children; the children grow up and leave home; and the husband and wife retire. Each of these changes in family structure affect its consumption decisions. We shall trace the family through its life cycle, identifying some of the important effects of life cycle stage on consumption practices.[5]

The *bachelor* stage begins when a single man or woman establishes a household apart from his or her parents. It includes individuals who are employed as well as college students. Consumers at this stage typically have relatively low incomes. But because they have few financial responsibilities, much of their income is available for discretionary spending. Bachelors tend to spend a substantial amount on automobiles and basic home furnishings such as kitchen equipment and furniture. They also spend substantial amounts

[5]This analysis is based on research reported by Reynolds and Wells (1977) and Wells and Gubar (1966).

TABLE 11.2. Frequency of Children's Attempts To Influence Purchases and Percentage of Mothers "Usually" Yielding

Product	Frequency of requests[a]				Percentage of yielding			
	5–7 years	8–10 years	11–12 years	Total[b]	5–7 years	8–10 years	11–12 years	Total[b]
Relevant foods								
Breakfast cereal	1.26	1.59	1.59	1.59	88	91	83	87
Snack foods	1.71	2.00	1.71	1.80	52	62	77	63
Candy	1.60	2.09	2.17	1.93	40	28	57	42
Soft drinks	2.00	2.03	2.00	2.01	38	47	54	46
Jello	2.54	2.94	2.97	2.80	40	41	26	36
Overall mean	1.82	2.13	2.16	2.03				
Overall percentage					51.6	53.8	59.4	54.8
Less relevant foods								
Bread	3.12	2.91	3.43	3.16	14	28	17	19
Coffee	3.93	3.91	3.97	3.94	2	0	0	1
Pet food	3.29	3.59	3.24	3.36	7	3	11	7
Overall mean	3.45	3.47	3.49	3.49				
Overall percentage					7.6	10.3	9.3	9.0
Durables, for child's use								
Game, toy	1.24	1.63	2.17	1.65	57	59	46	54
Clothing	2.76	2.47	2.29	2.52	21	34	57	37
Bicycle	2.48	2.59	2.77	2.61	7	9	9	8
Hot wheels	2.43	2.41	3.20	2.67	29	19	17	22
Record album	3.36	2.63	2.23	2.78	12	16	46	24
Camera	3.91	3.75	3.71	3.80	2	3	0	2
Overall mean	2.70	2.58	2.73	2.67				
Overall percentage					25.6	28.0	35.0	29.4
Notions, toiletries								
Toothpaste	2.29	2.31	2.60	2.39	36	44	40	39
Bath soap	3.10	2.97	3.46	3.17	9	9	9	9
Shampoo	3.48	3.31	3.03	3.28	17	6	23	16
Aspirin	3.64	3.78	3.97	3.79	5	6	0	4
Overall mean	3.13	3.09	3.26	3.16				
Overall percentage					16.8	16.3	18.0	17.0
Other products								
Automobile	3.55	3.66	3.51	3.57	2	0	0	12
Gasoline brand	3.64	3.63	3.83	3.70	2	0	3	2
Laundry soap	3.69	3.75	3.71	3.72	2	0	3	2
Household cleaner	3.71	3.84	3.74	3.76	2	3	0	2
Overall mean	3.65	3.72	3.70	3.69				
Overall percentage					2.0	.75	1.50	1.75

[a] On a scale from 1 = Often to 4 = Never.

[b] 5–7 years, $n = 43$; 8–10 years, $n = 32$; 11–12 years, $n = 34$; $n = 109$.

SOURCE: Ward and Wackman, 1972.

of money on clothing, particularly high fashion apparel. They allocate a considerable portion of their incomes to vacations and other leisure time pursuits.

Once individuals marry, they enter the second stage of the family life cycle, *newly married couples*. As a couple they are typically better off financially than they were as bachelors (or are likely to be in the near future) because both the husband and wife are employed. Like bachelors, they are heavy spenders on cars and vacations. Newlyweds also exhibit the highest purchase rate of any group for durables such as refrigerators, stoves, and furniture.

The third stage, known as *Full Nest I*, includes families whose youngest child is under six. These families typically have very limited discretionary income. Home purchases are at a peak during this stage and considerable resources are spent for durables such as washers, dryers, and televisions, as well as for children's food and toys. Frequently these purchases are made without the benefit of the wife's income. Full Nest I families thus tend to feel dissatisfied with their financial positions and the amount of money they have saved.

The financial situation improves for families in *Full Nest II*, where the youngest child is six or older. The family again has two wage earners. This group constitutes an important market for cleaning products as well as bicycles, pianos, and music lessons.

The family's financial position improves still further in *Empty Nest I* when all children have left home. During this stage of the life cycle, couples spend heavily on home improvements and travel. They are a particularly important market for luxury items such as expensive jewelry, automobiles, and furniture.

The final stage, *Empty Nest II*, is one in which there are no children living at home and the family head is retired. People at this stage experience a significant decline in income. They may sell their home and rent an apartment. They are likely to spend their discretionary income on travel as well as medical products and services.

The family life cycle concept suggests that a consumer's age is not sufficient to predict consumption. One must also consider the composition of the family. The presence of children and children's ages have a significant effect on consumption. Thus a thirty year-old in Full Nest I is likely to exhibit consumption behaviors that are more similar to a forty year old in Full Nest I than to a thirty year old in the bachelor stage.

The life cycle concept explains, at least in part, why some families are overprivileged in relation to other social class members, while others are underprivileged. At certain stages of the life cycle, such as Empty Nest I, some families in all social classes are overprivileged in that they have considerable discretionary incomes. Thus consumption patterns may be similar across classes. Cross class similarity in consumption is also likely for underprivileged families such as those in Full Nest II. These observations underscore the fact that all consumption patterns are not unique to particular social classes. A common culture, stage in the life cycle and other factors induce some cross class purchase similarities.

SUMMARY

In this chapter, the influence of two types of group membership on consumers' behavior was examined. Groups belonging to different social strata can be classified in demographic terms such as occupation and income. But a deep understanding of social class differences requires a knowledge of the thoughts each class has acquired via socialization. The observation that upper middle class members value individuality and achievement, that lower middle class members value morality and that upper lower class individuals rely on luck has implications for decisions ranging from choice of a spouse to product consumption.

A second type of group membership that affects consumption is the family. Members of a family assume one or more buying center roles, acting as a gatekeeper, influencer, decider, purchaser, or user. The buying center roles assumed by various family members depends upon the type of product and the stage in the purchase decision. A family's stage in the life cycle is an important determinant of the types of products they are likely to demand.

The description of social class and family influences on consumption behavior underscores the fact that individual decision making is strongly affected by group membership. The thoughts consumers activate in the process of making purchase choices are affected by their family and social class membership.

QUESTIONS

1. In Table 11.1 scientists are rated as having greater occupational prestige than engineers who, in turn, have greater prestige than machinists. Explain the reasons for these ratings.

2. What accounts for the fact that United States Supreme Court Justices have greater occupational prestige than members of the board of directors of a large corporation, and that lawyers have greater occupational prestige than accountants?

3. An analysis of the demand for microwave ovens reveals that disproportionate sales are made to families of professionals (lawyers, accountants) earning $40,000 or more and skilled tradespeople (plumbers, electricians) earning $25,000 to $30,000. How do you account for this pattern of response?

4. Explain the fact that a wife's education is a better predictor of family income and social class than a husband's education.

5. Identify the social class most likely to respond favorably to the following marketing programs. Choose among the upper middle, lower middle, and upper lower classes and support your choice.
    a. A game that teaches children the value of being organized
    b. A game that promotes creative solutions to problems
    c. A State lottery where there are instant winners
    d. A coordinated living room suite
    e. Coordinated jogging outfits
    f. Multi-colored men's brief underwear

6. Explain why consumers are exhibiting greater diversity than ever before in their choice of brands.

7. What buying center role is each family member likely to assume for the following purchases: an automobile; a snack; salt; and a home.

8. What is meant by "passive dictation?" What role does a passive dictator play in the buying center?

9. What conclusion can be derived from the discussion of relative income and life cycle stage about absolute income and chronological age as predictors of consumers' behavior?

Part V

The discussion so far has dealt with how consumers acquire, organize, and utilize information to make decisions as well as with how individuals and groups differ in processing information. The emphasis has been on understanding why consumers behave as they do. In this part of the book, the emphasis shifts. The focus now is on using our knowledge about consumers' behavior as a basis for designing strategies to influence consumers' consumption choices.

Strategies to influence consumer behavior begin with a consideration of product strategy. In Chapter Twelve, product strategies to stimulate demand for new and existing products are discussed. Chapter Thirteen considers the issue of message strategies in terms of communication content, execution, and structure. Chapter Fourteen examines communicators and modality of communication strategies for influencing consumers' behaviors. Throughout, the information processing principles discussed earlier in the book are used as a basis for devising marketing strategy.

Influencing Consumer Decision Making

Chapter 12

Product Strategy

Product strategy is typically the starting point for developing marketing strategy. The features of the product and its package dictate, to a large extent, the price that will be charged for it, where it is distributed, and how it is promoted. Coffee-Mate, a nondairy creamer, is a top-of-the-line brand in its category. This product characteristic dictates the strategy used to market the brand. Considerable white space on the package label is used to connote quality or purity. Coffee-Mate's quality dictates a premium price in relation to other brands of nondairy creamers. Distribution is limited to outlets that sustain the quality attribute. Thus Coffee-Mate has not sought entry into discount stores, even though category demand is likely to be substantial in such outlets. Promotion emphasizes quality by comparing Coffee-Mate to milk.

In this chapter, the problem of developing effective product strategies is examined. A product is defined as a collection of attributes that affect information processing and consumption choices. This broad definition of a product implies that factors such as the price charged, the package design, and in-store presentation are integral parts of product strategy. The impact of these product features on consumers' response is considered first. Then, strategies for enhancing consumers' adoption of new products are examined. Characteristics of the product and market that affect new product demand are identified and their implications for strategy suggested.

PRODUCT CHARACTERISTICS INFLUENCING CHOICE

What is Coca-Cola? One way to describe it is a caramel-colored, sweet, carbonated beverage. But to consumers it is more than this. Coca-Cola is a mystical soft drink. In talking about Coke, consumers say things such as, "Do you know that if you put a piece of bacon in a glass of Coke, the bacon will disintegrate. And Coke is great for shining car bumpers. If it can do these things, think of all the seductive things it might do in my stomach."[1] Consumers have a different view of Pepsi-Cola. For a long time it was viewed as the economical drink. This is because it came in a much larger bottle than Coke, but was priced the same.

Despite the distinct images consumers have for Coke and Pepsi, they have difficulty distinguishing between them on the basis of physical attributes. In blind tests where the brand is not identified, most consumers cannot distinguish between Coke and Pepsi in terms of color, carbonation, or flavor. Something beyond a product's physical characteristics is involved in consumers' view of it.

The above discussion suggests that viewing products simply as physical objects is too restrictive. Consumers have beliefs about products that are not solely a function of their physical characteristics. This is particularly the case for products like cigarettes and soft drinks, where there are many similar products competing with each other making it difficult to discern actual differences. In these situations, the image fostered by the price, the package design, and the manner in which the product is distributed become part of the product. The impact of these product characteristics is considered in detail.

Price as a Product Cue

A product's price is an important characteristic affecting consumer demand.[2] Economists have devoted considerable attention to the relationship between a product's price and the quantity demanded. They have hypothesized that in order to maximize utility people will buy more as price drops. This hypothesis has been examined empirically. Characteristic of these studies, the same brand is offered at different prices in matched stores over a specified time period. At the end of the study, sales at the different price levels are compared. The typical finding is that price is inversely related to the quantity sold (see for example, Applebaum and Spears, 1950; Hawkins, 1957; Greig et al., 1958; Stout, 1969); lower prices evoke greater demand.

It is not surprising to find that consumers exhibit a tendency to purchase more of a product as its price falls. From an information processing perspective, when other things are held constant, consumers abstract lower price to infer greater value. What is noteworthy is the fact that in a substantial number of situations price is not inversely related to quantity demand. In some instances it has been observed that price does not influence demand. In others, increasing price stimulates demand and lowering price reduces it.

[1]This analysis was developed by Sidney Levy.
[2]For a detailed discussion of price as a cue, see Olson, 1977.

Failure To Use Price in Decision Making. A factor that accounts for people's failure to use price information as a basis for consumption choices is that often price information is not processed. In studies addressing this issue, it has been found that consumers often do not check price. Wells and Lo Sciuto (1966) unobtrusively monitored whether or not people checked the prices of various products before purchasing them. They reported that about twenty-five percent of shoppers checked the prices of detergent, seventeen percent checked the price of candy, and thirteen percent checked the price of cereal. And in studies where consumers were asked to indicate the price of frequently purchased items such as breakfast cereal, their estimates were often inaccurate (Gabor and Granger, 1961; Progressive Grocer, 1964a).

Clearly if consumers do not process price information, they will not use it to make choices. To increase the likelihood of price utilization, the signal strength of the price must be increased. But how is this to be achieved? One answer to this question is provided by Weber's Law. It states that people will be sensitive to price changes when those changes reach a "just noticeable difference" or JND. In the case of price, a JND is a constant fraction where the numerator is the change in price required for it to be noticed and the denominator is the original price. For example, suppose for regular ketchup originally priced at eighty cents an eight cent price change is required before it is noticed by consumers. In this case the JND is .10. According to Weber's law, a large size ketchup selling at $1.20 would require a twelve cent price change before it is noticed by consumers.

Analysis of JNDs underscores the fact that the signal strength of a price cue may be increased by increasing the magnitude of a price change from its original value. Moreover, it indicates that the higher the original price, the greater is the absolute price change needed for consumers to notice it. But there is compelling evidence that merely increasing the signal strength of the price cue is not sufficient to insure its processing and use in decision making. This evidence, which emerges from research on unit pricing, suggests that the manner in which price information is presented is an important determinant of its use.

Unit pricing refers to the practice of displaying price information in terms of some common denominator. For example, the price of soft drinks might be represented in cost per ounce, and the price of detergent in cost per pound. Unit prices are typically displayed in a supermarket directly below each brand in a product category. The intent is to overcome consumers' inability to select the most economical choice among brands of different sizes (Friedman, 1967; Grant, 1969).

Research on unit pricing indicates that such information displays are not used by the majority of consumers (see Carmen (1972), Monroe and La Placa (1972) for a review of unit pricing studies). In a study conducted by Granger and Bellson (1972), two hundred housewives were asked to participate in a simulated shopping trip for detergent. They were confronted with seven brands of detergent, each available in different sizes. These brands were ones that were typically purchased by housewives. The unit price for each brand and size was presented. It was found that lowering the unit price of a particular size of detergent increased demand for that size. For example, about twenty-five percent of the research participants selected the family size detergent when its unit price was lower than other sizes, whereas only twelve percent selected the family size when the unit price was the same as for other sizes. Similarly, thirty percent of respondents selected the regular size detergent when its unit price was lower than other sizes, whereas only seven percent chose this size when the price of different sizes was the same. Apparently no more than thirty percent of consumers used unit pricing information in making their choice.

One problem with unit price is the way information is displayed. It requires consumers to process pricing information by examining the unit price displayed under each brand in a product category. Consumers appear to be unwilling to engage in such an arduous task. When a list is posted, which ranks brands according to their unit prices (for example, dishwashing liquids ranging in price from 36 cents to 90.7 cents), consumers make more extensive use of the information (Russo, 1977; Russo, Krieser, and Miyashito, 1975).

To summarize, the price of a product may not be inversely related to demand because consumers do not process price information. The processing and use of price information may be increased by making the signal strength of the price cue stronger; that is, by increasing the magnitude of the price difference from some baseline. The way price information is displayed also affects its processing and utilization. Providing consumers with a price list comparing the cost of various choice alternatives enhances the processing and use of price information as a basis for decision making.

Cognitive Analysis of High Prices. Increasing the signal strength of price information and using easily processed price displays are likely to enhance the utilization of price information. But this does not necessarily imply that charging a high price will reduce demand. Consumers may abstract the physical cue—high price—so that it causes the retrieval of thoughts about high quality. To the extent that they desire a high quality product, they will choose the higher-priced alternative.

There is considerable support for the contention that price is used as an indicator of quality. In one study, for example, it was found that people used price to judge the quality of what they believed to be three brands of beer. The higher-priced beer was judged to be of superior quality, despite the fact that all three brands came from the same brew and batch (McConnell, 1968a, 1968b, 1968c). A similar price-quality relationship has been observed in other studies (Leavitt, 1954; Stafford and Enis, 1969). Moreover, it has been demonstrated that high price can stimulate demand. Leavitt reported that people frequently selected the higher-priced alternative of razor blades and cooking sherry.

Consumers use price as an index of quality and select a higher-priced item to the extent quality is desired. But such use of price seems to be limited to situations where consumers cannot assess quality by other means. Thus, when consumers are familiar with a brand name, it is likely to be used to assess quality rather than price (Gardner, 1971; Jacoby et al., 1971). This implies that price is likely to be an indicator of quality when a product is initially introduced and consumers have no means beyond price to assess its quality.

Cognitive Analysis of Lowered Prices. The analysis of how consumers react to a high-priced product allows us to anticipate how they would react to a product that is priced below what they would normally expect. If high price serves as a cue to enhance perceived quality, and therefore demand, it follows that a low price would have the opposite effect. Abnormally low prices should stimulate demand. But such prices would also cause people purchasing a product at the low price to discount product features (for example, quality) as the sole reason for purchase. The fact that the product is inexpensive becomes a major reason for purchase. If price is later raised, repurchase will decline. People will no longer have one of the major factors that motivated initial purchase when they are repurchasing.

In a test of the prediction that low price inhibits demand, Doob and his co-workers (1969) had supermarkets offer new private branded products including mouthwash, toothpaste, light bulbs, and aluminum foil to customers at a competitive or low introductory price. The products were either continuously sold at the competitive price or first sold at the low introductory price for nine days and, thereafter, priced competitively. The findings for mouthwash were typical of the overall results of the study. As you would expect, the sales response was greater in stores where the brand was offered at a low price than where it was offered at a competitive price (Figure 12.1). However, when the price was equalized in all stores after nine days, the originally regularly-priced mouthwash

Figure 12.1. Findings of the Doob Study for Mouthwash

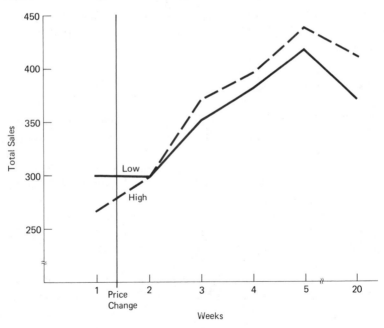

SOURCE: Doob et al., 1969.

outsold the one that was initially priced lower during the remaining weeks of the study.

Other studies provide additional support for the contention that low prices undermine repurchase of a product when the price is later raised. Dodson, Tybout, and Sternthal (1978) found that people who had loyally purchased a particular brand of flour or margarine were less loyal to that brand after they had purchased it on a cents-off the package or media coupon deal. Scott (1977) found that giving people a substantial economic incentive to gain their support for a social cause reduced their subsequent willingness to support that cause in relation to people who had not been given a substantial incentive.

Summary. The conclusion of our analysis is that only under a limited set of circumstances is price inversely related to demand. Price may have no influence on demand because this cue is not processed and utilized. In this case, increasing the signal strength of the price cue and presenting price information in a form that can be readily processed enhances its use.

Even if price information is used, price may not be inversely related to demand. When other cues to judge a product's quality are not available, price information may be abstracted and used for this purpose. To the extent that high quality is an important determinant of choice, the price-demand relationship will be positive. A negative price-demand relationship does emerge when a low price is later raised because people attribute their purchase to a low price that is no longer available. It should be noted, however, that these outcomes are likely to be observed only when a particular brand is not distinguishable from other alternatives on a basis other than price. Presumably, demand for a clearly inferior brand will not be stimulated by using a high price strategy. Nor will a low price strategy undermine the repurchase of a superior brand when price is later raised.

Product Presentation

Another set of characteristics that affect consumer information processing and choice relate to product presentation. The amount of space devoted to a product and a product's location on the shelf affect the extent to which consumers are aware of it. Product location may also influence consumer response. The use of special displays affects product awareness and may be used in evaluating a product's worth. Characteristics of the product package such as its size and composition are used to make inferences about its value. Finally, characteristics of the product itself may influence evaluation and consumer choice. Thus, strategies related to shelf space, product location, package characteristics, and the product *per se* are likely to influence consumer demand.

Shelf Space. Intuitively one might expect the amount of space devoted to a brand to be positively related to consumer demand. By increasing the space available to a brand, the signal strength of the brand is increased; the brand is more visible to consumers. In addition, as the amount of space increases, the likelihood of stockouts diminishes; more product is available for purchase. Thus it seems appropriate to devise strategies that increase the number of shelf-facings or units exposed on an aisle.

The belief that demand is related to the amount of shelf space is supported by formal research. Frank and Massy (1970) reported that in low volume retail outlets a one unit change in shelf space resulted in a three percent change in sales. In high volume stores, a unit change in shelf space resulted in a sixty percent change in sales. Curhan (1972) also found a relationship between the amount of shelf space allocated to a brand and consumers' demand for that brand. His results indicated that a five percent change in shelf space produced a one percent change in sales.

Thus, there is substantial evidence to support the contention that shelf space is related to demand.[3] This does not imply, however, that changing shelf space can always be expected to affect sales. Beyond a certain number of shelf facings, increasing the number of facings is unlikely to increase consumer awareness of a brand significantly or affect the stockout situation. This is perhaps why it has been observed that eight, twelve, and sixteen shelf-facings yielded the same sales response (Cox, 1970).

Changes in shelf facings also are not expected to affect the demand for all products. When a product or brand is one that consumers are willing to search for extensively, the number of shelf facings should have a minimal effect on sales. This accounts for the finding that the number of shelf facings did not affect the demand for Preparation H suppositories (Kotzan and Evanson, 1969). People who intended to purchase this brand sought it out regardless of its visibility.

Shelf Height. A product presentation factor that is closely related to shelf space is shelf height. Making products readily visible increases the likelihood of exposure to them and thus enhances demand. Studies conducted by *Progressive Grocer* (1964b, 1964c, 1971) indicate that for most products a "higher the better" rule applies. Eye level is best, followed by waist level and then knee level or lower. Height, however, does not affect consumer demand for heavily promoted products, where consumers will search for them regardless of the shelf height at which they are located. Finally, large, bulky, and heavy products such as twenty-five pound bags of dry dog food sell better when located on lower shelves.

Displays. Special displays are frequently used in retail stores to present product offerings. Among the more commonly used displays are end-of-aisle displays, free standing gondolas, and signs of various descriptions. From an information processing view, these displays are expected to stimulate demand because they stimulate product awareness and imply value.

Studies of the sales effect of displays indicate that they do affect sales. Merchandising felt tip pens in a wire carrousel yielded twenty percent greater sales than presenting the same product in the traditional bin or rack (West and McClure, 1969). Similarly, carton sales of cigarettes were greater when displayed in end-of-aisle racks than when stocked in regular grocery shelving (Kennedy, 1970).

Special displays not only increase the chances that consumers will see the product, they also imply that the products displayed are a special value. Apparently, consumers

---

[3]See Leone and Schultz (1980) for a detailed discussion of shelf-facing issue.

have associated special displays with economy. A more direct way to achieve this perception is by using in-store promotional signs. In one study, "as advertised" signs increased sales by one hundred twenty-four percent, and "cents-off" signs resulted in a twenty-three percent sales increase (*Progressive Grocer,* 1971). The presence of three-dimensional displays for coffee and gelatin desserts hung from supermarket ceilings increased sales of these products twelve fold.

Displays have effects beyond influencing consumer awareness and evaluation of a product. There is some evidence indicating that certain types of displays reduce pilferage. Kennedy (1970) found that pilferage (as a percent of sales) was significantly higher for cigarettes stocked on regular grocery shelves than for cigarettes located in end-aisle racks. Apparently the use of displays to increase the visibility of a product also makes stealing less appealing.

Packaging. Both the size and the composition of a product's package affect demand. In studies of package size, it has been found that larger packages stimulate sales. For example, sales of cheese were twenty percent greater for packages of up to two pounds than when package sizes were all one pound or less (Smith, Clement, and Hoofnage, 1956).

Although it appears that the size of a package affects demand, the reason for this relationship is unclear. It may be that larger packages make the product appear more substantial, thus connoting a better buy. Or the larger quantity of product per package may make the product appear more attractive because of the more substantial quantity. Or the use of a large package may attract attention and choice because of its novelty. Any or all of these factors could explain the fact that larger package sizes stimulate demand.

Package composition also affects consumer choice. In an interesting study, Brown (1958) presented freshly baked bread to consumers. The bread was wrapped in cellophane or wax paper. In paired comparisons, consumers judged the identical bread wrapped in cellophane to be fresher twice as often as when it was wrapped in wax paper. Either the transparency or the texture of the cellophane (or both) served as a cue that connoted freshness to consumers. In another study, it was found that package color influenced product evaluation (see Pinson, 1978). Consumers were asked to sample four cups of coffee. A brown, yellow, red, or blue can was placed beside each cup of coffee. After tasting each coffee, most consumers reported that the coffee from the brown can was too strong, the one from the yellow can was weak, the one from the red can was the richest, and the one from the blue can was mild. These differences in perception emerged despite the fact that all cups contained the same coffee.

Product Cues. A final set of product characteristics that may influence consumer choice is the physical features of the product itself. As will be recalled from the discussion in Chapter Seven, consumers abstract physical cues into subjective ones and use the latter to evaluate a product. A product's color, the noise it emits, and other physical cues are used to infer who the product is intended for; that is, whether it is appropriate for a man or woman, an upscale or downscale consumer, or some group with other characteristics.

For example, brown connotes a product is appropriate for men, whereas green connotes a product is appropriate for women. Purple and gold suggest a product for upscale consumers.

Physical product cues are also abstracted to assess a product's qualities. Noise is used to evaluate power, and color is used to assess flavor and freshness. For example, consumers offered an assortment of mostly red apples, partly red apples, or a combination of the two, purchased more apples when the assortment was of mostly red apples (Smith and Frye, 1964). Red connoted that apples were ripe.

In selecting physical cues to convey that a product is appropriate for a particular target it is important to choose cues that will not undermine evaluation of some performance characteristic. For example, a brown bar soap may connote its appropriateness for males. But the brown color may also cause people to view it as noncleansing. Similarly, in using a physical cue to convey some product characteristic, it is important that the cue not undermine the product's appropriateness for the target. Thus, a cigarette made with green paper might convey its freshness, but would be inappropriate if a male audience were being targeted.

Summary. Our analysis of product characteristics suggests a variety of strategies to stimulate consumer information processing and product demand. Consumers' in-store exposure to the relative price of competing brands is enhanced by listing the unit prices of these brands in order of magnitude. Product awareness can be stimulated by increasing the number of shelf facings, up to a certain number of facings; beyond this point, additional ones add little to exposure or demand. Eye level shelf height and special displays are also useful in stimulating product awareness.

Demand may also be stimulated by adapting product strategy to the way consumers organize information. A relatively high price may be used to connote quality, when other cues for assessing quality are absent. A relatively low price may stimulate demand, but undermine repeat purchase when price is later raised to a competitive level. Displays and large size packages may increase demand because they connote a bargain to consumers. Finally, the package composition and the physical characteristics of the product itself can be used to emphasize a product's attributes and who the product is for.

NEW PRODUCT STRATEGY

The impact of product characteristics on consumer information processing and choice discussed in the last section is of interest whether strategy is being developed for new or existing products. There are, however, several concerns beyond the ones previously discussed that are particularly germane to planning a new product introduction. Because a product is new, the strategist does not have data indicating the rate at which consumers will adopt it. This concern is addressed by examining the impact of new product characteristics on information acquisition. A new product also poses the problem of whom to target. Although the profile of consumers who are likely to purchase new products varies from product to product, there are some characteristics that distinguish new product adopters from the rest of the population. Finally, in planning the introduction of a new product, consideration must be given to how competitive offerings will affect consumers' demand for the new product.

In this section, we shall discuss the effect of product characteristics, consumer characteristics, and the nature of competition on new product adoption. This information enables the strategist to assess the rate at which a new product is likely to be accepted and to devise strategies to speed up the rate of new product adoption. In addition, it suggests a targeting strategy for new product introductions.

New Product Characteristics and Adoption

Some new products are adopted rapidly by consumers, while others are accepted more slowly or not at all.[4] Blade razors with twin blades microscopically close together and food processors were adopted rapidly by consumers. In contrast computers, room air conditioners, and vodka were accepted more slowly. And, some products such as the Edsel automobile, Corfam shoes, and Sodaburst in-home sodas were retracted from the market shortly after introduction because of their limited appeal.

The rate at which new products are likely to be adopted can be anticipated by evaluating a new product's *complexity, communicability, relative advantage, compatibility* and *divisibility* (Rogers and Shoemaker, 1971). Each of these characteristics is necessary but not sufficient to influence adoption. We shall first define these characteristics and then indicate why they affect new product adoption.

Complexity refers to the difficulty involved in using a product. The more complex a product, the slower its rate of adoption. This factor accounts for the slow rate at which computers were purchased when they were introduced three decades ago. The product was sufficiently complicated as to cause resistance to adopting it. In contrast, the simplicity of food processors and twin-bladed razors contributed to their rapid adoption.

Communicability refers to the extent to which the use of a product and the results obtained by using it are observable or can be described to others. The greater a new product's communicability, the more rapidly it will be adopted by consumers. This factor is apt to present a problem in the marketing of many personal care items, which provide benefits that are not generally topics of conversation, or that are not readily observable.

Relative advantage refers to the ability of a product to perform some function in a superior fashion to existing products. The extent to which a new product has some advantage over existing ones is positively related to the rate of its adoption. For example, blade razors with twin blades on the same side provided a closer shave than blade razors without this feature. Moreover, this relative advantage was readily communicated by demonstrating in commercials that the first blade lifted the facial hair and the second cut it off at the skin line. Relative advantage, communicability, and simplicity thus served to speed the adoption of twin-bladed razors.

In essence, relative advantage echos the old adage "build a better mousetrap and

---

[4]For a detailed discussion of this issue, see Robertson (1971), Rogers (1976), Rogers and Shoemaker (1971).

people will beat a path to your door." But relative advantage is not sufficient to insure rapid new product adoption. The product must also be compatible with a consumer's views and behavior. It took more than a decade for vodka to receive acceptance by a substantial segment of the American population because it was not compatible with consumers' view of hard liquor. Unlike other liquors, vodka is colorless and has a rather mellow flavor.

Getting back to mousetraps, it should be noted that someone did build a better mousetrap. It was much more effective in catching mice than the standard trap. It cost a little bit more but not enough so that the price would be a deterrent to purchase. It did not sell very well. The reason for poor sales was that the trap was not compatible with existing patterns of product use. Typically, after a mouse has been caught in a trap, consumers toss both the trap and the mouse in the garbage can rather than extricate the dead mouse and re-use the trap. Even though the improved trap did not cost much more, it looked expensive. Consumers could not bring themselves to discard it, but they also did not want to deal with a dead mouse.

The point of this illustration is that relative advantage is not sufficient to insure new product adoption. It must also be compatible with the way consumers behave. On the other hand, the strategist must be careful not to make a new product compatible with consumers' behavior at the expense of having a distinct difference between the new product and existing ones. Products frequently fail because they are of a "me too" variety, offering no point of difference in relation to competitive products. What is needed is a product that achieves both *compatibility* and has a relative advantage.

A final new product characteristic that affects the rate of adoption is *divisibility,* or the extent to which a product can be tried in small quantities. Divisibility is positively related to the rate of new product adoption. The slow rate of computer adoption is, in part, related to the fact that it could not be tried in limited quantity or with limited financial obligation. For many other products, divisibility is relatively easy to achieve. Food and household cleaning products, for example, are made divisible by offering samples at a nominal cost or free-of-charge. Automobiles are made divisible by offering test drives. Likewise, durables such as televisions and stereos are made divisible by offering free in-home trials.

The foregoing analysis suggests that the manager can anticipate the rate of new product adoption by evaluating it in terms of complexity, communicability, relative advantage, compatibility, and divisibility. If a product does not perform well on these characteristics the product may require modification, or other strategies may be devised to improve performance. Alternatively, it may be necessary to accept a slow rate of adoption and plan production, promotion, and distribution accordingly.

Consider, for example, the Frost 8/80 case described in Chapter One. Consumers were slow to adopt this product. One problem was that Frost 8/80 did not perform well on the compatibility characteristic. Consumers did not know what to think about or how to use a product that looked like vodka and tasted like whiskey. This problem might have been solved by changing the color of Frost 8/80 so it looked like other whiskeys. But this might have made it difficult to communicate Frost 8/80's unique characteristic—that it was less harsh-tasting than other whiskeys. This problem could be addressed by a divisibility strategy. By offering consumers free samples, they could learn about Frost 8/80's unique attribute from their own experience. This strategy might not have been successful in speeding the rate of product adoption because it was still incompatible with how consumers view whiskey. The taste of Frost 8/80 would be incompatible with what is expected from whiskey. Thus the appropriate occasions for consuming it would be uncertain. In this event, the decision might be made to accept a slow rate of adoption or to retract the product.

To this point, we have focused on the nature of the product characteristics that affect their adoption and we have considered how the strategist may make use of this information. But, we have said little about *why* the five product characteristics discussed are determinants of adoption rate. This issue can be addressed from an information processing perspective.

New product adoption requires consumers to acquire information. The facility with which this information can be acquired affects the adoption rate. The five characteristics outlined earlier each influence the extent of information acquisition. Complexity and communicability determine the extent to which information about a new product will be represented in memory. Complex products and those lacking communicability inhibit the reception of information about them that is needed to make a decision. Relative advantage provides positive thoughts about a product that serve as a basis for favorable evaluation. Compatibility limits the number of unfavorable thoughts consumers are likely to have about a new product. Finally, divisibility allows consumers to generate their own repertoire of product-related thoughts on the basis of their experience with the new product.

Targets for New Product Adoption

The rate of new product adoption may be influenced by judicious choice of a target, as well as by appropriate selection of new product features. To identify the target for new product introductions, it is useful to understand the process by which information about and trial of a new product spreads throughout the population. This process is referred to as the diffusion of innovations. It has been studied for products such as new farming methods, new medicines, and new telephone systems (Robertson, 1971; Rogers and Shoemaker, 1971).

The Diffusion Process. The diffusion process was investigated by Whyte (1954) in the early 1950s. His study centered on the adoption of room air conditioners in Philadelphia. At the time, air conditioners were a new product. He observed that on some blocks, as many as thirty-five percent of the homes had room air conditioners. On others, less than five percent of the homes had room air conditioners. This variation could not be explained adequately in terms of differences in affluence or marketing effort. The homes on all blocks were homogeneous with respect to demographic profile and the market information they received. Whyte also noted that the pattern of adoption was quite distinct. It would travel up and down one side of a street and across the backyard to the adjacent street. Only infrequently was adoption on one side of a street associated with adoption on the other side. It was as if the street were a barrier that inhibited adoption.

These observations were interpreted as evidence for a two-step flow explanation of the diffusion process. According to this view, information about new products, such as air conditioners, is initially disseminated by product producers to opinion leaders via the mass media. This constitutes step one. Opinion leaders are knowledgeable about a new product because they have acquired information about it and because they have adopted it. Opinion leaders disseminate the new product knowledge they have to the mass public via word-of-mouth. This is step two (see Lazarsfeld, Berelson, and Gaudet, 1948).

The two-step flow accounts for Whyte's observations of the adoption of room air conditioners. The proportion of people adopting room air conditioners varied on different blocks because some blocks had more opinion leaders than others. Because opinion leaders disseminated information that stimulated air conditioner purchase there was greater air conditioner adoption on blocks with more opinion leaders than on blocks with only a few opinion leaders. Moreover, opinion leaders transmitted their knowledge about air conditioners to those with whom they came into frequent contact. Contact was most frequent with the people who lived on the same side of the street and across the backyard. This is because adult contacts most frequently occurred in the process of monitoring their children's activities, and children were not allowed to cross the street.

The two-step flow suggests that the key to rapid diffusion of an innovation is to reach opinion leaders. Assuming that a new product has some perceived relative advantage over existing ones, by reaching opinion leaders information would be rapidly diffused to the entire population. Given the importance of opinion leaders, much research effort has been devoted to identifying their characteristics. Some of the characteristics most frequently found to be associated with opinion leadership are examined in the next section.

Characteristics of Opinion Leaders. Opinion leaders are thought to differ from the rest of the population in several ways.[5] Their timing of new product purchases is distinct from others in the population. Opinion leaders also have greater ability than others to acquire information about innovations, as well as to acquire the new products they desire. Also, they have greater motivation to engage in the acquisition of information and products.

Opinion leaders are typically not the first to acquire new products. This is done by a group called innovators. As Figure 12.2 shows, innovators constitute a small percentage of the population. They are not opinion leaders because their decision-making style is too risky to influence others in the population. Innovators are willing and able to afford the social and financial risk associated with a wrong decision. In contrast, early adopters tend to include a disproportionately large number of opinion leaders (Baumgarten, 1975; Jacoby, 1972). Early adopters are more risk-averse than innovators in their new product purchases. Thus they are viewed by the remainder of the population as more reliable sources of information than innovators. Members of the early majority tend to be cautious in their adoption of new products, waiting for word-of-mouth about product performance. The late majority is composed of people who are skeptical about new products. Their new product adoption is motivated by social pressure from peers and the lack of availability

---

[5]For a detailed discussion of opinion leader characteristics, see Rogers and Stanfield (1968) and Rogers and Shoemaker (1971).

Figure 12.2. Time Course of New Product Adoption

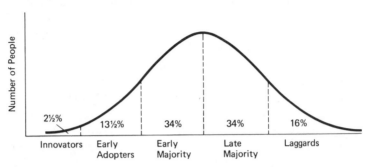

SOURCE: Rogers and Shoemaker, 1971.

of the products they had been using. Finally, laggards resist purchasing new products. Laggards acquire new products only after they are well-established in the marketplace, if at all.

To serve the role of opinion leader, an individual must be among early adopters of a new product. To be an early adopter an individual must have access to information about new products. It is not surprising to find that opinion leaders have broader exposure to information. They participate more in organizations and have greater exposure to print media than does the mass public (that is, early majority, late majority, and laggards). As a result of these multiple sources of information, opinion leaders are more likely to be aware of new products than others in the population.

Opinion leadership also requires the ability to purchase and use new products. This requirement accounts for the observation that opinion leaders have more discretionary income than the mass public. They are financially able to afford the risk of a poor new product choice. The required ability to use new products also explains why opinion leaders tend to be younger than the remainder of the population. As we noted in Chapter Nine, older people experience greater difficulty than their younger counterparts in mastering unfamiliar tasks such as operating new products.

A final requirement for opinion leadership is the motivation to acquire information about new products and to purchase them. It has been found that opinion leaders exhibit a greater need for change and achievement. Thus they actively seek out information that will enable them to have new experiences and perform well. Moreover, opinion leaders' motivation will help overcome resistance to new product acceptance due to its complexity, communicability, compatibility, and divisibility.

To reiterate, opinion leaders are more likely than others to process and use new product information. Specifically, they are more likely to be exposed to information about new products than others. They also have the financial means to accommodate the risk involved in new product purchase. Finally, opinion leaders are motivated to engage in information search and new product purchase.

Applicability of the Two-Step Flow. The two-step flow implies that rapid adoption of new products can be achieved by making opinion leaders aware of them via mass media. Opinion leaders have substantial exposure to these information sources. In turn, opinion leaders can disseminate information about a new product to the mass public via word-of-mouth. For example, when the Ford Motor Company introduced the Mustang in 1964, it gave free loaners to fraternity and sorority members. The notion was that these people would serve as opinion leaders, who would disseminate information about the Mustang.

There are, nevertheless, several factors that question the strategic value of using the two-step flow as the basis for marketing strategy. One problem is that opinion leaders for one product category are unlikely to be opinion leaders for another. Opinion leaders for television sets are unlikely to be opinion leaders for diapers. Opinion leaders tend to be like the general public but more experienced with a product category. Also, it is unlikely that the same individual will have substantial experience in a broad range of product categories. Thus, it becomes necessary to identify opinion leaders for each product category in which they are to be employed as a basis for rapid new product diffusion. This task may be too expensive for many firms to undertake.

A second factor that limits the strategic value of the two-step flow is the observation that information flow is bidirectional. Not only do opinion leaders convey information about a new product to the mass public, but also the mass public seeks information from those they consider to be opinion leaders. This observation implies that there is no need to develop strategies that specifically target opinion leaders. Communications directed at opinion leaders as well as the mass public may stimulate the mass public to seek out information from people they consider opinion leaders. Such an approach takes advantage of the fact that opinion leaders disseminate product information, without incurring the cost of identifying them and devising communication programs to reach them exclusively.

Competitive Analysis

Until now, our analysis of product strategy has emphasized how consumers interpret product cues and how they differ in adopting new products. We have neglected to indicate how competitive strategies affect new product strategy. This issue is addressed by considering an approach developed by the Hendry Corporation (Butler, 1973).

The Hendry approach introduces competitive effects into the product strategy decision by considering the structure of the market. Market structure reflects how consumers view the alternative brand offerings in a product category. Although there are many different types of market structures, two that appear quite often are brand structure and product form structure. It should be noted that these are "pure types." Real market structures are apt to contain elements of both. The following example illustrates brand and product structure for margarine.

The margarine market includes a number of different brands. These are represented by the letters A, B, C, and D in Figure 12.3. Margarine also comes in two forms, tub and stick. This gives rise to two market structures. One is a brand structure. Here consumers' primary choice is of a brand, not of a form. For example, a consumer may select Brand A in *either* stick or tub form. The other structure, product form, gives primary consideration to the form—stick or tub—and not to the brand. Thus, under a

Figure 12.3. Brand and Product Market Structures

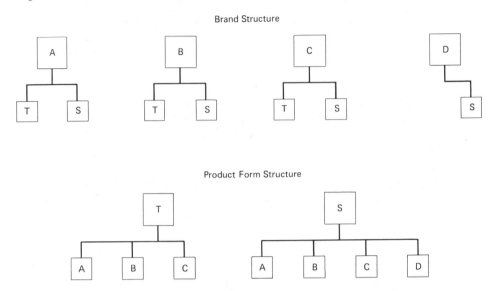

product form structure a consumer may allocate margarine purchases to Brands A and C, always selecting tub.

Figure 12.3 indicates that Brand D does not presently offer margarine in a tub. The question becomes, under what market structure will the introduction of a tub by Brand D be most successful? The answer is product form structure, but let us examine why. If brand structure dominates, it means that consumers tend to buy certain brands in either form. If Brand D introduced a tub margarine most of the customers for D's tub would come from D's present consumers. Consumers who purchase Brands A, B, or C tend to divide their purchases among the tub and stick forms offered by A, B, and C. They are far less likely to be attracted to D's tub.

Now consider the case in which the product form structure prevails. There is a group of consumers who prefer margarine in tub form and divide their purchase among the available tub brands (A, B, and C). By introducing a tub margarine, Brand D would attract consumers who presently buy Brands A, B, and C in tubs rather than from present purchasers of Brand D stick margarine. Thus, if the underlying structure were determined to be a brand structure, the usefulness of Brand D offering a margarine in a tub would be questionable. It may cannibalize sales of its current product. If, however, a product form structure prevailed, then it would become advantageous for D to offer a tub, but only under certain competitive conditions.

The market structure analysis suggests two ways information can be stored in long-term memory. The margarine address may be linked directly to brand addresses, which in turn are linked to product form addresses. Alternatively, the margarine address may be linked directly to product form addresses which are then linked to brand addresses.

Figure 12.4. Unpolarized Market

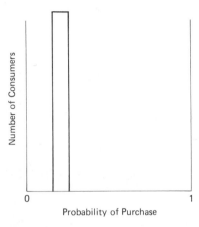

SOURCE: Butler, 1973

Which of these information storage strategies consumers will use in a particular situation is an empirical question. Current theories are not adequate to identify the conditions under which brand and product form storage are likely to emerge.

Once the market structure is determined empirically, the viability of a new product introduction can be assessed. This involves an analysis of the polarity of market structures. A market is said to be unpolarized when all consumers have the same probability of purchasing a specific brand (for example, Brand A in Figure 12.4) In essence, Figure 12.4 implies that when a market is unpolarized, consumers are exhibiting uncertainty by choosing a particular brand only a fraction of the time and by engaging in brand switching the remainder of the time. In contrast, a totally polarized market structure is one where consumers are certain. As Figure 12.5 shows, they purchase a particular brand (e.g.,

Figure 12.5. Totally Polarized Market

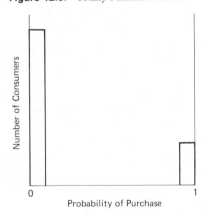

SOURCE: Butler, 1973

Figure 12.6. Consumer Preference Profile

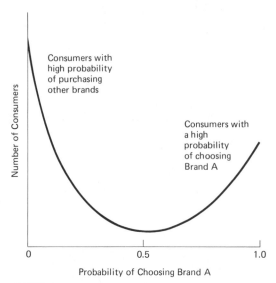

SOURCE: Butler, 1973.

Brand A) either with a probability of one or a probability of zero. Real market structures typically fall between these extremes, with different consumers having different probabilities of purchasing a brand, ranging from zero to one hundred percent (Figure 12.6).

When a new product is introduced, it is going to realize most of its sales from the middle area of the distribution, that is, those consumers who do not have a particularly high or a particularly low probability of choosing a given brand (in this case, A). As Figure 12.7 a,b,c, shows, vulnerability of a particular brand tends to decrease as the number of brands available to consumers increases. This has a particularly interesting implication for consumers' behavior. In essence, in product categories where there are many brands there is apt to be little switching and high brand loyalty. With a large number of purchase alternatives consumers are able to find a brand that uniquely satisfies their needs. Because their unique needs are satisfied they have little reason to switch to another brand.

It should be emphasized that only in the long run will there be less brand switching as the number of brands increases. In the short run, a large number of brands will cause uncertainty. As we discussed in Chapter Five, uncertainty will emerge because consumers will not have the breadth and depth of experience necessary to be sure of their choice when many brand alternatives exist. As their experience mounts certainty will occur, particularly because the availability of multiple brands increases the likelihood of information consistency; consumers will find a brand that delivers the attributes they desire.

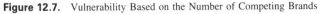

Figure 12.7. Vulnerability Based on the Number of Competing Brands

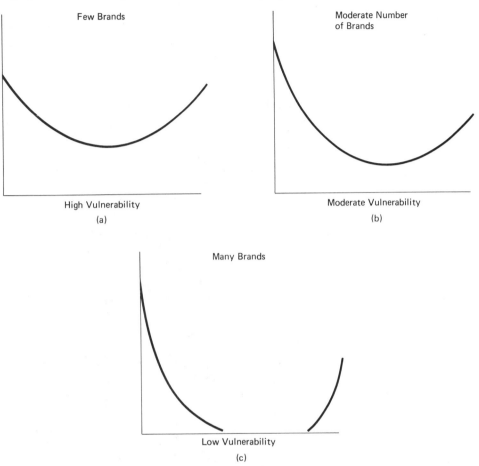

SOURCE: Butler, 1973

With the notion of polarity in mind, let us return to the problem of introducing a new margarine. The best opportunity for Brand D to introduce a new tub margarine would occur when a product form structure prevailed and there is low polarity. In this case, consumers are willing to switch brands, and the likelihood of Brand D cannibalizing its stick sales is low. Somewhat less attractive would be a tub introduction when a brand form structure prevailed and polarity was low. Here some cannibalism can be expected. When the dominant structure was a brand form and polarity was high, introducing a tub would be a very unattractive strategy for Brand D. These conditions all but insure cannibalism of Brand D stick sales.

SUMMARY

Product strategy is based on an understanding of how consumers interpret product cues. One important cue is price. Although there is some evidence that price is inversely related to demand, this is not always the case. When price cues are weak, consumers do not use them in making choices. Thus, price has no effect on demand. Even when price is a strong cue, the inverse price demand relationship may not hold. A high price may increase demand if it is viewed as an indicator of product quality and consumers want high quality. A low price may stimulate demand, but inhibit repeat purchase when price is later raised.

Other product cues may also affect information processing and consumer demand. Product awareness in-store can be enhanced by using a substantial number of shelf facings, using eye-level shelf height, and special displays. Moreover, displays may stimulate purchase because they connote a good value. Finally, the product package and the product's characteristics *per se* provide information about who the product is for and how it will perform.

Special consideration is required in developing new product strategy. This entails examining the product features and consumer characteristics that influence the rate of new product adoption. Products that are simple, are easy to communicate about, have a relative advantage, are compatible with consumers' behavior, and are divisible will be adopted most rapidly. Consumers who are like the mass public but are more experienced can also serve as agents for speeding the rate of new product adoption. These opinion leaders tend to be exposed to a substantial amount of new product information, have the resources to purchase new products and have the motivation to do so. Although it may be useful to focus promotional attention on opinion leaders to stimulate new product diffusion, the cost involved in identifying these individuals may make other approaches more viable.

Finally, the nature of competition must be considered in devising new product strategy. Determination of the viability of a new product introduction requires a knowledge of how consumers represent a market in memory. They may represent a market as a brand structure or product form structure. Which of these structures is employed in specific instances is an empirical question. Once the memory structure is identified, the likely success of a new product introduction can be assessed by examining market polarity.

QUESTIONS

1. The price of Del Monte peaches is permanently lowered five percent so that they sell at a lower price than other national brands of peaches. This price reduction induces no change in the demand for Del Monte peaches. What strategy would you suggest to stimulate demand for Del Monte peaches? Provide a rationale for your choice of strategy.

2. Explain the outcome resulting from each of the following strategies.

   a. In some outlets, a new tire is marketed at a price that is ten percent higher than comparable competitive tires. In other outlets it is competitively priced. Sales are significantly greater where the price is higher, despite the fact that all stores in which the new tire is marketed are comparable.

b. To increase sales, a flour producer lowers price ten percent below competitors' price. Sales increase five percent. After a month, price is returned to its initial level and sales fall twenty percent.

3. Outline product presentation strategies you would use to increase awareness of a product sold in a supermarket, such as coffee or detergent.

4. Outline product presentation strategies you would use to convince consumers that a brand of bread was fresh; a brand of detergent was for men; and a brand of toothpaste was economical.

5. For each of the following pairs of new products choose the one you believe will be adopted at a more rapid rate. Indicate the reason for your choice.

a. Eye glasses that become sunglasses in response to sunlight *or* eye glasses with interchangeable lenses.

b. Automobiles that give forty miles per gallon *or* electrically powered automobiles.

c. Computerized in-home energy control systems *or* computerized business energy control systems.

6. What factors do you believe account for the failure of the following new products:

a. Corfam shoes
b. Frost 8/80
c. Edsel automobile

7. Outline the characteristics that typify opinion leaders.

8. What are the problems in using the two-step flow as a basis for diffusing new products?

9. Suppose the coffee market has the following structure, where A, B, and C are three competing firms.

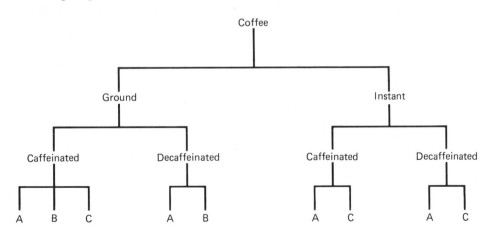

a. What type of new coffee should firm C consider first? Indicate whether it should be ground or instant and caffeinated or decaffeinated. Defend your choice.

b. What type of new coffee should firm B consider? Assume that the instant caffeinated market is highly polarized, whereas the other three markets are unpolarized.

Chapter 13

Message Strategies

When Carin Gendell, the brand manager for Big Bag Cookie Mix, came back from lunch, Sara Newman was waiting for her. Sara was in marketing research and had been working with Carin on the launch of the Big Bag brand cookie mix. The purpose of today's meeting was to plan the introductory advertising for Big Bag.

Big Bag is an easy-to-prepare cookie mix. Six dozen cookies can be made by adding eggs and butter to the Big Bag mix and baking it for ten minutes. Big Bag was to be offered in four flavors: chocolate chip, double chocolate, peanut butter and sugar—at a price of $1.79. Two competitors had been in the market for six months, offering a chocolate chip flavor in packages that yielded only three dozen cookies. Competitors' brands sold for 89 cents.

Through the grapevine Carin had learned that competitors were about to add three flavors to their cookie mix line. She felt it was imperative to introduce Big Bag before this happened. Delay would undoubtedly mean that Big Bag would get lost among the multitude of available brands and flavors. Carin hoped that today's meeting would set the stage for a successful Big Bag introduction.

Carin and Sara had met frequently during the past several months to develop the marketing plan for Big Bag. On the basis of Sara's research it was decided that women eighteen to forty-four years of age with children would be the target market. These consumers indicated that when they made cookies it was usually in batches of five dozen or more. As one consumer said, "If I make less than five or six dozen they are gone in a day. All that work and they are gone in a day." This information was the basis for offering Big Bag in quantities sufficient to make six dozen. The name Big Bag reinforced this feature.

Carin thought the advertising should stress convenience—how easy the mix was to use. Also, the ability to make six dozen cookies from one box seemed to be important to consumers and distinguished Big Bag from its competitors. But she wanted to know what other attributes might be emphasized to promote trial of Big Bag before making a decision. Sara Newman had spent the last several weeks collecting the needed information.

Sara: We conducted a one-week in home test of Big Bag. Four hundred households representative of our target were used. After trying Big Bag, people were asked to list the things they liked most about it. Here is what we found:

Likes Mentioned	Percentage of Respondents Mentioning Likes
Easy to prepare	80%
Good Flavor	50%
Makes Convenient Number of Cookies	10%
Nutritious	2%

Carin: It seems clear that we should stress ease-of-preparation and good flavor. Our earlier research indicated these were important determinants of cookie mix brand choice.

Sara: Not so fast. I also administered a questionnaire to our respondents asking how important it is that a cookie mix be nutritious. Eighty percent said it was important or very important. And Big Bag is the only cookie mix that fortifies the mix with vitamins. So maybe we should stress nutrition in advertising too.

Carin: So you think we should stress nutrition, ease-of-preparation, and flavor?

Sara: Right. Flavor should be stressed. In a blind taste test where respondents didn't know which brand they were trying, they preferred the flavor of Big Bag two to one over the two competitors' brands.

Carin: OK. What about the execution of the Big Bag message? I was thinking of using a humorous approach.

Sara: I have no data on that. But I wonder whether you can tell people about ease-of-preparation, flavor, and nutrition and still manage to deliver it in a humorous manner. Won't the humor get in the way?

Carin: You may have a point there. Do you have any suggestions about how often we should advertise?

Sara: Competitors are advertising very heavily, so we'll need a lot of repetition. I can't tell you exactly how much. But it will be seasonal. Seventy percent of the cookie consumption occurs during two periods–October through December and February through April.

In this chapter, we shall discuss issues raised in the Big Bag scenario. First, guidelines for selecting message content are discussed. These pertain to deciding what should be said in order to persuade people. Although many aspects of the message content decision are specific to the product, consumers, and competitive environment under consideration, there are rules and procedures that transcend contexts. Message execution strategies are considered next. These pertain to how the message content is presented. The use of executions such as humor and threat are examined. Then guidelines for message structure are presented. Strategies pertaining to the number of times a message should be presented and the order in which various bits of information should be presented are discussed. In the final section, the role of nonverbal communications or silent messages is assessed. Facial expressions, body gestures, eye contact, the use of physical space as well as the specific words chosen to convey information all provide message recipients with clues that help them interpret the meaning and accuracy of a communication. As we shall see, knowledge about nonverbal communications is of particular importance in personal selling situations.

Throughout the chapter, message strategies are interpreted from an information processing perspective. The persuasive effect of varying message content, execution, and structure is examined in terms of their effect on information retrieval, rehearsal, and decision making.

MESSAGE CONTENT STRATEGIES

The decision about what to say to influence consumers' behavior is usually determined by conducting research in the context of interest. Marketing research identified ease-of-preparation, flavor, and nutrition as being appropriate for the central content of Big Bag messages. Similarly, H&R Block conducted a survey to identify the major difficulties people had in completing their tax return. The seventeen problems mentioned most frequently formed the basis for the H&R Block advertising campaign. In each commercial, the president of H&R Block presented one of the seventeen tax-related problems mentioned by consumers and described how his firm could help resolve the problem.

Research specific to the context of interest is needed to identify appropriate message content. However, evidence emerging from research that transcends contexts helps the manager evaluate message content alternatives and rule out weak content strategies. Knowledge of how individuals acquire, organize, and use information is useful in evaluating the appropriateness of various message content strategies.

Consumer Oriented vs. Product Oriented Attribute Selection

One approach to developing the message is to include all the attributes possessed by a brand and allow consumers to select those attributes they deem important for brand evaluation. In advertising for Big Bag this would mean conveying information about Big Bag's convenient package size, ease-of-preparation, good flavor, and nutrition. The problem with this approach is that it runs afoul of consumers' processing capabilities. As we noted in our discussion of information processing, the short-term memory store is characterized by limited capacity. Only a certain number of thoughts can be processed per time unit. Thus, presentation of a substantial number of attributes is likely to result in the processing of some subset. There is no assurance that consumers will process those brand features which provide the strongest advocacy for the brand being promoted.

The problem of processing limitation can be at least partially overcome by increasing the time available for processing. In effect, this would allow consumers the time necessary to store incoming information in long-term memory. Operationally, this may be achieved by using a print medium (for example, magazines or newspapers) to communicate brand information. Because the processing of print information is self-paced, individuals have the time necessary to engage in complete processing.

Increasing the time available for processing is less feasible when information presentation is externally paced as is the case in television advertising. Given the cost of television time, increasing the length of the commercial to allow processing of multiple brand features often is prohibitively expensive. In this situation, the best strategy is to select the one or two attributes most likely to be persuasive.

The approach typically considered first in selecting among attributes is a consumer-oriented procedure. Attributes that are key determinants of consumers' brand choice are identified. Then in the message formulation, these attributes of the brand are stressed. In the case of Big Bag, this would entail emphasizing taste and ease-of-preparation, both of which are important determinants of brand choice. This approach is consumer oriented in that it capitalizes on an existing belief held by consumers.

In some instances it may be inappropriate to pursue a consumer-oriented content selection procedure. This is the case when the brand does not possess the attributes on which a consumer's decision turns, or when a competitor has preempted the brand by already emphasizing an attribute that determines choice. Under these circumstances, it may be necessary to employ a product oriented procedure. This involves convincing consumers that an attribute possessed by a brand is an important determinant of choice. For example, if consumers did not view a cookie mix box that yielded six dozen as being preferable to two yielding three dozen, Big Bag might attempt to convince consumers that the package size (six dozen vs. three dozen) is an important consideration in deciding what brand of cookie mix to select.

The product oriented approach is less attractive than a consumer oriented approach because it is generally more costly to execute. A product oriented approach requires people to change their perception of an attribute's role in the choice process. This perception is often resistant to change as it may be based on a history of experience. In contrast, a consumer oriented approach makes no attempt at changing the perceived role of attributes in the choice process. Rather, it involves forming or changing an individual's evaluation of a brand on attributes a consumer already considers to be choice determinants. Brand evaluations are more susceptible to change than attributes because they are usually less tied to a long history of experiences.

From a conceptual standpoint, it should be recognized that the consumer and product oriented approaches are based on our understanding of information organization. As you will recall from Chapter Seven, consumers' preferences were a function of their beliefs about the extent to which an object possesses some attribute and an assessment of the attribute. The consumer oriented approach attempts to change beliefs by linking an object with an attribute that guides decision making. In contrast, the product oriented strategy entails altering attribute assessment, so that the attribute already linked to a brand in the consumer's mind motivates purchase.

Message Discrepancy

Consumer oriented and product oriented approaches help the manager decide what attributes to select. However, they do not provide guidance as to how extreme the claim on those attributes should be.[1] Suppose Big Bag's ease-of-preparation is selected as an attribute to stress in a persuasive appeal. What degree of ease-of-preparation should be presented? From our knowledge of information processing, it is anticipated that taking an extremely discrepant position from what people currently believe (for example, Big Bag is as easy-to-prepare as ready-to-eat cereal), will simply stimulate counterargumentation and communication rejection. In contrast, by assuming a position that is very close to individuals' current beliefs (for example, Big Bag is easier to prepare than cookies made from scratch), they will maintain their current beliefs.

Consider a study that dealt with changing people's beliefs about the hours of sleep they needed per night (Bochner and Insko, 1966). In a pretest, it was observed that most students believed they needed about eight hours of sleep per night. Subjects were given a three page essay which advocated a specific number of hours of sleep per night. Depending upon the treatment to which subjects were assigned, the number of hours suggested was between eight and zero hours. Furthermore, for half the subjects the message was attributed to a highly credible Nobel prize-winning physiologist, and for the remainder to a moderately credible YMCA director.

Figure 13.1 depicts the findings of this study. When the source was the highly credible Nobel prize winner, subjects shifted their attitudes about the hours of sleep needed to a greater extent when the discrepancy between their initial belief and that advocated by the communicator increased (that is, they believed they needed less sleep as the number of hours of sleep advocated was reduced). There was a slight but nonsignificant decline in their attitude change when zero hours of sleep was recommended. In contrast, for subjects who were presented the same communication attributed to the YMCA director, a moderately discrepant position was most persuasive.

Other studies have generally confirmed these findings. Attitude change is a linearly increasing function of discrepancy when the communicator is highly credible (Aronson, Turner, and Carlsmith, 1963; Bergin, 1962; Brewer and Crano, 1978; Choo, 1964; Hill, 1963; Johnson and Steiner, 1968). However, in one study where the discrepancy between subjects' beliefs and those advocated by a highly credible source was very extreme, subjects did exhibit a decline in attitude change at extreme discrepancies (Koslin, Stoops, and Loh, 1967). Also, consistent with the findings of the sleep experiment, the relationship between discrepancy and attitude change is usually curvilinear (inverted U) when the communicator is not highly credible (Aronson, Turner, and Carlsmith, 1963; Brewer and Crano, 1968; Koslin, Stoops, and Loh, 1967).

[1]See Insko (1967) and Sternthal, Phillips and Dholakia (1978) for detailed reviews of the discrepancy literature.

Figure 13.1. The Persuasive Effect of Discrepant Communications Presented by High and Low Credibility Communicators

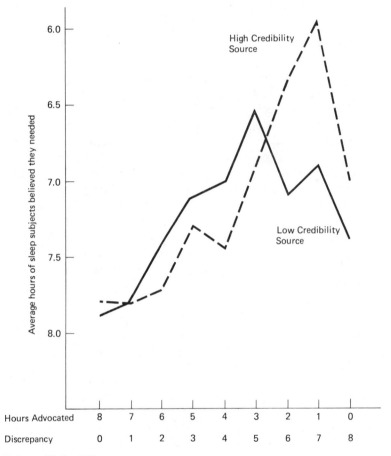

SOURCE: Bochner and Insko, 1966.

From a practical standpoint, these findings suggest that the marketer employ a moderate level of discrepancy in order to maximize persuasion. After all, in most cases marketing communicators are not highly credible. However, existing theory does not allow us to make an *a priori* prediction regarding the specific amount of discrepancy that is optimal. Rather, trial and error must be used to determine that level. As an illustration of these points, consider the car battery producer who wished to convince consumers about the superiority of his brand. To do this, a message was developed showing that the battery could start twelve cars all of which had dead batteries. Although this demonstration was a valid presentation of the battery's power, consumers were not influenced by it. People either did not believe the battery could start twelve cars, or they felt they did not need to pay the price it would cost for a battery that was that powerful. By systematically changing the number of cars that the battery was depicted as being able to start, the manufacturer found that showing five cars being started by the battery induced maximum persuasion.

Attributes Sensitive to Social Norms

Consumers sometimes overstate the importance of certain attributes in guiding their brand choice. This inaccuracy in response is particularly prominent when an attribute is related to a social norm. Consider the importance accorded nutrition in the cookie mix scenario described earlier. It may be that nutrition is an important determinant of brand choice. But there is also a rival explanation. Consumers may have been responding to the social norm that prescribes they purchase products that maintain the physical well-being of their family. In order to appear as though they are in compliance with this norm, consumers overstate the importance of this attribute in decision making. In actuality, it may have little effect on brand choice.

One way to detect whether consumers are responding so as to be in compliance with a social norm is to examine the way in which an attribute emerges in research. In the Big Bag example, a very small percent (two percent) of the respondents *spontaneously* mentioned nutrition. In contrast, when they were directly questioned about the importance of nutrition as a determinant of brand choice, eighty percent indicated that it was an important determinant of purchase. Why the discrepancy? The specific mention of nutrition evoked a social norm, which led to an evaluation of nutrition as an important choice determinant. On the other hand, asking consumers to produce spontaneously the factors guiding decision making did not make the norm salient. Thus nutrition did not emerge as a determinant of brand choice in this situation.

Opposing Attributes

Until now, the discussion of message content has focused on the selection of a single attribute. Very often more than one attribute is presented as a basis for persuasion. In these instances, it is important to assure that the presentation of one attribute does not undermine the presentation of a second attribute. Consider, for example, presenting ease-of-preparation and flavor as the reasons to buy Big Bag cookie mix. Demonstrating ease-of-preparation may be interpreted as a cue that stimulates the retrieval of flavor reservations. From their experience people have learned that easy-to-prepare foods usually do not taste good. This may undermine any attempt to persuade people about Big Bag's superior flavor.

There are several ways to resolve this problem. One is to focus on a single attribute in a particular campaign, say flavor. Once people are convinced that a brand is superior-tasting, a second attribute such as ease-of-preparation may be introduced successfully. Another approach is to alter the undermining attribute so it is no longer at odds with a second attribute. In presenting their Lite beer, Miller stressed its good flavor and the fact that it was less filling than regular beer. The reason it is less filling is because it has fewer calories. Presumably Miller stressed less filling rather than fewer calories, because the latter attribute would have evoked flavor reservations. Low calorie beverages do not taste as good as the carbohydrate-rich variety. Less filling ones, however, do not evoke flavor reservations.

The fact that one attribute may undermine another can be anticipated from an understanding of the information processing and organization processes discussed earlier. For example, a physical attribute such as ease-of-preparation is abstracted to connote convenience. But because consumers have frequently found that convenience is associated with poor flavor these attributes are stored together in memory. Thus, the evocation of convenience via a persuasive appeal also evokes negative thoughts about flavor.

MESSAGE EXECUTION

Communication content is not the only factor that affects message persuasiveness. The manner in which a message is executed is also important. Execution refers to the type of message environment used to convey information about product attributes. Three execution devices are examined in this section: threatening appeals, humorous appeals, and labeling. From an information processing perspective, these devices may be employed to affect the storage and retrieval of information and thus alter the persuasiveness of an appeal.

Threatening Appeals

Threatening physical consequences for non-compliant behavior would seem to be a viable influence strategy. After all, admonitions to children such as "don't touch the hot stove, you'll burn yourself" seem to be effective without much repetition. Thus, it was surprising when Janis and Feshbach (1953) found that increasing threat reduced persuasion. In the high threat condition subjects were told about the terrible consequences of poor dental hygiene—teeth falling out, bleeding gums, receding lower jaw, and the like. Furthermore, gory pictures of people who had not practiced proper dental hygiene were used to support the verbal arguments. In the low threat condition, the consequences were less serious and were accompanied by drawings of the effects of improper brushing. Using a similar approach, other researchers have replicated Janis and Feshbach's finding that increasing threat of physical consequences caused a decline in persuasion, whether the topic was dental hygiene, tuberculosis, or smoking (Leventhal, 1970).

The implication for marketing communications was clear: Do not use threatening appeals. However, since the mid-1960s the pervasive finding has been that increasing threat increased influence. This reawakened interest in threat as a practical device for persuasion.[2] Ray and Wilkie (1970) suggested that the disparity in the findings relating threat to persuasion could be resolved by hypothesizing a nonmonotonic (inverted u)

---

[2] See Ray and Wilkie (1970) and Sternthal and Craig (1974) for a review of the threat literature.

relationship. As Figure 13.2a shows, increasing threat from a low to a moderate level increases persuasion. But further increasing threat from a moderate to a high level causes a decline in persuasion. This contention is based on the premise that threat serves two functions. It acts as a drive to increase the probability of message reception as well as a cue that reduces the likelihood of message acceptance (Figure 13.2b). Assuming that persuasion is the product of the probabilities of information reception and acceptance, increasing threat initially increases persuasion; people become more vigilant to the communication. However, as threat continues to be increased, its persuasive impact declines; people become hypervigilant and look for loopholes in the threatening appeal or some other means of denial (Janis, 1967).

This threat-drive explanation is illustrated in Figure 13.2. When threat is low, there

Figure 13.2. Explanation for the Persuasive Effect of Threatening Physical Consequences

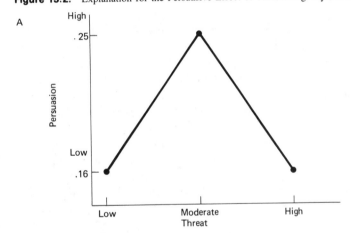

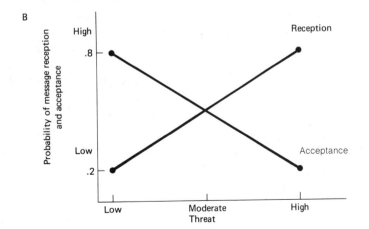

Figure 13.3. Parallel Response Model

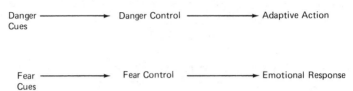

is little persuasion (.16 or the probability of reception, .2, multiplied by the probability of acceptance, .8). When threat is moderate, persuasion is greatest (.25, or the probability of reception, .5, multiplied by the probability of acceptance, .5). Beyond this level, increasing threat reduces persuasion, as seen when at a very high level of threat, persuasion is low again (.16, or the probability of reception, .8, multiplied by the probability of acceptance, .2).

This explanation accounts for the positive and negative threat-persuasion findings reported in the literature. It suggests that the strategist employ some moderate amount of threat to be maximally persuasive. However, the drive-threat explanation is open to criticism. It offers an explanation that is so general that it can be fitted to almost any finding without making accurate *a priori* predictions in specific situations. If a positive threat-persuasion relationship is observed, it is contended that relatively low levels of threat must have been involved, whereas if a negative relationship is found it is argued that high levels of threat must have been present in the appeal.

One way to overcome the lack of specificity in the threat-drive explanation is to interpret the effects of threat in terms of a parallel response process (Leventhal, 1970). According to this explanation, the processing of threatening appeals involves two parallel but independent processes. One is *danger control*. It processes information about what constitutes danger and how to cope with it (Figure 13.3). The output of the danger control process is adaptive action that controls danger. The other process is *fear control*. It processes emotional cues such as statements describing the dire consequences resulting from noncompliance with the message advocated. Processing via fear control leads to actions that are effective in coping with anxiety. These actions may or may not be effective in coping with the danger. In fact, in some situations, actions that reduce anxiety inhibit adaptive actions.

An example will clarify the parallel response process. Consider the following radio commercials:

Anti - Drug Project

(Sung)

God save the soul of a boy bound for glory
He had a lot of life to live

He had a lot of love to give

God save the soul of a boy bound for glory

So very very far from home.

(Spoken)

Raymond Anderson, 18. High on something, jumped or fell

out of an abandoned tenement March 20.

Antoinette Deshmo, 17. Tried heroin for the first time at

a college party. Overdosed and died February 1st.

Barbara Montoban, 15. Died March 14, in the hospital after taking

50 Nembutal tablets.

Michael Shuff. Injected lethal dose of heroin at school. Died

later at the home of a friend . . . .

(Sung)

Save all my brothers

Save all my sisters

Save all the people I know

God save the soul of a boy bound for glory

So very very far from home.

(Spoken)

If you got a friend on drugs get him off.

It's hard to bury a friend.

SOURCE: The Advertising Council

Rat Control

Rats live off garbage

To get at it they will scale walls, climb rooftops,

swim half-a-mile underwater. The trick is not to let

them get at it. Which means putting your garbage in a garbage can

with the lid on tight. The way the Department of Health sees it,

if we keep our garbage away from rats we stand a far better chance

of keeping rats away from us. Starve a rat today!

SOURCE: New York Department of Health

Which of the two radio commercials would you expect to be more effective? From the standpoint of the parallel response interpretation of threat effects, the rat control commercial is superior. It focuses on what constitutes danger by identifying the situations in which rat infiltration can be expected. It also provides a means for coping with danger—

put the garbage in a can with the lid on tight. The anti-drug commercial is less likely to be persuasive. It emphasizes the dire consequences of drug abuse. This appeal is likely to evoke fear control and actions to cope with the anxiety induced by the commercial. The coping response of drug users may be to stop using drugs, which would be an adaptive action. However, an equally likely response is for the drug user to "shoot up" to reduce anxiety.

To reiterate, the parallel response view suggests that in using threat strategies emphasis should be given to cues that help people identify and cope with danger. In contrast, information about the consequences of failing to comply with the message advocacy is likely to evoke actions to cope with emotion. These actions may be ineffective in coping with danger. In essence, these recommendations are tantamount to suggesting that the threatening elements be minimized in presenting threat appeals. Also, information about what constitutes danger and how to deal with it should be emphasized.

Other findings of use to the practitioner are also consistent with the parallel response view:

1. Recommendations about how to cope with danger that the audience perceives to be effective will enhance the persuasiveness of a communication (Leventhal, 1970).
2. Increasing threat increases persuasion when the threatening appeal is delivered by a highly credible source. When communication credibility is low, no amount of threat is persuasive (Hewgill and Miller, 1965; Miller and Hewgill, 1966).
3. People who are highly vulnerable to a threatening appeal (for example, smokers, when the appeal deals with the link between smoking and cancer), are less persuaded as threat increases, while people who are relatively unaffected by a message are more persuaded given a greater level of threat. Thus, highly threatening messages are appropriate to keep nonsmokers from taking up the habit, and low threat is preferable if the purpose is to get people to stop smoking (Berkowitz and Cottingham, 1960; Leventhal, Singer, and Jones, 1965; Leventhal, Jones, and Trembly, 1966).

The parallel response view provides a viable explanation for the persuasive effects of threatening appeals. Nevertheless, it is useful to reinterpret parallel response in information processing terms because the latter theory provides a more detailed description of the process by which threat affects persuasion. According to information processing theory, the presentation of a message that identifies danger and recommends ways of coping with danger stimulates the processing of message thoughts. Because these thoughts are consistent with the communicator's advocacy, persuasion ensues.

Information processing theory also implies that persuasion will be substantial when an individual's thought repertoire is not activated. This can occur when a highly credible spokesperson delivers a threatening appeal. This source blocks the retrieval of individuals' own thoughts, thus enhancing persuasion. In addition, the presentation of a highly threatening appeal is persuasive when message recipients are people who are not highly vulnerable to the threat posed in the message because these people are unlikely to have the motivation to generate counterarguments.

Threatening appeals are unlikely to be effective when they focus on the dire consequences of noncompliance, are delivered by a low credibility source, or are presented to a highly vulnerable audience. In these circumstances, people activate their own thought repertoire. These thoughts are likely to be effective in coping with the anxiety induced by the threatening appeal. But these own thoughts are not necessarily ones that will lead to advocacy-consistent action.

Until now, the discussion has centered on the effects of physical threats. Most of the research done pertains to this type of threat appeal. However, in light of the relatively few instances when physical threat can be used in marketing contexts, it is also useful to consider the effects of threatening social consequences.

Consider a television commercial depicting several couples playing party games in a living room setting. As the commercial proceeds, an attractive young woman is shown using her neck and chin to dislodge an apple held by a man against his neck with his chin. Just as she is about to succeed, she jumps back in horror, shrieks "ring around the collar," and looks accusingly at a woman who is apparently the man's wife. The festivities come to an abrupt halt and the woman caught being derelict in her duty shrinks with embarrassment. In the next scene, it is clear that the woman has remedied the problem by using the advertised brand of detergent. Relieved, she proclaims "no more ring around the collar," much to the delight of her husband.

The use of social disapproval is common in advertising. In fact, advertisers have for a long time used social disapproval to alert consumers to the consequences of such dreaded social diseases as halitosis, dishpan hands, and the wet head. These appeals may be effective because they focus consumers' attention on the expectations of others. As we have already noted, the perceived opinions of others (that is, social normative beliefs) are often important determinants of consumers' behavior. Considering the expectations of others serves not only to increase the likelihood that individuals will gain the acceptance of others, but also allows them to check the accuracy of their own position by comparing it with the position perceived to be held by significant others.

Although widely used by advertising practitioners, there is little formal research that compares the persuasiveness of social threat appeals and other types of messages. Nevertheless, the evidence that does exist tends to confirm the use of social threat under certain conditions. Powell and Miller (1967) found that when a highly credible communicator presented the message, threat of social disapproval was substantially more effective in changing people's attitudes toward giving blood to the Red Cross than either social approval or straightforward appeals. When the appeal was attributed to a low credibility communicator, however, the straightforward message was most persuasive. Thus, it seems appropriate to use threat of social consequences in situations where the communicator is perceived to be relatively credible.

Humorous Messages

Humor is perhaps the vehicle most often used by mass communications to persuade consumers.[3] Yet the evidence regarding the effectiveness of humor is equivocal. Humorous ads for Volkswagen and Benson & Hedges are not only creative but also have been commercially successful. However, many equally creative ads have been failures.

The equivocal findings regarding the effects of humor have resulted in a heated debate. Proponents of humor argue that it is a universal language that allows the com-

---

[3]See Sternthal and Craig (1973) for a review of the humor literature.

municator to speak to an audience at its own level. Opponents contend that humor is not universal; what is funny in New York or Chicago often fails to amuse in Peoria. Furthermore, it is argued that humorous messages wear out quickly on repetition, and require too much space or time to develop.

To assess the effects of humorous messages in a more rigorous manner, let us consider the effects of humor on information processing. Humor is likely to increase the attention paid to a communication (Leavitt, 1970). At the same time the humor may be sufficiently distracting that people fail to process persuasive arguments. This is likely to be the case in the following excerpt from a radio commercial for Arahas Hotel.

Person 1:   What can people do at the Arahas Hotel?

Person 2:   Well there are two Olympic size pools to refresh them and four restaurants to satisfy almost any taste.

Person 1:   But can they . . . (next words drowned out by beeping sound similar to one used by television talk show censors).

Person 2:   No. No. We can't tell them about that. But we can tell them that there are three bands for their dancing pleasure and . . .

Person 1:   But can they . . . (next words drowned out by beeping sound).

Person 2:   We can't talk about that. But we can tell them that three days and two nights cost only $34.50.

Although people typically recalled that this commercial told about the different activities and services available at the Arahas Hotel, few recalled them specifically. Virtually all people questioned mentioned that they recalled the beeping, and were busy completing the drowned-out portion with their own fantasies while the commercial proceeded to mention other attributes of the Hotel.

One way to insure that a humorous appeal is not so distracting as to cause message recipients to ignore the message content is to focus the humor on the salient product attribute. In the Volkswagen ad the humor is directed at the attributes of the car, which is a main selling feature (Figure 13.4). Similarly the humor used in the Benson & Hedges ad focuses on the distinguishing feature of the brand, its length (Figure 13.5). In addition, the use of multiple executions where the same brand attributes are presented in different settings may be effective in stimulating the processing of humorous appeals.

Given that humor is not sufficiently distracting to inhibit information processing, it may be an effective means of persuasion. Specifically, humor may serve as a mild distractor that inhibits those audience members who are initially opposed to the message from generating and rehearsing counterarguments. In turn, this reduction in counterargumentation could enhance message acceptance and persuasion (Sternthal and Craig, 1973). Some strategists caution however, that humor is likely to be effective in gaining message acceptance only if it is directed at the product and not the potential user (Monica, 1971). This argument has credence from an information processing perspective. Depicting the product user as unintelligent, selfish, or as possessing other undesirable characteristics may evoke counterarguments and message rejection. However, when humor is at the expense of the product user but is good-natured, it does not induce counterargumentation.

Figure 13.4. Volkswagen Ad

They don't make them like they used to.

They may still look like they used to, but that doesn't mean we still make them that way.

We used to have a tiny rear window. Now there's a big one.

We used to have a plain old rear seat. Now there's one that folds down.

Over the years, engine power has been increased by 76%.

A dual brake system has been added.

The heater is much improved.

Fact is, over the years, over 2,200 such improvements have been made. Yet, you have to be some sort of a car nut to tell a new one from an old one.

Which, of course, was the plan.

In 1949, when we decided not to outdate the bug, some of the big auto names making big, fancy changes were Kaiser, Hudson and Nash.

Not that we were right and they were wrong, but one thing's for sure: They don't make them like they used to either.

SOURCE: Courtesy of Volkswagen of America.

Figure 13.5. Benson & Hedges Ad

SOURCE: Reprinted by permission of Philip Morris Incorporated.

Indeed, the highly successful Benson & Hedges ad campaign pokes fun at both the user and the brand.

In light of the observation that humorous appeals are more likely to inhibit comprehension and facilitate attention and acceptance (given sufficient comprehension) than straightforward appeals, it is not surprising that humorous appeals have generally been found to be no more persuasive than straightforward messages (Kennedy, 1972; Kilpela, 1961; Pokorny and Gruner, 1969). What persuasive power humorous appeals lose because they inhibit comprehension is offset by enhancing message attention and acceptance. From a managerial perspective this suggests that the use of humor should be confined to situations where message recipients are familiar with the product and brand attributes. Thus humor is likely to be inappropriate when introducing a substantially new product, or when there are a large number of facts people must understand in order to be persuaded.

Labeling

The execution devices discussed so far are appropriate in both mass communication and personal contact situations. In contrast, labeling is most suitable when persuasion occurs in a face-to-tace context. In using a labeling approach, the communicator interprets individuals' behavior or verbal statements in such a way that label recipients view themselves as the type of people who would perform the behavior desired by the communicator.

The persuasive power of the labeling approach is demonstrated in a study reported by Swinyard and Ray (1977). As part of their investigation, they contacted Palo Alto, California residents and presented a message pertaining to the donation of blood to the Red Cross. People assigned to the labeling treatment were then told: "Thank you for your time in listening about the Red Cross. I wish more of the people I met were as interested in their fellow man as you appear to be." Those assigned to receive no label were merely thanked for listening to the appeal. Research participants were later contacted by phone and asked which of five organizations they would select if they were going to do volunteer work. The percent selecting the Red Cross served as the dependent measure.

Swinyard and Ray found that people who had previously been labeled were more likely to indicate their preference to do volunteer work for the Red Cross than people who had not been labeled. Presumably, labeling drew people's attention to their behavior, which indicated their concern for the Red Cross. When they were next asked to engage in a behavior where the Red Cross was pertinent, they retrieved thoughts about their previous actions and used them to guide subsequent behavior. For nonlabeled people, concern for the Red Cross was not made salient and therefore not retrieved in responding to the phone request.

Swinyard and Ray's findings demonstrate the persuasive power of labeling in influencing individuals' intentions. Miller, Brickman, and Bolen (1975) examined the effect of labeling on actual behavior and compared it to a standard persuasion approach. In this study, the group of public school students assigned to the labeling condition were told repeatedly that they were neat and tidy people. The teacher commended the class for being ecology-minded; the principal told students how orderly their room appeared; the janitors left a note to the class saying how easy it was to clean the floor in their room.

Figure 13.6. Effect of Labeling and Persuasion on Immediate and Long-Term Littering Behavior

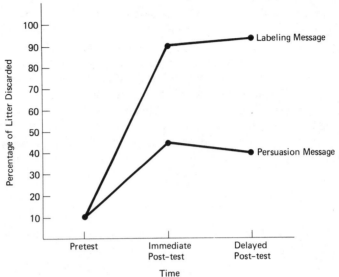

SOURCE: Adapted from Miller, Brickman, and Bolen, 1975.

A second group received persuasive messages. Essentially, this involved specifying the reasons students should be ecology-minded.

To determine the effect of these strategies the experimenters purposely littered the classroom with candy wrappers and measured the percent of these wrappers students discarded in the waste basket. As Figure 13.6 indicates, the students who were to recieve the persuasion and labeling messages did not differ in the percent of litter discarded before receiving the messages. After the messages were received, those given the labeling message discarded significantly more litter than those given the persuasion message. Further, this finding was observed both immediately after and two weeks after (delayed post-test) they had been given the communication.

Despite the substantial evidence suggesting that a labeling message strategy is a powerful persuasive device, several precautions are necessary if it is to be used effectively. First, it should be used in situations where people are uncertain about their disposition concerning the issue in question. If people have developed a negative feeling about a particular brand on the basis of using that brand, attempting to convince them that they are the type of person who will use the brand is likely to be ineffective, regardless of the expertise of the communicator conferring the label. In fact, in such situations persuasion strategies such as distraction, two-sided communications, and threat are probably more effective than a labeling approach.

A second requirement in using labeling is that the communicator be perceived by the message recipients as having the expertise or knowledge to confer the label. Otherwise it is unlikely that they will accept the label as an accurate description of themselves. Swinyard and Ray's communicators were credible because they had witnessed research participants' reaction to their message about the Red Cross. Miller *et al.* used the students' teacher, principal, and janitor to confer the label. These sources were credible because they would necessarily have knowledge to comment on students' tidiness.

Whatever the means employed, it is important to insure that the communicator is perceived to have the knowledge to confer a label. This is readily achieved when the influence attempt occurs in a face-to-face situation. The information needed can be gathered by talking to the person who is to be influenced or by getting him to comply with a small request. Then a label can be conferred so that it is tailored to the individual's response. On the other hand, it is quite difficult to convince the audience that the communicator knows them when a mass communication is employed. For this reason, it is most appropriate to use labeling in personal selling situations.

MESSAGE STRUCTURE

Once the strategist has decided about the content and execution of a message, consideration turns to the message structure. How often to present the communication and when to present it are two important structural issues. Each of these issues is examined from an information processing perspective.

Message Repetition

A basic tenet of the advertising industry is that message repetition is necessary to stimulate sales. This assertion is supported by a variety of investigations. In a correlational study, Starch (1962) analyzed the sales response to print advertising for 105 brands in thirteen product categories. He found that four insertions per year was the turning point between a decrease and an increase in brand purchases (Table 13.1). In a controlled field experiment, Becknell and McIsaac (1963) reported that the introduction of Teflon cookware supported by heavy advertising repetition yielded greater sales than when the introduction was not supported by heavy advertising. Discontinuing advertising also had a detrimental effect on sales. Finally, in a laboratory setting, Sawyer (1971) observed that repetition of print ads had a positive, though modest effect on the redemption of coupons for the advertised brand.

On the basis of these data it seems evident that repeating a persuasive message is

TABLE 13.1. Relationship of Print Advertising Pages to Sales Change

Pages in One Year	Sales Change
13	+6.8%
8	+5.5%
5	+1.2%
4	no change
1	−3.7%
0	−6.0%

SOURCE: Starch, 1962.

related to a greater likelihood of purchase. In this section, we shall examine why this is the case by describing the effect of repetition on information processing. In addition, we shall qualify the repetition effect by identifying situations in which message repetition reduces the effectiveness of an appeal.

Repetition and Information Processing. Repetition of a persuasive message increases the likelihood that its contents will be stored in memory.[4] Politz (1960) found that individuals exposed to two issues of the *Saturday Evening Post* exhibited much greater familiarity with the brands and claims included in the issues than those exposed to one issue. This effect was particularly apparent for brands that were familiar to respondents.

In part then, the positive effect of repetition on sales is explained by the fact that repeating a persuasive communication enhances the probability of storing the message content. It suggests that communication strategists can increase learning of their advocacy by increasing repetitions. This prescription is not highly practical in that most strategists are faced with a limited budget. Given this limitation, it becomes important to consider the timing of communication repetitions.

Suppose a budget is available for thirteen communication presentations annually.[5] One way to proceed is to employ a *concentrated* schedule; one communication is presented each week for thirteen weeks. As Figure 13.7 shows, message recall increases rapidly during the period of message presentations. After the last message presentation, recall drops rapidly. This concentrated repetition schedule is particularly useful when the objective is to gain immediate impact. This objective emerges when a product is seasonal or when the objective is to gain widespread knowledge of a new product before competitors enter the market.

An alternative strategy involves spreading the exposures over the entire year. By using this *continuity schedule,* the level of audience recall ultimately achieved is usually less than that attained using a concentrated schedule, but is substantial throughout the year. Figure 13.8 illustrates this effect for a schedule where thirteen exposures are administered at four-week intervals. Over time, the percentage of people recalling the ad increases. By the end of the year about half of the message recipients recall the ad. Note, too, that the degree of forgetting between exposures, as indicated by downward sloping lines in the sawtooth curve, becomes markedly less as exposures mount. A continuity strategy is particularly appropriate for an established product where message repetition is necessary to stimulate repurchase of the brand. For example, the average consumer purchases nine different brands of ready-to-eat cereal during the course of a year. To insure that their brand is among the set considered at any point in time, manufacturers of ready-to-eat cereals typically use a continuity strategy.

In many instances, it is useful to pursue a third strategy called *flighting*. Flighting involves selecting several time periods for substantial message repetition. At other times no message repetitions are presented. For example, the Big Bag cookie mix schedule

---

[4]For a detailed review of the repetition effects on information processing, see Sawyer (1980), and Mitchell and Olson (1977).

[5]This discussion is based on the work of Zielske (1959).

Figure 13.7. Concentrated Schedule—Thirteen Exposures at Weekly Intervals

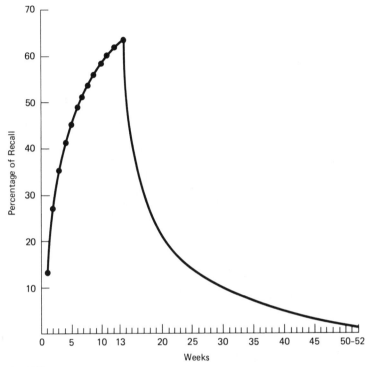

SOURCE: Zielske, 1959.

might involve a fall flight with six message presentations between October and December and seven between February and April. There would be no message presentations during the remaining six months. The idea of this approach is to gain the impact of a concentration strategy while benefiting from the maintenance of a continuity strategy.

When enough resources are available a variant of flighting called *pulsing* is used. Like flighting, pulsing involves selecting several time periods for substantial message repetition. At other times, message repetition is reduced to a low level when pulsing is being used. Pulsing is thus more expensive than flighting but yields greater continuity in message delivery.

Repetition serves to increase learning of the communication content. By varying the timing of the repetitions, the strategist can enhance the extent to which people learn message information. Moreover, repetition can be used to enhance people's attitude toward the position advocated in an appeal. McCullough and Ostrom (1974) showed subjects five different print ads for Yardley After Shave. These ads stressed the same attribute but differed in execution. After each ad, message recipients recorded their thoughts about the product. It was found that repetition increases the number of positive thoughts people had about Yardley After Shave.

In the McCullough and Ostrom study, repetition caused an increasingly positive

279

Figure 13.8. Continuity Schedule—Thirteen Exposures at Four Week Intervals

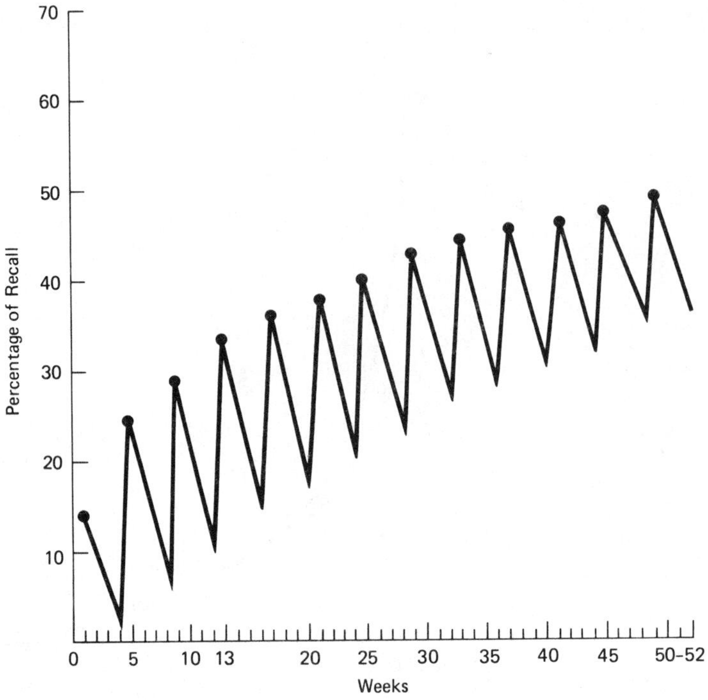

SOURCE: Zielske, 1959.

attitude toward the message advocacy. By varying the execution, subjects' attention was held on message thoughts. Thus, additional exposures enhanced the retrieval and rehearsal of information about Yardley After Shave. When asked to indicate their thoughts, subjects were able to generate more and more message thoughts when given additional exposures.

Qualifying Repetition Effects. So far, we have observed that the greater the repetition, the more positive the outcome. Repetition enhances retrieval and rehearsal of message thoughts and thus stimulates a message-consistent response. However, it should be noted that this conclusion holds only under a limited set of conditions. We shall now examine some of the factors that qualify the assertion that more repetition is better.

One factor that appears to influence the effect of repetition is the message recipient's initial disposition toward the appeal. When the audience is initially quite negative toward a message issue, repeating the appeal appears to increase their negative attitude toward it (Saegert, Swap, and Zajonc, 1973). Apparently, the repetition acts as a cue that stimulates the rehearsal of message recipients' repertoire of thoughts. Because the person's initial disposition is negative, the thoughts retrieved are negative. The greater the number of repetitions, the greater the retrieval of negative thoughts and the less positive a person becomes toward the message issue.

A second factor that qualifies the repetition effect is message content. Ray and Sawyer (1971) presented subjects with either intrusive hard sell ads that tended to deliver all information in a single exposure, or soft sell ads. They observed that repetition of the soft sell ads resulted in an increase in people's intention to purchase the advertised brand. In contrast, repetition of the hard sell ads had no effect on purchase intention. Apparently, additional esposures to the hard sell ad had little utility and therefore did not influence purchase intentions.

A third factor that qualifies the effect of repetition is the amount of repetition used. As we have seen, in response to initial message repetitions people store the communication content. When asked their feelings about the message issue, this content is retrieved and rehearsed and consequently persuasion occurs. However, if very substantial levels of repetition are used, *wearout* is observed. Wearout refers to an absolute decline in message effectiveness caused by very high levels of message repetition.

Initial investigations of the wearout phenomenon suggested that wearout was due to inattention and that wearout in recall of a message could be forestalled by insuring attention (Craig, Sternthal, and Leavitt, 1976; Grass and Wallace, 1969).[6] This was achieved by varying the execution of the message in successive exposures while maintaining the same message content. Thus, the wearout in recall observed when the same appeal was presented repeatedly could be overcome by varying the situations depicted in the message while delivering the same product attributes.

More recent research has questioned the adequacy of the inattention explanation of wearout. Calder and Sternthal (1980) had subjects view television commercials in a context that was intended to maximize attention. The commercials were imbedded in highly entertaining programs. The commercial repetitions were spread out over a several week period. The commercial executions for a particular brand were varied; three different commercials for each brand were used. Despite the presence of all of these devices to enhance attention wearout occurred. Very high levels of repetition resulted in a more negative evaluation of the advertised brand than lower repetition levels.

The Calder-Sternthal study sheds doubt on the adequacy of the inattention explanation of wearout. Even under conditions where message attention was likely to be high, wearout in product evaluation occurred. From an information processing viewpoint, this finding can be explained as follows. Initial exposures to a communication for a brand cause people to store the message information and use it in evaluating the advertised product. However, beyond a certain point, even different commercial executions have little utility; people have learned the communicated information. Thus message recipients begin to retrieve their own repertoire of thoughts. These thoughts are likely to be more negative than the ones contained in the message—which is specifically designed to persuade. As a result of retrieving their own thoughts rather than message thoughts, product evaluation declines.

Support for this interpretation is provided in a study by Cacioppo and Petty (1979). They presented subjects with either one, three, or five repetitions of the same communication. When repetitions were increased from one to three, attitude toward the message

---

[6]See Greenberg and Suttoni (1973) for a review of the advertising wearout literature.

issue became more positive. Further increasing repetition resulted in wearout. Consistent with the information processing view, the number of support arguments increased and the number of counterarguments decreased when repetitions were increased from one to three, whereas the opposite pattern was observed when repetition was increased from three to five; the number of support arguments declined and the number of counterarguments increased.

On the basis of the Calder-Sternthal study it seems apparent that such attention-getting devices as multiple executions are not adequate to forestall wearout. The question is, what strategies are likely to overcome this problem? From the information processing perspective, strategies are required that stimulate the processing and retrieval of message thoughts rather than the communication recipient's own thoughts. One way to achieve this entails presenting new information. For example, in one campaign Trans World Airline emphasized on-time arrivals in one communication, and low priced fares in another. Focusing different messages on *unique attributes* is likely to stimulate the storage and retrieval of message thoughts and, therefore, inhibit wearout.

One of the observations emerging from recent wearout studies is that repetition stimulates the retrieval of the message recipients own thoughts. Although these thoughts are often not favorable to the advocacy, this is not always the case. Consider a study in which college students were sent either one or three letters from the university's health service (Kapferer, 1975). The letters informed the students that they could have their blood pressure checked free of charge during a particular time period and presented reasons why students should take advantage of this service. As one might expect, repetition enhanced compliance with the request. In fact, three times as many students had their blood pressure checked when sent three letters rather than one letter. Surprisingly, however, there was no difference in information processing between those receiving one and three letters. Both groups had processed very little of the contents of the communication other than where they should go and get their blood pressure checked.

What then accounts for the greater effect of three letters? Apparently, students who received three letters asked themselves "Why is the health service so persistent about wanting me to get my blood pressure checked? They must know something that I don't." Repetition caused communication recipients to retrieve thoughts that happened to be consistent with the message advocacy. Of course, repetition is unlikely to have this effect in most commercial contexts where repeated solicitation is perceived by the recipient to be caused by some self-serving motive of the communicator such as profit and not by a sincere interest in the recipient's welfare. Indeed, repeated mail solicitations from those selling magazines, books, bank services, and other commercial products or services usually end up in the waste basket—often unopened.

Order of Presentation

Communication practitioners evidence substantial concern regarding where their messages appear in relation to those of competitors. They often are willing to pay more for advertising placements on the inside and back covers of magazines and at the beginning or end of a series of television commercials. This practice is predicated on the belief that order of presentation affects the attention paid to a message. Physiological measures of attention lend some credence to this view.

Order of presentation also affects the persuasiveness of a message even when all appeals are likely to be attended.[7] Investigations demonstrating this phenomenon typically involve the presentation of arguments both for and against a particular issue. In some cases a primacy effect has been observed; that is, the argument that is presented first (whether for or against the issue) is most persuasive. In other cases, a recency effect has been reported; those arguments presented at the end of the message are most persuasive. Finally, in some cases the order of presentation appears not to make a difference.

These discrepant findings can be explained in terms of the delay between messages advocating different positions and between the last message and measurement of the attitude change induced by the messages. Consider the relatively simple case where two messages are presented, one advocating the purchase of brand A, the other advocating the purchase of brand B. If the two messages are presented one after the other, and they are equally compelling, some people will evaluate brand A more favorably and some will prefer brand B if evaluation immediately follows the message presentation (Table 13.2). If, however, there is a delay after the messages are presented before an evaluation is made, a primacy effect is likely; a disproportionate number of people will exhibit a preference for the brand that was presented first—whether it be A or B. Finally, if there is a delay between the messages, and evaluation immediately follows the last message presented, a recency effect is likely; the last presented brand will be preferred. More generally stated, when evaluation is made immediately after a series of persuasive messages, the longer the delay between competing messages the greater the recency effect. Conversely, the greater the delay between the presentation of the last appeal and evaluation the greater the likelihood of a primacy effect (Insko, 1964).

The effect of order can be explained in terms of information processing. The information presented first is processed and stored in long-term memory. The information

TABLE 13.2. Primacy vs. Recency

Effect	Example				Choice
Primacy/Recency	A	B	E		A or B
	B	A	E		A or B
Primacy	A	B	X	E	A
	B	A	X	E	B
Recency	A	X	B	E	B
	B	X	A	E	A

A = message for brand A
B = message for brand B
E = evaluation of message recipient's attitude
X = delay in days or weeks

[7]See Miller and Campbell (1959) and Insko (1964) for a review of the order effects literature.

presented last is held in the short-term memory store. When evaluation follows immediately after, the message presented last is still in short-term memory. Thus, both messages are available for making a choice and no systematic primacy or recency effect is observed. In contrast, when there is a delay between the messages and evaluation the message presented last is lost from short-term memory, which can only hold information temporarily. The message presented first was stored in long-term memory so it is retrieved and guides choice (that is, a primacy effect). Finally, when the delay intercedes between messages and evaluation immediately follows the second message, the message presented last determines choice. Although the first message is likely to have been stored in long-term memory, the delay makes it difficult to retrieve. The message presented last is likely to still be in the short-term store and is therefore readily accessible as a basis for evaluation.

It should be noted that in many applied instances it is difficult to take advantage of the knowledge about order effects represented in Table 13.2. This is because a manager cannot control competitors' placements of messages or the timing of consumer decision making. In light of these limitations, managers often resort to substantial message repetition to insure the availability of information about their brands.

SILENT MESSAGES

The discussion of message strategy presented in this chapter has focused on the persuasive effects of verbal communications. Because we have all been trained to say things that are socially acceptable, it is often difficult for a message recipient to determine the true meaning of a communication simply by examining what the communicator said. In these situations, nonverbal cues such as voice intonation, gestures, eye contact, and the use of physical space help an individual decipher the meaning of a communication. These silent messages are particularly valuable for interpreting the true meaning, when to smile, how much eye contact to maintain, or how far to stand from people with whom they are conversing.

Consider the job interview strategy used by Bill, a person who is knowledgable about the effects of nonverbal cues. He has established a set of guidelines about personal appearance which he follows in the interview situation.

> . . . I bought a conservative grey suit for interviewing. However, often I wear a brightly colored tie with it. I wear my hair at ear length—white walls around the ears are unnecessary and shoulder length hair is inappropriate. My shoes have a military shine and my pants have a sharp crease . . .

Once in the interview, Bill uses other nonverbal cues that he feels will enhance his attractiveness as a candidate.

> . . . I shake the interviewer's hand firmly and look him in the eye as I state my name. I take a seat that is at a right angle to the interviewer's seat. If there is not a chair in this position, I move one into it. I try to speak in a relatively loud voice, keep my hands away from my face, and maintain eye contact, especially when the interviewer is speaking. I nod my head

and smile when I understand or agree with a point, but I won't necessarily do this in response to everything the interviewer says . . .

Now let us examine an excerpt from an interview itself.

Interviewer: (with hand over his mouth) Frankly Bill, you have the same qualifications as the other nine people I interviewed today. Why should I hire you?

Bill: (maintaining eye contact with the interviewer) It's true that my grade point is about the same as *those* people. But I believe my disposition is better suited to brand management than theirs.

Interviewer: (Putting feet up on the desk and leaning back in his chair) Why is that?

Bill: (leaning forward and smiling) Well, I've been very successful at achieving goals I've set for myself. I became treasurer of my fraternity because we were broke. I organized an alumni banquet which netted us $800. I also . . .

Interviewer: (Yawning) O.K. I see our time is almost up. Do you have any questions you would like me to answer?

Bill: Yes. I'm looking for a company that is growing. What is the growth rate of your firm?

Interviewer: The industry is experiencing a twenty percent growth rate. The marketing department has been expanding. Their need is for people who will progress from brand management positions to general management positions.

Bill left the interview with a negative feeling about the interviewer's firm. He felt that they were not a growth-oriented company, and that there was not close coordination in the firm. He felt things just did not click between himself and the interviewer. The interviewer acknowledged that Bill was bright and seemed capable. However, he felt Bill was too aggressive a person to fit into his organization. He pointed out that unlike other firms that seemed to prefer aggressive goal-oriented people, their style called for a more submissive type at the entering level.

The interview situation, like many other persuasive marketing contexts, is one where participants have carefully rehearsed what they say to persuade others. Thus much of the evaluation of the other party depends on the interpretation of the nonverbal cues that accompany verbal communication. In this section, we shall examine three types of silent messages: proxemics, kinesic behavior, and paralanguage.[8] Proxemics deals with how people use physical space as a means of conveying information. In the interview scenario, Bill's placement of his chair was a manifestation of proxemic behavior. Kinesic behavior involves the use of body positioning and movement as well as eye contact to indicate one's feeling. The interviewer's yawns and leaning back in his chair constitute kinesic behaviors that convey a feeling of social distance. Finally, paralanguage refers to the particular choice of words to transmit information. The interviewer's response to Bill's question about the growth rate of his firm with the statement "the industry is experiencing a twenty percent growth rate" conveys information beyond the literal meaning of the words used. As we shall see, an understanding of proxemic, kinesic, and

---

[8]This taxonomy is adapted from the one due to Duncan (1969). For a review of the nonverbal communication literature, see Bonoma and Felder (1977) and Hulbert and Capon (1972).

paralanguage cues is particularly useful for transmitting and interpreting verbal messages in face-to-face contexts; it can also be applied in a mass communication setting.

Proxemics

One important aspect of how people use space to convey information, or proxemic behavior, is the distance communicators choose to stand from each other. In North America, there are a set of well-defined norms relating personal space to the attitude toward the person with whom you are communicating. People who are intimate tend to stand at a distance of one half to one and one-half feet from each other, while more casual acquaintances generally stand two and one-half to four feet apart. Even greater distances (seven to twelve feet) are used when there is a consulting relationship (Hall, 1966).

Two types of research have been used to demonstrate the relationship between attitude toward the person one is engaging in conversation and distance. One involves having people role-play various degrees of a negative and positive attitude toward another and observing the distance at which the individual stands from the other person. It has been found that the distance subjects choose to stand from another person increases as the attitude they are asked to assume becomes more negative. Similarly, when subjects are asked to assess the interpersonal attitudes of people in conversation, they rate the attitudes more negatively as the distance between the people increases (Mehrabian, 1971). You may confirm these findings by doing your own study. Next time you are engaged in a conversation with an acquaintance, slowly encroach upon his or her personal space. Unless you are romantically linked, you will find that the person backs up to ensure the appropriate personal space. If you continue your encroachment tactics you can systematically move a person across the room; or the person may abruptly leave, suspicious of your designs. Indeed, Americans are often made uncomfortable by persons from European countries where the norms dictate more proximity than is comfortable for Americans.

From a strategic standpoint, it is important to understand the norms regarding personal space because they influence the way in which consumers behave. In conversation, personal space is defined by the relationship with the other person. In other situations, physical barriers may be used to define personal space. Several examples will illustrate this point.[9]

1. The Restaurant—During the lunch hour rush all seats in a downtown restaurant are occupied, even though only seventy percent of the restaurant's capacity is being used. Customers placed briefcases, umbrellas, and coats on unoccupied chairs at their table to insure that the hostess would not seat strangers at their table. Management urged patrons to use the free coat-checking service and installed more small tables to overcome this problem.
2. The University Study Hall—The administration of a university decided not to build a study hall facility, reasoning that the twenty classrooms which could seat over one thousand students would be ample for those who wished to study in them at night. It was

[9]These illustrations are adapted from Mehrabian (1971).

found that the building when serving as a study hall accommodated only twenty students—one per classroom.

3. The Bus Stop Bench—Despite the presence of a nine foot bench at bus stops which would comfortably seat five or six people, seldom did more than two people use the bench at one time. One person generally sat at each end (where personal space was defined at least on one side). Management painted white stripes eighteen inches apart on the bench, substantially increasing utilization.

4. The Oil Company Commercial—A television commercial was aired in which the brand spokesperson and a potential customer stood face-to-face at a distance of less than one foot while the spokesperson proclaimed the virtues of the brand. Message recipients were made so uncomfortable by this ad because of the violation of personal space that it had to be retracted.

These examples illustrate the fact that people pursue strategies in consuming that are likely to insure the personal space they deem appropriate. Very often this entails using physical landmarks such as a table, the walls of a room, or the end of a bench to define their space. Because the need for personal space often results in underutilization of management's resources, a knowledge of personal space norms can be used to anticipate and overcome this threat.

In some situations, consumers adjust their personal space norms because of the nature of the situation. If you frequently go to the same movie theatre you might have observed that the lobby holds many more people when an X-rated movie is playing than when a G-rated movie is showing. This may occur because the G-rated movie attracts more families who define a personal space between themselves that is sufficient for conversation. On the other hand, the audience for X-rated movies is composed of smaller groups of people with less control over personal space and less need for room to converse. In part, this personal space needed for conversation is related to the need for eye contact among those engaged in conversation. We shall now examine eye contact and other kinesic or body language behaviors.

Kinesic Behavior

Kinesic behavior is another aspect of non-verbal communication; it includes eye contact, head nods, gestures, and posture. Eye contact between people engaged in conversation generally lasts between one and seven seconds before people look away from one another. Each person spends between thirty and sixty percent of the conversation time looking at the other person, though mutual eye contact generally ranges from between ten and thirty percent of the conversation time (Sommer, 1969). Furthermore, people look more often and longer when listening than when speaking.

One of the functions of eye contact is regulatory. When a speaker is finished speaking he looks at the listener, signaling that it is appropriate for the other person to respond. He looks away from the listener at the outset of the speech to signal he is about to talk and also so that he will not be distracted by the listener while collecting his thoughts.

More interesting from the marketing strategist's perspective is the expressive function served by eye contact. Greater eye contact between communicators is generally associated with greater liking (Exline, 1963; Exline, Gray and Schuette, 1965). Though both men and women exhibit this pattern, women tend to engage in more eye contact and exhibit greater variability in the amount of eye contact used than do men; that is, women have less eye contact with disliked people than do men and more eye contact with people they like than men (Duncan, 1969; Mehrabian, 1971, 1972). Perhaps this is why it is particularly uncomfortable for women to converse with people wearing dark sunglasses— an important cue regarding the other person's feelings is lost.

Thus people use both distance and eye contact to convey their feelings. Sometimes, in fact, both these cues are used together. As the positive attitude between communicators increases both the distance between them and eye contact decreases. As people move relatively close together prolonged eye contact would become uncomfortable. In such instances, we find a decrease in eye contact to compensate for the physical proximity between communicators. As a result, eye contact increases as the attitude between communicators increases from negative to neutral. Beyond that point, increases in positive attitude may result in slightly reduced eye contact to compensate for the closer distance between communicators.

The ability to use eye contact is important in personal selling situations. The seller can use eye contact to indicate a positive attitude toward the buyer. Moreover, by being sensitive to the degree of contact used by the buyer, he can gauge the buyer's reaction to his appeal. To do this, he may interpret other kinesic behaviors beyond eye contact. Specifically, the use of head nods, gestures, and a pleasant voice as well as substantial eye contact indicate liking, whereas the absence of these cues is indicative of disliking. In addition, body position cues give some indication of a person's feeling of dominance or submissiveness. A sideways lean and asymmetry in the way an individual positions his arms and legs indicate a relaxation associated with a dominant feeling. In contrast, an erect posture with hands and legs symetrically placed generally indicates a submissive feeling.

The liking-disliking and dominant-submissive dimensions are shown in Figure 13.9. Often people exhibit cues related to each of these dimensions at the same time. If people emit some cues related to liking and submissiveness, they are labeled as respectful. However, people exhibiting an extreme number of cues related to liking and submissiveness are perceived to be ingratiating; a salesman who nods agreement with everything a buyer says, smiling and gesturing in a positive manner, is often perceived to be phony. In contrast, people who give cues suggesting disliking and submissiveness are regarded as fearful, while fewer cues suggesting disliking and submission result in labeling a person as tense or vigilant. Further, a combination of dominance and disliking cues is interpreted as aggressiveness, while dominance and liking is labeled charitable (Figure 13.9).

The adept salesperson can tailor the nonverbal cues so that his verbal appeals are maximally effective. If the customer is aggressive, using cues that convey respect may be most effective. If, however, the buyer is fearful, cues suggesting charitability may be most influential. Whatever the situation, the important point to recognize is that nonverbal cues can have a significant effect on the persuasiveness of a verbal communication.

A knowledge of eye contact can also be used to influence mass consumption. For

Figure 13.9. Determination of Personality Using Nonverbal Cues

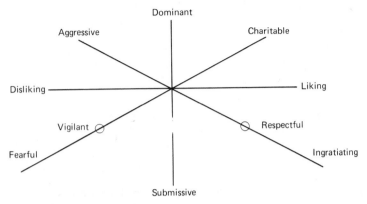

SOURCE: Adapted from Mehrabian, 1971.

example, seating arrangements that allow people to sit at right angles to each other enhances communication because it provides the opportunity for the eye contact needed for feedback but also reduces prolonged eye contact that is uncomfortable. Thus the use of service counters in restaurants promotes rapid turnover of the clientele, whereas serving people at tables or booths where the distance between the communicators is substantial encourages patrons to linger and talk.

Paralanguage

Paralanguage refers to the way in which we choose to convey information. Yawns, grunts, loudness, tempo, and the specific words used are all part of the paralanguage that affect the interpretation of a persuasive message. Of particular concern here will be an examination of the meaning conveyed by the word choice. Specifically, we shall describe paralanguage with respect to forms of reference, over-inclusion, and euphemisms.

The form of reference used by a communicator can be used to interpret his or her feeling. Consider the following forms of reference that might be used by a purchaser after speaking to a distributor:

We talked
He and I talked
I talked to him
I had to talk to him

Although these statements convey essentially the same information, the words used give an indication of the purchaser's feelings toward the distributor. "We talked" and "He and I talked" suggest that the purchaser views the distribution to be on an equal standing. In contrast, "I talked to him" suggests that the purchaser initiated the action and may be dominant in the relationship. Finally, "I had to talk to him" appears to reflect the purchaser's negative attitude toward the distributor. Consider the feeling conveyed by Bill's mother when she refers to his fiancée as follows:

> My daughter-in-law to-be
> Bill's fiancée
> Bill's lady friend
> That thing

There are several common ways to use forms of reference to connote feeling. Words like "here" and "this" convey the feeling of closeness and liking, while the use of words "there" and "that" indicate distance and dislike (Table 13.3). Similarly, the use of the active voice (He tells me) suggests a more positive feeling than does the passive voice (I am told by him). When several of these forms of reference are combined, the speaker's feeling is readily inferred. A statement such as "I have been working with that distributor" conveys a less positive feeling about the distributor than does the statement "I am working with this distributor."

Another way to convey feeling using paralanguage is to employ an overinclusion strategy. Suppose a manufacturer asks his distributor how a particular product is moving. If the manufacturer's business is highly valued by the distributor he might answer that business is slow rather than saying that the product is a disaster. This is tantamount to saying your product is not moving well but I still think it is a good product. Overinclusion is an effective means of diffusing responsiblity by attributing it to more than one source.

Finally, euphemisms may be used to minimize the negative aspects of a communication. The use of euphemisms is common in marketing communications to consumers. Advertisers state that tickets are "available at . . ." rather than "sold at . . ." to make the exchange sound more palatable. Funeral homes represent their services as involving "laying to rest those who passed away," which is more acceptable than saying "burying the dead."

Although any particular nonverbal cue is easily misinterpreted, the presence of several cues, whether they are proxemic, kinesic, or paralanguage cues, helps an individual more accurately interpret the verbal portion of a communication. People who have mastered the silent messages they transmit can use them to complement their verbal appeals. Indeed, the success of Ed McMahon, Danny Thomas, and others as spokespeople is, in

TABLE 13.3.   Paralanguage: The Choice of Words To Convey Distance

Closeness	Distance
Here he is	*There* he is
This distributor carries a competitive line of brands	*That* distributor carries a competitive line of brands
He tells me	I am told by him

part, attributable to their ability to use nonverbal cues to support their verbal arguments for purchasing a product.

Let us reconsider the job interview scenario described earlier in light of the discussion of nonverbal cues. Bill's strategy for selecting where he would sit in the interview room was appropriate. By sitting at right angles to the interviewer he would easily have the eye contact necessary to indicate attention and understanding, but not so much eye contact that he would have to engage actively in looking away from the interviewer. Bill's feeling that the interview did not go well was probably justified. The interviewer placed his feet on the desk, leaned back, and yawned, all indicating social distance or dislike. This response occurred despite Bill's attempts to indicate his liking and interest in the company—he leaned forward, smiled, and nodded his head discriminately. Bill's doubts about the firm's growth also seem well-founded. In response to Bill's question about the firm's growth, the interviewer overincluded and talked about industry growth. The interviewer also gave evidence that he was not closely affiliated with the marketing department by referring to "their need" rather than "our need." In sum, a knowledge of the meaning of nonverbal communications facilitates correct interpretation of ambiguous messages and allows communicators to reinforce the feeling they are trying to convey with verbal communications.

SUMMARY

In this chapter, we have examined strategies for enhancing the effectiveness of persuasive appeals. Although the content of these appeals is specific to the situation being considered, there are several guidelines that apply to most situations. Initially, an attempt should be made to select attributes from a consumer perspective. In situations where this is not feasible, a product-oriented procedure is appropriate. The product attributes should be positioned so that they are moderately discrepant from information recipients' initial beliefs. Attributes that reflect social norms should be used with caution. The use of two or more attributes having opposing connotations should be avoided.

A second important consideration in developing effective messages involves decisions about message execution. Three execution strategies were considered in this chapter—threat, humor, and labeling. Threat appeals should focus on helping the message recipient identify and cope with danger. Emphasis on the dire consequences of not complying with the message advocacy should be avoided. In using humor as an executional device, care must be exercised to use multiple message executions, focus the humor on a major product attribute, and direct the humor at the product rather than the product user. Finally, labeling strategies are likely to be effective in personal selling situations where the communicator has the credibility to confer a label and label recipients are uncertain about their feelings on an issue.

A third consideration in developing effective message strategies entails making decisions about structural factors such as the level of repetition and order of presentation. Up to a point, repetition has a positive effect on consumers' response. Beyond this point, however, wearout occurs. Wearout is likely to be minimized by adding new information to the communication as repetitions mount. The effect of presentation order is a function of (1) the time interval between a firm's appeal and that of competitors, and (2) the time interval between these appeals and consumer evaluation. It is best to be first in presenting a message when both messages are received in close proximity and evaluation occurs some time later. It is best to follow a competitor's appeal when there is a substantial interval between competitive appeals and evaluation occurs soon after the last appeal is presented.

In the concluding section of this chapter, the value of understanding silent messages is examined. By using proxemics, kinesics, and paralanguage judiciously, communication strategists can enhance the impact of their advocacy. Failure to understand the meaning of nonverbal cues may result in undermining the verbal portion of a communication.

QUESTIONS

1. For each of the following product categories indicate whether threatening appeals would be appropriate and why: life insurance; deodorant; perfume; smoke detector; breakfast cereal; and detergent.

2. Suggest an approach that could be used to determine the optimal number of message repetitions.

3. If a package goods marketer were advertising a new mouthwash on television, should the strongest arguments be at the end or the beginning of the commercial?

4. Observe a sales interaction. How are silent messages being used?

5. What is the relationship between message discrepancy and persuasion? Does it depend on other factors?

6. What are some humorous ads? Are they effective? Why?

7. How might a labeling strategy be applied in personal selling?

8. Which is likely to be most effective, a concentrated schedule or a continuity schedule? What do you have to be careful about with a concentrated schedule?

Chapter 14

Communication Source and Modality Strategies

As we noted in the last chapter, the judicious choice of message content, execution, and structure are necessary to produce effective communications. But well designed messages may not be sufficient to influence consumers' behavior. The extent to which message recipients use the information conveyed in an appeal depends on their perception of the communicator and the characteristics of the communication modality (that is, print, broadcast). For example, in the early 1970s Quaker Oats introduced Mikey as a spokesperson for Life cereal in an effort to stimulate sales which had experienced little growth for a number of years. Mikey was a three-year-old child who was portrayed as disliking all cereal except Life. Although other elements of the Life campaign were essentially unaltered, sales of the brand increased substantially. In another instance, Sears found that switching their advertising from television to print substantially increased the demand for their line of home furnishings. These illustrations provide testimony for the fact that persuasive communications require the selection of appropriate spokespersons to convey compelling messages through suitable media.

In this chapter, we consider the effect of message source and modality on communication persuasiveness. This entails describing the role of these factors in consumer information processing. On the basis of this analysis, the communication source and modality strategies that are likely to maximize persuasion in different situations are identified.

THE COMMUNICATION SOURCE

Marketing strategists appear to believe that a communicator's character has a significant impact on an appeal's persuasiveness.[1] Advertisers select consumers who typify the target audience to present testimonials about their satisfaction with the advertiser's product. Manufacturers seek the seal of approval from independent product testing agencies to substantiate their claims. Politicians running for office often solicit the endorsement of well-known individuals and prestigious organizations.

In all of these illustrations, the strategy is to select sources whose credibility maximizes message influence. Credibility refers to three attributes of a communicator's character. One is *attractiveness*. Individuals who are judged to be dynamic, likable, and interesting are considered attractive. A second dimension of credibility is *expertise*. This refers to the extent to which a spokesperson is perceived to be capable of making correct assertions. People who are professional, trained, and qualified are generally perceived as expert. The third dimension of credibility, *trustworthiness*, refers to the degree to which message recipients perceive the assertions made by a source to be valid. Honest, just, and moral people are typically seen as trustworthy.

Strategists have typically approached the communicator selection problem by attempting to maximize the source's credibility. The rationale is that the higher the credibility, the more likely a message is to be influential. But recent evidence questions the wisdom of this approach. High credibility is an effective persuasive device in a limited number of situations. In other instances, credibility either does not affect consumer persuasion or it inhibits persuasion. This suggests that attempts to enhance the source's credibility are not always conducive to maximizing persuasion. In this section, we shall identify the situations in which it is useful and detrimental to employ source enhancement strategies.

Source Attractiveness

Celebrities are often used as spokespeople for products and services. O.J. Simpson is the spokesperson for Hertz rent-a-car, Danny Thomas for Maxwell House coffee, Avery Schriver for Frito-Lay, and Ed McMahon for Alpo dog food. These and other attractive sources stimulate attention to a communication, enhancing the storage of message information. This does not imply, however, that attractive sources are more persuasive than communicators with less of this attribute. The use of celebrities may distract an audience from processing information important in influencing consumers' behavior. For example, Pizza Hut aired a commercial featuring Rich Little, a well known comedian. Viewers of this commercial exhibited good recall of the fact that Rich Little was the spokesperson, but had much poorer recall of the main selling proposition—that Pizza Hut was open for lunch.

---

[1]Detailed reviews of communicator's effect on persuasion are provided by Anderson and Clevenger (1963), Simons, Berkowitz, and Moyer (1970) and Sternthal, Phillips, and Dholakia, (1978).

One strategy for reducing the likelihood that a spokesperson distracts people from processing message information is to select communicators who are associated with the product attribute being promoted. John Houseman is perceived to be a serious, hardworking, and highly analytical person, perhaps because of his role as a law professor in *The Paper Chase*. He is an appropriate spokesperson for the Smith-Barney financial institution in television commercials because he personifies that firm's hard-working and analytical attributes. Members of the Pittsburgh Steeler's football team are appropriate spokespeople for luggage because they personify important product attributes—ruggedness and durability.

A more difficult problem to overcome in using attractive sources is that they are often not viewed as experts for the products they are sponsoring. Consumers may question Danny Thomas' knowledge about coffee or Ed McMahon's expertise about dog food. As a result, message recipients may be motivated to generate counterarguments and not be persuaded by the appeal.

In sum, it appears that attractive sources facilitate information storage. But the thoughts stored may be about the source and not the reasons for complying with his or her advocacy. The use of sources who personify important product features may minimize this problem. However, if an attractive source is perceived to lack expertise, message recipients may retrieve and rehearse counterarguments, and thus reject the source's advocacy.

Despite the fact that attractive sources are not likely to be highly persuasive, they are used frequently as spokespeople in advertising. In part, this is because advertising effectiveness is judged on the basis of recall, and attractive sources all but insure substantial recall of at least some elements of an appeal. When a more compelling criterion such as attitude toward a product or purchase is used to evaluate communication effectiveness, an attractive source may be ineffective. The other dimensions of source credibility, trust and expertise, must be considered. These are examined below. In the remainder of this chapter, credibility will refer to the trust and expertise dimensions.

Expertise and Trust as Persuasive Facilitators and Nonliabilities

One of the most reliable effects observed in the communication literature is that highly trustworthy and/or expert sources induce greater persuasion than sources who are less trustworthy or expert. Although high credibility sources do not make a message more memorable than low credibility sources, they yield more positive attitudes toward the position advocated in a message than less credible communicators. High credibility sources also induce more behavioral compliance. Illustrative of this latter finding is a study reported by Brock (1965). He varied credibility by systematically manipulating the degree of similarity between the source and the message recipients. This was achieved by having paint store salespeople determine how customers intended to use the paint they were going to purchase. Salespeople then indicated that they had experience with the intended use (high credibility) or did not have such experience (low credibility). Once a customer had stated his intent to purchase, the salesperson suggested either a higher or lower priced paint. When the salesperson and customer shared attitudes about how the paint would perform, the customer followed the salesperson's suggestion to a much greater extent than when attitudes were dissimilar. This occurred regardless of whether the higher or lower priced paint was recommended.

On the basis of the Brock study and many others similar to it, one might conclude that a highly credible source is more persuasive than a less credible source. However, this conclusion requires qualification. In terms of information processing, credibility affects persuasion by influencing information retrieval from long-term memory. Specifically, a highly credible source inhibits the retrieval and rehearsal of individuals' own thought repertoires. Presumably, when a communicator is highly trustworthy and/or expert, people have little motivation to check the veracity of the source's assertions by retrieving and rehearsing their own thoughts. When the source is less credible, message recipients are motivated to assess their beliefs about the information presented and therefore retrieve and rehearse their own thoughts. Thus, to the extent that own thoughts oppose those presented in a message, a highly credible source is more persuasive than a source lower in credibility. In practical terms, this suggests that it is useful to employ a highly credible source when the target audience has negative thoughts about the position advanced in an appeal, and when alternative devices to inhibit conterargumentation are not available or appropriate.

The superior persuasive power of a highly credible source depends on the presence of factors beyond message recipients' negative disposition toward an appeal. The amount of time that passes between a communicator's presentation and recipients' reactions to it, the timing of the source's introduction, and the type of message used all affect the relative persuasiveness of a high and low credibility source when the audience is negatively disposed toward a message. Each of these factors is considered below.

This analysis identifies situations in which a highly credible source is more persuasive than a low credibility source. On the basis of this information, the strategist can discern the circumstances in which it is useful to pursue strategies to enhance credibility. In addition, the analysis specifies ways to increase the persuasiveness of a low credibility source. This knowledge is important to the marketing strategist because in many instances it is difficult to find a highly credible spokesperson. Message recipients know that the communicator is motivated by self-interest to present an appeal and, therefore, do not trust him fully.

Time between the Source's Presentation and Reaction.

Although the communication source may have a substantial effect on immediate attitude change, marketing strategists are more concerned with the persistence of attitude change over time. If the greater immediate influence of a high credibility source in relation to a low credibility source does not persist over time, there would be little reason for marketers to attempt enhancement of the source's trustworthiness and expertise, (unless immediate consumer action were anticipated).

The persistence of the credibility effect has been examined by varying the delay between message presentations. In an early investigation dealing with individuals' reactions and the time between the source's presentation and the measurement of individuals' reactions, Hovland, Lumsdaine, and Sheffield (1949) examined the persuasive effect of a low credibility source. Some enlisted men were shown a film supporting the Allied effort during World War II, while others (that is, the no-message control group) were not shown the film. The film was sponsored by the Army, presumably a low credibility source. Message-related attitudes were measured either five days or nine weeks later. The results indicated that the differences between the group receiving the film and the no-message control group were substantially greater in the nine week post-test than in the one administered five days after the film was shown. This phenomenon was termed the *sleeper effect*, because it appeared that a film sponsored by a low credibility source manifested greater persuasive impact with the passage of time.

From an information processing perspective, the sleeper effect is interpreted in terms of the relative memorability of a source and a message. Messages tend to be more memorable than their sources because messages are associated with more thoughts in memory. For this reason, people often present information to the very individuals from whom they originally heard the information; the message is memorable, but the source is not.

Sleeper effect research has centered on demonstrating the sleeper effect by exper- imentally varying source credibility as well as the temporal delay before the administration of the attitude measures. Subjects were exposed to a persuasive message attributed to either a low or high credibility source, and the effect of the appeal on attitudes was measured both immediately after the communication and after some extended delay. The findings of these studies provide virtually no support for the sleeper effect as it was originally conceived (Capon and Hulbert, 1973). The low credibility source typically induced little initial attitude change and did not become significantly more persuasive through time (Figure 14.1). Rather, it has been frequently observed that the initial greater persuasiveness of a high credibility source relative to one of low credibility does not persist over time. This outcome is most likely attributable to a maturational effect; the highly credibility source has a substantial immediate persuasive effect upon respondents that decays with the passage of time (Figure 14.1).

The repeated failure to demonstrate the sleeper effect has led some investigators to question its existence (Capon and Hulbert, 1973; Gillig and Greenwald, 1974). Others have contended that methodological inadequacies account for the inability to exhibit the phenomenon (Gruder *et al.*, 1978).[2] Regardless of which of these positions is correct, the use of a strategy that seeks to enhance the persuasiveness of a low credibility source by relying on the passage of time appears to be unattractive. In many contexts, message processing requires its repetition. Under such circumstances, it has been found that a highly credible source is more influential than a low credibility source (Johnson and Watkins, 1971). Moreover, even if a sleeper effect occurs, and a low credibility source becomes more persuasive over time, there is no assurance that this strategy will be as effective as repeating a message delivered by a highly credible communicator.

---

[2]Several published studies have demonstrated that persuasion increases over time (Gruder *et al.*, 1978; Watts and Holt, 1979). But these investigations did not involve the manipulation of source credibility.

Figure 14.1. The Sleeper Effect

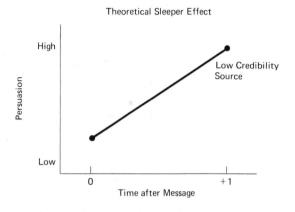

Theoretical Sleeper Effect

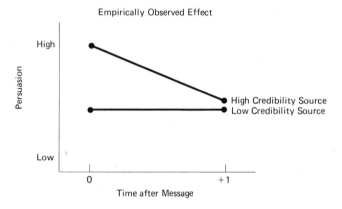

Empirically Observed Effect

Timing of the Source Introduction. Another approach to enhancing the persuasiveness of a low credibility source entails varying the timing of the source's introduction. A highly credible source is more persuasive than a low credibility source when the source is introduced at the outset of a message. But these sources are equally persuasive when the source's identification is deferred until the end of the message. Delaying identification serves to reduce the persuasiveness of a highly credible source and increase the influence of a low credibility source (see Sternthal *et al.*, 1978).

These findings are predicted by information processing theory. When a source is not identified until the end of a message, it comes too late to affect information retrieval and rehearsal. Thus delaying identification of a highly credible source prevents high credibility sources from inhibiting counterargumentation and less credible sources from facilitating it.

Introducing the communicator at the end of an appeal is useful when message recipients oppose the message advocacy and the source is not highly credible. For example, it was found that people were unconvinced about the effectiveness of Tums, an antacid. They questioned whether such a small tablet could be effective. To offset these counterarguments a TV commercial was developed which showed a large pill. The brand name Tums, which we shall view as the source in this instance, was not identified. Rather, the audio message indicated how the product performed while the pill was shown turning slowly. By the end of the commercial, the pill had revolved sufficiently to expose the brand name. The effectiveness of this device for Tums attests to the value of delaying source identification.

Despite its value as a persuasive device, deferring the source's introduction has several liabilities. One problem is that it often reduces the likelihood of information reception. Apparently, brand and other source identification at the outset of a commercial orients people so that they can locate and retrieve thoughts relevant to the message information. When this orienting information is deferred until the end of the message, it is important to use some other vehicle so that message recipients quickly comprehend what the appeal is going to be about.

Even if information reception is insured, delaying the identification of a low credibility source is a less than optimal strategy. Although it increases the persuasiveness of a low credibility source, it may not yield the same degree of influence as a high credibility communicator who is introduced at the outset of a message. Thus, the use of a source deferral strategy should be used in situations where it is not feasible to enhance source credibility directly.

Message Factors. In the previous chapter, we examined the combined effects of source credibility and message discrepancy, as well as the joint effects of credibility and threat. We shall review these findings briefly to underscore the importance of coordinating message and source. Two other message factors, incongruity and evidence, are also examined.

Source credibility has a systematic persuasive effect when an appeal is relatively discrepant. In this instance, a highly credible source induces more persuasion than a less credible communicator. With less discrepant appeals, there is no systematic effect of credibility. Highly credible sources are less persuasive than they would be with a more discrepant message and low credibility sources are more persuasive. These findings are consistent with expectations from information processing theory. High credibility is effective in blocking counterargument retrieval, which is most likely to occur when there is considerable message discrepancy. When a message is less discrepant, there are few counterarguments retrieved, and credibility has no effect on persuasion.

From a strategic perspective, evidence pertaining to the joint effects of credibility and message discrepancy suggest that it is useful to recruit highly credible sources if the message to be presented is highly discrepant. In situations where it is not possible to employ a highly credible communicator, moderately discrepant appeals should be used; less credible communicators are most persuasive when the message is moderately discrepant.

Studies pertaining to the joint effect of source credibility and threat also indicate the importance of orchestrating source and message to maximize persuasion. When a highly threatening message is used, a highly credible source is substantially more persuasive than a low credibility communicator. When a message threat is relatively low, a highly credible source still has greater persuasive power than a less credible source, though the magnitude of this difference is often less than is obtained for highly threatening appeals. These findings suggest that the use of a threat approach requires a highly credible spokesperson. Regardless of whether the threat is mild or severe, it induces counterarguing. A highly credible source can minimize retrieval of negative thoughts, whereas a less credible communicator cannot.

A third credibility-message combination involves the presentation of information that is incongruous with the source's best interest. Walster, Aronson, and Abrahams (1966) demonstrated that a highly credible prosecutor who argued in favor of more court power, which was in his best interest (that is, a congruous message), was much more persuasive than a low credibility criminal who argued for reduced court power, which was in his best interest. On the other hand, when these sources presented incongruous messages (that is, the prosecutor argued for less court power and the criminal for more court power) the prosecutor and criminal were about equally persuasive. This result emerged because the low credibility criminal became much more persuasive by using incongruity; the highly credible prosecutor was about as persuasive whether his message was congruous or incongruous with his best interest.

This finding is consistent with the information processing view. The prosecutor, by virtue of his position, had the credibility necessary to inhibit message recipient's retrieval of counterarguments. The low credibility source was successful in blocking counterargumentation only when he assumed an incongruent position. In effect, by presenting a message that was incongruous with his own interests, the low credibility criminal was likely to have become trustworthy. In turn, this increase in trustworthiness inhibited counterarguing.

The use of an incongruous message is seldom used by marketing strategists. The successful implementation of incongruity causes message recipients to accept a position in direct opposition to the communicator's best interests. Variants of the incongruity strategy are more suitable when the aim is to stimulate demand. One variant entails using a source who currently supports a position that is incongruous with his or her past behavior. Research pertaining to the use of such converts as spokespersons indicates that they induce greater influence for their view than do sources who have assumed a stance consistently favoring the position they advocate (Dutton, 1973; Levine and Valle, 1975). Apparently, by altering one's position, credibility is enhanced and counterargumentation is inhibited. This may explain Mikey's effectiveness as a spokesperson for Life cereal. Mikey was depicted as a convert; someone who hated all cereals, but liked Life cereal.

Another useful variant of the incongruity strategy involves the use of partial congruity. Although no investigations have been reported which manipulate both source credibility and the degree of congruity, studies pertaining to one-sided versus two-sided appeals are pertinent to the issue of partial congruity effects. Two-sided appeals may be regarded as partially congruous messages because arguments both favorable and unfavorable to the speaker's position are presented. It has been found that a two-sided message induces more persuasion than a one-sided appeal providing that the unfavorable information (1) is presented first, (2) is refuted in a compelling manner by the favorable information, and (3) cites only those unfavorable arguments that are already known to the audience (Hass and Linder, 1972). Presumably, a two-sided appeal that follows these prescriptions is effective because the presentation of information contrary to one's own best interests establishes trust at the outset of the message. This inhibits counterarguing and stimulates the processing of the message arguments that follow, which are in the spokesperson's best interests.

The final message device considered in this section involves the use of evidence. It entails providing supportive factual information that originates from a source other than the speaker (McCroskey, 1969). McCroskey (1969, 1970) observed that a highly credible source induced greater persuasion than a low credibility communicator when no evidence was used to support their advocacy. When evidence was used it had no effect on the persuasiveness of the credible source, but substantially increased the influence of a low credibility source. In fact, the low credibility source was about as persuasive as the highly credible source providing that he used unfamiliar evidence to support his position.

These findings imply that when evidence to support the message position is not available, it is worthwhile pursuing highly credible sources as spokespeople. However, when a spokesperson lacks credibility, the use of unfamiliar evidence is a highly potent strategy for two reasons. First, unfamilar evidence is effective because people focus on the evidence *per se* rather than the source. Thus, low credibility is not a liability. Second, the unfamilar evidence serves to inhibit counterargumentation. Familar evidence is ineffective since it is likely to have been already considered by message recipients in developing counterarguments.

The value of using evidence is illustrated by Gillette's strategy in stimulating demand for Flexmatic, an electric razor. Flexmatic had an eight percent share of the market when it introduced an advertising campaign that provided evidence for the superiority of this brand. The advertising reported the results of a clinical study which indicated that Flexmatic gave a closer shave than competitors' electric razors. In response to this campaign, Flexmatic's share of market rose to sixteen percent. Although all of this increase was not attributable to the use of evidence, this case demonstrates the persuasive potency of using unfamiliar evidence.

Summary and Implications. When message recipients oppose the position advocated in a message, they are likely to retrieve and rehearse counterarguments. A highly trustworthy and expert source can inhibit counterargumentation, whereas a less credible source cannot. As a result, a highly credible source is more persuasive. But this result is obtained in only a limited number of situations. These are summarized in Table 14.1. In these circumstances, it is useful to recruit a highly credible spokesperson to deliver an appeal.

When circumstances dictate the use of highly credible spokespersons, several strategies are available. One is to use testimonials made by product users. People should be selected who are knowledgeable about the subject of their testimonial, who appear truthful in stating their opinions, and who use the product in the same way as the audience does. Advertising for the analgesic, Tylenol, illustrates the effective use of testimonials. People

TABLE 14.1. The Joint Effects of Source Credibility and Other Variables

High Credibility Facilitates Persuasion When:
Response to an appeal is immediate
Source is identified at the outset of an appeal
Message discrepancy is substantial
Threatening appeals are used

A Low Credibility Source's Persuasiveness is Enhanced by:
Delaying the time between message presentation and response
Deferring source identification until the end of a message
Employing messages that are moderately discrepant from audience's initial position
Employing incongruous messages
Using unfamiliar evidence

experiencing headaches were recruited and asked to try Tylenol. Their description of the headache pain they suffered before taking Tylenol and their testimonials about Tylenol's effectiveness in relieving their headaches were recorded by a hidden camera. These testimonials were used as the basis for an effective advertising campaign.

A second strategy that is useful when a high credibility spokesperson is called for involves the use of testimonials given by people who have a reputation for being trustworthy and expert. E.F. Hutton, a company that offers financial services, employed the late John Paul Getty as a spokesperson in their advertising. Getty's expertise in financial matters was implied by his reputation as one of the world's richest men. He was also likely to have been viewed as trustworthy in that he had little to gain and much to lose by misrepresenting the value and quality of E.F. Hutton's services.

Finally, group consensus can be used as a means of gaining high credibility. When a substantial number of people share an opinion it confers expertise and trust on the source, even if each group member alone is not highly credible. A study by Asch (1951) illustrates the power of consensual information. A group of nine people were seated at a table, ostensibly to take part in a psychological experiment of visual judgment. Subjects were shown three lines on a card and asked to indicate the one that was closest to a single line drawn on a second card. Subjects went around the room and indicated their choices out loud. The same task was then repeated for a different set of lines. This task was quite easy and subjects had little difficulty in making the appropriate match.

In actuality eight of the nine subjects were confederates of the experimenter. They were seated so that the real subject (who did not know that the others were confederates) gave his response last. On the third trial these confederates each selected the same wrong line as being most similar to the standard line. Faced with this group consensus, subjects voiced the same wrong answers on about one third of the trials, even though they knew the answer was wrong. Some subjects never conformed, others always did, and some conformed on some trials but not on others. This high degree of conformity to group opinion in a situation where physical reality is easily determined makes it likely that even greater influence is achieved when reality is subjective.

Communication strategists make extensive use of consensual information in attempting to enhance persuasion. Sales people emphasize the popularity of a particular product in the hope that this consensual data will stimulate demand. When the World Football League began operation in 1974, management used this means of source enhancement to gain acceptance for their product. Crowds of twenty thousand were reported when only some ten thousand people were actually present. Large numbers of free tickets were given away for games on national television so that viewers would believe that the league had attracted a large following. Although such misrepresentations are questionable on ethical grounds, they do illustrate the use of consensual strategy.

In using a consensual strategy, it is important to consider who will serve as the spokespersons. If message recipients view the spokespersons as atypical, the use of a consensual strategy is likely to be ineffective (Wells and Harvey, 1977). The failure of the consensus strategy employed by the World Football League may have been attributable to this problem; message recipients did not perceive those who attended World Football League games to be representative of the population or like themselves.

Even if a consensual strategy is properly executed, it is not likely to be as effective as testimonials by typical consumers or by people known for their credibility (Wells and Harvey, 1977). This observation is anticipated by information processing theory. According to this view, the greater the ease with which a stimulus evokes a mental image, the more memorable it is. In turn, the greater the memorability of a stimulus the more likely it is to evoke stimulus-related thoughts which cause the message recipient to accept the advocacy. Presenting the experiences of a single person is likely to enhance the availability of thoughts about an issue to a greater extent that providing statistical information on the opinion of a relevant population.

Our analysis also has strategic implications in situations where it may not be feasible to employ a highly credible source. The appropriate spokesperson may not be available, or may be too expensive to employ. When these situations occur, it is appropriate to use strategies that enhance the persuasiveness of sources who lack credibility. These strategies are summarized in Table 14.1.

Credibility as a Persuasive Liability

Until now, the focus has been on situations where credibility enhanced, or, at least, did not undermine social influence. In this section, we consider situations in which a highly credible source is a persuasive liability. This entails examining situations where message recipients have a favorable opinion toward the message advocacy, and where individuals' own behavior is an important cue in assessing their attitudes.

Favorable Initial Opinion. In several investigations, it has been found that message recipients who are favorably disposed to an appeal are more persuaded by a moderately credible communicator than a highly credible source (see Sternthal *et al.*, 1978). This result is anticipated from information processing theory. As will be recalled, it was hypothesized that high credibility serves to inhibit the retrieval and rehearsal of thoughts from memory, whereas a less credible source does not have this effect. When the thoughts people have in memory are positive, high credibility inhibits their retrieval. Presumably, when a highly credible source advocates a view that message recipients favor, they are not highly motivated to retrieve thoughts. When the source is less credible, people may feel obliged to help the communicator by bolstering his arguments with their own. As a consequence, individuals generate more positive thoughts and are more persuaded when the communication is delivered by a source who is not highly credible.

The finding that high credibility is a persuasive liability when message recipients favor the issue qualifies the conditions under which it is appropriate to seek highly credible spokespeople. Such sources may enhance persuasion when the target audience is not favorably disposed to the appeal. High credibility sources are inappropriate when the audience favors the message issue. This is not to say that the least trustworthy and expert communicator available should be sought when an audience favors the message issue. This may cause people to question the soundness of their position, generate counterarguments, and reject the message. What is needed is a source who is sufficiently credible to block counterargumentation but not so credible as to inhibit support argumentation.

One's Own Behavior as a Cue. A second situation in which high credibility is a persuasive liability occurs when message recipients' own behavior is an important consideration in determining their attitude. Consider a situation where people purchase a product advocated by a highly credible source. Their attitude toward this product is not likely to be very positive in this instance because purchasers are uncertain whether the source's credibility or their liking for the product caused their purchase. Thus, some counterargumentation is likely. In contrast, if purchase resulted from an advocacy by a low credibility source, people are certain that their feeling about the product and not the source caused their behavior. As a result, few counterarguments are likely to be generated and persuasion is substantial. In effect, the less credible source is more persuasive.

This line of reasoning has been confirmed in several investigations (Dholakia and Sternthal, 1977; Powell, 1965; Tybout, 1978). It suggests that when individuals use their own behavior as a cue in assessing their attitudes, the selection of highly credible spokespeople is not appropriate. Rather, communicators should be selected who are sufficiently credible to evoke behavior, but not so credible that they are viewed as the cause of behavior.

COMMUNICATION MODALITY

A variety of communication modalities are available to transmit persuasive messages. Among the most frequently used modalities are broadcast media such as radio and television and print media such as magazines and newspapers. The selection of appropriate modalities is a complex and multifaceted decision. Consumers' media exposure habits and their processing behavior in response to information conveyed by different media must be considered. Competitors strategy also affects modality choice. Also, the modalities selected must be consistent with a firm's distribution and pricing strategy.

In this section, we shall describe the various factors that guide modality selection. Our analysis begins with an assessment of how consumers' behavior affects the strategist's choice of communication modality. This involves considering the traditional approach to media selection and extending it using principles derived from information processing theory. Discussed next is the effect of competitors' modality choices on a firm's media selection decisions. Finally, we describe the impact of distribution and pricing strategies on modality choice.

Consumer Response

Exposure as a Criterion for Modality Selection. The traditional approach to modality selection entails choosing those media which efficiently reach a desired target. The criterion for selection is exposure. Suppose 7UP is interested in identifying media that will reach current users of that brand efficiently. To address this issue, a demographic profile of current 7UP users is required. This can be obtained from data provided by syndicated services such as Simmons Market Research Bureau (SMRB) or Mediamark Research Inc. (MRI). Inspection of these data indicate that 7UP users have the following demographic profile:

Age:	18–34
Income:	$8,000 and up
Education:	College
Geographic Location:	Northeast, North Central, West

By specifying the profile of the target, the manager is in a position to evaluate the appropriateness of various media in exposing the target market to 7UP communications. Again, syndicated service data can be used for this purpose. They specify the demographic profiles of the audiences for various media. Table 14.2 shows the audiences best reached by three vehicles. It suggests that Magazine A is most effective in reaching current 7UP users. Whether it is also most efficient depends upon the cost of an insertion in each vehicle.

Although it is useful to select media that efficiently expose a desired audience to a communication, basing media selection solely on an exposure criterion is inappropriate. Such an approach assumes that once individuals are exposed to information it will be processed in the same way regardless of communication modality. There is, however, substantial evidence to suggest that the communication modality has a significant effect on information processing. We shall examine processing differences in information pre-

TABLE 14.2. Audiences for Three Vehicles

	Magazine A	TV Program A	TV Program B
Age	18–44	18–44	35 and up
Income	$8000–20,000	under $8000	$15,000 and up
Education	College	High school or less	College
Geographic	Regional editions available	Regional spots at station break	Regional spots at station break

sented audio-visually (for example, television), auditorally (for example, radio), and visually (for example, print).

Modality Differences in Information Processing.   Individuals' ability to represent incoming information in memory is affected by the modality used to transmit information.[3] One reason for this occurrence is that the rate of information transmission often differs among media. Processing of print information, such as an ad appearing in a newspaper or magazine, is self-paced. Message recipients process print information at a rate they find appropriate. In contrast, broadcast information that is auditory, such as radio commercials, or audiovisual, such as television commercials, involves externally paced presentations. The rate of information presentation is controlled by the communicator and not the message recipient.

The differences in pacing between print and broadcast media affect the processing of information in certain situations. As one might expect, when a message is difficult to understand, the ability to self-pace printed information makes it easier to recall than externally paced broadcast information (Chaiken and Eagley, 1976). Self-pacing provides the time necessary to interpret a complex message. When the same message is made easy-to-understand, the media differences in message processing are diminished (Chaiken and Eagley, 1976). In effect, the advantage of self-pacing is lost when messages can be readily understood.

The foregoing analysis suggests that it is important to insure easy message understanding when broadcast media are used. This can be achieved by careful selection of the language used in a broadcast appeal. When the broadcast involves television, the visual portion of the message can be used to facilitate understanding. Slowing down the rate of broadcast presentations is a less attractive alternative for coping with the pacing problem. Not only is it a costly strategy, but it also may have adverse effects on information processing. Increasing the time available for processing may provide message recipients with an opportunity to rehearse their own repertoire of message-related thoughts (see Wright, 1974). To the extent these thoughts are composed of counteragruments, slowing the rate of presentation is likely to cause message rejection.

Different modalities also vary in their effects on the availability of processed information. It has been found consistently that information transmitted pictorially is better recalled than information transmitted by some verbal means. (See Kieras, 1978). For example, when people are shown a large number of pictures, each representing an animal, for example, their recall of the objects is better than when the names of the same objects are verbally presented. Moreover, the transmission of information via pictures accompanied by verbal statements yields superior recall of the objects presented than transmissions involving only verbal statements, providing that the pictorial and verbal representations are closely related to each other (Donaldson, 1976; Levin, Bender, and Lesgold, 1976, Siegal and Allik, 1973). When the pictures and verbal statements are not closely related, recall is poorer than when verbal statements are presented alone (Sadowski, 1972).

---

[3]See Kisielius (1980) for a detailed discussion of modality effects.

There is not widespread agreement on the explanation for the effects reported above. A promising account for pictorial superiority in recall effect involves an examination of the differences in processing pictorial and verbal information. It is believed that because most pictorial representations are rich in the number of cues they provide, they trigger the retrieval and rehearsal of a substantial number of thoughts in memory (Kieras, 1978). These thoughts preserve the features of the objects presented in the pictorial representation and preserve the temporal sequence of events depicted. In contrast, purely verbal representations are likely to evoke relatively few thoughts. Because pictorial representations typically evoke more thoughts than verbal representations, pictorially presented information is likely to be better recalled.

An examination of how pictorial and verbal information is processed also explains the effectiveness of verbal representations accompanied by pictures in relation to verbal representations transmitted alone. A stimulus that includes a verbal and pictorial representation is stored sequentially. The pictorial representation is stored first in long-term memory. During this time, the verbal part of the message is held in short-term memory. Once the pictorial information is stored, the verbal information is rehearsed and registered in long-term memory. If the pictorial and verbal information are closely related, the retrieval and rehearsal of thoughts evoked by the pictorial information facilitates subsequent processing of the verbal information. Because related pictorial and verbal representations evoke more thought retrieval and rehearsal than verbal representations alone, the former yields better recall. However, if the pictorial and verbal representations are not closely related to each other, the cognitive resources required to retrieve and rehearse disparate bits of information may exceed the message recipient's processing capacity. Thus, pictorial representations limit message learning in relation to verbal representations alone.

The foregoing analysis implies that television communications should be better learned than radio communications of the same information. Television appeals involve the processing of both verbal and pictorial representations, whereas radio involves only the processing of verbal representations. If the pictorial and verbal representations are coordinated, television communications should evoke a greater number of associations about the object of advocacy than radio communications. The greater the number of associations or thoughts about a message, the more readily it is recalled.

It might be anticipated that because pictorial information is better recalled than verbal information, transmission of information pictorially would result in greater persuasion. This is likely to be the case when the pictorial information reinforces the verbal information. Here pictures make message thoughts more available. But pictorial representations also can undermine persuasion (Kisieluis, 1980). This results because pictorial representations are complex stimuli that are difficult to control. They may provide cues that unintentionally evoke message recipients' repertoire of unfavorable thoughts to the object pictured as well as message thoughts. In contrast, verbal representations are highly precise and are, therefore, more readily controlled. The associations evoked by verbal representations are thus more likely to be ones presented in the communication.

Several strategies are available to control the adverse effects of pictorial representations on communication effectiveness. One is to pre-test pictorial representations to insure that they do not evoke message recipients' repertoire of unfavorable thoughts. Another is to speed up the rate of communication presentation. Devices are now available for compressing information with minimal distortion. This strategy should reduce the evocation of message recipients' own thoughts. Caution is necessary in selecting the rate of presentation, because very fast rates of presentation may shut down the processing of message thoughts as well as the audience's own repertoire of thoughts.

Our analysis not only suggests how to make communications involving pictorial representations (such as television messages) more persuasive, it also indicates how to enhance the persuasiveness of verbal representations (such as radio messages). The approach involves increasing the number of associations evoked by a verbal representation. This can be achieved by providing enough descriptive detail in a radio message so that people readily construct images when they hear it. Alternatively, a media schedule might be developed where television messages are used at the outset of a campaign to facilitate the generation of object-related thoughts. Later, radio commercials could be employed in the hope that the associations created by the television campaign would be evoked in response to the radio appeal. Both strategies are attractive because they permit the use of radio, a less expensive medium, without compromising the processing of message information. But in using either strategy, it is important to limit the evocation of message recipients' own repertoire of counterarguments.

Competitive Environment

The choice of communication modality is affected by the competitive environment. When competitors gravitate to a particular modality to convey product messages, a firm has two strategies available to insure the impact of its own communications. One is to use the same modality as competitors are using. As we noted in the previous chapter, when this strategy is pursued it is important that sufficient communication frequency be used to distinguish a firm's brand from those of competitors. Sears used this approach successfully in advertising its home furnishing line. It advertised predominantly in print, the modality used by most of Sears' competitors. The success of this strategy was predicated on the fact that Sears had adequate resources to insure that their communication was processed despite the presence of competitors' appeals.

A second approach useful in dealing with competitors is to select media that are not frequently used by competitors. This may entail the selection of modalities that yield less than optimal consumer exposure. (Perhaps this is why competitors do not use such media.) Even if such a liability were present, it may be more than offset providing the firm's use of a particular modality was unique. Apparently, use of a medium not used by competitors allows message information to be more readily associated with the message source. Lanier used radio advertising to inform consumers about their line of dictating equipment in an industry where industrial print media were the dominant modality. This strategy was, in part, responsible for the rapid emergence of Lanier as a major company in the dictating equipment field.

The strategies suggested for combating competitive media strategy are based on the hierarchical network representation of long-term memory developed in Chapter Five. Because competitors are closely related in memory, using the same communication modality may cause the message conveyed by one competitor to become associated with another. By using different communication modalities than competitors, a point of distinction is provided that helps the message recipient store communicated information with the appropriate source. Similarly, by using frequent communication the chances that information will be stored at the appropriate node are enhanced.

Other Factors in Modality Selection

Two other factors that influence modality choice are worthy of mention. One is a firm's market coverage or distribution. Modalities which match market coverage are preferred to ones that outstrip distribution. Thus, network television would be an inappropriate modality to deliver a communication for a firm with regional distribution. The other factor is price volatility. When a product is susceptible to rapid price change and this fact must be made known to consumers, certain modalities are inappropriate. Specifically, modalities requiring long lead times such as network television and magazines are not highly attractive when prices are volatile. In this situation newspapers and radio, which are highly flexible and allow last minute modifications, are preferred.

SUMMARY

The persuasive impact of an appeal depends upon the manager's ability to orchestrate the communication, its source, and the modalities used to convey message information. Attractive sources facilitate the storage of information. Trustworthy and expert sources help persuade those who are negatively predisposed to the message issue, but are a liability when message recipients are positively disposed to the issue or when recipients consider the fact that they complied with a source's advocacy in evaluating a product or service. These effects occur in large measure because source credibility effects the retrieval of information from memory.

The communication modality also affects message persuasiveness. In selecting modalities it is important to consider their impact on information processing. Information reception is facilitated by using self-paced print media. Storage and retrieval of message information is enhanced by enabling people to image critical communication content. This can be achieved by using visualizations or detailed verbal descriptions in message presentations. Finally, modality selection is determined by competitors strategies. To insure that an appeal is linked to the sponsoring firm one may use frequent message repetition or select a modality that is not being used by competitors.

QUESTIONS

1. What managerial goal is achieved by employing attractive sources? What are the liabilities in relying on attractive sources as spokespersons for persuasive appeals?

2. Suppose the target for a product message is people who do not have a favorable disposition toward the product. What type of sources would you select to persuade the message recipients to purchase the advertised product? Why would you select the sources you have identified?

3. What strategies would you consider if the spokesperson for an appeal were viewed as lacking trustworthiness? (Assume that you cannot change the spokesperson). For each strategy selected use your understanding of information processing to defend your choices.

4. Under what conditions is a highly credible source a persuasive liability? Explain why credibility has this effect in each case identified.

5. Is audience exposure an adequate criterion for modality selection? Defend your position drawing on your understanding of how modalities affect information processing.

6. What accounts for the greater effectiveness of print in conveying information in relation to radio messages? How can this advantage be offset when radio messages are used?

7. What accounts for the greater effectiveness of television messages in relation to radio? What strategies are likely to be effective in offsetting the deficit exhibited by radio presentations?

8. What strategies are available to offset the adverse effects of having competitors use the same modality as your firm for conveying persuasive communications? How would the strategy selected be affected by the financial ability of your firm in relation to that of competitors?

Part VI

Part VI summarizes the main features of the information processing view. The relationships among variables involved in processing information are described and the strategic marketing implications emerging from this analysis are identified. The application of information processing principles in addressing marketing problems is highlighted further in two illustrative cases.

Summary and Conclusion

Chapter 15

Information Processing Theory: Marketing Strategy

In this book, consumers' behavior is interpreted from an information processing perspective. Purchase and consumption decisions are viewed in terms of how individuals acquire, organize, and use information. Specifically, in Parts I and II we presented an overview of the information processing view, indicated how information processing guided consumer research, and related the information processing view to other theoretical positions. Part III provided a detailed account of consumer information acquisition, organization, and utilization processes. Part IV added detail to this account by describing the impact of individual differences and groups on information processing and consumption. Part V focused on strategies emerging from the information processing view. In so doing, we added further descriptive detail regarding consumer information processing.

In this chapter, we review the main features of information processing theory and highlight some of the strategic implications it suggests. This discussion summarizes the theory and its application in a wide variety of settings. In addition, we illustrate the application of information processing theory in two specific contexts: controlling the effects of adverse rumors and stimulating energy conservation.

CONSUMER INFORMATION PROCESSING

Information processing theory views consumers' behavior as a goal-oriented activity. Consumers want to make informed purchase decisions. They want to know what attributes are likely or unlikely to be provided by a particular consumption choice. To achieve their goal, consumers use information acquired from others, as well as information derived from their own experiences. The decision-making process involves the representation of incoming information as thoughts in memory. These thoughts, or object-attribute associations, may be used immediately as a basis for product evaluation and choice, or they may be stored in memory for later evaluation. Consumers also may evoke the retrieval of thoughts previously stored that are relevant to product evaluation, or they may evoke original thoughts not previously associated with a product. Whatever the origin of the thoughts that are activated at a particular point in time, they require organization if they are to be used in consumer decision making. The processes by which information is acquired, organized, and used are reviewed and the strategic implications of this description are specified.

Exposure and Reception

Consumers must be exposed to information if it is to influence their behavior. One approach to exposure is to assume that consumers are passive; that is, they do not actively seek out information, but process information they happen to be exposed to. To the extent this assumption is correct, it is useful to make information readily available as a means of insuring exposure. This may entail devoting significant resources to presenting information via mass media and personal selling. For many products, it may also involve enhancing exposure through the extensive use of in-store strategies such as increasing the number of shelf facings, securing eye-level shelf height, and using special displays. If this is not feasible, attempts to motivate consumers to search for information may be employed. Search for information can be evoked by questioning consumers' certainty about their current knowledge and emphasizing the economic, social, or psychological risk associated with a wrong decision.

Information to which people are exposed may or may not be processed. If attention is paid to incoming information, it is represented in a temporary memory store called short-term memory. Attention is high when the strength of the incoming information signal is strong and when the incoming information is pertinent. Thus, two strategies emerge when information processing is inhibited because communicated thoughts are not registered in memory. One is to increase signal strength, which may be achieved by increasing the frequency of incoming information. The other is to change the information presented so that the thoughts conveyed are more pertinent to message recipients. This latter strategy may require a change in the product so that it has features pertinent to consumers, or it may merely require altering which of the current features of a product are emphasized.

Retrieval and Rehearsal

Incoming information represented as thoughts in short-term memory (STM) may be used immediately to make a judgment. Alternatively, the message thoughts registered in STM may stimulate the *retrieval* of relevant own thoughts from long-term memory

(LTM). To the extent that message thoughts and own thoughts are *rehearsed,* they are represented in some permanent form in LTM for later use in decision making. We shall consider the nature and implications of retrieval and rehearsal processes.

The retrieval of thoughts from LTM is facilitated by the fact that memory is organized. Specifically, LTM is structured so as to preserve the meaning of objects. This is believed to entail representing object-attributable associations at one or more addresses in memory. These addresses are made readily accessible by virtue of their hierarchical arrangement. Memory is believed to be arranged so that brand thoughts are hierarchically organized under product category addresses. Thus, thoughts about Coast soap that have been previously processed can be retrieved by considering, say, a personal cleaning products memory address. These thoughts, in turn, might activate addresses pertaining to soaps and ultimately those pertaining to Coast.

Long-term memory also is organized to preserve sequences of events or episodes people have experienced. Although the specific details of this type of thought storage are not well understood, it appears that scenarios composed of thoughts are constructed to represent everyday occurrences. Because such episodes are represented by many object-attribute associations, they often are readily available in memory.

The retrieval of thoughts stored in LTM frequently is initiated by the thoughts currently available in STM. These latter thoughts may facilitate the location of addresses in LTM where relevant associations are stored as well as stimulate the retrieval of the thoughts stored at these addresses. The thoughts retrieved and represented in STM may then stimulate further thought retrieval from LTM. When the thoughts represented in STM are ambiguous, they trigger the retrieval of the most available thoughts. Thoughts' availability depends upon recency of storage; memory appears to operate on a "last-in-first-out" principle, that is, information most recently processed is most accessible. Availability also is affected by the number of convergent thoughts one has about some object. The more thoughts pertaining to a product characteristic of an object, the more available that characteristic is for retrieval and representation in STM.

The evaluation of a product or some other object is based on the thoughts registered in STM. These thoughts may be message thoughts representing incoming information, or own thoughts representing previously stored associations. In situations where decisions are not made at the time of presentation of incoming information, message and own thoughts can be stored for later retrieval by a rehearsal process. Rehearsal involves the active association of attributes with an object. The availability of thoughts is enhanced by rehearsal, because rehearsal fosters both recency of storage and the number of convergent associations.

Our description of retrieval and rehearsal implies that decision making is a constructive process. Individuals most often do not base decisions on a faithful representation of incoming information. Rather, decisions are based on people's own repertoire of thoughts as well as message thoughts. Moreover, the thoughts that serve as a basis of decision making are often the product of abstraction and aggregation. Associations between some object and physical attribute are abstracted to infer a thought linking an object and subjective attribute. Thoughts are also aggregated or combined in various ways to render a product judgment. Individuals may use a linear compensatory, disjunctive, conjunctive, lexicographic, or some other aggregation rule. By invoking the processes of abstraction and aggregation, an individual can construct thoughts that are distinct from those represented in incoming information or from those previously stored in long-term memory.

Although our primary focus has been on how object-attribute associations affect decision making, it should be noted that other types of thoughts can influence choice. Thoughts relating some object to some role a person fulfills, which we have termed personal normative beliefs, can affect decision making. Thoughts associating an object to the associations perceived to be held by significant others, or social normative beliefs, also can influence choice.

The favorableness of product evaluation and the likelihood of consumption depend on the valence of the thoughts people have represented in short-term memory at the time of decision making. Evaluation is likely to be favorable to the extent that a decision is based on message thoughts or positive own thoughts. Favorability of evaluation also increases to the extent that counteradvocacy own thoughts are suppressed.

The description of retrieval and rehearsal processes has important implications for the design of marketing strategy. Initially we shall consider strategies that are useful in influencing the behavior when the target is composed of people who are favorably disposed to a product. Then influence strategies are identified that are appropriate when the target is not favorable to a product offering. Finally the implications of the retrieval and rehearsal processes for marketing program evaluation are examined.

The description of LTM structure has implications for positioning strategy. It implies that product positioning efforts begin by assessing the category address that is consistent with a brand and yields the greatest demand. Such positioning is attractive to the extent that a firm can distinguish its brand on attributes important to consumers from similarly positioned competitors. Selecting a position of greatest demand also is warranted when a firm has sufficient resources to insure that the promotion of an attribute shared by competitors is associated with the firm's brand, or when distinctiveness can be achieved by some other means. If this is not possible, positions that yield less demand but allow a competitive distinction on attributes important to consumers should be considered.

The description of retrieval and rehearsal suggests several strategies to enhance the permanent representation of incoming information in LTM. One strategy pertains to address identification. It is important to identify the context or issue at the outset of a communication so that information recipients can locate and activate the address to which incoming information is to be associated. If the context is not evident to the audience until the end of the communication, a permanent trace of its content is unlikely because the appropriate memorial address is not known until it is too late to associate it with incoming information. Message recipients may guess what a communication is about and store information in that context. But if their guess is wrong, the stored information is unlikely to be retrieved when evaluating the object advocated in the communication. Indeed, advertisers have repeatedly found that late identification of their brand and the product category in a commercial results in limited processing of message information.

The permanent representation of incoming information also may be fostered by implementing other communication strategies. Frequent presentation of information may be a useful device in that it is likely to activate many object-attribute associations and increase the probability of recent storage. In addition, pictorial representations such as those used in visual media (for example, television, print pictures) may be used to stimulate the processing of incoming information. In the absence of pictorial representations, the processing of incoming information may be induced by several other imaging strategies. When information transmission is auditory (as is the case for radio messages), vivid verbal descriptions of an object's attributes and the context in which the object is used are particularly useful devices. Additionally, the processing of auditory communications and verbal presentations can be enhanced by suggesting that the audience conjure up mental images of the information presented. If an audience has no strong pictorial representation about an object, an effective imaging strategy may be to present pictorial information initially and then use an auditory medium to trigger the activation of this representation. Operationally, this might be achieved by launching a communication campaign with television and printed pictorial information and introducing radio only after the target audience has had an opportunity to store the visualization. Finally, the representation of marketer information may be stimulated by using some type of incentive to induce purchase.

The use of repetition, imaging, and behavior inducement strategies are appropriate when the target audience is favorably disposed to a brand. These strategies enhance the availability of message thoughts. They also may enhance the availability of own thoughts. But this does not pose a problem when the target is favorably disposed because own thoughts are likely to be composed of support arguments. In contrast, when the target audience is not favorably disposed to a brand, the evocation of own thoughts may undermine influence. Indeed, we have seen that increasing repetition, imagery, and incentives can have an adverse effect on brand evaluation and purchase.

When individuals are likely to retrieve and rehearse negative own thoughts, two strategies are useful. One entails presenting cues that block own thought activation. Devices such as highly credible spokespeople, evidence supporting an advocacy, two-sided appeals, and distraction are appropriate for this purpose. A second strategy entails providing cues that increase the likelihood of retrieving positive own thoughts about a product. The product name, package, logo, price, and other physical features should be assessed in terms of the thoughts they are likely to induce. For example, hot dogs that are darker in color and spicier than most other brands of hot dogs imply maturity. Such products appeal to consumers who desire an adult hot dog. In contrast, to appeal to a more youthful target, a light pink and more bland-tasting hot dog would be appropriate.

The selective retrieval of own thoughts favorable to a product may also be achieved by providing cues that evoke social or personal normative beliefs. By stressing the expectations of others, or reminding the consumer of a product's value in discharging some role obligation, positive own thoughts may be evoked. The intent of such cues is to inhibit the retrieval and rehearsal of individuals' negative object-attribute associations that otherwise might be activated in response to incoming information.

Finally, a knowledge of individuals' aggregation rules imply specific product and communication strategies. For example, if consumers employ linear compensatory aggregation, influence can be achieved by developing products that dominate competitive offerings on one or more of the product features most important to consumers, and by emphasizing these features in promoting the product. Less important features can be neglected in designing a product, because competitive dominance on such features will be offset by the firm's superiority on the features critical to making a choice. If, however, consumers use a conjunctive aggregation approach, it is important that a product meet some minimal standard on all characteristics serving as the basis for evaluation.

Individual and Group Differences

Our description of information processing has focused on the mechanism by which information is represented, stored, and retrieved. The explanation is based on the assumption that individuals have thoughts stored in memory and that these thoughts are used in object evaluation. The origin of these thoughts is not described. Nor is the process which causes different people to hold different thoughts addressed. An understanding of individual and group differences is useful in this regard.

At the most basic level, it may be contended that the differences in thoughts people have stored reflect different exposure opportunities. In turn, differences in information exposure opportunities reflect variations in how people are socialized. Individuals socialized in an upper middle class environment value individuality and achievement. Lower middle class people value orderliness and morality. And upper lower class individuals believe in luck. These orientations are represented in memory and influence individuals' response to products and communications. Products offering consumers a way of expressing their individuality are likely to appeal to upper middle class members, who have many positive associations with this attribute. In contrast, products offering orderliness and neatness are likely to attract lower middle class members who have stored favorable associations with these characteristics.

Socialization not only affects the content of thoughts individuals store in memory, but also the way in which they process information. As children undergo cognitive development, there are certain anxieties and frustrations that are not completely resolved. In later life, these unresolved anxieties are manifested in terms of particular information storage and retrieval strategies. For example, individuals with an oral fixation may exhibit gullibility. In processing terms, their evaluations depend on incoming information to a much greater extent than on the retrieval of their own previously stored thought repertoire. People with an oral fixation may also exhibit an aggressive biting response mode. For these people, retrieval of their own thought repertoire is the basis for evaluation and response.

An understanding of the effect of socialization on consumer response is of value to marketing regulators and strategists. Regulators justify their scrutiny over media communications on the basis that some individuals cannot resist persuasion. Thus the regulators' role is to insure that incoming information is valid. Strategists are interested in educating consumers to employ own thought retrieval strategies so as to minimize the effect of competitive propaganda. Such strategies may entail providing consumers with the arguments necessary to combat competitive appeals and teaching consumers to rely on their own thought repertoire in response to a persuasive appeal.

PROBLEM SOLVING FROM AN INFORMATION PROCESSING PERSPECTIVE

So far, we have reviewed consumer decision making from an information processing perspective and noted the strategic implications emerging from this theory. The implications identified are ones applicable in a wide variety of circumstances. Now, we shall change our perspective, and illustrate how specific problems can be interpreted and addressed from an information processing viewpoint. The problems chosen for discussion are ones that are both common and difficult to resolve.

Controlling the Effects of Rumors

Companies are often faced with rumors associating their product with undesirable characteristics.[1] Although these rumors are not true, they appear to have an adverse effect on consumers' behavior. In what is perhaps the best documented case, the McDonald's fast food restaurant chain was rumored to be using red worm meat in its hamburgers. The rumor was not true. But McDonald's sales were reported to be down by as much as thirty percent in those regions where the worm rumor circulated.

McDonald's experience is not an isolated occurrence. A substantial number of firms have confronted the problem of dispelling rumors linking their products to undesirable attributes. Gillette was faced with a rumor that their hairdryers were made with asbestos, a cancer-producing agent. General Foods had to contend with the rumor that Pop Rocks, a candy filled with carbon dioxide, caused children to explode when it was consumed in combination with soft drinks. (It was also rumored that some parents were testing the veracity of this assertion, using their children as subjects.) As in the case of McDonald's, the rumors about Gillette hairdryers and Pop Rocks were untrue but threatening to sales.

Information processing theory is useful in addressing the rumor problem. It not only suggests approaches that are likely to be effective in dispelling the adverse effect of a rumor, it also alerts the strategist to approaches that are likely to be unsuccessful. Consider, for example, the refutation approach used by McDonald's to combat the rumor that their hamburgers were made with worms. McDonald's store managers posted a letter from the Secretary of Agriculture stating that "hamburger produced by these [McDonald's] establishments is wholesome, properly identified, and in compliance with standards prescribed by Food Safety and Quality Service regulations." Television and print advertisements emphasizing "100 percent pure beef" were intensified. Public relations statements by McDonald's personnel noted that "It doesn't make sense, even from a financial viewpoint. Red worms cost between $5 and $8 a pound. Hamburger meat costs just over a dollar a pound. You'd have to be nuts to put worms in your hamburgers. You just couldn't afford it."

This refutation strategy did little to dispel the effect of the rumor that McDonald's made its hamburgers with worm meat. As the advertising manager for McDonald's System

---

[1]This illustration is based on a study reported by Tybout, Calder, and Sternthal (1981).

of Ohio Incorporated observed, "It's [the refutation strategy] not doing any good. The calls are still coming in. Business is still not back."

McDonald's experience in using refutation to combat the effect of an adverse rumor is anticipated from information processing theory. People exposed to a rumor linking McDonald's to worms are likely to have stored this association in memory. The presentation of information refuting the rumor may stimulate the retrieval of this association, resulting in an unfavorable evaluation of McDonald's. Or, consumers may retrieve thoughts such as "McDonald's hamburgers are not made with worms." Such thoughts are likely to be less positive about McDonald's than the ones consumers would have retrieved in the absence of the refutation.

Information processing theory also suggests several strategies that are likely to be effective in combating adverse rumor effects. One is a storage strategy. In the context of the McDonald's worm rumor, storage involves relating worms to objects other than McDonald's and particularly to objects that are positively evaluated. For example, when called upon to respond to the worm rumor, McDonald's public relations personnel might have noted that worms were considered a delicacy used in salads, to make cookies and the like. A controlled experimental test of this approach indicated that it dispelled the effect of the adverse McDonald's worm rumor. The storage strategy may have made worms positively valued, so that its association with McDonald's hamburgers would not be negatively evaluated. Alternatively, it may have caused the storage of worms with objects other than McDonald's hamburgers. Or, both of these outcomes may have occurred.

Another approach to combating the adverse effect of a rumor involves a retrieval strategy. Consumers are provided with cues that minimize the chances that they will retrieve object-rumor associations. In the case of McDonald's worm rumor, a retrieval strategy may entail advertising products in the line other than hamburgers. Alternatively, consumers can be asked in advertising to think about their favorite McDonald's and the things they like best about it. In a controlled experiment, such devices have been found to be effective in dispelling the McDonald's worm rumor. This outcome emerges because people are directed to think about characteristics of McDonalds other than the one related to the rumor.

The point of this illustration is that information processing theory is a useful basis for strategy. It helps the manager to distinguish the strategies that are likely to be effective in addressing a problem from those that are unlikely to work. Note, however, that information processing theory does not indicate precisely how a strategy is to be operationalized. This task is left to the discretion of the manager. Thus, information processing theory suggests that storage and retrieval strategies are likely to be more effective than a refutation strategy in combating the adverse effects of rumors. The specific storage and retrieval strategies to be implemented, however, are left to the manager's ingenuity.

Stimulating Energy Conservation

The information processing perspective developed in this text can also be applied to general problems facing society. One such area where this perspective has considerable potential is in dealing with energy problems. While technological solutions hold considerable promise for the longer term, conserving energy offers the best immediate alternative. One source estimates that the United States could consume thirty to forty percent less energy and still enjoy the same standard of living (Yergin, 1979). Consequently, the problem becomes how to persuade people to conserve energy. To illustrate the approach, an example of the successful application of a consumer information processing strategy is presented (Craig and McCann, 1978).

Summer brownouts and blackouts are an infrequent but insistent reminder of our energy problems. The tremendous load placed on a utility's generation and distribution system by air conditioners is the root of the problem. Over the past twenty years, there has been a dramatic growth in the use of air conditioners and a concomitant increase in electricity consumption. Utilities must often use older and less efficient generating capacity to meet summer peak demand, thus contributing even more to the waste of scarce energy resources. The problem is to convince consumers to use less electricity for air conditioning purposes.

A program to achieve energy conservation involves a number of distinct steps. First, the focal behavior has to be identified. Second, the component behaviors that comprise the focal behavior have to be determined. Third, the target consumers (that is, those best able to respond to the communications program) must be identified. Fourth, relevant appeals must be developed to convince the target audience to conserve energy. Finally, a method to assess whether the communications program had any effect must be devised.

To implement this approach, some idea is needed about the component behaviors pertaining to the focal behavior—use of air conditioners. One way to obtain this information is to solicit the opinions of experts. Table 15.1 enumerates eleven air conditioning behaviors that can affect electricity conservation suggested by experts in this field. All but the last component behavior can be accommodated immediately by consumers. Buying a unit with a high EER rating is more of a long run conservation behavior.

In addition to knowing what can be done to conserve energy, it is important to identify the consumers most able to engage in these behaviors. The prime group is obviously households that have air conditioning units. These individuals tend to be younger, have higher incomes, more education, and live in larger dwellings than those who do not have air conditioners (Craig, 1980). Alternatively, this group can be defined as households that consume more than five thousand kilowatts per year, with summer consumption at least twenty percent greater than winter consumption (Craig and McCann, 1978). The advantage of this latter definition is that it allows precise targeting of messages as part of normal bill enclosures.

After the target group had been defined, it was a question of designing a communication program to persuade them to conserve electricity. A knowledge of how consumers process information was important at this juncture. Because it was anticipated that consumers would activate counterarguments to an appeal advocating electricity conservation, it was expected that a highly credible spokesperson would enhance the effectiveness of persuasive communication. Given consumers' limited knowledge about electricity conservation it was thought that a message would be made more effective if it were repeated. Both these strategies were used to achieve energy conservation.

A basic message was designed incorporating the eleven component behaviors shown

TABLE 15.1. Component Conservation Behaviors To Save Electricity When Using Air Conditioning

When you use your air conditioners, do not overcool. Set to control room temperature at about seventy-eight degrees, or no more than fifteen degrees cooler than outside temperature. If your air conditioner has low, medium, and high settings—use medium.

Turn off your air conditioner when no one is going to be home. If you must go home to a cool house or apartment, it is cheaper—in terms of both money and energy—to invest in a timer to turn your air conditioner on about an hour before you expect to get in than to leave it on all day.

Keep all doors and windows closed while your air conditioner is in use. You do not want to cool the great outdoors. Also be sure closet doors are closed, and shut off rooms not in use.

Reduce the use of heat producing appliances. When running your air conditioner limit the use of ovens, dishwashers, dryers, and so on, to the cooler parts of the day. Also remember that lights are a heat source, and turn them off when they are not needed.

Close drapes or draw shades and blinds on the sunny side of your home to cut incoming heat. Light colored draperies or ones with light linings will cut off more heat than dark ones.

Locate your window unit carefully for cooling effectiveness. A window in the middle of the area to be cooled is the best place. Avoid corners and hallways as locations. Make sure large pieces of furniture do not block circulation of air into and from the unit.

Use portable fans with window air conditioners to reduce need for additional units.

Plan no-cook meals on hot days, when possible, to avoid heating the kitchen. When you can, use a small appliance, such as an electric skillet, instead of the oven.

When you service your air conditioner: Clean or replace the air filter. All air conditioners have filters that clean the air. If the filter is clogged and dirty, the air conditioner will have to work harder and longer to cool your home. Most filters are easy to clean or can be replaced inexpensively.

Clean the fins and coils. Dirt and grime in the air collect on the fins and coils. This layer of dirt makes the unit run longer than it would if it were clean. If you have access to your air conditioner from the outside simply clean it every month or so.

Buy an air conditioner with a high EER (Energy Efficiency Rating). The operating cost of an air conditioner depends on its EER rating, usually between 5 and 12. The higher a unit's EER, the more cooling power it produces per watt used and the lower its operating cost.

in Table 15.1. Given the need to convey an extensive amount of information, a self-paced medium was appropriate. Therefore, a print message was developed. It was included as an enclosure along with consumers' utility bills. The basic appeal was that it would cost much more to use the air conditioner this summer than in previous summers and here were eleven ways to lower the cost. Some consumers received this message identified as coming from the utility (that is, Con Edison), while others received the same message from the more credible chairman of the New York Public Service Commission. Some consumers received the message only once (at the beginning of August) while others received it twice (again at the beginning of September).

In assessing the effectiveness of the communication program, the most important

Figure 15.1. Effect of Source and Repetition on Requests for Energy Conservation Information

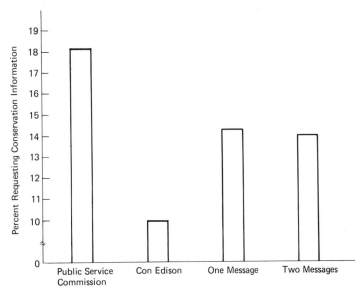

SOURCE: Adapted from Craig and McCann, 1978.

measure is whether people consumed less electricity during the test periods. It is also important, however, to see how much interest in conservation the communication prompted. Thus, two measures of effectiveness were used: (1) the number of consumers who requested more information about ways to reduce their energy consumption, and (2) the actual kilowatt hours consumed during August and September. Figure 15.1 shows the percent of people who requested additional information about energy conservation. Significantly more people requested information when the message came from a source of higher overall credibility (18.1 percent vs. 10 percent). The critical measure is how much electricity was consumed. Figure 15.2 shows the differences between source treatments. In July, before the experiment started, there was no difference in the electricity consumption of the two groups. All groups received the message at the beginning of August. During the month of August the group receiving the message identified as coming from the New York Public Service Commission consumed significantly less electricity. In the month of September there was a sharp drop in electricity consumption for all groups in response to lower ambient temperatures. Because everyone reduced their consumption it was not possibly to determine whether the second message had any effect.

It is fairly clear that the effectiveness of a communication advocating energy conservation can be enhanced by using a high credibility source. This relationship held whether the outcome were measured in terms of requests for energy conservation information or actual reduction in the amount of energy consumed. This argues for the use of the most credible spokespersons possible when attempting to persuade people to conserve energy. In contrast, repetition of the message had no effect. This does not mean,

Figure 15.2. Plot of Source Effect Pre-experiment Month and Two Post-experiment Months

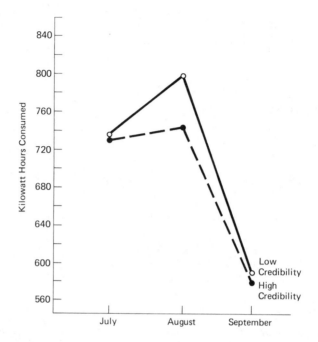

SOURCE: Adapted from Craig and McCann, 1978.

however, that people should not be reminded of what they can do to conserve energy. The overall drop in ambient temperature may have negated the repetition impact. Repetition might have enhanced communication effectiveness if the temperature had remained high.

Further, this study suggests that a knowledge of how consumers process information can be valuable in designing effective influence programs. A knowledge of the theory provides an indication of what strategy is likely to be most effective. But, the incorporation of theoretically based strategies into the overall marketing program does not provide a test of the theory's adequacy. For example, the fact that repetition of the message did not result in increased conservation should not be taken as a repudiation of information processing theory. Environmental factors (in this case, temperature) may have obscured outcomes predicted by information processing theory. Or, the number of repetitions used may have been insufficient to produce outcomes predicted by information processing theory. These observations underscore the fact that theory provides strategic direction. Strategic effectiveness depends, however, not only on selecting appropriate theories as a basis for strategy, but also effective implementation. Effective implementation is a matter of managerial ingenuity and experience.

SUMMARY

This chapter summarizes the information processing view and identifies strategies that are useful in influencing consumers' behavior. Consumers are viewed as goal-oriented individuals who seek information to make judicious choices. Information acquired from others and on the basis of past experience is organized and used for this purpose. Effective consumer influence strategies require the provision of information favorable to a product, service, or other object. Effective strategies also require that unfavorable information about a product be addressed. Both of these requirements may be met by appropriate use of product, price, distribution, and promotion instruments.

QUESTIONS

1. Identify two strategies you would select to overcome the following marketing problems. Defend your choice in terms of information processing theory.

   a. Consumers are not aware of a brand.
   b. Consumers' evaluation of a brand becomes more negative when they are presented with television communications suggesting that consumers purchase the brand.
   c. Consumers are not persuaded by an appeal where the brand and product category are identified late in the message.

2. What accounts for the ineffectiveness of the refutation strategy used by McDonald's to combat the worm rumor?

3. Develop strategies that you believe would be effective in combating the effect of the rumor linking McDonald's hamburgers and worm meat. Defend your choice of strategy on the basis of your knowledge about consumer information processing.

4. What accounts for the finding that the communication source affected the amount of electricity consumption? Why was message repetition an ineffective strategy?

5. "Theory is useful in identifying appropriate marketing strategy. It cannot insure that the strategies selected in this way will be effective." Explain this statement.

Bibliography

ADVERTISING RESEARCH FOUNDATION, "Are There Consumer Types—An Attempt to Predict Buying Behavior from Demographic and Personality Traits," Supervised Study 28, New York: ARF, 1964.

AJZEN, I., AND M. FISHBEIN, "The Prediction of Behavioral Intentions in a Choice Situation," *Journal of Experimental Social Psychology,* 5, 1969, 400–16.

———, "The Prediction of Behavior from Attitudinal and Normative Variables," *Journal of Experimental Social Psychology,* 6, 1970, 466–87.

———, "Attitudes and Normative Beliefs as Factors Influencing Behavioral Intentions," *Journal of Personality and Social Psychology,* 21, 1972, 1–9.

———, "Attitudinal and Normative Variables as Predictors of Specific Behaviors," *Journal of Personality and Social Psychology,* 27, 1973, 41–57.

ALEXIS, M., G. HAINES, AND L. SIMON, "Consumer Information Processing: The Case of Women's Clothing," *Marketing and the New Science of Planning,* Chicago: American Marketing Association, 1968, 197–205.

ANDERSON, K., AND T. CLEVENGER, "A Summary of Experimental Research in Ethos," *Speech Monographs,* 30, 1963, 59–78.

ANDERSON, N., "Averaging Versus Adding as a Stimulus-Combination Rule in Impression Formation," *Journal of Experimental Psychology,* 70, 1965, 394–400.

ANDREASEN, A. R., "Attitudes and Customer Behavior: A Decision Model," in *New Research in Marketing,* ed. L. Preston, Berkeley, CA: Institute of Business and Economic Research, 1965.

APPLEBAUM, W., AND R. SPEARS, "Controlled Experimentation in Marketing Research," *Journal of Marketing,* 14, 1950, 505–17.

ARNDT, J., "Perceived Risk, Sociometric Integration, and Word-of-Mouth Communication in the Adoption of a New Food Product," in *Risk-Taking and Information-Handling in Consumer Behavior,* ed. D. Cox, Boston: Harvard University Press, 1967.

ARONSON, E., J. TURNER, AND J. CARLSMITH, "Communication Credibility and Communication Discrepancies as Determinants of Opinion Change," *Journal of Abnormal and Social Psychology,* 67, 1963, 31–37.

ASCH, S., "Effects of Group Pressure upon the Modification and Distortion of Judgments," in *Groups, Leadership and Men,* ed. H. Guetzkow, Pittsburgh, PA: Carnegie Press, 1951.

BAGOZZI, R., A. TYBOUT, C. S. CRAIG, AND B. STERNTHAL, "The Construct Validity of the Tripartite Classification of Attitudes," *Journal of Marketing Research,* 16, 1979, 88–95.

———, and M. Van Loo, "Fertility as Consumption: Theories from the Behavioral Sciences," *Journal of Consumer Behavior,* 4, 1978, 199–228.

BAUER, R., "Consumer Behavior as Risk-Taking" in *Risk-Taking and Information-Handling in Consumer Behavior,* ed. D. Cox, Boston: Harvard University Press, 1967.

BAUMGARTEN, S., "The Innovative Communicator in the Diffusion Process," *Journal of Marketing Research,* 12, 1975, 12–18.

BECKNELL, J., AND R. R. MCISAAC, "Test Marketing Cookware Coated With Teflon," *Journal of Advertising Research,* 3, 1963, 2–8.

BERGIN, A., "The Effect of Dissonant Persuasive Communications upon Changes in a Self-Referring Attitude," *Journal of Personality,* 30, 1962, 423–38.

BEM, D., "Self-Perception Theory," in *Advances in Experimental Social Psychology,* ed. L. Berkowitz, New York: Academic Press, 1972.

———, AND A. ALLEN, "On Predicting Some of the People Some of the Time: The Search for Cross-Situational Consistencies in Behavior," *Psychological Review,* 81, 1974, 506–20.

BENHAM, T., "Polling for a Presidential Candidate: Some Observations of the 1964 Campaign," *Public Opinion Quarterly,* 29, 1965, 185–99.

BERELSON, B., P. LAZARSFELD, AND W. MCPHEE, *Voting: A Study of Opinion Formation in a Presidential Election,* Chicago: University of Chicago Press, 1954.

BERKOWITZ, L., AND D. COTTINGHAM, "The Interest Value and Relevance of Fear Arousing Communications," *Journal of Abnormal and Social Psychology,* 60, 1960, 37–43.

BERNSTEIN, P., "Psychographics is Still an Issue on Madison Avenue," *Fortune,* January 16, 1978.

BETTMAN, J., "Information Processing Models of Consumer Behavior," *Journal of Marketing Research,* 7, 1970, 370–76.

———, "Issues in Designing Consumer Information Environments," *Journal of Consumer Research,* 2, 1975, 169–77.

———, and P. KAKKAR, "Effects of Information Presentation Format on Consumer Information Acquisition Strategies," *Journal of Consumer Research,* 3, 1977, 233–40.

———, *An Information Processing Theory of Consumer Choice.* Reading, MA: Addison-Wesley, 1979.

BLATT, J., L. SPENCER, AND S. WARD, "A Cognitive Developmental Study of Children's Reactions to Television Advertising," *Television and Social Behavior, Vol. 4, Television in Day-to-Day Life: Patterns of Use,* eds. E. Rubinstein, G. Comstock, and J. Murray, Washington, D.C.: Department of Health, Education and Welfare (HEW), 1972. pp. 452–67.

BLUM, P., "How Population Trends Can Help You Anticipate Changes in Consumer Markets," *The Research File,* Ogilvy & Mather, 1977.

BOCHNER, S., AND C. INSKO, "Communicator Discrepancy, Source Credibility, and Opinion Change," *Journal of Personality and Social Psychology,* 4, 1966, 614–21.

BONOMA, T., AND L. FELDER, "Nonverbal Communication in Marketing: Toward a Communicational Analysis," *Journal of Marketing Research,* 14, 1977, 169–80.

BRANSFORD, J., AND M. JOHNSON, "Considerations of Some Problems of Comprehension," in *Visual Information Processing*, ed. W. Chase, New York: Academic Press, 1973.

BREWER, M., AND W. CRANO, "Attitude Change as a Function of Discrepancy and Source of Influence," *Journal of Social Psychology*, 76, 1968, 13–18.

BRISLIN, R., AND K. OLMSTEAD, "An Evaluation of Two Models Designed to Predict Behavior." Paper presented at the APA meeting, Montreal, 1973.

BRITT, S., *Psychological Principles of Marketing and Consumer Behavior*. Lexington, MA: Lexington Books, 1978.

BROCK, T., "Communication-Recipient Similarity and Decision Change," *Journal of Personality and Social Psychology*, 1, 1965, 650–54.

———, S. ALBERT, AND L. BECKER, "Familiarity, Utility and Supportiveness as Determinants of Information Receptivity," *Journal of Personality and Social Psychology*, 14, 1970, 292–301.

BRUNER, J., J. GOODNOW, AND G. AUSTIN, *A Study of Thinking*, New York: John Wiley, 1956.

BROWN, R., "Wrapper Influence on the Perception of Freshness in Bread," *Journal of Applied Psychology*, 42, 1958, 257–60.

BUCKLIN, L., "Testing Propensities to Shop," *Journal of Marketing*, 30, 1966, 22–27.

———, "Consumer Search, Role Enactment, and Market Efficiency," *Journal of Business*, 42, 1969, 416–38.

BUTLER, D., "Evaluating New Product Opportunity." Paper presented at the American Marketing Association International Conference, St. Louis, MO, April 25, 1973.

BUTZ, W., AND M. WARD, "Baby Boom and Baby Bust: A New View," *American Demographics*, 1, 1979, 11–17.

CACIOPPO, J., "Cognitive and Neurophysiological Responses Accompanying Anticipation of Discrepant Communications." Unpublished manuscript, Ohio State University, 1977.

CALDER, B., "Focus Groups and the Nature of Qualitative Research," *Journal of Marketing Research*, 14, 1977, 353–64.

———, C. INSKO, AND B. YANDELL, "The Relation of Cognitive and Memorial Processes to Persuasion in a Simulated Jury Trial," *Journal of Applied Social Psychology*, 4, 1974, 62–93.

———, AND B. STERNTHAL, "Television Advertising Wearout: An Information Processing View," *Journal of Marketing Research*, 17, 1980, 173–86.

CANN, A., S. SHERMAN, AND R. E. ELKES, "Effects of Initial Request Size and Timing of a Second Request on Compliance: The Foot in the Door and the Door in the Face," *Journal of Personality and Social Psychology*, 32, 1975, 774–82.

CAPON, N., AND J. HULBERT, "The Sleeper Effect, An Awakening," *Public Opinion Quarterly*, 37, 1973, 333–58.

CARMEN, J., "A Summary of Empirical Research on Unit Pricing," *Journal of Retailing*, 48, 1972–73, 63–71.

CHAIKEN, S., AND A. EAGLY, "Communication Modality as a Determinant of Message Persuasiveness and Message Comprehensibility," *Journal of Personality and Social Psychology*, 34, 1976, 605–14.

CHERRY, E., "Some Experiments on the Recognition of Speech with One and with Two Ears," *Journal of the Acoustical Society of America*, 25, 1953, 975–79.

CHOO, T., "Communicator Credibility and Communication Discrepancy as Determinants of Opinion Change," *Journal of Social Psychology*, 64, 1964, 65–76.

CIALDINI, R., AND K. ASCANI, "Test of a Concession Procedure for Inducing Verbal, Behavioral, and Further Compliance with a Request to Give Blood," *Journal of Applied Psychology*, 61, 1976, 295–300.

————, AND D. SCHROEDER, "Increasing Compliance by Legitimizing Paltry Contributions: When Even a Penny Helps," *Journal of Personality and Social Psychology,* 34, 1976, 599–604.

————, J. VINCENT, S. LEWIS, J. CATALAN, D. WHEELER, AND B. DARBY, "Reciprocal Concessions Procedure for Inducing Compliance: The Door-in-the-Face-Technique," *Journal of Personality and Social Psychology,* 31, 1975, 206–15.

COHEN, A., "Some Implications of Self Esteem for Social Influence," in *Personality and Persuasibility,* eds. C. Hovland and I. Janis, New Haven: Yale University Press, 1959, 102–20.

COHEN, J., "An Interpersonal Orientation to the Study of Consumer Behavior," *Journal of Marketing Research,* 4, 1967, 270–78.

————, "Toward an Integrated Use of Expectancy-Value Attitude Models." Chicago: Association for Consumer Research, 1972.

————, M. FISHBEIN, AND O. AHTOLA, "The Nature and Uses of Expectancy-Value Models in Consumer Attitude Research," *Journal of Marketing Research,* 9, 1972, 456–60.

COLEMAN, R., "The Significance of Social Stratification in Selling," in *Marketing: A Mature Discipline,* ed. M. Bell, Chicago: American Marketing Association, 1961.

————, AND B. NEUGARTEN, *Social Status in the City.* San Francisco: Jossey Bass, 1971.

COOK, T., AND D. CAMPBELL, *The Design and Analysis of Quasi-Experiments for Field Settings.* Chicago: Rand McNally, 1979.

COX, D., *Risk-Taking and Information-Handling in Consumer Behavior.* Boston: Harvard University Press, 1967.

COX, K., "The Effect of Shelf Space on the Sales of Branded Products," *Journal of Marketing Research,* 7, 1970, 55–58.

CRAIG, C. S., *Consumer Reactions to Price Changes: An Experimental Investigation.* Unpublished doctoral dissertation, Ohio State University, 1971.

————, "Discretionary Consumption of Electricity." Working paper, June 1980.

————, AND J. MCCANN, "Assessing Communication Effects on Energy Conservation," *Journal of Consumer Research,* 5, 1978, 82–88.

————, B. STERNTHAL, AND C. LEAVITT, "Advertising Wearout: An Experimental Analysis," *Journal of Marketing Research,* 13, 1976, 365–72.

CRAIK, F., AND R. LOCKHART, "Levels of Processing: A Framework for Memory Research," *Journal of Verbal Learning and Verbal Behavior,* 11, 1972, 671–84.

CURHAN, R., "The Relationship between Shelf Space and Unit Sales in Supermarkets," *Journal of Marketing Research,* 9, 1972, 406–12.

DABBS, J., AND H. LEVENTHAL, "Effects of Varying the Recommendations in a Fear-Arousing Communication," *Journal of Personality and Social Psychology,* 4, 1966, 525–531.

DAVIS, H., "Dimensions of Marital Roles in Consumer Decision Making," *Journal of Marketing Research,* 7, 1970, 168–77.

————, "Decision Making Within the Household," *Journal of Consumer Research,* 2, 1976, 241–60.

DAWES, R., "Social Selection Based on Multi-Dimensional Criteria," *Journal of Abnormal and Social Psychology,* 68, 1964, 104–09.

————, AND B. CORRIGAN, "Linear Models in Decision Making," *Psychological Bulletin,* 81, 1974, 95–106.

DAY, G., *Buyer Attitudes and Brand Choice Behavior,* New York: Free Press, 1970.

DEJONG, W., "An Examination of Self-perception Mediation of the Foot-in-the-Door Effect," *Journal of Personality and Social Psychology,* 37, 1979, 2221–39.

DHOLAKIA, R., AND B. STERNTHAL, "Highly Credible Sources: Persuasive Facilitators or Persuasive Liabilities?" *Journal of Consumer Research,* 3, 1977, 223–32.

DICHTER, E., *Handbook of Consumer Motivations*, New York: McGraw-Hill, 1964.

DIXON, N., *Subliminal Perception: The Nature of a Controversy*, London: McGraw-Hill, 1971.

DODSON, J., A. TYBOUT, AND B. STERNTHAL, "Impact of Deals and Deal Retraction on Brand Switching," *Journal of Marketing Research*, 15, 1978, 72–81.

DOMMERMUTH, W., "The Shopping Matrix and Marketing Strategy," *Journal of Marketing Research*, 2, 1965, 128–32.

DONALDSON, J., "Channel Variation and Effects of Attitudes Towards Physically Handicapped Individuals," *AV Communication Review*, 24, 1976, 135–44.

DOOB, A., J. CARLSMITH, J. FREEDMAN, T. LANDAUER, AND S. TOM, "Effect of Initial Selling Price on Subsequent Sales," *Journal of Personality and Social Psychology*, 11, 1969, 345–50.

DOUGLAS, S., "Cross-National Comparisons and Consumer Stereotypes: A Case Study of Working and Non-Working Wives in the U.S. and France," *Journal of Consumer Research*, 3, 1976, 12–20.

DUNCAN, S., "Nonverbal Communication," *Psychological Bulletin*, 72, 1969, 118–37.

DUTTON, D., "The Maverick Effect: Increased Communicator Credibility as a Result of Abandoning a Career," *Canadian Journal of Behavioral Science*, 5, 1973, 145–51.

EASTERLIN, R., AND M. WACHTER, "The Coming Upswing in Fertility," *American Demographics*, 1, 1979, 12–15.

EINHORN, H., "The Use of Nonlinear, Noncompensatory Models in Decision Making," *Psychological Bulletin*, 73, 1971, 221–30.

———, "Expert Measurement and Mechanical Combination," *Organizational Behavior and Human Performance*, 7, 1972, 86–106.

———, S. KOMORITA, AND B. ROSEN, "Multidimensional Models for the Evaluation of Political Candidates," *Journal of Experimental Social Psychology*, 8, 1972, 58–73.

ELMS, A., "Role Playing, Incentive, and Dissonance," *Psychological Bulletin*, 68, 1967, 132–48.

ENGEL, J., D. KOLLAT, AND R. BLACKWELL, *Consumer Behavior*, New York: Dryden Press, 1968, 1973, 1978.

EXLINE, R., "Exploration in the Process of Person Perception: Visual Interaction in Relation to Competition, Sex, and Need for Affection," *Journal of Personality*, 31, 1963, 1–20.

———, D. GRAY, AND D. SCHUTTE, "Visual Behavior in a Dyad as Affected by Interview Content and Sex of Respondent," *Journal of Personality and Social Psychology*, 1, 1965, 201–09.

FEDERAL TRADE COMMISSION, "Food Advertising: Proposed Trade Regulation Rule and Staff Statement," Federal Register, 39, November 11, 1974, 39842–62.

FISHBEIN, M., "Attitude and the Prediction of Behavior," in *Readings in Attitude Theory and Measurement*, ed. M. Fishbein, New York: John Wiley, 1967.

———, *Readings in Attitude Theory and Measurement*. New York: John Wiley, 1967.

———, AND I. AJZEN, "Attitudes toward Objects as Predictors of Single and Multiple Behavioral Criteria," *Psychological Review*, 81, 1974, 59–74.

———, *Belief, Attitude, Intention and Behavior: An Introduction to Theory and Research*. Reading, MA: Addison-Wesley, 1975.

FOULKE, E., "Listening Comprehension as a Function of Word Rate," *Journal of Communication*, 18, 1968, 198–206.

FRANK, R., AND W. MASSY, "Shelf Position and Space Effects on Sales," *Journal of Marketing Research*, 7, 1970, 59–66.

FREEDMAN, J., J. CARLSMITH, AND D. SEARS, *Social Psychology*. Englewood Cliffs, NJ: Prentice-Hall, Inc. 1970.

———, AND S. FRASER, "Compliance without Pressure: The Foot-in-the-Door Technique," *Journal of Personality and Social Psychology*, 4, 1966, 195–202.

FRIEDMAN, M., "Consumer Confusion in the Selection of Supermarket Products," *Journal of Applied Psychology,* 50, 1966, 529–34.

GABOR, A., AND C. GRANGER, "On the Price Consciousness of Consumers," *Applied Statistics,* 10, 1961, 170–88.

GARDNER, D., "Is There A Generalized Price-Quality Relationship?" *Journal of Marketing Research,* 8, 1971, 241–43.

GILLIG, P., AND A. GREENWALD, "Is It Time to Lay the Sleeper Effect to Rest?" *Journal of Personality and Social Psychology,* 29, 1974, 132–39.

GOLDHABER, G., "Listener Comprehension of Compressed Speech as a Function of the Academic Grade Level of the Subjects," *Journal of Communication,* 20, 1970, 167–73.

GRAMBOIS, D., "A Study of the Family Decision Making Process in the Purchase of Major Durable Household Goods." Unpublished doctoral dissertation, Indiana University, 1962.

GRANGER, C., AND A. BILLSON, "Consumers' Attitudes toward Package Size and Price," *Journal of Marketing Research,* 9, 1972, 239–48.

GRANT, B., "Truth in Pricing." Report to Mayor J.V. Lindsay, New York City, September, 1969.

GRASS, R., AND W. WALLACE, "Satiation Effects of TV Commercials," *Journal of Advertising Research,* 9, 1969, 3–8.

GREENBERG, A., AND C. SUTTONI, "Television Commercial Wearout," *Journal of Advertising Research,* 13, 1973, 47–54.

GREENWALD, A., "Cognitive Learning, Cognitive Response to Persuasion, and Attitude Change," in *Psychological Foundations of Attitudes,* eds. A. Greenwald, T. Brock, and T. Ostrom, New York: Academic Press, 1968.

———, AND R. ALBERT, "Acceptance and Recall of Improvised Arguments," *Journal of Personality and Social Psychology,* 8, 1968, 31–34.

GREY, J., AND A. WEDDERBURN, "Grouping Strategies with Simultaneous Stimuli," *Quarterly Journal of Experimental Psychology,* 12, 1960, 180–84.

GRIEG, W., F. STRAND, AND H. LARZELERE, "Relative Retail Sales and Elasticity of Demand for Dehydrated Mashed Potato Products," Agricultural Economics Department Cooperative Extension Service, Michigan State University, East Lansing, July, 1958.

GRUDER, C., T. COOK, K. HENNIGAN, R. FLAY, C. ALESSIS, AND J. HALAMAJ, "Empirical Tests of the Absolute Sleeper Effect Predicted from the Discounting Cue Hypothesis," *Journal of Personality and Social Psychology,* 36, 1978, 1061–74.

HALL, C., AND G. LINDZEY, *Theories of Personality,* 3rd ed., New York: John Wiley, 1978.

HALL, E., *The Hidden Dimensions.* New York: Doubleday, 1966.

HANSEN, F., *Consumer Choice Behavior.* New York: Free Press, 1972.

HASS, R., AND D. LINDER, "Counterargument Availability and the Effects of Message Structure on Persuasion," *Journal of Personality and Social Psychology,* 23, 1972, 219–33.

HAUG, M., "Social-Class Measurement: A Methodological Critique," in *Issues in Social Inequality,* ed. G. Thielbar and S. Feldman, Boston: 1977.

HAWKINS, E., "Methods of Estimating Demand," *Journal of Marketing,* 21, 1957, 428–38.

HEMPEL, D., "Search Behavior and Information Utilization in the Home Buying Process," in *Marketing Involvement in Society and the Economy,* ed. P. McDonald, Chicago: American Marketing Association, 1969.

———, "Family Buying Decisions: A Cross Cultural Perspective," *Journal of Marketing Research,* 11, 1974, 295–302.

HESLIN, R., B. BLAKE, AND J. ROTTON, "Information Search as a Function of Stimulus Uncertainty and the Importance of the Response," *Journal of Personality and Social Psychology,* 23, 1972, 333–39.

HEWGILL, M., AND G. MILLER, "Source Credibility and Response in Fear-Arousing Communication," *Speech Monographs*, 32, 1965, 95–101.

HILL, A., "Credibility, Discrepancy, and Latitude of Communication as Dimensions of Dissonance Influencing Attitude Change," *Australian Journal of Psychology*, 15, 1963, 124–32.

HISRICH, R., AND M. PETERS, "Selecting the Superior Segmentation Correlate," *Journal of Marketing*, 38, 1974, 60–63.

HODGES, R., P. SIEGEL, AND P. ROSSI, "Occupational Prestige in the United States: 1925–1963," in *Class, Status and Power*, eds. R. Bendix and S. Lyrset, 2nd ed., New York: Free Press, 1966.

HOVLAND, C., A. LUMSDAINE, AND F. SHEFFIELD, *Experiments on Mass Communication*, Princeton, NJ: Princeton University Press, 1949.

HOWARD, J., *Marketing: Executive and Buyer Behavior*, New York: Columbia University Press, 1963.

———, *Marketing Theory*, Boston: Allyn and Bacon, 1965.

———, AND L. OSTLUND, *Buyer Behavior: Theoretical and Empirical Foundations*, New York: Knopf, 1973.

———, AND J. SHETH, *The Theory of Buyer Behavior*. New York: John Wiley, 1969.

HUGHES, D., S. TINIC, P. NAERT, "Analyzing Consumer Information Processing," in *Marketing Involvement in Society and the Economy*, ed. P. McDonald, Chicago: American Marketing Association, 1969.

HULBERT, J., AND N. CAPON, "Interpersonal Communication in Marketing: An Overview," *Journal of Marketing Research*, 9, 1972, 27–34.

INSKO, C., "Primacy vs. Recency in Persuasion as a Function of the Timing of Arguments and Measures," *Journal of Abnormal and Social Psychology*, 69, 1964, 381–91.

———, *Theories of Attitude Change*, New York: Appleton-Century-Crofts, 1967.

JACOBY, J., "Opinion Leadership and Innovativeness: Overlap and Validity," Proceedings of the Third Annual Conference of the Association for Consumer Research, ed. M. Venkatesan, 1972.

———, J. OLSON, AND R. HADDOCK, "Price, Brand Name and Product Characteristics as Determinants of Perceived Quality," *Journal of Applied Psychology*, 55, 1971, 470–79.

———, D. SPELLER, AND C. BERNING, "Brand Choice as a Function of Information Load: Replication and Extension," *Journal of Consumer Research*, 1, 1974, 33–42.

———, D. SPELLER, AND D. KOHN, "Brand Choice Behavior as a Function of Information Load," *Journal of Marketing Research*, 11, 1974, 63–69.

JANIS, I., "Effects of Fear-Arousal in Attitude Change: Recent Developments in Theory and Experimental Research," in *Advances in Experimental Social Psychology*, 3, ed. L. Berkowitz, New York: Academic Press, 1967.

———, AND S. FESHBACH, "Effects of Fear-Arousing Communications," *Journal of Abnormal and Social Psychology*, 48, 1953, 78–92.

———, AND P. FIELD, "Sex Differences and Personality Factors Related to Persuasibility," in *Personality and Persuasibility*, eds. C. Hovland and I. Janis, New Haven, CT: Yale University Press, 1959.

JOHNSON, H., AND I. STEINER, "The Effects of Source on Response to Negative Information about One's Self," *Journal of Social Psychology*, 74, 1968, 215–24.

———, AND T. WATKINS, "The Effects of Message Repetition on Immediate and Delayed Attitude Change," *Psychonomic Science*, 22, 1971, 101–03.

KAPFERER, J., "Repetition, Persistence of Induced Attitude Change, and Retention of the Inducing Message Content." Unpublished doctoral dissertation, Northwestern University, 1975.

KASSARJIAN, H., "Personality and Consumer Behavior: A Review," *Journal of Marketing Research*, 8, 1971, 409–19.

KATONA, G., *Psychological Analyses of Economic Behavior.* New York: McGraw-Hill, 1951.

——, *The Mass Consumption Society.* New York: McGraw-Hill, 1964.

——, AND E. MUELLER, "A Study of Purchase Decisions in Consumer Behavior," in *Consumer Behavior,* ed. L. Clark, New York: New York University Press, 1954.

——, "A Study of Purchase Decisions," in *Consumer Behavior: The Dynamics of Consumer Reaction,* ed. L. Clark, New York: New York University Press, 1955.

KELLEY, H., "The Processes of Causal Attribution," *American Psychologist,* 28, 1973, 107–28.

KENNEDY, A., "An Experimental Study of the Effect of Humorous Message Content upon Ethos and Persuasion." Unpublished doctoral dissertation, University of Michigan, 1972.

KENNEDY, J., "The Effect of Display Location on the Sales and Pilferage of Cigarettes," *Journal of Marketing Research,* 7, 1970, 210–15.

KEY, B., *Subliminal Seduction,* New York: Signet, 1974.

KIERAS, D., "Beyond Pictures and Words: Alternative Information Processing Models for Imagery Effects in Verbal Memory," *Psychological Bulletin,* 85, 1978, 532–54.

KILPELA, D., "An Experimental Study of the Effects of Humor on Persuasion." Unpublished master's thesis, Wayne State University, 1961.

KISIELIUS, J., "Imagery Effects on Persuasion." Unpublished manuscript, Northwestern University, 1980.

KLEINMUNTZ, B., "The Processing of Clinical Information by Man and Machine," in *Formal Representation of Human Judgement,* ed. B. Kleinmuntz, New York: John Wiley, 1968.

KOLLAT, D., R. BLACKWELL, AND J. ROBESON, *Strategic Marketing,* New York: Holt, Rinehart and Winston, 1972.

KORNZWEIG, N., "Behavior Change as a Function of Fear Arousal and Personality." Unpublished doctoral dissertation, Yale University, 1967.

KOSLIN, B., J. STOOPS, AND W. LOH, "Source Characteristics and Communication Discrepancy as Determinants of Attitude Change and Conformity," *Journal of Experimental Social Psychology,* 3, 1967, 230–42.

KOTZAN, J., AND R. EVANSON, "Responsiveness of Drug Store Sales to Shelf Space Allocations," *Journal of Marketing Research,* 6, 1969, 465–469.

KRUGMAN, H., "The Impact of Television Advertising: Learning without Involvement," *Public Opinion Quarterly,* 29, 1965, 349–56.

——, "Why Three Exposures May Be Enough," *Journal of Advertising Research,* 12, 1972, 11–14.

——, "Memory without Recall, Exposure without Perception," *Journal of Advertising Research,* 17, 1977, 7–12.

LA PIERE, R., "Attitudes vs. Actions," *Social Forces,* 20, 1934, 230–37.

LAZARSFELD, P., B. BERELSON, AND H. GAUDET, *The People's Choice,* New York: Columbia University Press, 1948.

LAZARUS, R., AND R. McCLEARY, "Autonomic Discrimination without Awareness: A Study of Subception," *Psychological Review,* 58, 1951, 113–22.

LEAVITT, C., "A Multidimensional Set of Rating Scales for Television Commercials," *Journal of Applied Psychology,* 54, 1970, 427–29.

LEAVITT, H., "A Note on Some Experimental Findings about the Meaning of Price," *Journal of Business,* 27, 1954, 205–10.

LEONE, R., AND R. SCHULTZ, "A Study of Marketing Generalizations," *Journal of Marketing,* 44, 1980, 10–18.

LEPPER, M., D. GREENE, AND R. NISBETT, "Undermining Children's Interest with Extrinsic Rewards: A Test of the Overjustification Hypothesis," *Journal of Personality and Social Psychology,* 28, 1973, 129–37.

LEVENTHAL, H., "Findings and Theory in the Study of Fear Communications," in *Advances in Experimental Social Psychology,* 5, ed. L. Berkowitz, New York: Academic Press, 1970.

————, S. JONES, AND G. TREMBLY, "Sex Differences in Attitude and Behavior Change under Conditions of Fear and Specific Instructions," *Journal of Experimental Social Psychology,* 2, 1966, 378–99.

————, R. SINGER, AND S. JONES, "The Effects of Fear and Specificity of Recommendation upon Attitudes and Behavior," *Journal of Personality and Social Psychology,* 2, 1965, 20–29.

————, AND G. TREMBLY, "Negative Emotions and Persuasion," *Journal of Personality,* 36, 1968, 154–68.

LEVIN, J., B. BENDER, AND A. LESGOLD, "Pictures, Repetition, and Young Children's Oral Prose Learning," *AV Communication Review,* 24, 1976, 367–80.

LEVINE, J., AND R. VALLE, "The Convert as a Credible Communicator," *Social Behavior and Personality,* 3, 1975, 81–90.

LEVY, S., *Marketplace Behavior—Its Meaning for Management,* New York: AMACOM, 1978.

LUTZ, R., "Changing Brand Attitudes Through Modification of Cognitive Structure," *Journal of Consumer Research,* 1, 1975, 49–59.

————, "An Experimental Investigation of Causal Relations Among Cognitions, Affect, and Behavioral Intention," *Journal of Consumer Research,* 3, 1977, 197–208.

LYNN, R., *Attention, Arousal, and the Orientation Reaction,* Oxford: Pergamon, 1966.

MANDELL, M., *Advertising* (2nd ed.), Englewood Cliffs, NJ: Prentice-Hall, Inc., 1974.

MARTINO, J., "Tools for Looking Ahead," Office of Research Analysis, Holloman Air Force Base, 1970.

McCANN, C., *Women and Department Store Newspaper Advertising,* Chicago: Social Research, 1957.

McCOLLOUGH, J., AND T. OSTROM, "Repetition of Highly Similar Messages and Attitude Change," *Journal of Applied Psychology,* 59, 1974, 395–97.

McCONNELL, J., "An Experimental Examination of the Price-Quality Relationship," *Journal of Business,* 41, 1968, 439–44.

————, "The Price-Quality Relationship in an Experimental Setting," *Journal of Marketing Research,* 5, 1968, 300–03.

————, "Effects of Pricing on Perception of Product Quality," *Journal of Applied Psychology,* 52, 1968, 313–14.

McCROSKEY, J., "A Summary of Experimental Research on the Effects of Evidence in Persuasive Communication," *Quarterly Journal of Speech,* 55, 1969, 169–76.

————, "The Effects of Evidence as an Inhibitor of Counter-Persuasion," *Speech Monographs,* 37, 1970, 188–94.

McGINNES, E., "Emotionality and Perceptual Defense," *Psychological Review,* 56, 1949, 244–51.

McGUIRE, W., "The Effectiveness of Supportive and Refutational Defenses in Immunizing and Restoring Beliefs Against Persuasion," *Sociometry,* 24, 1961, 184–97.

————, "Inducing Resistance to Persuasion: Some Contemporary Approaches," in *Advances in Experimental Social Psychology,* Vol. 1, ed. L. Berkowitz, New York: Academic Press, 1964.

————, AND D. PAPAGEORGIS, "The Relative Efficacy of Various Types of Prior Belief-Defense in Producing Immunity Against Persuasion," *Journal of Abnormal and Social Psychology,* 62, 1961, 327–37.

MEHRABIAN, A., *Silent Messages*. Belmont, CA: Wadsworth, 1971.

———, *Nonverbal Communications*. Chicago: Aldine, 1972.

MILLER, G., "The Magical Number Seven, Plus or Minus Two: Some Limits on Our Capacity for Processing Information," *Psychological Review,* 63, 1956, 81–97.

MILLER, G., AND M. HEWGILL, "Some Recent Research on Fear-Arousing Message Appeals," *Speech Monographs,* 33, 1966, 377–91.

MILLER, N., AND D. CAMPBELL, "Recency and Primacy in Persuasion as a Function of the Timing of Speeches and Measurement," *Journal of Abnormal and Social Psychology,* 59, 1959, 1–9.

MILLER, R., P. BRICKMAN, AND D. BOLEN, "Attribution vs. Persuasion as a Means of Modifying Behavior," *Journal of Personality and Social Psychology,* 31, 1975, 430–41.

MILLS, J., "The Effect of Certainty on Exposure to Information Prior to Commitment," *Journal of Experimental Social Psychology,* 1, 1965, 348–55.

———, E. ARONSON, AND H. ROBINSON, "Selectivity in Exposure to Information," *Journal of Abnormal and Social Psychology,* 59, 1959, 250–53.

———, AND J. JELLISON, "Avoidance of Discrepant Information Prior to Commitment," *Journal of Personality and Social Psychology,* 8, 1968, 59–62.

MINIARD, P., AND J. COHEN, "Isolating Attitudinal and Normative Influences in Behavioral Intention Models," *Journal of Marketing Research,* 16, 1979, 102–10.

MISCHEL, W., "Toward a Cognitive Social Learning Reconceptualization of Personality," *Psychological Review,* 80, 1973, 252–83.

MITCHELL, A., AND J. OLSON, "Cognitive Effects of Advertising Repetition," in *Advances in Consumer Research,* Vol. 4, ed. W.D. Perreault, Jr., Atlanta: Association for Consumer Research, 1977.

MONICA, C., "Six Rules to Help You Make Funny TV Commercials," *Advertising Age,* 42, 1971, 46.

MONROE, K., AND P. LA PLACA, "What Are the Benefits of Unit Pricing?" *Journal of Marketing,* 36, 1972, 16–22.

MONTGOMERY, D., "New Product Distribution Analysis of Supermarket Buyer Decision," *Journal of Marketing Research,* 12, 1975, 255–64.

MORAY, N., "Attention in Dichotic Listening: Affective Cues and the Effect of Instructions," *Quarterly Journal of Experimental Psychology,* 11, 1959, 59–60.

MURDOCK, B., "The Retention of Individual Items," *Journal of Experimental Psychology,* 62, 1961, 618–625.

MURRAY, H., *Explorations in Personality,* New York: Oxford University Press, 1938.

MYERS, J., AND J. GUTMAN, "Life Style: The Essence of Social Class," in *Life Style and Psychographics,* ed. W. Wells, Chicago: American Marketing Association, 1974.

———, AND J. MOUNT, "More on Social Class vs. Income as Correlates of Buying Behavior," *Journal of Marketing,* 37, 1973, 71–73.

———, R. STANTON, AND A. HAUG, "Correlates of Buying Behavior: Social Class vs. Income," *Journal of Marketing,* 35, 1971, 8–15.

NICOSIA, F., *Consumer Decision Processes*. Englewood Cliffs, NJ: Prentice-Hall, Inc., 1966.

NORMAN, D., *Models of Human Memory*. New York: Academic Press, 1970.

OLSON, J., "Price as an Informational Cue: Effects on Product Evaluations," in *Consumer and Industrial Buying Behavior,* eds. A. Woodside, J. Sheth, and P. Bennett, New York: North-Holland, 1977.

———, "Theories of Information Encoding and Storage: Implications for Consumer Research," in *The Effect of Information on Consumer and Market Behavior,* ed. A. Mitchell, Chicago: American Marketing Association, 1978.

PAYNE, J., "Task Complexity and Contingent Processing in Decision Making: An Information Search and Protocol Analysis," *Organizational Behavior and Human Performance,* 16, 1976, 366–87.

PETERS, W., "Relative Occupational Class Income: A Significant Variable in the Marketing of Automobiles," *Journal of Marketing,* 34, 1970, 74–77.

PETTY, R., T. OSTROM, AND T. BROCK (eds.), *Cognitive Responses in Persuasive Communication: A Text in Attitude Change,* New York: McGraw-Hill, 1980.

PHILLIPS, L. AND B. CALDER, "Evaluating Consumer Protection Programs: Part I. Weak but Commonly Used Research Designs," *Journal of Consumer Affairs,* 13, 1979, 157–85.

———, "Evaluating Consumer Protection Programs: II. Promising Methods," *Journal of Consumer Affairs,* 14, 1980, 9–36.

———, AND B. STERNTHAL, "Age Differences in Information Processing: A Perspective on the Aged Consumer," *Journal of Marketing Research,* 14, 1977, 444–57.

PINSON, C., "Abstraction of Physical Attributes." Unpublished paper, Northwestern University, 1978.

———, "The Nature of Judgements about Products." Unpublished manuscript, Northwestern University, 1978.

PLINER, P., H. HART, J. KOHL, AND D. SAARI, "Compliance without Pressure: Some Further Data on the Foot-in-the-Door Technique," *Journal of Experimental Social Psychology,* 10, 1974, 17–22.

PLUMMER, J., "Applications of Life Style Research to the Creation of Advertising Campaigns," in *Life Style and Psychographics,* ed. W. Wells, Chicago: American Marketing Association, 1974.

POKORNY, G., AND C. GRUNER, "An Experimental Study of the Effect of Satire Used as Support in a Persuasive Speech," *Western Speech,* 33, 1969, 204–11.

POLITZ MEDIA STUDIES, *The Rochester Study,* New York: *Saturday Evening Post,* 1960.

POWELL, F., "Source Credibility and Behavioral Compliance as Determinants of Attitude Change," *Journal of Personality and Social Psychology,* 2, 1965, 669–76.

———, AND G. MILLER, "Social Approval and Disapproval Cues in Anxiety-Arousing Communications," *Speech Monographs,* 34, 1967, 152n59.

PRAS, B., AND J. SUMMERS, "A Comparison of Linear and Nonlinear Evaluation Process Models," *Journal of Marketing Research,* 12, 1975, 276–81.

PRASAD, V., "Socio-economic Product Risk and Patronage Preferences of Retail Shoppers," *Journal of Marketing,* 39, 1975, 42–47.

PROGRESSIVE GROCER, "How Much Do Customers Know About Prices?" February, 1964a, pp. 104–06.

PROGRESSIVE GROCER, "Shelf Merchandising Strategy: A Key to Increased Sales," March, 1964b, pp. 121–25.

PROGRESSIVE GROCER, "Shelf Attitudes Affect Buying Attitudes," March, 1964c, p. 126.

PROGRESSIVE GROCER, "How to Make Displays More Sales Productive," February, 1971.

RAY, M., AND A. SAWYER, "Repetition in Media Models: A Laboratory Technique," *Journal of Marketing Research,* 8, 1971, 20–29.

———, IN COLLABORATION WITH A. SAWYER, M. ROTHSCHILD, R. HEELER, E. STRONG, AND J. REED, "Marketing Communication and the Hierarchy-of-Effects," in *New Models for Mass Communication Research,* ed. M.P. Clarke, Beverly Hills, CA: Sage Publications, 1973.

———, AND W. WILKIE, "Fear: The Potential of an Appeal Neglected by Marketing?" *Journal of Marketing,* 34, 1970, 54–62.

REINGEN, P., AND J. KERNAN, "Compliance with an Interview Request: A Foot-in-the-Door, Self-Perception Interpretation," *Journal of Marketing Research,* 14, 1977, 365–69.

REYNOLDS, F., AND W. WELLS, *Consumer Behavior.* New York: McGraw-Hill, 1977.

RICH, S., AND S. JAIN, "Social Class and Life Cycle as Predictors of Shopping Behavior," *Journal of Marketing Research, 5,* 1968, 41–49.

ROBERTSON, T., *Innovation Behavior and Communication,* New York: Holt, Rinehart & Winston, 1971.

———, AND J. ROSSITER, "Children and Commercial Persuasion: An Attribution Theory Analysis," *Journal of Consumer Research, 1,* 1974, 13–20.

ROEDDER, D., "Age Differences in Children's Information Processing: Theoretical Sources and Policy Implications," *Journal of Consumer Research.* In press.

ROGERS, E., "New Product Adoption and Diffusion," *Journal of Consumer Research, 2,* 1976, 290–301.

———, AND F. SHOEMAKER, *The Communication of Innovations: A Cross Cultural Approach,* New York: Free Press, 1971.

———, AND J. STANFIELD, "Adoption and Diffusion of New Products: Emerging Generalizations and Hypotheses," in *Application of the Sciences in Marketing Management,* ed. F.M. Bass, C. King and E.A. Pessemeir, New York: John Wiley, 1968.

ROSEN, S., "Postdecision Affinity for Incompatible Information," *Journal of Abnormal and Social Psychology, 63,* 1961, 188–90.

ROSENBERG, M., "Cognitive Structure and Attitudinal Affect," *Journal of Abnormal and Social Psychology, 53,* 1956, 367–72.

ROTTON, J., R. HESLIN, AND B. BLAKE, "Some Determinants of Confidence and Information Seeking." Paper presented at the annual meeting of the Western Psychological Association, Los Angeles, 1970.

RUMELHART, D., *Introduction to Human Information Processing,* New York: John Wiley, 1977.

RUSS, F., "Consumer Evaluation of Alternative Product Models." Unpublished doctoral dissertation, Carnegie-Mellon University, 1971.

RUSSO, J., "More Information is Better: A Reevaluation of Jacoby, Speller, and Kohn," *Journal of Consumer Research, 1,* 1974, 68–72.

———, "The Value of Unit Price Information," *Journal of Marketing Research, 14,* 1977, 193–201.

———, AND B. DOSHER, "Dimensional Evaluation: A Heuristic for Binary Choice." Unpublished working paper, Department of Psychology, University of California, San Diego, 1975.

———, G. KRIESER, AND S. MIYASHICA, "An Effective Display of Unit Price Information," *Journal of Marketing, 39,* 1975, 11–19.

———, AND L. ROSEN, "An Eye Fixation Analysis of Multi-Alternative Choice," *Memory and Cognition, 3,* 1975, 267–76.

RYAN, M., AND E.H. BONFIELD, "The Fishbein Extended Model and Consumer Behavior," *Journal of Consumer Research, 2,* 1975, 118–36.

SADOWSKI, R., "Immediate Recall of TV Commercial Elements—Revisited," *Journal of Broadcasting, 16,* 1972, 277–87.

SAEGERT, S., W. SWAP, R. ZAJONC, "Exposure, Contact, and Interpersonal Attraction," *Journal of Personality and Social Psychology, 25,* 1973, 234–42.

SAWYER, A., "A Laboratory Experimental Investigation of the Effects of Advertising." Unpublished doctoral dissertation, Stanford University, 1971.

———, "Repetition and Cognitive Response," in *Cognitive Responses to Persuasion,* ed. R. Petty, T. Ostrom, and T. Brock, New York: McGraw-Hill, 1980.

SCHRAMM, W., AND R. CARTER, "Effectiveness of a Political Telethon," *Public Opinion Quarterly, 23,* 1959, 121–26.

SCHWARTZ, S., AND R. TESSLER, "A Test of a Model for Reducing Measured Attitude-Behavior Discrepancies," *Journal of Personality and Social Psychology,* 24, 1972, 225–36.

SCISSORS, J., AND J. PETRAY, *Advertising Media Planning,* Chicago: Crain Books, 1976.

SCOTT, C., "Past Behavior Incentives and Maintained Behavior Change: A Field Study of Self-Attribution Theory." Unpublished doctoral dissertation, Northwestern University, 1975.

———, "The Effects of Trial and Incentives on Repeat Purchase Behavior," *Journal of Marketing Research,* 13, 1976, 263–69.

———, "Modifying Socially-Conscious Behavior: The Foot-in-the-Door-Technique," *Journal of Consumer Research,* 4, 1977, 156–64.

———, AND A. TYBOUT, "The Effect of Uncertainty and Incentives on Consumer Response." Unpublished manuscript, Northwestern University, 1978.

SEARS, D., "Political Behavior," in *Handbook of Social Psychology,* Vol. 5., eds. G. Lindzey and E. Aronson, Reading, MA: Addison-Wesley, 1969.

———, AND J. FREEDMAN, "Selective Exposure to Information: A Critical Review," *Public Opinion Quarterly,* 31, 1967, 194–213.

SELIGMAN, C., M. BUSH, AND K. KIRSCH, "Relationship between Compliance in the Foot-in-the-Door Paradigm and Size of First Request," *Journal of Personality and Social Psychology,* 33, 1976, 517–20.

SHIFFRIN, R., D. PISONI, AND K. CASTANEDA-MENDEZ, "Is Attention Shared Between the Ears?" *Cognitive Psychology,* 6, 1974, 190–215.

SIEGEL, A., AND J. ALLIK, "A Developmental Study of Visual and Auditory Short-Term Memory," *Journal of Verbal Learning and Verbal Behavior,* 12, 1973, 409–18.

SIMMONS, R., AND M. ROSENBERG, "Functions of Childrens' Perceptions of the Stratification System," *American Sociological Review,* 36, 1971, 235–49.

SIMON, H., "A Behavioral Model of Rational Choice," *Quarterly Journal of Economics,* 69, 1955, 99–118.

SIMON, S., N. BERKOWITZ, AND R. MOYER, "Similarity, Credibility, and Attitude Change: A Review and a Theory," *Psychological Bulletin,* 73, 1970, 1–16.

SKOLNICK, P., AND R. HESLIN, "Quality Versus Difficulty: Alternative Interpretations of the Relationship between Self-Esteem and Persuasibility," *Journal of Personality,* 39, 1971, 242–51.

SLOVIC, P., AND S. LICHTENSTEIN, "Comparison of Bayesian and Regression Approaches to the Study of Information Processing in Judgement," *Organizational Behavior and Human Performance,* 6, 1971, 651–730.

SMITH, H., W. CLEMENT, AND W. HOOFNAGE, *Merchandising Natural Cheddar Cheese in Retail Food Stores,* MRR-115, U.S. Department of Agriculture, April 1956, in W.S. Hoofnage, "Experimental Design in Measuring the Effectiveness of Promotion," *Journal of Marketing Research,* 2, 1965, 154–62.

———, AND R. FRYE, *How Color of Red Delicious Apples Affects Their Sales,* MRR-618, U.S. Department of Agriculture, February 1964, in W.S. Hoffnage, "Experimental Designs in Measuring the Effectiveness of Promotion," *Journal of Marketing Research,* 2, 1965, 154–62.

SNYDER, M., AND M. CUNNINGHAM, "To Comply or Not Comply: Testing the Self-Perception Explanation of the Foot-in-the-Door Phenomenon," *Journal of Personality and Social Psychology,* 31, 1975, 64–67.

SOMMER, R., *Personal Space: The Behavioral Basis of Design,* Englewood Cliffs, NJ: Prentice-Hall, Inc., 1969.

SORENSEN, A., "The Structure of Intergenerational Mobility," *American Sociological Review,* 40, 1975, 456–71.

STAFFORD, J., AND B. ENIS, "The Price Quality Relationship: An Extension," *Journal of Marketing Research*, 6, 1969, 456–58.

STARCH, D., "What Is the Best Frequency of Advertisements?" Daniel Starch Tested Copy, 1962.

STERNTHAL, B., AND C.S. CRAIG, "Humor in Advertising," *Journal of Marketing*, 37, 1973, 12–18.

———, "Fear Appeals: Revisited and Revised," *Journal of Consumer Research*, 1, 1974, 22–34.

———, "Marketing Experimentation," in *Marketing Research: Fundamentals and Dynamics*, G. Zaltman and P. Burger, Hinsdale, Illinois: Dryden Press, 1975.

STERNTHAL, B., R. DHOLAKIA AND C. LEAVITT, "The Persuasive Effects of Source Credibility: Tests of Cognitive Response," *Journal of Consumer Research*, 4, 1978, 252–60.

———, L. PHILLIPS, AND R. DHOLAKIA, "The Persuasive Effect of Source Credibility: A Situational Analysis," *Public Opinion Quarterly*, 42, 1978, 285–314.

STOUT, R., "Developing Data to Estimate Price-Quality Relationships," *Journal of Marketing*, 32, 1969, 34–36.

SVENSON, O., "Coded Think Aloud Protocols Obtained When Making A Choice to Purchase One of Seven Hypothetically Offered Houses: Some Examples." Unpublished paper, University of Stockholm, 1974.

SWINTH, R., J. GAUMNITZ, AND C. RODRIGUEZ, "Decision Making Processes: Using Discrimination Nets for Security Selection," *Decision Sciences*, 6, 1975, 439–48.

SWINYARD, W., AND M. RAY, "Advertising-Selling Interactions: An Attribution Theory Experiment," *Journal of Marketing Research*, 14, 1977, 509–16.

TAEUBER, C., "A Changing America," *American Demographics*, 1, 1979, 9–15.

TITTLE, C., AND R. HILL, "Attitude Measurement and Prediction of Behavior: An Evaluation of Conditions and Measurement Techniques," *Sociometry*, 30, 1967, 199–213.

TOUSSAINT, I., "A Classified Summary of Listening, 1950–1959," *Journal of Communication*, 10, 1960, 125–34.

TYBOUT, A., "Relative Effectiveness of Three Behavioral Influence Strategies as Supplements to Persuasion in a Marketing Context," *Journal of Marketing Research*, 15, 1978, 229–42.

———, B. CALDER, AND B. STERNTHAL, "Using Information Processing Theory to Design Effective Marketing Strategies," *Journal of Marketing Research*, 18, 1981, 73–79.

VAN RAAIJ, W., "Direct Monitoring of Consumer Information Processing by Eye Movement Recorder." Unpublished paper, Tilburg University, 1976.

VROOM, V., *Work and Motivation*. New York: John Wiley, 1964.

WALSTER, E., E. ARONSON, AND D. ABRAHAMS, "On Increasing the Persuasiveness of a Low Prestige Communicator," *Journal of Experimental Social Psychology*, 2, 1966, 325–42.

WARD, S., G. REALE, AND D. LEVINSON, "Children's Perceptions, Explanations, and Judgments of Television Advertising: A Further Explanation," in *Television and Social Behavior, Vol. 4, Television in Day-to-Day Life: Patterns of Use*, eds. E. Rubinstein, G. Comstock, and J. Murray, Washington, D.C.: U.S. Department of HEW, 1972.

———, AND D. WACKMAN, "Purchase Influence Attempts and Parental Yielding," *Journal of Marketing Research*, 9, 1972, 316–19.

———, D. WACKMAN, AND E. WARTELLA, *How Children Learn to Buy: The Development of Consumer Information Processing Skills*, Beverly Hills, CA: Sage Publications, Inc. 1977.

WARNER, L., M. MEEKER, AND K. EELS, Social Class in America: *A Manual of Procedure for the Measurement of Social Status*, New York: Harper & Row, 1960.

WATTS, W., "Relative Persistence of Opinion Change Induced by Active Compared to Passive Participation," *Journal of Personality and Social Psychology*, 5, 1967, 4–15.

————, AND L. HOLT, "Persistence of Opinion Change Induced under Conditions of Forewarning and Distraction," *Journal of Personality and Social Psychology,* 37, 1979, 778–89.

WEBB, E., D. CAMPBELL, R. SCHWARTZ, AND L. SECHREST, *Unobtrusive Measures: Nonreactive Research in the Social Sciences,* Chicago: Rand McNally, 1965.

WEBSTER, F., AND Y. WIND, "A General Model for Understanding Organizational Buying Behavior," *Journal of Marketing,* 36, 1972, 12–19.

WELLS, G., AND J. HARVEY, "Do People Use Consensus Information in Making Causal Attributions?" *Journal of Personality and Social Psychology,* 35, 1977, 279–93.

WELLS, W., "Psychographics: A Critical Review," *Journal of Marketing Research,* 12, 1975, 196–213.

————, AND A. BEARD, "Personality and Consumer Behavior," in *Consumer Behavior: Theoretical Sources,* eds. S. Ward and T. Robertson, Englewood Cliffs, NJ: Prentice-Hall, Inc., 1973.

————, AND G. GUBAR, "The Life Cycle Concept," *Journal of Marketing Research,* 3, 1966, 355–63.

————, AND L. LoSCIUTO, "Direct Observation of Purchasing Behavior," *Journal of Marketing Research,* 3, 1966, 226–33.

WEST, E., AND P. MCCLURE, "Sales Effect of a New Counter Display," *Journal of Advertising Research,* 9, 1969, 29–34.

WESTOVER, I., "A Comparison of Listening and Reading as a Means of Testing," *Journal of Education Research,* 52, 1958, 23–26.

WHEELESS, L., "The Effects of Comprehension Loss on Persuasion," *Speech Monographs,* 38, 1971, 327–30.

WHYTE, W., "The Web of Word of Mouth," *Fortune,* 50, 1954, 140–43, 204–12.

WICKER, A., "Attitudes vs. Actions: The Relationship of Verbal and Overt Behavioral Responses to Attitude Objects," *Journal of Social Issues,* 25, 1969, 41–78.

————, "An Examination of the 'Other Variables' Explanation of Attitude-Behavior Inconsistency," *Journal of Personality and Social Psychology,* 19, 1971, 18–30.

WILLIAMS, D., "An Information Processing Theory of Individual Consumer Purchasing Behavior." Unpublished doctoral dissertation, Northwestern University, 1976.

WILKIE, W., AND E. PESSEMIER, "Issues in Marketing's Use of Multi-Attribute Models," *Journal of Marketing Research,* 10, 1973, 428–41.

WILSON, D., H. L. MATHEWS, AND J. W. HARVEY, "An Empirical Test of the Fishbein Behavioral Intention Model," *Journal of Consumer Research,* 1, 1975, 39–48.

WILSON, I., "What One Company Is Doing about Today's Demands on Business," in *Changing Business-Society Interrelationships,* ed. G.A. Steiner, Los Angeles, CA: Graduate School of Management, UCLA, 1975.

WILSON, W., "Unobtrusive Induction of Positive Attitudes." Unpublished doctoral dissertation, University of Michigan, 1975.

WOODSIDE, A., "Dominance and Conflict in Family Purchasing Decisions," Association for Consumer Research, 1972, pp. 650–59.

WRIGHT, P., "Analyzing Media Effects on Advertising Responses," *Public Opinion Quarterly,* 38, 1974, 192–205.

————, "Consumer Choice Strategies: Simplifying Vs. Optimizing," *Journal of Marketing Research,* 12, 1975, 60–67.

————, "Message-Evoked Thoughts: Persuasion Research Using Thought Verbalizations," *Journal of Consumer Research,* 7, 1980, 151–75.

YALCH, R., "The Prediction of Behavior: A Field Study of Self-Perception Theory." Unpublished doctoral dissertation, Northwestern University, 1974.

YERGIN, D., "Conservation: The Key Energy Source," in *Energy Future,* eds. R. Stobaugh and D. Yergin, New York: Random House, 1979.

YOUNG, S., "Psychographics Research and Marketing Relevancy," in *Attitude Research Reaches New Heights,* eds. C. King and D. Tigert, Chicago: American Marketing Association, 1971.

ZALTMAN, G., AND M. WALLENDORF, *Consumer Behavior: Basic Findings and Management Implications,* New York: John Wiley, 1979.

ZIELSKE, H., "The Remembering and Forgetting of Advertising," *Journal of Marketing,* 23, 1959, 239–43.

Indices

Author Index

A

Abrahams, D., 300
Advertising Research Foundation, 186
Ahtola, O., 141
Ajzen, I., 142, 156, 158, 159, 160, 165
Albert, S., 85, 103
Alessis, C., 297
Alexis, M., 147
Allen, A., 189, 192
Allik, J., 306
Anderson, K., 294
Anderson, N., 143
Andreasen, A., 44
Applebaum, W., 238
Arndt, J., 43
Aronson, E., 84, 263, 300
Ascani, K., 119
Asch, S., 302
Austin, G., 150

B

Bagozzi, R., 167, 201
Bauer, R., 42
Baumgarten, S., 249
Beard, A., 41, 189, 190
Bechnell, J., 277
Becker, L., 85
Bellson, A., 239
Bem, D., 117, 189, 192
Bender, B., 306
Benham, T., 81
Berelson, B., 81, 249
Bergin, A., 263
Berkowitz, L., 270
Berkowitz, N., 294
Berning, C., 150
Bernstein, P., 216
Bettman, J., 6, 44, 144, 151, 152
Blackwell, R., 44–46, 51–54, 109

Blake, B., 86
Blatt, J., 196
Blum, P., 205
Bochner, S., 263
Bolen, D., 275
Bonfield, E., 156, 167
Bonoma, T., 285
Bransford, J., 95
Brewer, M., 263
Brickman, P., 275
Brislin, R., 160, 166, 167
Britt, S., 44
Brock, T., 85, 97, 295
Brown, R., 244
Bruner, J., 150
Bucklin, L., 87
Bush, M., 129
Business Week, 204
Butler, D., 251
Butz, W., 202

C

Cacioppo, J., 102, 281
Calder, B., 24, 30, 42, 104, 107, 281, 319
Campbell, D., 23, 30, 283
Cann, A., 119
Capon, N., 285, 297
Carlsmith, J., 83, 241, 263
Carmen, J., 239
Carter, R., 83
Castaneda-Mendez, K., 93
Catalan, J., 121
Chaiken, S., 306
Cherry, E., 92
Choo, T., 263
Cialdini, R., 119, 121
Clement, W., 244
Clevenger, T., 294
Cohen, A., 193
Cohen, J., 141, 167, 186

Coleman, R., 220, 221
Cook, T., 30, 297
Corrigan, B., 145
Cottingham, D., 270
Cox, D., 42, 43
Cox, K., 243
Craig, C. S., 28, 41, 107, 163, 167, 266, 271, 272, 281, 321, 323, 324
Craik, F., 99
Crano, W., 263
Cunningham, M., 119, 121, 129
Curhan, R., 243

D

Darby, B., 121
Davis, H., 228
Dawes, R., 145, 148
Day, G., 156
DeJong, W., 117
Dholakia, R., 106, 123, 263, 294, 298, 303, 304
Dichter, E., 41
Dixon, N., 170
Dodson, J., 242
Dommermuth, W., 43
Donaldson, J., 306
Doob, A., 241
Dosher, B., 151
Douglas, S., 208
Duncan, S., 285, 288
Dutton, D., 300

E

Eagly, A., 306
Easterlin, R., 201
Einhorn, H., 144, 148, 150, 151
Elkes, R., 119

Elms, A., 103
Engel, J., 44–46, 51–54
Enis, B., 240
Evanson, R., 243
Exline, R., 288

F

Federal Trade Commission, 152
Felder, L., 285
Feshbach, S., 266
Field, P., 193
Fishbein, M., 141, 142, 156, 158, 159,
    160, 163, 165
Flay, R., 297
Foulke, E., 95
Frank, R., 243
Fraser, S., 117
Freedman, J., 83, 117, 241
Friedman, M., 239
Frye, R., 244

G

Gabor, A., 239
Gardner, D., 240
Gaudet, H., 81, 249
Gaumnitz, J., 147
Gillig, P., 297
Goldhaber, G., 95
Goodnow, J., 150
Granbois, D., 87
Granger, C., 239
Grant, B., 239
Grass, R., 281
Gray, D., 288
Greenberg, A., 281
Greene, D., 123
Greenwald, A., 62, 103, 297

Grey, J., 93
Grieg, W., 238
Gruder, C., 297
Gruner, C., 275
Gubar, G., 229
Gutman, J., 220

H

Haddock, R., 240
Haines, G., 147
Halamaj, J., 297
Hall, C., 186, 286
Hansen, F., 44
Hart, H., 118
Harvey, J., 160, 303
Hass, R., 301
Haug, A., 220
Haug, M., 221
Hawkins, E., 238
Heeler, R., 127
Hempel, D., 86, 228
Hennigan, K., 297
Heslin, R., 86, 194, 195
Hewgill, M., 270
Hill, A., 263
Hill, R., 159
Hisrich, R., 220
Hodges, R., 219
Holt, L., 297
Hoofnage, W., 244
Hovland, C., 297
Howard, J., 44, 49–54, 193
Hughes, D., 86
Hulbert, J., 285, 297

I

Insko, C., 104, 263, 283

J

Jacoby, J., 150, 240, 249
Jain, S., 222
Janis, I., 193, 266, 267
Johnson, H., 263, 297
Johnson, M., 95

K

Kakkar, P., 151
Kapferer, J., 163, 282
Kassarjain, H., 186
Katona, G., 86, 87, 146
Kelley, H., 117
Kennedy, A., 275
Kennedy, J., 243, 244
Kernan, J., 129
Key, B., 170
Kieras, D., 99, 306, 307
Kilpela, D., 275
Kirsch, K., 129
Kisielius, Y., 306, 307
Kleinmuntz, B., 147
Kohl, J., 118
Kohn, D., 150
Kollat, D., 44–46, 51–54, 109
Komorita, S., 148
Koslin, B., 263
Kotzan, J., 243
Krieser, G., 240
Krugman, H., 127, 128

L

Landauer, T., 241
LaPiere, R., 157

LaPlaca, P., 239
Larzelere, H., 238
Lazarsfeld, P., 81, 249
Lazarus, R., 169
Leavitt, C., 106, 107, 272, 281, 298, 303
Leavitt, H., 240
Leone, R., 243
Lepper, M., 123
Lesgold, A., 306
Leventhal, H., 266, 268, 270
Levin, J., 306
Levine, J., 300
Levinson, D., 196
Levy, S., 141, 216, 217, 221, 222, 238
Lewis, S., 121
Lichtenstein, S., 142, 144
Light, L., 213
Linder, D., 301
Lindzey, G., 186
Lockhart, R., 99
Loh, W., 263
Lo Sciuto, L., 239
Lumsdaine, A., 297
Lutz, R., 141, 156
Lynn, R., 89

M

McCann, C., 219
McCann, J., 163, 321, 323, 324
McCleary, R., 169
McClure, P., 243
McConnell, J., 240
McCroskey, J., 301
McCullough, L., 279
McGinnies, E., 169
McGuire, W., 104, 105
McIsaac, R., 277
McPhee, W., 81
Mandell, M., 9

Martino, J., 178
Massy, W., 243
Mathews, H., 160
Mehrabian, A., 286, 288
Miller, G., 270, 271
Miller, G.A., 97
Miller, N., 283
Miller, R., 275
Mills, J., 84, 85
Miniard, P., 167
Mischel, W., 189
Mitchell, A., 278
Miyashica, S., 240
Monica, C., 272
Monroe, K., 239
Montgomery, D., 147
Moray, N., 93
Mount, J., 220
Moyer, R., 294
Mueller, E., 87, 146
Murdock, B., 97
Murray, H., 42
Myers, J., 220

N

Naert, P., 86
Neugarten, B., 221
Nicosia, F., 44
Nisbett, R., 123
Norman, D., 91

O

Olmstead, K., 160, 166, 167
Olson, J., 6, 238, 240, 278
Ostlund, L., 44, 49–54
Ostrom, T., 97, 279

P

Papageorgis, D., 105
Payne, J., 147
Pessemier, E., 144
Peters, M., 220
Peters, W., 220
Petray, J., 20
Petty, R., 97, 281
Phillips, L., 30, 197, 263, 294
Pinson, C., 244
Pisoni, D., 93
Pliner, P., 118
Plummer, J., 189–91
Pokorny, G., 275
Politz, A., 278
Powell, F., 271, 304
Prasad, V., 222
Progressive Grocer, 239, 243, 244

R

Ray, M., 127, 266, 275, 281
Reale, G., 196
Reed, J., 127
Reingen, P., 129
Reynolds, F., 229
Rich, S., 222
Robertson, T., 196, 246, 248
Robeson, J., 109
Robinson, H., 84
Rodriguez, C., 147
Roedder, D., 196
Rogers, E., 246, 248, 249
Rosen, B., 84
Rosen, S., 151
Rosenberg, M., 142, 212
Rossi, P., 219
Rossiter, J., 196
Rothschild, M., 127

Rotton, J., 86
Rumelhart, D., 91, 94, 98, 102
Russ, F., 147, 148, 150, 151
Russo, J., 150, 151, 240
Ryan, M., 156, 167

S

Saari, D., 118
Sadowski, R., 306
Saegert, S., 280
Sawyer, A., 127, 277, 278, 281
Schramm, W., 83
Schultz, R., 243
Schutte, D., 288
Schwartz, R., 23
Schwartz, S., 160, 165
Scissors, J., 20
Scott, C., 9, 117, 126, 129, 163, 242
Sears, D., 82, 83
Sechrest, L., 23
Seligman, C., 129
Sheffield, F., 297
Sherman, S., 119
Sheth, J., 49, 193
Shiffrin, R., 93
Shoemaker, F., 246, 248, 249
Siegel, A., 306
Siegel, P., 219
Simmons, R., 221
Simon, H., 147
Simon, L., 147
Simons, N., 294
Singer, R., 270
Skolnick, P., 194–95
Slovic, P., 142, 144
Smith, H., 244, 245
Snyder, M., 119, 121, 129
Sommer, J., 287
Sorensen, A., 225
Spears, R., 238

Speller, D., 150
Spencer, L., 196
Stafford, J., 240
Stanfield, J., 249
Stanton, R., 220
Starch, D., 277
Steiner, I., 263
Sternthal, B., 28, 106, 107, 123, 167,
    197, 242, 263, 266, 271, 272,
    281, 294, 298, 303, 304, 319
Stoops, J., 263
Stout, R., 238
Strand, F., 238
Strong, E., 127
Suttoni, C., 281
Svenson, O., 151
Swap, W., 280
Swinth, R., 147
Swinyard, W., 275

T

Tessler, R., 160, 165
Tinic, S., 86
Tittle, C., 159
Tom, S., 241
Toussaint, I., 95
Trembly, G., 270
Turner, J., 263
Tybout, A., 127, 163, 167, 242, 304,
    319

V

Valle, R., 300
Van Loo, M., 201
Van Raaij, W., 151
Vincent, J., 121
Vroom, V., 158

W

Wachter, M., 201
Wackman, D., 196, 230
Wallace, W., 281
Wallendorf, M., 216
Walster, E., 300
Ward, M., 202
Ward, S., 196, 230
Warner, L., 221
Wartella, E., 196
Watkins, T., 297
Watts, W., 103, 297
Webb, E., 23
Webster, F., 7, 44, 46–48, 51–54, 226
Wedderburn, A., 93
Wells, G., 303
Wells, W., 41, 189, 190, 192, 229, 239
West, E., 243
Westover, I., 95
Wheeler, D., 121
Wheeless, L., 96
Whyte, W., 248
Wicker, A., 156, 165, 166, 167
Wilkie, W., 144, 266

Williams, D., 56
Wilson, D., 160
Wilson, I., 169, 172
Wind, Y., 7, 44, 46–48, 51–54, 226
Woodside, A., 228
Wright, P., 74, 144, 150, 306

Y

Yalch, R., 76, 162
Yandell, B., 104
Yergin, D., 321
Young, S., 191, 192

Z

Zajonc, R., 280
Zaltman, G., 216
Zielske, H., 278

Subject Index

A

Abstraction, 132–44, 244–45
Activities, interests and opinions (*see* Psychographics)
Additive linear model, 143–46
Adoption of new products:
  consumer characteristics for, 248–51
  product characteristics for, 246–48
Age, 195–98
Aggregation:
  complexity and, 149–50
  conjunctive, 148
  disjunctive, 148–49
  implications of, 151–53
  information format, 151
  lexicographic, 146–48
  linear, 142–46
  perceived risk and, 150–51
Alternative bias, 151
Anal fixation, 188
Anal stage, 187
Archival research, 17–20
Arousal, 61, 88–91
Attention, 61, 91–94
Attitude:
  measurement of, 74–76, 159–60
  prediction of behavior from, 156–63
  toward the act, 159–60
  toward the object, 68, 159–60
Attribute bias, 151
Attribute selection, 261–63, 265–66
Attribution theory (*see* Self-perception theory)
Autonomic, 228

B

Baby boom, 201–4
Bachelor stage, 229
Behavior:
  measurement of general, 161–63
  measurement of specific, 161
  multiple act criterion, 162
  prediction of, 155–81
  prediction of long-term, 170–80
  repeated measure criterion, 162
  single act criterion, 161
Behavioral intention, 165
Birth order, 206
Birth rate (*see* Fertility rates)
Body language, 284–89
Brand development index (BDI), 17–18
Brand structure, 251–55
Buying center, 48, 226–27

C

Cannibalism, 108, 252–55
Category development index (CDI),
  18–19
Certainty, 85–86
Children's information processing,
  196–97
Cognitive analysis (*see* Information
  processing)
Cognitive response (*see* Information
  processing)
Communicability, 246
Communication modality:
  and competitive environment, 308
  and distribution, 309
  exposure criterion, 305–6
  and persuasion, 306–8
  picture processing, 306–8

Communicator credibility (*see* Source
  credibility)
Compatibility, 247
Compensatory process, 143
Complexity, 246
Comprehension, 94–97
Compressed speech, 95–97
Concentration, 278
Conjunctive, 148
CONPAAD, 73–74
Consumer behavior:
  comparison of models of, 51–54
  definition of, 6–7
  Engel-Kollat-Blackwell model of,
    44–46
  Howard-Ostlund model of, 49–51
  microeconomic model of, 40–41
  prediction of behavior model, 166–68
  psychoanalytic model of, 41–42
  Webster-Wind model of, 46–48
Consumer information processing (*see*
  Information processing)
Continuity, 278
Cued processors, 196–97

D

Danger control, 268
Decider, 226–27
Decision complexity, 149–50
Decision importance, 86–88
Defense mechanisms, 41, 187–89
Delphi method, 173–76
Depth interviewing, 25, 42
Diffusion of innovations, 246–51
Discrepant messages, 263–65
Disjunctive, 148–49
Displays, 243–44
Diverse, 205–6
Divisibility, 247

Dollars to opportunity, 111
Dollars to sales, 111
Door-in-the-face, 119, 121–22

E

Early adopters, 249–50
Early majority, 249–50
Education, 211–13
Ego, 41, 187
Elderly consumers' information
    processing, 197–98
Empty nest I, II, 231
Energy conservation, 320–24
Engel-Kollat-Blackwell model, 44–46
Environmental forecasting, 172–75
Experimentation:
    before-after, 30–31
    time series, 31–32
    true experiments, 28–30
Expertise (*see* Source credibility)
Extraneous events:
    concept of, 69, 165–66
    measurement of, 76
Eye contact, 287–89

F

Family decision making, 226–29
Family life cycle, 229–31
Fear appeals (*see* Threatening appeals)
Fear control, 208
Feelings of inadequacy, 193
Fertility rates, 201–5
Flighting, 278–79
Focus groups, 25, 42
Foot-in-the-door technique, 117–20

Forecasting:
    correlational approach to, 178
    environmental, 172–75
    growth curves, 176–78
    technological, 176–78
    trend curves, 176–78
Frequency effects (*see* Repetition)
Freudian theory, 185–89
Full nest I, II, 231

G

Galvanic skin response (GSR), 73, 169
Gatekeeper, 226–27
Gender, cues suggesting, 135–38
General behavior, 161–63
Genital stage, 188
Growth curves, 176–78

H

Household size, 205–8
Howard-Ostlund, 49–51
Humorous appeals, 271–75

I

Id, 41
Income, 211–13, 220–21
Index numbers, 21–22
Individual differences, 12–13, 69–70,
    189–98, 318
Influence, 226–27

Information acquisition, 8–11
  measurement of, 72–76
  from others, 59–65
  from own experience, 65–66,
    116–22, 124–29, 304
Information organization, 11, 66–68,
    132–53
  effect of circumstance on, 149–51
Information processing:
  age differences in, 195–98
  cognitive analysis, 62–65, 94–107,
    314–18
  cognitive response, 97–102
  exposure to information, 60–61,
    82–88, 305–6
  implications of, 70–72, 107–13,
    314–18
  information reception, 61–62, 88–94,
    314
  interpretation of Freud, 188–89
  measurement of, 72–77
  multiple processes view, 127–29
  of new product information, 246–48
  pictorial, 306–8
  of price information, 240–42
  and repetition, 278–82
  single process view, 124–27
  and source credibility, 296
Information seeking:
  certainty as a determinant of, 85–86
  decision importance as a determinant
    of, 86–88
Information utilization, 11–12, 68–
    69
  measurement of, 76–77
Innovators, 249–50

J

Just noticeable difference (JND), 239

K

Kinesic, 285, 287–89

L

Labeling, 275–77
Laggards, 250
Late majority, 249–50
Lexicographic, 146–48
Lifestyle (*see* Psychographics)
Limited processors, 196–97
Linear model, 142–46
Long-term memory (*see* Information
    processing, cognitive analysis;
    memory; Rehearsal; Retrieval)
Lower middle class, 222
Low involvement, 127–29

M

Market segmentation, 111–13
Market structures:
  brand structures, 251–55
  polarity of, 253–55
  product form structures, 253–55
Marriage, 205–6
Marriage rate, 207
Measurement:
  of attitude, 74–76, 159–60
  of behavior, 76, 161–63
  of cognitive response, 74
  of exposure, 72
  of extraneous events, 76, 165–66
  of motivation to comply, 164
  of normative beliefs, 76, 163–65
  of reception, 73

Memory:
  long-term, 98–102
  short-term, 97–102
Message discrepancy, 263–65
Message strategy:
  attribute selection, 261–63, 265–66
  consumer-oriented, 261–63
  humorous appeals, 271–75
  labeling, 275–77
  product-oriented, 261–63
  threatening appeals, 266–71
Migration (*see* Population)
Mobility (*see* Population)
Modality (*see* Communication modality)
Models of consumer behavior (*see*
    Consumer behavior)
Motivation to comply, 164
Multiple act behavior measure, 162
Multiple processes view, 127–29

N

Newly married stage, 230
New products, 245–55
Noncompensatory models, 146–49
Nonverbal communication (*see* Silent
    messages)
Normative beliefs:
  measurement of, 76, 163–65
  personal, 68, 164–65
  social, 68, 163–64

O

Observation research, 23–24
Occupation, 211–13, 217–20
Occupational status, 217–20
Opinion leaders, 249–51
Opportunity-to-see, 72

Oral fixation, 188–89
Oral stage, 187
Order of presentation, 282–84
Overprivileged, 220

P

Packaging, 244
Paralanguage, 285, 289–91
Parallel response model, 268–71
Parent-child relations, 229–30
Passive dictation, 229
Perceived risk, 42–43, 150–51
Performance, cues suggesting, 138–41
Personality:
  development, 187–89
  impact on information processing,
    192–95
  inventories, 189
  structure, 186–87
  tailored measures of, 189–92
Personal space, 286–87
Phallic fixation, 188
Phallic stage, 187
Polarity of market structures, 253–55
Population:
  migration, 209–11
  mobility, 209–11
  projections, 203
Positioning, 107–11
Price:
  effect of lowering, 241–42
  failure to use in consumer decision
    making, 239–40
  and information processing, 240–42
  and JND, 239
  and quality, 240
  and quantity, 238
  and unit pricing, 239–40
  and Weber's Law, 239
Primacy, 102–3, 283–84

Product:
    characteristics affecting adoption,
      246–55
    competitive analysis, 251–55
    diffusion, 246–51
    displays, 243–44
    and market structures, 251–55
    new, 245–55
    packaging, 244
    shelf height, 243
    shelf space, 242–43
Product form structures, 251–55
Proxemics, 285–87
Psychoanalytic theory, 41–42, 185–89
Psychographics, 189–92
Pulsing, 279
Pupil dilation, 73
Purchaser, 226–27

R

Recall, 112–13
Recency, 102–3, 283–84
Rehearsal, 102–7
Relative advantage, 246
Repeated measure of behavior, 161
Repetition, 277–82, 322–24
Research:
    descriptive, 17–24
    evaluative, 28–32
    explanatory, 24–27
    theoretical, 32–34
Retrieval, 102–7
Rumors, 319–20

S

Satisficing, 147
Self-confidence (*see* Self-esteem)

Self-esteem, 193–95
Self-pacing, 197–98, 306
Self-perception theory, 117–31
    augmentation, 123
    discounting, 123
    effect of circumstances, 122–27
    effect of incentives, 123, 126–27
    effect of source credibility, 123
    implications of, 129–30
Sentence completion, 42
Shadowing, 92–94
Shelf height, 243
Shelf space, 242–43
Short-term memory (*see* Information
    processing, cognitive analysis;
    memory; Retrieval; Rehearsal)
Silent messages, 284–91
Single act behavior measure, 161
Single process view, 124–27
Sleeper effect, 296–98
Social class:
    cues suggesting, 138, 141
    determinants of, 216–21
    indices of, 221
    lower middle, 222
    upper lower, 221–22
    upper middle, 222–25
Social stratification, 216–26
Source credibility:
    and attractiveness, 294–95
    dimensions of, 294
    and discrepancy, 263–65
    and energy conservation, 322–24
    expertise and trust, 295–304
    joint effects with other variables,
      301–3
    as a liability, 303–4
    and similarity, 295–96
    and the sleeper effect, 296–98
    and the timing of the source
      introduction, 298–99
    and use of evidence, 301
Specific behavior, 161
Strategic processors, 196–97

Sublimation, 41–42
Subliminal information presentation, 168–70
Superego, 41, 187
Survey research, 20–22
Syncratic decision making, 228

T

Technological forecasting, 176–78
Test marketing, 28–29
Thematic apperception test (TAT), 42
Thoughts defined, 62
Threatening appeals:
    effects of, 266–71
    parallel response model of, 268–71
    threat drive model of, 267–68
Trend curves, 176–78
Trust (*see* Source credibility)

Two-sided communication, 300–301
Two-step flow, 248–51

U

Underprivileged, 220
Unit pricing, 239–40
Unobtrusive measures, 23–24, 163
Upper lower class, 222–25
Upper middle class, 221–22
User, 226–27

W

Warner's ISC, 221
Wearout, 281–82
Weber's Law, 239
Webster-Wind model, 46–48
Women in the work force, 208–9